MW01629774

Ernst Ludwig Kirchner . Jens Ferdinand Willumsen

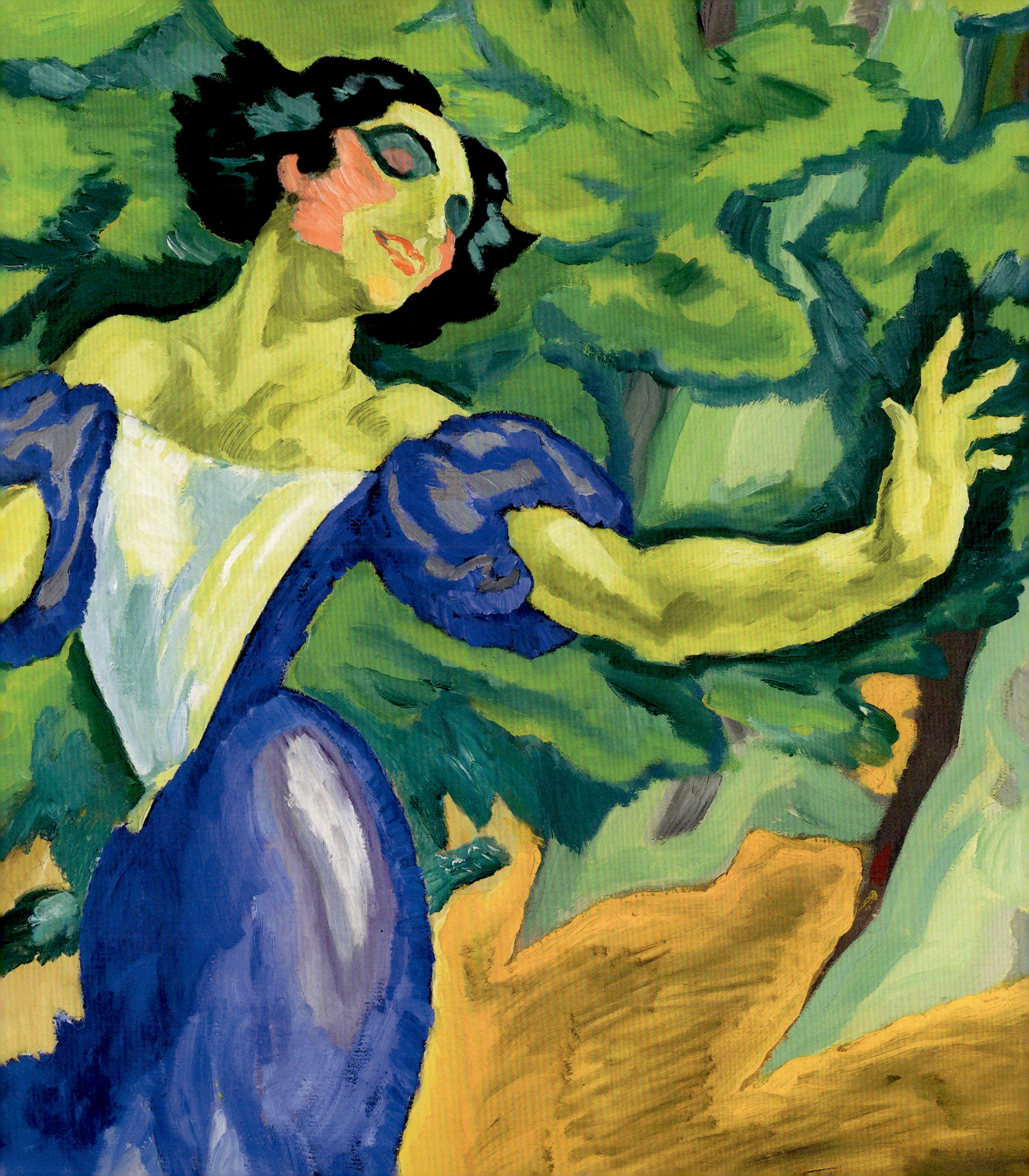

The Late Works of
Ernst Ludwig Kirchner and
Jens Ferdinand Willumsen

STAGING NATURE AND LIFE

HATJE
CANTZ

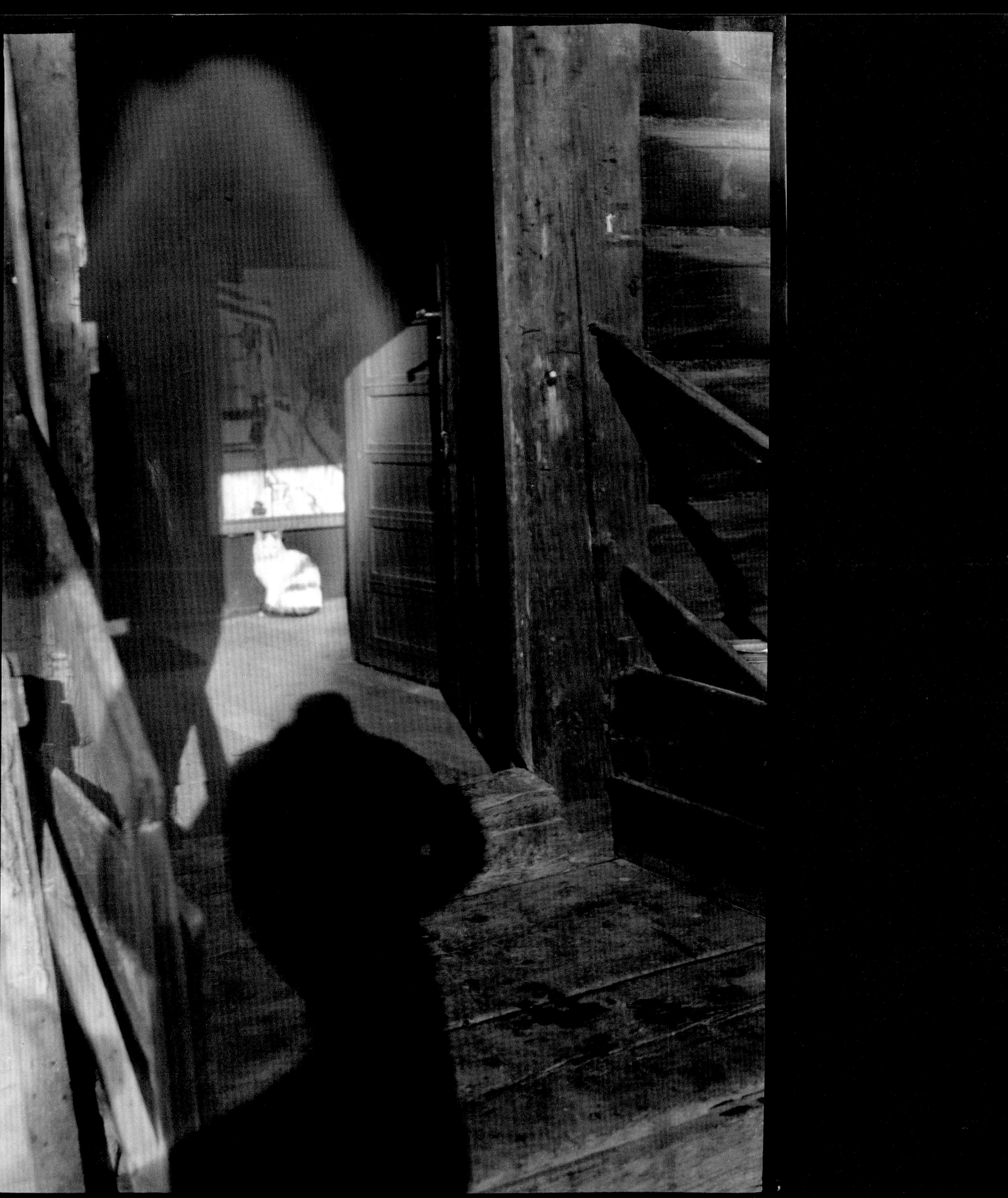

Contents

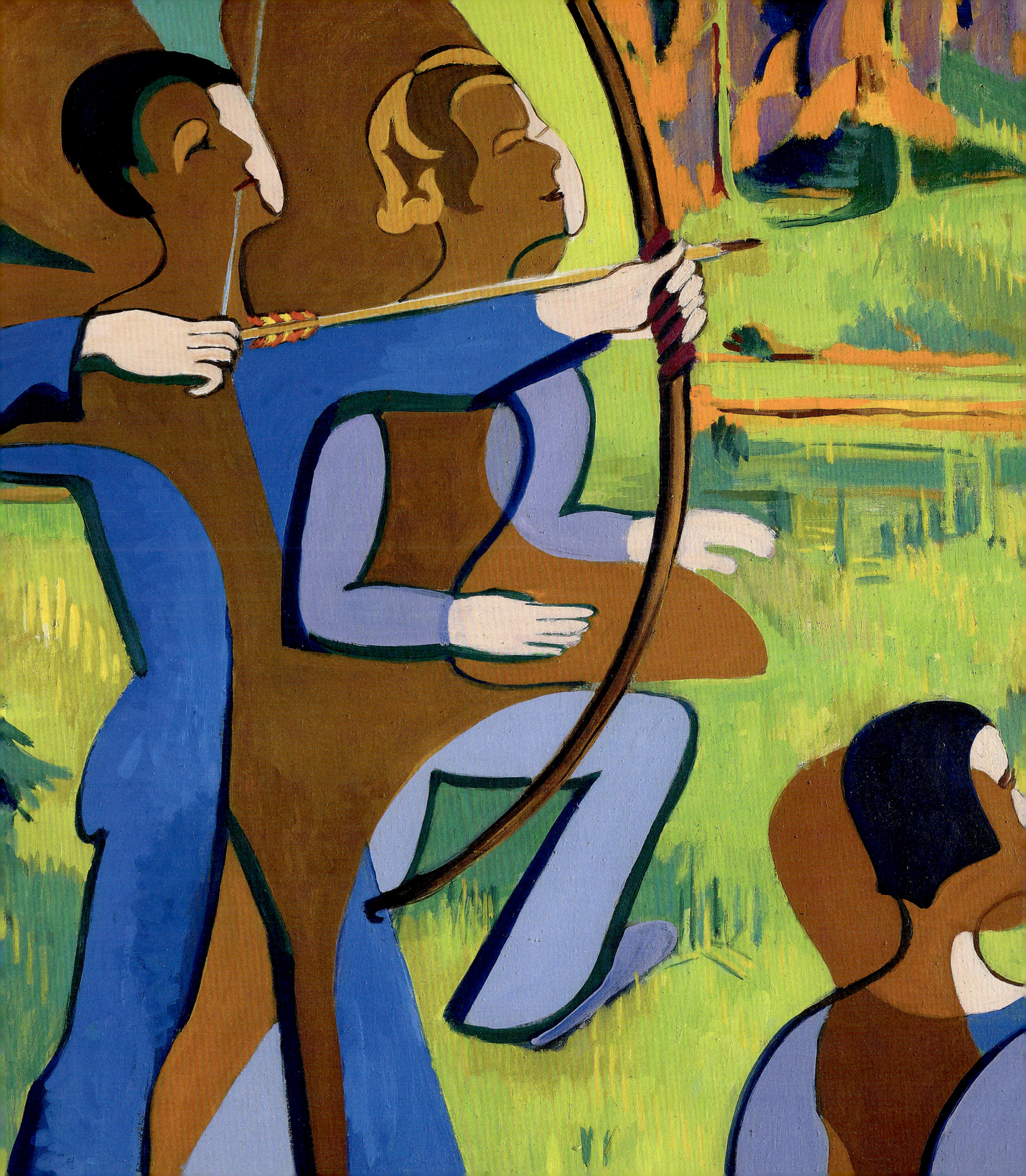

Foreword

Ernst Ludwig Kirchner
Detail of *Bogenschützen* (Archers), 1935–37
Oil on canvas, 195 × 150 cm
Kirchner Museum Davos

The Danish artist J.F. Willumsen (1863–1958) created works that share the dynamic composition, explosive colors, and expressive style of German Expressionism. Yet Willumsen's relationship to the Expressionist movement, which flourished in Germany and Austria in the early decades of the twentieth century but had very little real impact in Denmark, has received only sporadic attention. Willumsen himself categorically denied being inspired by German art and culture, and in his memoirs explicitly distanced himself from what he called the "Teutonic" style. In an international art-historical context he has primarily been associated with the French Symbolism of the eighteen-nineties, whereas the works he created after the turn of the century have often been seen as independent of contemporary trends on the European art scene and highly individual in style. If we start to scratch the surface, however, it emerges that Willumsen had a significant amount of contact with the German art world. Before the outbreak of World War I he exhibited regularly in Germany at major exhibitions such as the Berlin Secession and Munich's international art exhibitions, but also at solo and group exhibitions. In 1906 the Brücke group of German artists invited him to exhibit with members of the group and artists such as the Norwegian painter Edvard Munch, an invitation Willumsen declined.

This marginalization of the influence of contemporary German art on Willumsen's oeuvre—by the artist himself as well as art historians—can be seen in the light of two world wars and the subsequent opposition to Germany and German culture. Willumsen's insistent pose as a solitary genius immune to the influence of other artists or art movements has also played its role in readings of his works in posterity.

The Late Works of Ernst Ludwig Kirchner and Jens Ferdinand Willumsen: Staging Nature and Life is the first time an exhibition and accompanying catalogue relate Willumsen's oeuvre to contemporary developments on the German art scene—more specifically to one of the most significant representatives of German Expressionism, the artist Ernst Ludwig Kirchner (1880–1938). The exhibition is also the first major presentation of Kirchner at a Danish museum.

The coupling of Kirchner and Willumsen is based on a remarkable visual affinity between their late works, opening a realm of similarities and connections between the two in terms of style, their view of art, and their identity as artists. These works from the late nineteen-tens to nineteen-thirties were created in the wake of the sway of Expressionism, at a juncture when new avant-garde movements dominated the art scene.

The artistic quests of Kirchner and Willumsen during this period followed the same path. Their works overlap in subject and style: figurative, intense in color, and expressive. Their paintings of people and mountains reflect the influence of the spread of the Vitalist movement in Europe at the time, as well as the widespread influence of Friedrich Nietzsche. Both artists staged nature and people in nature in their paintings, but they also staged themselves as artists. From their self-imposed exile—Kirchner in Davos and Willumsen in the South of France—they sought recognition as artistic geniuses with a talent that extended beyond their own lifetime, something they believed should earn them a position among the great masters of art history. They tried to control the reception of their oeuvre and legacy through shameless self-mythologizing. Rarely, however, did their own evaluation of their work and that of art critics coincide, although there were exceptions. For the author Carl Einstein (1885–1940), who otherwise rejected Expressionism, Kirchner possessed a unique power as an artist. Einstein's analysis is key to understanding Kirchner's self-image. Both Kirchner and Willumsen sought to influence the reception of their works by publishing texts of their own—Kirchner even going to the extreme of using a pseudonym.

With these parallels in sight, as well as the differences that inevitably emerge when juxtaposing the works of two artists, the exhibition addresses the following themes, which are also among the ideas explored in the catalogue texts.

The City in Close-Up and Panorama: During the nineteen-twenties and nineteen-thirties both Willumsen and Kirchner made a series of paintings of the city and city crowds, Willumsen focusing on Venice and Rome, and Kirchner on Berlin and towns in Switzerland. Their portrayals of urban landscapes explore the explosive expansion of the city, the perception of time, and the atmosphere of urban nightlife. The paintings, which include close-ups of crowds and panoramas, are dominated by vibrant colors and a striking use of light. Kirchner's city is lit by electric lamps and the cold glow of neon signs, whereas Willumsen's is illuminated by the yellow glow of the moon and colorful fireworks against the night sky of Venice.

The Liberated Body: Inspiration from Vitalism's celebration of bodily energy and vigor can be seen in the interest of both artists in dance. Kirchner and Willumsen were equally fascinated by the free, expressive movements of modern dance, using drawing, photography, prints, and paintings to explore bodily exertion. Both artists also portray other forms of outdoor physical activity: ball games, hiking, and the archer, which like the dancer was a recurrent figure in the writings of Nietzsche.

Mountain Aesthetics: Mountains are a frequent motif in the works of Kirchner and Willumsen, and there are striking visual similarities between the intense use of color and the highly simplified, almost graphic style of their mountainscapes. In different ways both artists' view of the mountains was inspired by Vitalist perceptions of the growth and cycle of nature as a source of life. Whereas Willumsen's interest in mountains focused primarily on the sublime landscape, Kirchner was more interested in authentic folk life in the midst of unspoiled nature.

Tradition and Modernity: Both Willumsen and Kirchner identified with the art and artists of the past. Kirchner saw himself as the heir of Albrecht Dürer, whereas Willumsen was fascinated by El Greco, and had a large collection of older art. Both artists shared the ambition of revitalizing the art of the past and finding a universal style, something also seen in their works depicting human life and everyday existence in a range of media. Kirchner was a painter, but also designed tapestries with stylized, naked bodies in nature: a paradisiacal, primeval idyll. Willumsen portrayed human life and its evolution, and depicted people living in harmony with nature. In some ways these works seem anti-modern, but they also represent bold reinterpretations of a tradition: a renewal of the quest for nature and authenticity in the wake of World War I.

There are also similarities in the reception of Willumsen and Kirchner's late works. Both artists had to wait to receive recognition for what they themselves saw as the full maturation of their art. It was their early works that secured them a place in art history. In Denmark, Willumsen became famous for his Symbolist works of the eighteen-nineties, and Kirchner had his international breakthrough with the Expressionism of the Brücke group. In recent years, however, interest in and appreciation of the later works of both artists have grown, something reflected in exhibitions and publications addressing and illuminating this period of their respective oeuvres. With *The Late Works of Ernst Ludwig Kirchner and Jens Ferdinand Willumsen: Staging Nature and Life* we hope to contribute to this rereading and reanalysis of the artists' late works.

This exhibition, bringing together the works of Willumsen and Kirchner, has been years in the making, and is based on an outstanding collaboration with the Kirchner Museum Davos in Switzerland, and the generous loan of a large part of their collection. We would like to extend our warmest thanks to the Ernst Ludwig Kirchner Foundation and Carla Burani, director of Kirchner Museum Davos, who has been an invaluable source of help and support during the process, as well as the former director of Kirchner Museum Davos, Thorsten Sadowsky, who has supported the project from its conception, and opened doors to crucial contacts. Similarly, we would like to express our gratitude to Wolfgang Henze, who with his extensive knowledge of Kirchner's oeuvre has been tirelessly generous and helpful in providing us with information on the artist's works, and contacts to the private collectors who own them.

Heartfelt thanks go to all the staff at Willumsen's Museum for their contribution to the exhibition and this publication. First and foremost Anne Gregersen, who has curated the exhibition and edited this comprehensive publication with expertise and dedication. During the process she has been assisted by museum manager Rune Jonassen, curator Louise Bugge Jacobsen, and museum assistant Seline Rørbæk. Thanks also to graphic designer Carl-H. K. Zakrisson for the beautiful layout of the publication, and exhibition architects Stine and Matilde Friese for the equally aesthetic design of the exhibition.

We would also like to thank the publication authors Anders Ehlers Dam, Uwe Fleckner, Anne Gregersen, Jill Lloyd, and Carsten Thau, whose perceptive texts bring new and interesting perspectives to the oeuvres of Kirchner and Willumsen alike. Jane Rowley and Kevin Cook we thank for their elegant translations and Martin Butler for the proofreading.

The exhibition and this publication have been made possible only thanks to the generous support of a number of Danish foundations. We would like to express our thanks to the Foundation of June 15th for enabling us to launch the project with their Exhibition Award for the exhibition concept in 2017. Their backing and generosity was followed by that of the Louis-Hansen Foundation, the Augustinus Foundation, the Beckett Foundation, the Knud Højgaard Foundation, and the Jorck Foundation, a fantastic level of support that has made it possible to source unique artworks from museums, galleries, and private collections in Europe, and show such an extensive range of Ernst Ludwig Kirchner's works for the first time in Denmark. We would also like to thank Goethe-Institut Dänemark for creating an interesting program based on the exhibition as part of the Danish-German Year of Culture 2020.

A willingness to lend major artworks to an exhibition can never be taken for granted, so it is with immense gratitude that we thank the museums, galleries, and private collectors for their exceptional generosity in making it possible for us to exhibit works from their collections. Besides Kirchner Museum Davos, we thank Galerie Henze & Ketterer, KUNSTEN Museum of Modern Art Aalborg, Museum Frieder Burda, Städel Museum, Victor Petersens Samling, as well as several private collectors. We would also like to extend our warm thanks to the board of the museum and our external partners near and far for their support and contributions in making both the exhibition and publication possible.

Lisbeth Lund
Museum Director, Willumsen's Museum

Pp. 10–11
J. F. Willumsen
Detail of *Markuspladsen. Venedig. Nat. Fantasi* (St Mark's Square. Venice. Night. Fantasy), 1929
Oil on canvas, 87 × 97 cm
Willumsen's Museum, Frederikssund

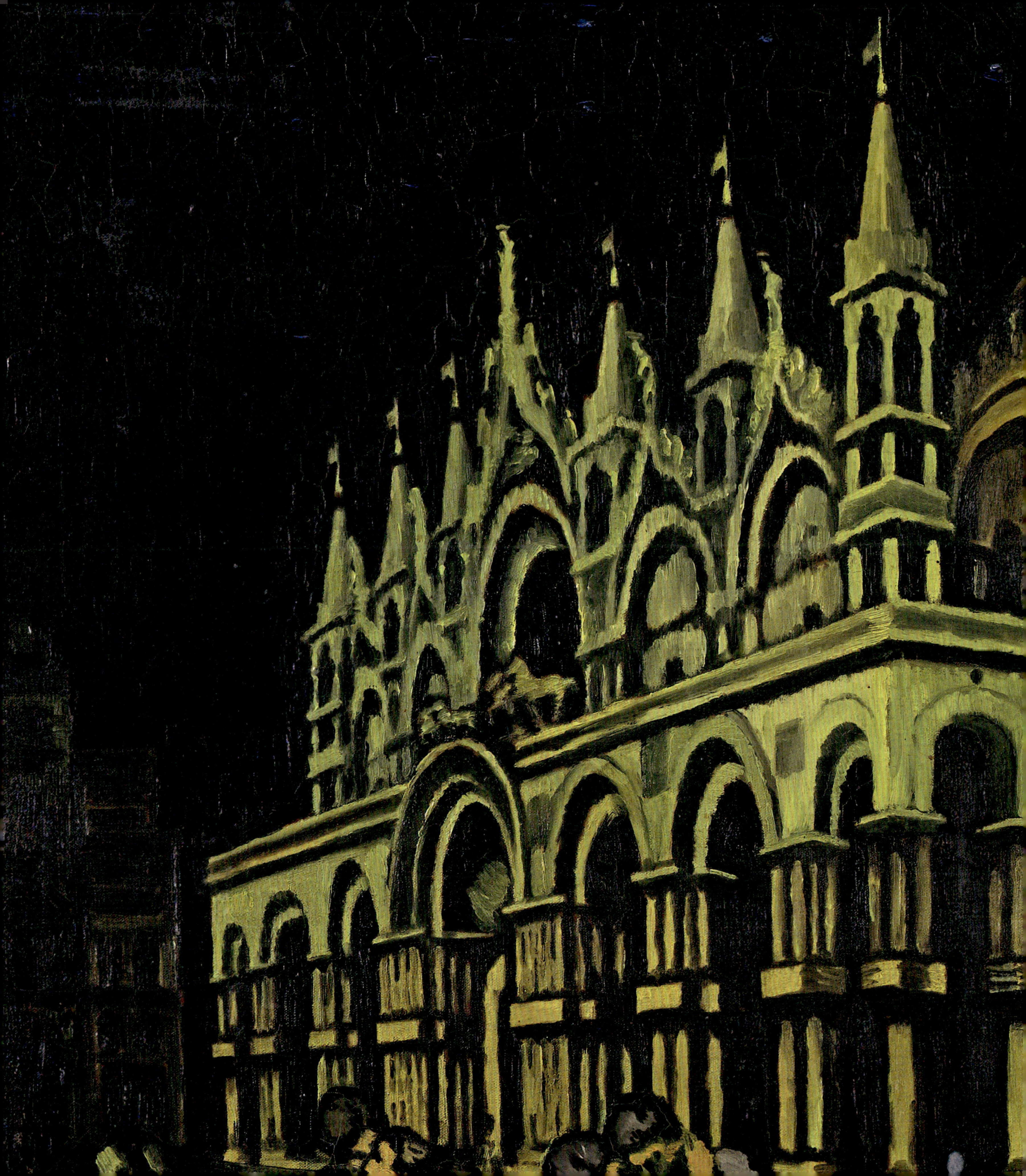

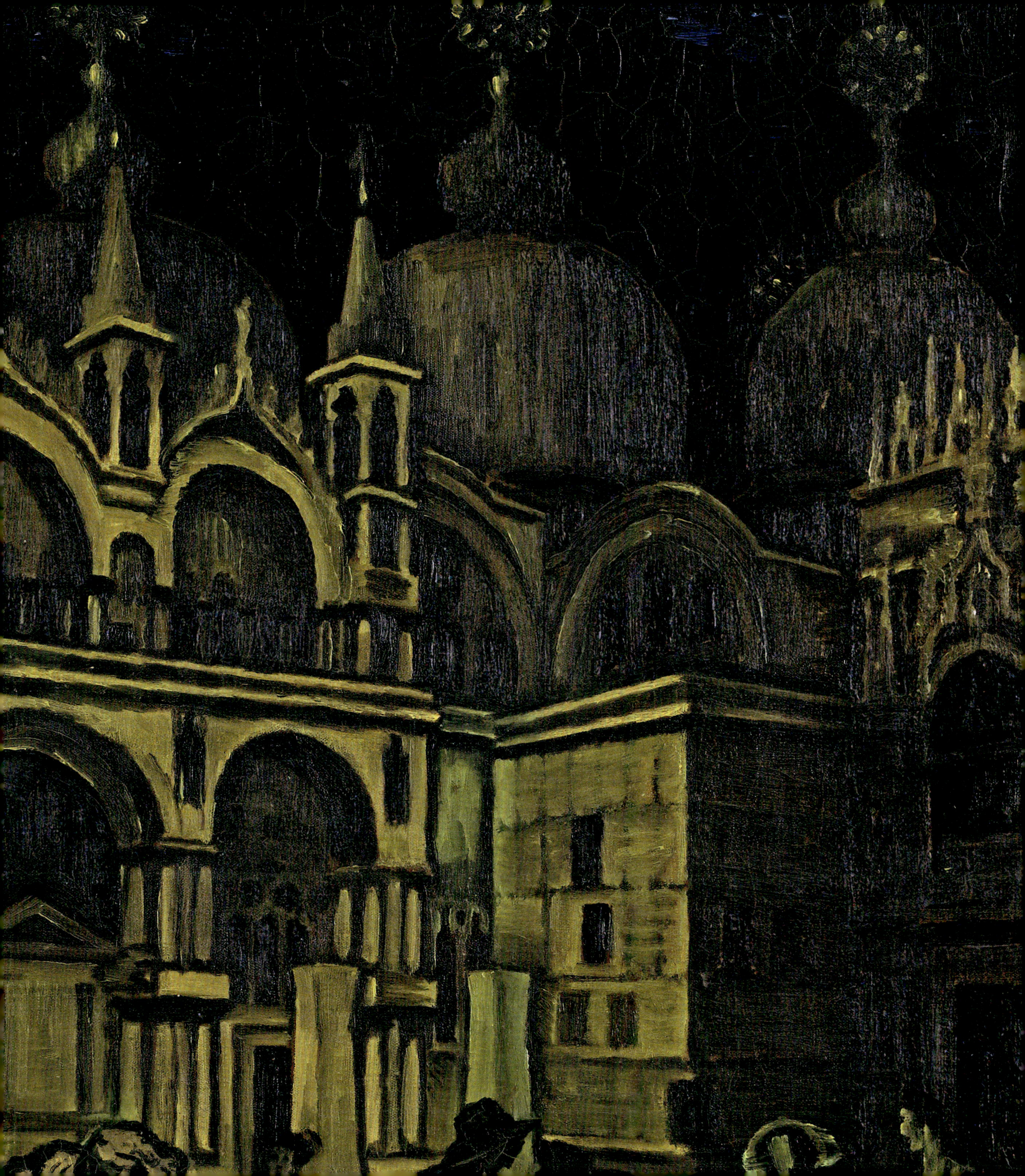

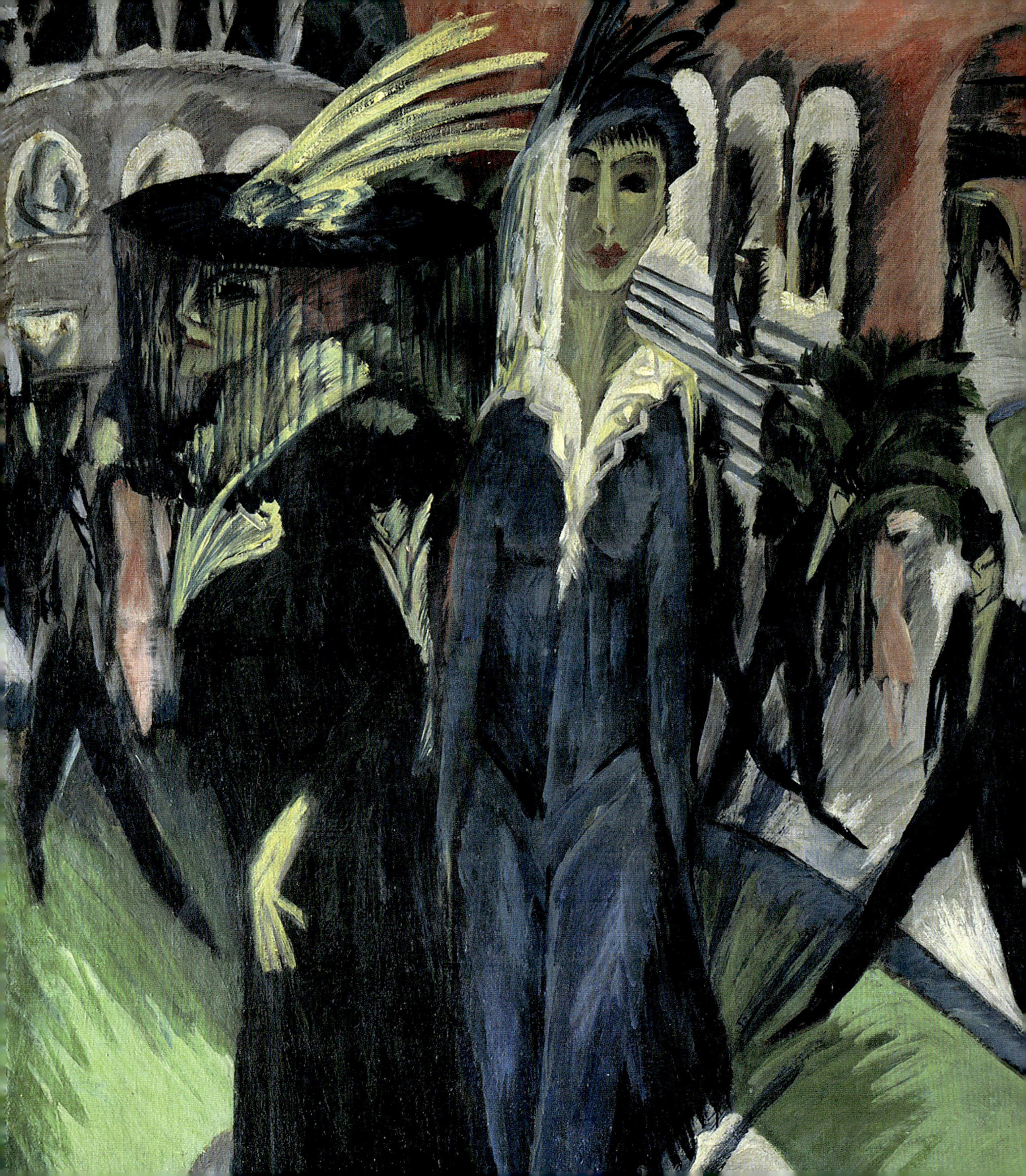

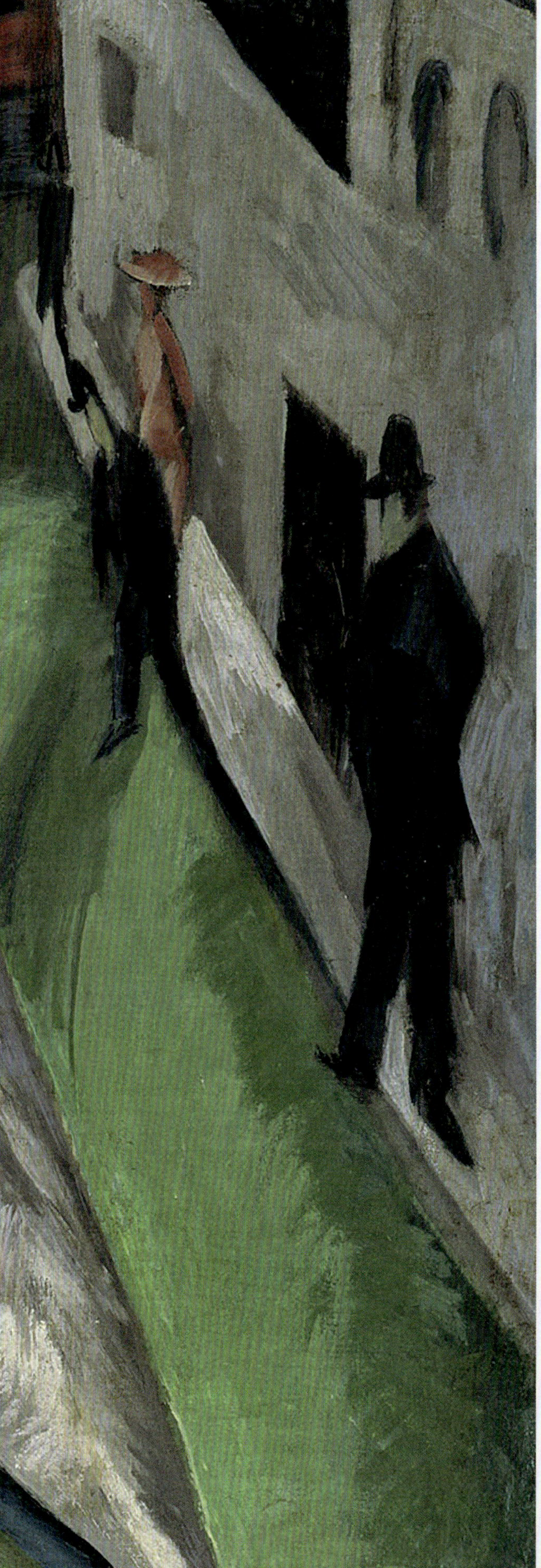

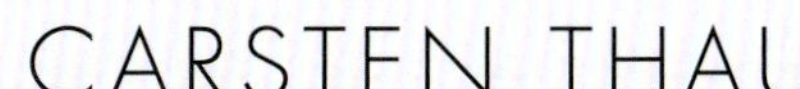

CARSTEN THAU

Refraction and Distortion: Dimensions of Time and Space in the City Paintings of Kirchner and Willumsen

Ernst Ludwig Kirchner
Detail of *Potsdamer Platz*, 1914
Oil on canvas, 200 × 150 cm
Nationalgalerie – Staatliche Museen, Berlin

I.

It is true of all visual arts throughout the twentieth century that works initially found objectionable in terms of their formal qualities become, with time, a natural part of aesthetic perception, an established norm. In this respect the works of Ernst Ludwig Kirchner and Jens Ferdinand Willumsen are an exception. They fascinate at the point of repulsion, repel as they fascinate. The experience of their cityscapes is one of ambivalence, not least due to their representation of spatiality and their confrontational use of color. The subject of the essay that follows is the dynamism, space, experience of time, and atmospheric dimensions of nightlife in the city paintings of Kirchner and Willumsen. The use of color as an element of idiosyncratic, artistic potentiation is discussed in conclusion.

II.

The Brücke artist group was founded in 1905 by four young architecture students in Dresden. During the first decade of the twentieth century the group endeavored to reconcile culture and nature by breaking out of academic insularity in a classical avant-garde attempt to build a bridge between life and art. The members of the group also wanted to catapult themselves into a new future, which among German artists in particular was inspired by a messianic dream of redemption. They had an ecstatic energy, and were such a tight-knit community that it is not always possible to identify the individual artist behind their works. The artistic explorations of the group were impregnated with impulses from Vincent van Gogh and Paul Gauguin, as well as Henri Matisse and Edvard Munch. The young artists tried in vain to involve the latter two in a direct collaboration. On the other hand, the Danish-German artist Emil Nolde Hansen, who was 30 years their senior, worked with the group for a year and a half.

The environment surrounding the Brücke artists was full of models, *femmes d'artistes*, the erotic atmosphere of the artist's studio, bodily candor, crudely made paintings confronting the viewer, outings with nude bathing, and utopian daydreams based on the Orientalism of the nineteenth century. The group also absorbed Édouard Manet and Charles Baudelaire's interest in prostitutes, as well as Gauguin's representations of sensual, "pre-civilized" women from Tahiti. Nature and the body were the most significant symbols of otherness for the members of the Brücke group. The same was true of Willumsen, as well as the contemporary group of artists in Denmark who called themselves "Hellenerne" (The Hellenes), to which Svend Hammershøi belonged, and who also pursued nude bathing and a "primeval" pact with nature, although without the same artistic radicality as the pioneers of European Modernism.[1] Throughout Europe during the period around World War I, not least in Germany, small *Lebensreform* colonies emerged with expressionist dancing, simple ancient robes, and ideas of a new culture based on craftmanship, local concepts of society, the cultivation of *Gesamtkunstwerk*, and the incorporation of elements and objects from other cultures, all part of the quest for authentic culture free of the vexations of industrial civilization.

Like other groups of the historical avant-garde, the Brücke artists formed a commune, were anti-bourgeois, and authored manifestos. The members of the group also insisted on launching their work at group exhibitions, as well as pursuing an experimental lifestyle in the utopian and liberated realm of the artist's studio. As part of the dissemination of their ideas, the Brücke artists worked with reproductive media such as woodcuts. The sharp outlines of these works, akin to those of posters or pictograms, also rubbed off on their works in oils. Within the group they spoke of using color as dynamite, an explosive detonated in the work to make the motif pulsate.[2] The Dionysian energy of the fast, rough, sharp contours of sketching coupled with the explosive release of color connects to their artist colleague Wassily Kandinsky's hope of imbuing the material with spirit ("eine Durchgeistung des Materials"), heralding the romanticization of materials that was long to hold sway over Nordic art and craftsmanship.[3] In accordance with the Vitalist impulse in color and material, at one point Kandinsky describes the shining

1. Rather than a radical subversive aesthetic, the Hellenes aspired to the authenticity of early Hellas. In German Romanticism, the issue of the modern loss of spontaneity measured against early Greek culture was addressed around the turn of the century by figures such as Friedrich Schiller. A continuation of the theme can be found in Karl Marx's *Grundrisse zur Kritik der politischen Ökonomie* (1859), where in the famous introduction he writes: "The Greeks were normal children." The modern loss of innocence in relationship to early Greek culture is similarly present in Friederich Nietzsche's *The Birth of Tragedy* (1872) and the philosophy of Martin Heidegger. The myth of the Grecian as something to be invoked and brought to life through grand gestures or a heavily mannered style is also present in Willumsen's art.

2. The term "dynamite" used by the group recalls Nietzsche's statement that in its radical departure from accepted norms, his philosophy was to act as dynamite. At one point Kirchner claims color to supersede form. On the colorist dimensions of Kirchner's woodcuts see Guenther Gercken, "Aus der Farbe Gestaltet," in Guenther Gercken and Magdalene M. Moeller, eds., *Ernst Ludwig Kirchner—Farbige Druckgraphik*, exh. cat. Brücke-Museum, Berlin/Museen Böttcherstrass, Bremen (Munich, 2008), p. 16ff.

3. In the nineteen-tens members of the Brücke group were in contact with Kandinsky's artist group Der Blaue Reiter, who they exhibited with in 1912. During the same period, Kirchner was in contact with future Bauhaus teachers, such as Oskar Schlemmer.

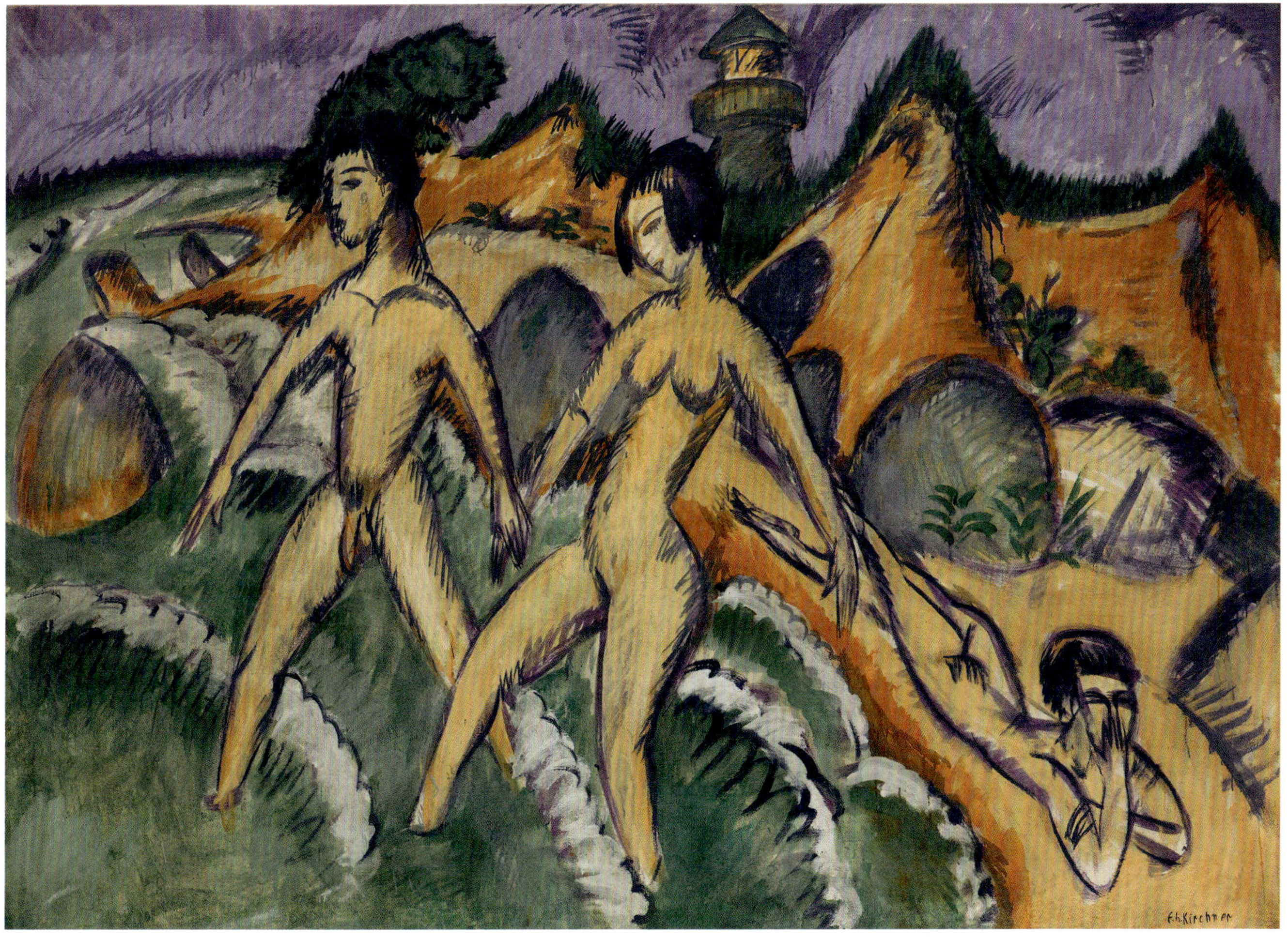

Fig. 1
Ernst Ludwig Kirchner
Ins Meer Schreitende
(Striding into the Sea), 1912
Oil on canvas,
146.4 × 200 cm
Staatsgalerie, Stuttgart

oils and vibrating colors he squeezes out of the tube as small, living creatures.[4]

III.

Kirchner's oeuvre in particular exists between two poles: on the one hand intense landscapes with people before the great temple of nature—a genre he cultivated early when on the island of Fehmarn in the Baltic—and on the other, people thrust onto the streets and squares of the metropolis, a modern maelstrom of crowds and traffic (figs. 1 and 2). In the novel *Lucky Per* by the Danish Nobel laureate Henrik Pontoppidan, published around the time Kirchner was living in Berlin, we find the following description of the frenzied pulse of the German capital:

> I have now looked around the "Unter den Linden" and am sitting in the café "Bauer" ... Outside, in the streets, there is a humming and a roaring that leaves no doubt I am in a world capital. I have the sense that I am sitting in the middle of a giant water wheel. This huge city is like a monstrous turbine that sucks up a stream of humanity and spits it out again after having consumed all its energy. What a concentration of living power! There is really something uplifting in feeling the floor beneath your feet vibrate with the discharged energy of two million men ... I have decided, provisionally, to stay here in Berlin. There is something in the life and energy here that energizes me internally. Herrrrich! It feels as if I have been charged by lightning and thunder.[5]

4. See Wassily Kandinsky, "Über die Formfrage," in Wassily Kandinsky and Franz Marc, eds., *Der Blaue Reiter Almanac* (Munich, 1912), p. 74.
5. Henrik Pontoppidan, *Lucky Per* [1898–1904], trans. Naomi Lebowitz (New York, 2010), p. 192.

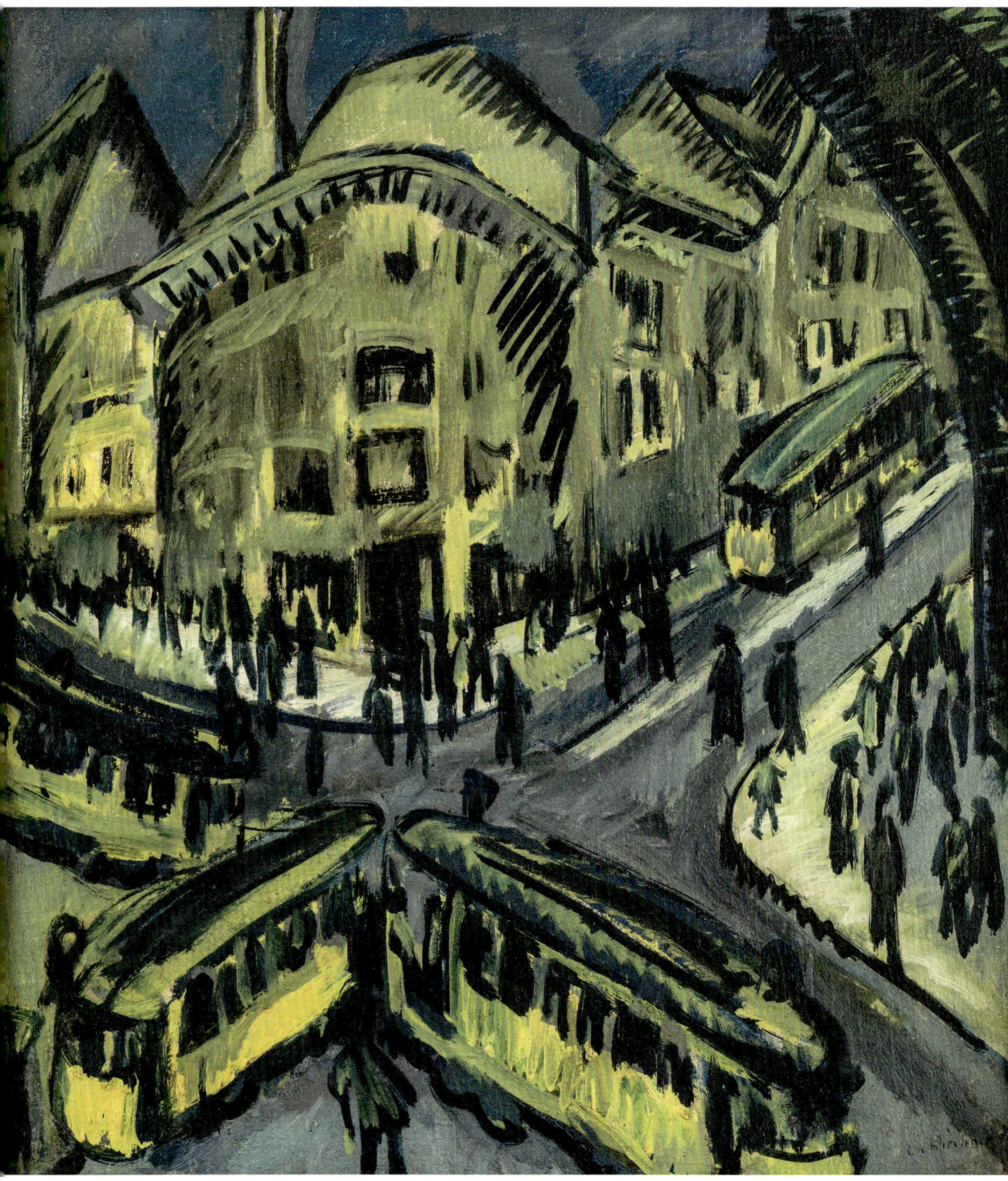

Fig. 2
Ernst Ludwig Kirchner
Nollendorfplatz Berlin
(Nollendorf Square, Berlin),
1912
Oil on canvas, 69 × 60 cm
Stiftung Stadtmuseum Berlin

As expressed indirectly in Pontoppidan's enthusiastic representation, Vitalism appears to be connected not only to an intensified sense of vitality in nature, the exhilarated metabolism of the body, ecstasy, and dancing desire, but also to the mighty machine of the metropolis.

IV.

Kirchner and the other Brücke artists moved to Berlin in 1911. Kirchner demonstrates a greater sensitivity to the chaos of the city than others in the group: its fragmentary flux of passers-by, bizarre physiognomies, aloof streetwalkers, and carriages and trams rattling through the alleys of the city under the glare of electric streetlamps erupting like yellow acid. Kirchner immerses himself in a flood of impressions, seeking out the riotous shockwaves of metropolitan life (fig. 3). He records his fleeting impressions in his sketchbook as he walks—glancing only sporadically at the page. His swiftly sketched snapshots overlap each other in a chaotic montage.

The French Fauvists, pioneered by Henri Matisse and André Derain, made their entrance the year the Brücke group was formed at the famous 1905 *Salon d'Automne* in Paris. For the members of the group, Matisse was an essential source of inspiration. Few French artists at the time dealt with the bustling traffic of the metropolis.[6] Matisse worked primarily with color-saturated canvasses and solid, juxtaposed brushstrokes to depict houses and landscapes in the provinces of the South of France, as well as interiors and portraits. This was in contrast to the works of his French predecessors, such as Claude Monet and Camille Pissarro, whose grainy, light-flooded boulevard paintings depict urban circulation from above the crowds to depict major traffic arteries like Boulevard Montmartre from a balcony perspective (fig. 4).

Monet and Pissarro represented the anonymous masses on foot and in carriages with short, abrupt black strokes that both mime the crowd—are its optical equivalent—and create a new convention for cityscapes: figures represented as black silhouettes in a form of hieroglyphic punctuation that reappears in a number of Kirchner's paintings. In Paris the rushing torrent of people and vehicles becomes an image of what French Vitalist philosopher Henri Bergson called *élan vital*, a dynamic, vital impulse concentrated in time that the philosopher saw pervading every aspect of life.[7] The spectacle of the boulevard with its chaos of perpetual motion could only be observed as a whole from an elevated point of view, sometimes with the head of the artist himself or someone in his place looking out from a balcony at the very edge of the painting.[8]

After the Fauvists, led by Matisse, had left the motif of the city and its frenetic dynamic behind, it was taken up again, in Germany by Kirchner. The Brücke artists were

6. André Derain did in fact paint a series of works from London. The works did not, however, focus on the busy traffic of the city, but on colorist depictions of the Thames and the city's bridges, buildings, etc.

7. Henri Bergson, *L´evolution créatrice* (Paris, 1907).

8. See "Gadens uendelige vibrationer – storbyen som perpetuum mobile," in Carsten Thau, *Arkitekturen som Tidsmaskine* (Copenhagen, 2001), pp. 83–101.

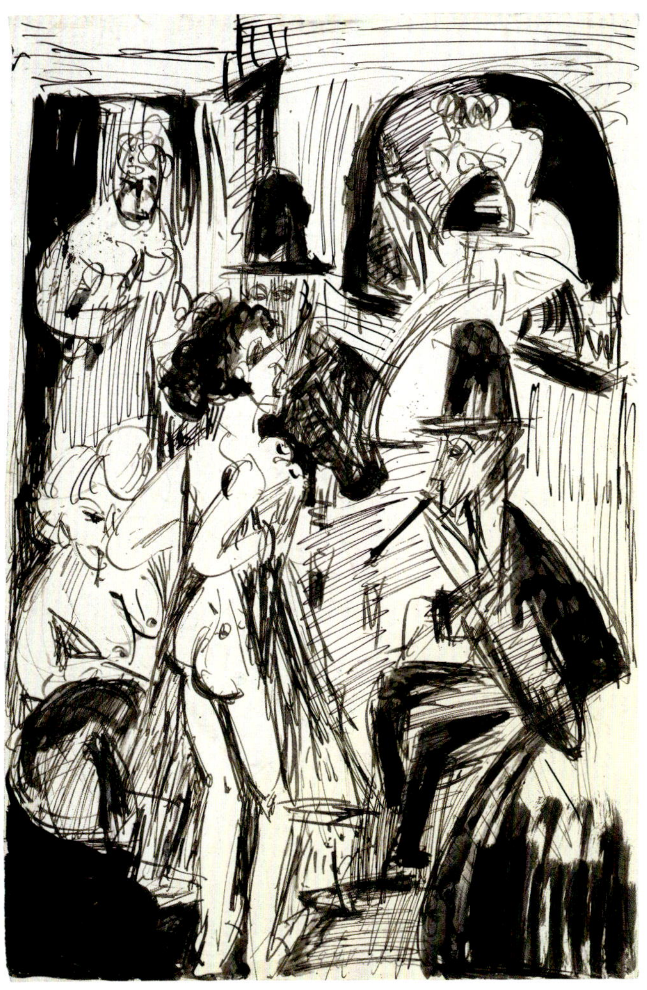

Fig. 3
Ernst Ludwig Kirchner
Bordell (Brothel), 1913
Watercolor, 49.8 × 33 cm
Brücke-Museum,
Karl und Emy Schmidt-Rottluff Stiftung, Berlin

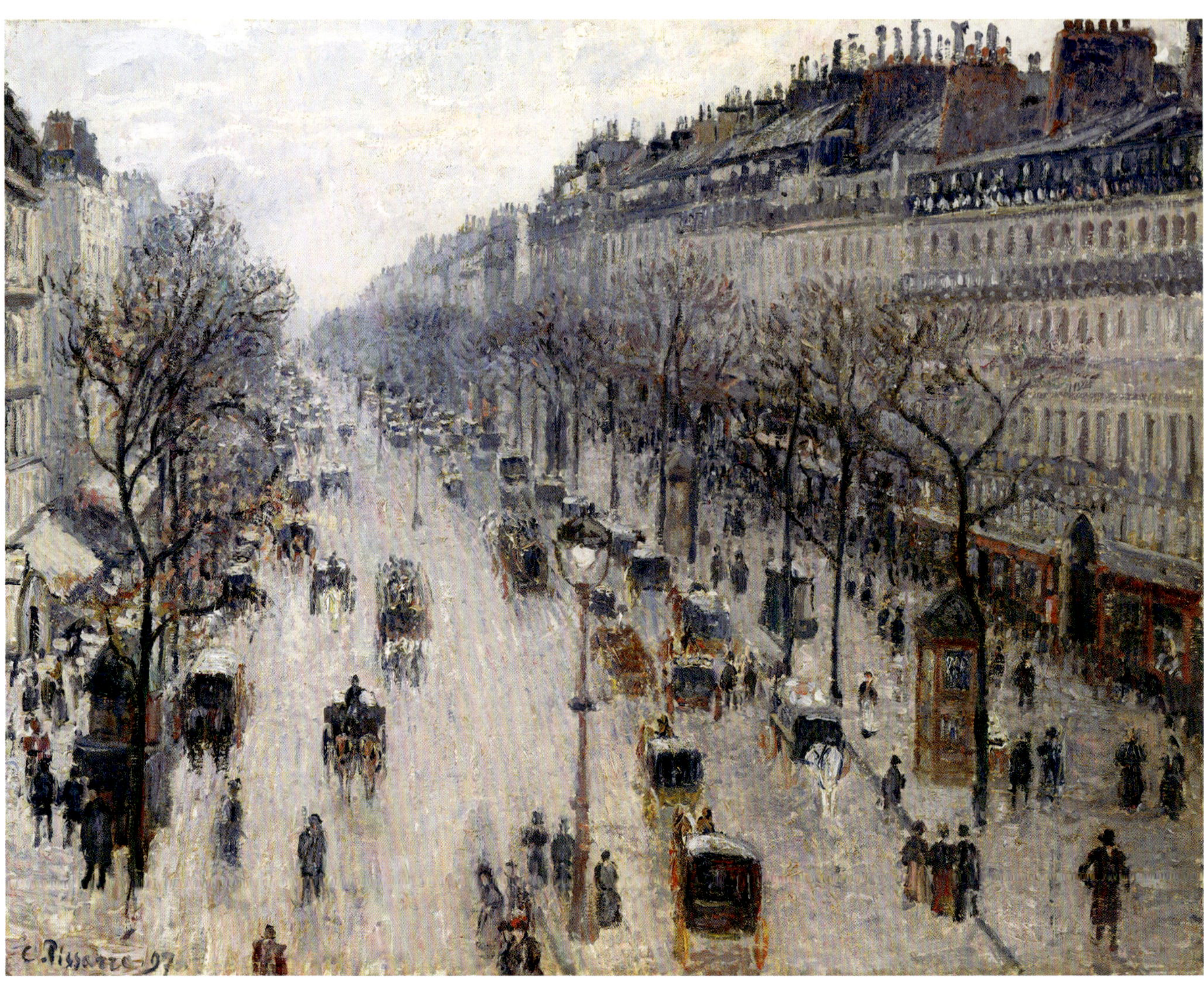

Fig. 4
Camille Pissarro
Boulevard Montmartre, un matin d'hiver (The Boulevard Montmartre on a Winter Morning), 1897
Oil on canvas, 64.8 × 81.3 cm
The Metropolitan Museum of Art, New York

familiar with the works of Monet and Pissarro, and Max Pechstein reportedly wrote home from Paris to say that if people wanted to see French art exhibited, they should travel to Germany. The city paintings of the Impressionists were widely exhibited in Germany during the first decade of the twentieth century. But whereas the Impressionists viewed the boulevard as a grand, panoramic landscape, Kirchner's perspective is down among the crowd in intense, close contact with others. He sketches on the move, governed by what Baudelaire called *beauté fugitive*: a sense of beauty that arises from the transitory and passing rather than any sense of permanence. Kirchner was familiar with Baudelaire's *Le peintre de la vie moderne*[9]—on Constantin Guys—but it is in his Berlin series, in the "spleen" of the works, that we see the spirit of Baudelaire's prose poem: the sense of the overlooked, the anonymous masses, the flaneur, the streetwalker, randomness, and chance. What is striking when Kirchner looks up is the way the painting warps and wraps around the disparate and disassociated crowd, frontally concentrated or tautly stretched across the city scene—a disparate set of people and vehicles with an identifiable monument such as the Brandenburg Gate or Potsdamer Platz as a stage for the composition (fig. 5).

A number of Willumsen's Venice paintings also depict similarly dispersed crowds of mutually distanced indi-

9. Charles Baudelaire, "The Painter of Modern Life," in *The Painter of Modern Life and Other Essays*, ed. and trans. Jonathan Mayne (London, 1964).

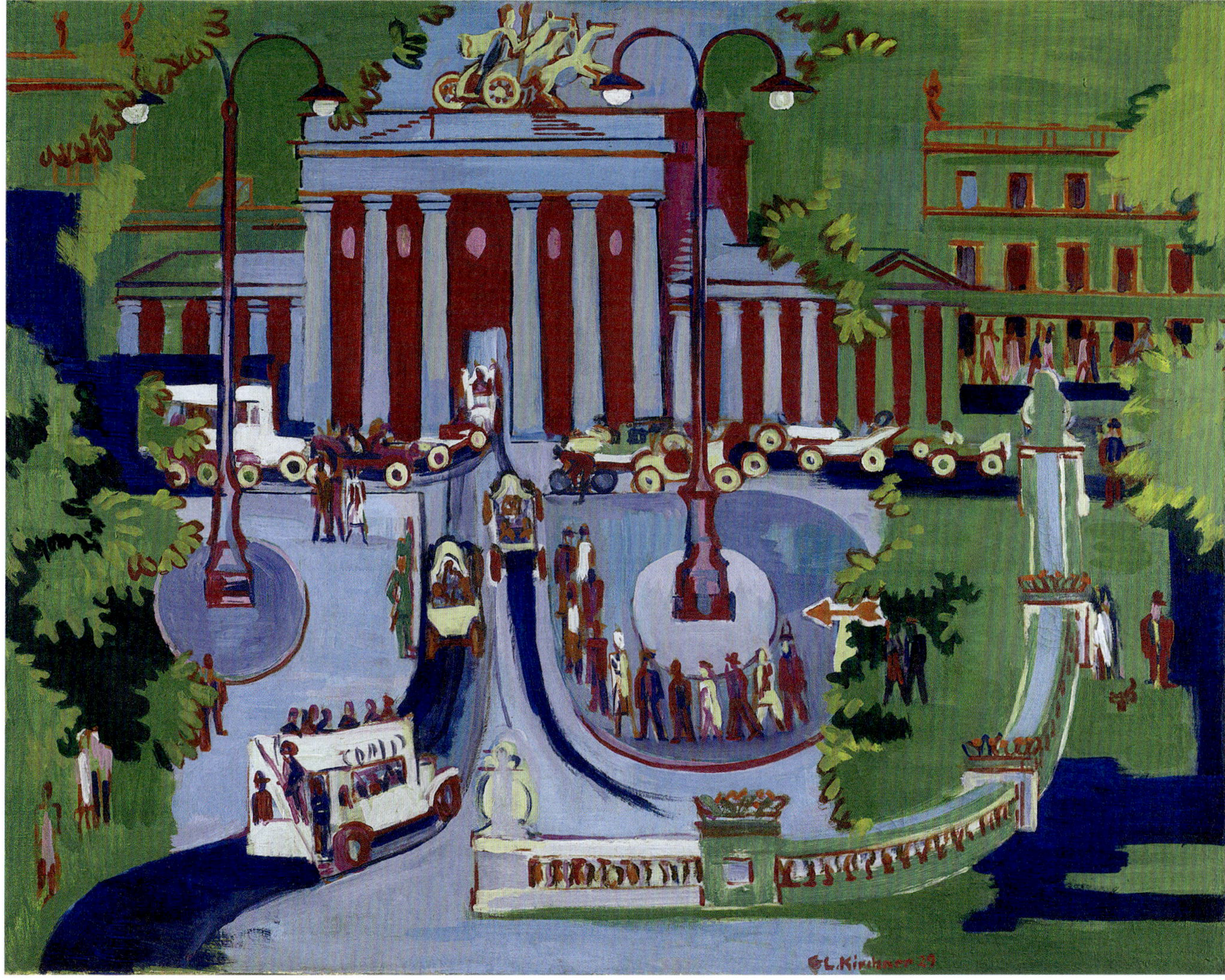

Fig. 5
Ernst Ludwig Kirchner
Brandenburger Tor
(Brandenburg Gate), 1929
Oil on canvas, 121 × 149.5 cm
Städel Museum, Frankfurt am Main

viduals in a prominent architectural setting in works such as *Markuspladsen. Venedig. Nat. Fantasi* (St Mark's Square. Venice. Night. Fantasy, fig. 6) and *Moloen med San Giorgio* (The Molo with San Giorgio, fig. 7). The people populating the paintings are a judicious mix of figures in a landscape, in the latter looking up at the Doge's Palace with a woman in evening dress in the foreground, a scene of fleeting passers-by at night.[10] The figures, presumably primarily tourists, create an atmosphere of elated desolation in a theatrical setting of mysteriously receding buildings, a romantic, polymorphic scene. Like Kirchner, in his Venice series Willumsen paints famous monuments such as Scuola Grande in San Marco and the columns of the Piazzetta. His more deserted or purely architectural paintings, as extreme as they might appear in the eerie moonlight,[11] are without the intense experience of modernity and city stress and strain of Kirchner's Berlin paintings. Naturally, perhaps, given that his subject—the lagoon city of Venice—is a smaller, more hushed urban setting. Neither do they possess the highly dramatic manipulation of perspective using spatial elements and boundaries seen in Kirchner's Berlin paintings of the nineteen-tens (fig. 8).

In this specific context Willumsen's city paintings are less radical. This is also true of a much earlier city scene, *Billede af livet på Paris' kajer* (Life on the Quays of Paris,

10. Akin to J. F. Willumsen's portraits of Michelle Bourret, who he lived with later in life.
11. As in the works of El Greco, the moon breaks through a frayed cloud above the San Trovaso Canal like an ominous flash, an optical astigmatism.

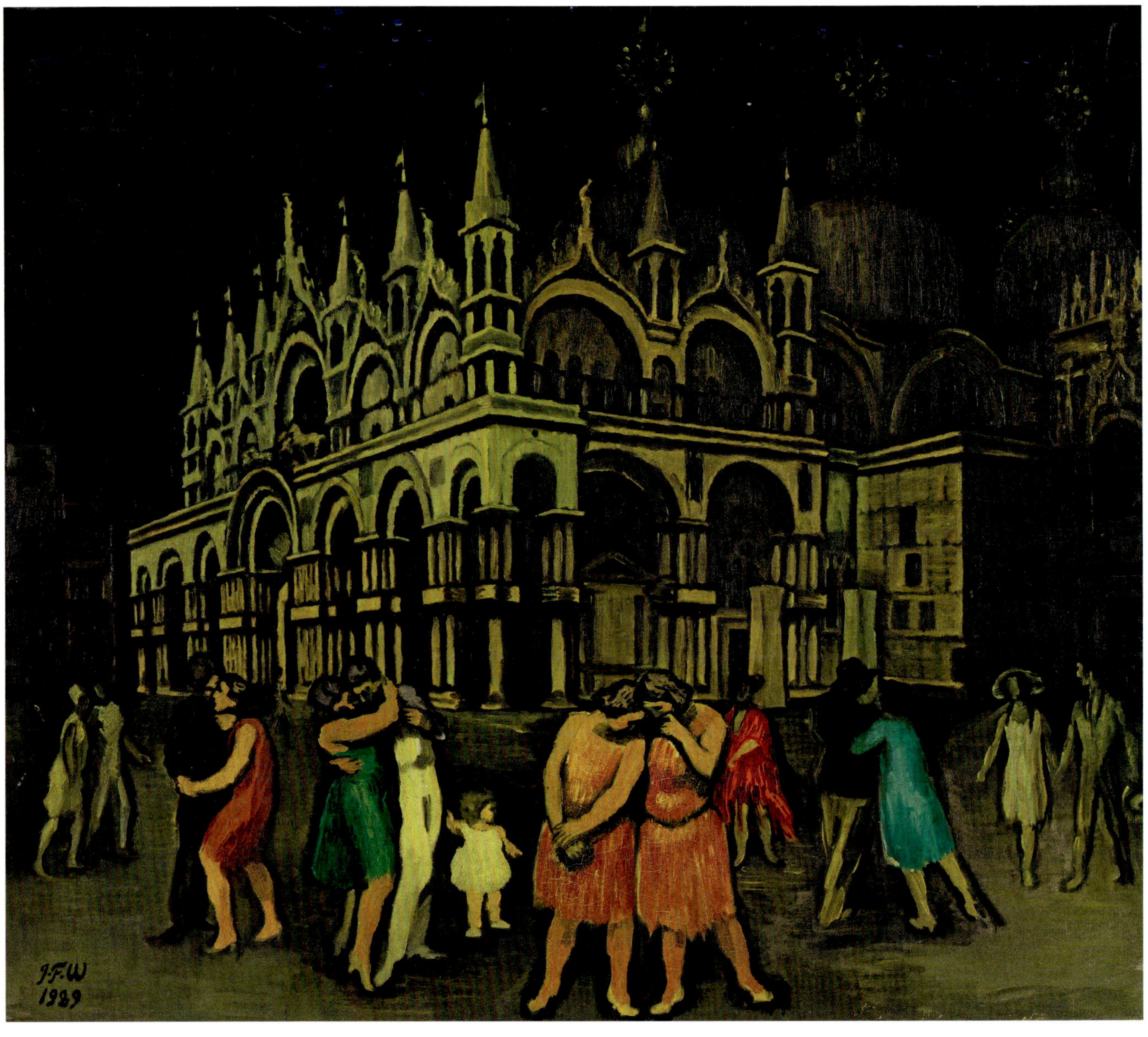

Fig. 6
J. F. Willumsen
Markuspladsen. Venedig. Nat. Fantasi (St Mark's Square. Venice. Night. Fantasy), 1929
Oil on canvas, 87 × 97 cm
Willumsen's Museum, Frederikssund

1890, fig. 9), which as a scene of life provides a charming view of people moving through the city on foot and in carriages. The painting is a captivating depiction of the city based on a photograph in an English magazine presenting life by the Seine and Notre Dame. The dramatic zigzagging composition is also based on the photograph. Willumsen himself describes his focus as "depicting the swarming life of people and carriages in black moving in every direction."[12] The Danish word for swarm was also included in the first title of his painting *La Fourmilière* (The Anthill).[13] It does not possess the same sense of flowing traffic (inspired by Monet and Pissarro) of Edvard Munch's canvasses of Rue de Rivoli and Rue Lafayette seen from a balcony of the following year, as their sublime profusion and sense of acceleration in the face of a colossal release of energy unequivocally radicalize the boulevard paintings of the Impressionists (figs. 10 and 11).[14]

12. See Leila Krogh, *J.F. Willumsen – over grænser*, exh. cat. Ordrupgaard, Charlottenlund/Musée d´Orsay, Paris (Charlottenlund, 2010), pp. 68–69.
13. Ibid.
14. See Thau 2001 (see note 8), p. 97.

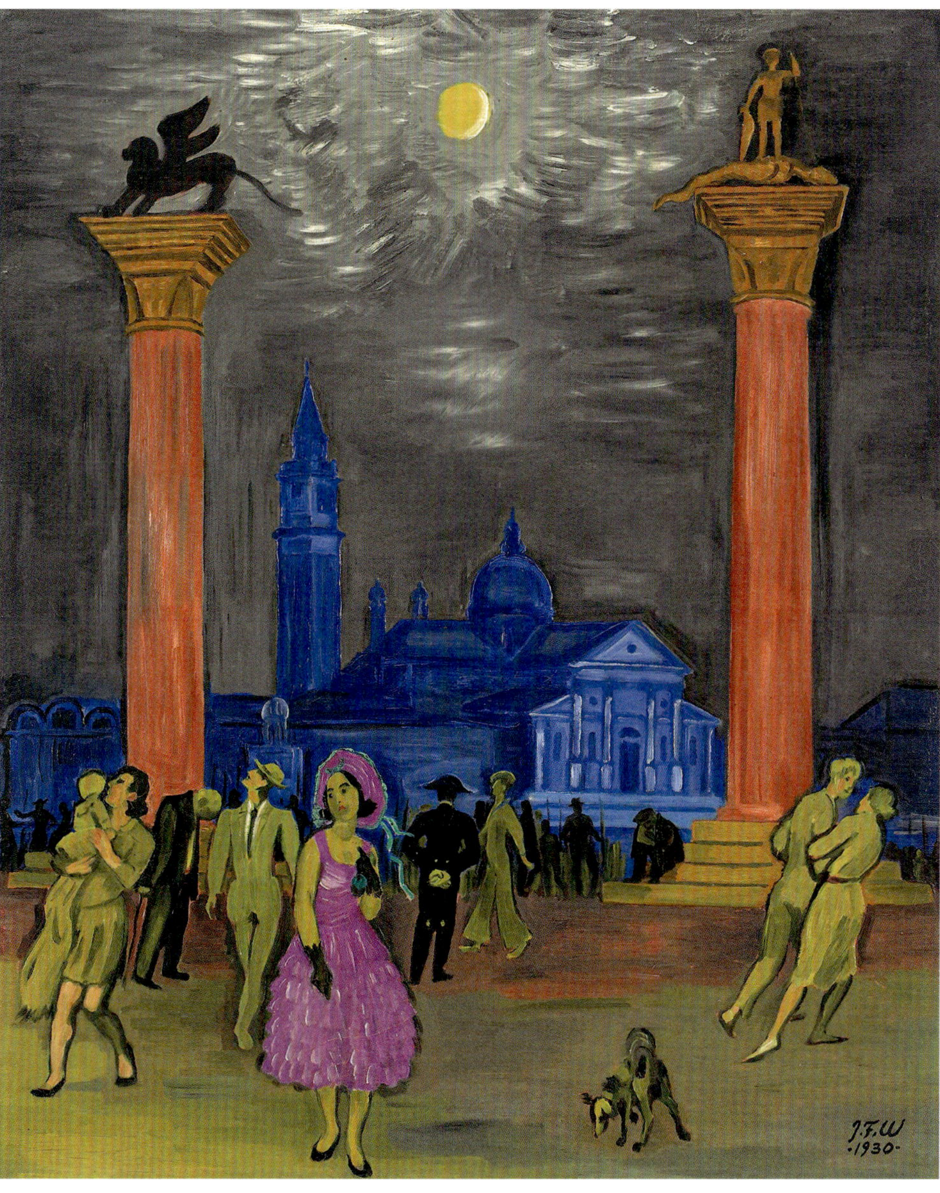

Fig. 7
J. F. Willumsen
Moloen med San Giorgio
(The Molo with San Giorgio), 1930
Oil on canvas, 92 × 73 cm
Willumsen's Museum, Frederikssund

V.

Whereas in his early works Willumsen apparently comes to terms with the city as a lifeworld, for a number of reasons Kirchner is more deeply affected, for instance when walking through the city after the Brücke group had fallen apart, facing the collapse of the utopian dream of an artists' collective that was to bring about a radically new society.

Kirchner describes the years between 1911 and 1914 as the loneliest time of his life, during which he was driven by restlessness into streets full of people and carriages day and night. Yet the more he was among people, the more acutely he felt his isolation and exclusion, despite the fact that nobody in the anonymous crowd could be claimed to be consciously excluding him. This caused despondency, a feeling that could only be dissipated with willpower and work. He learned how to make himself invisible from all the lonely people brushing past each other, yet acting as if they were invisible to each other.

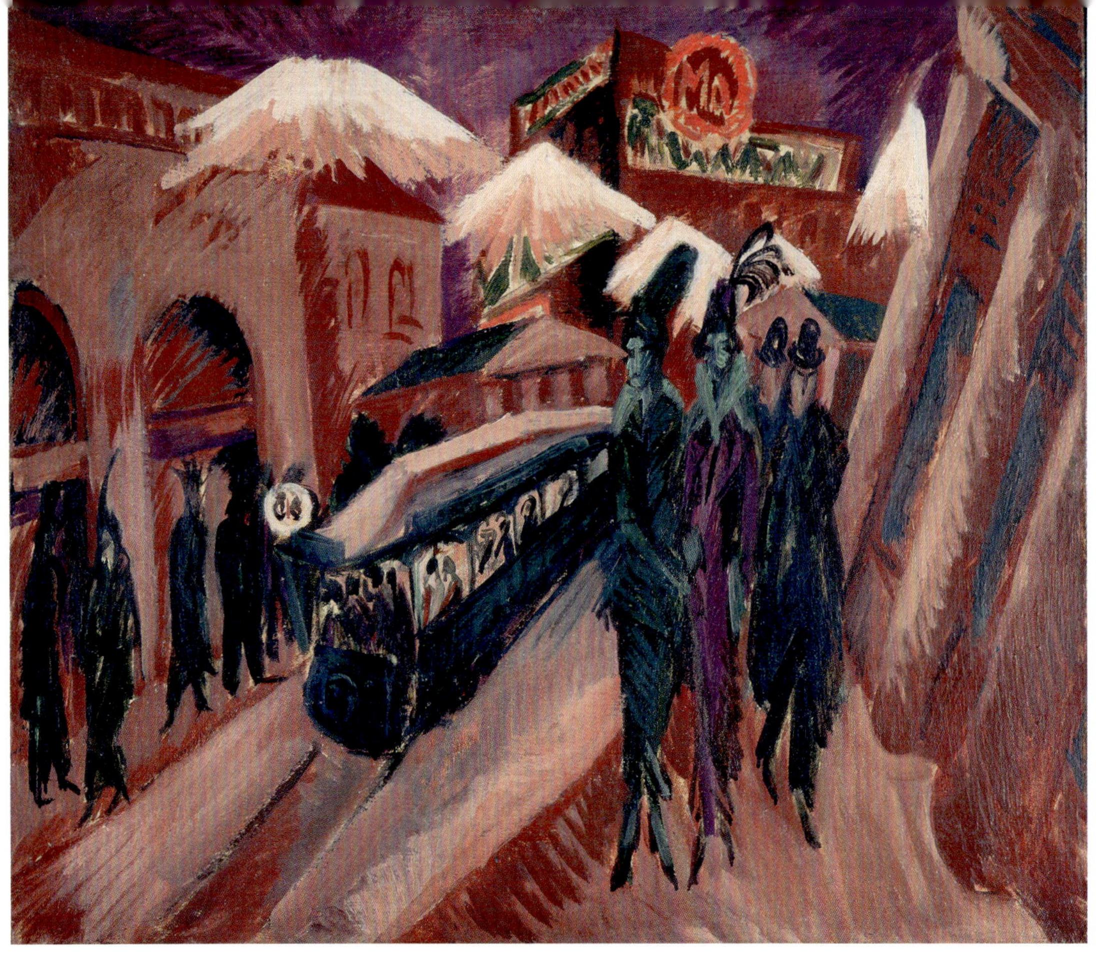

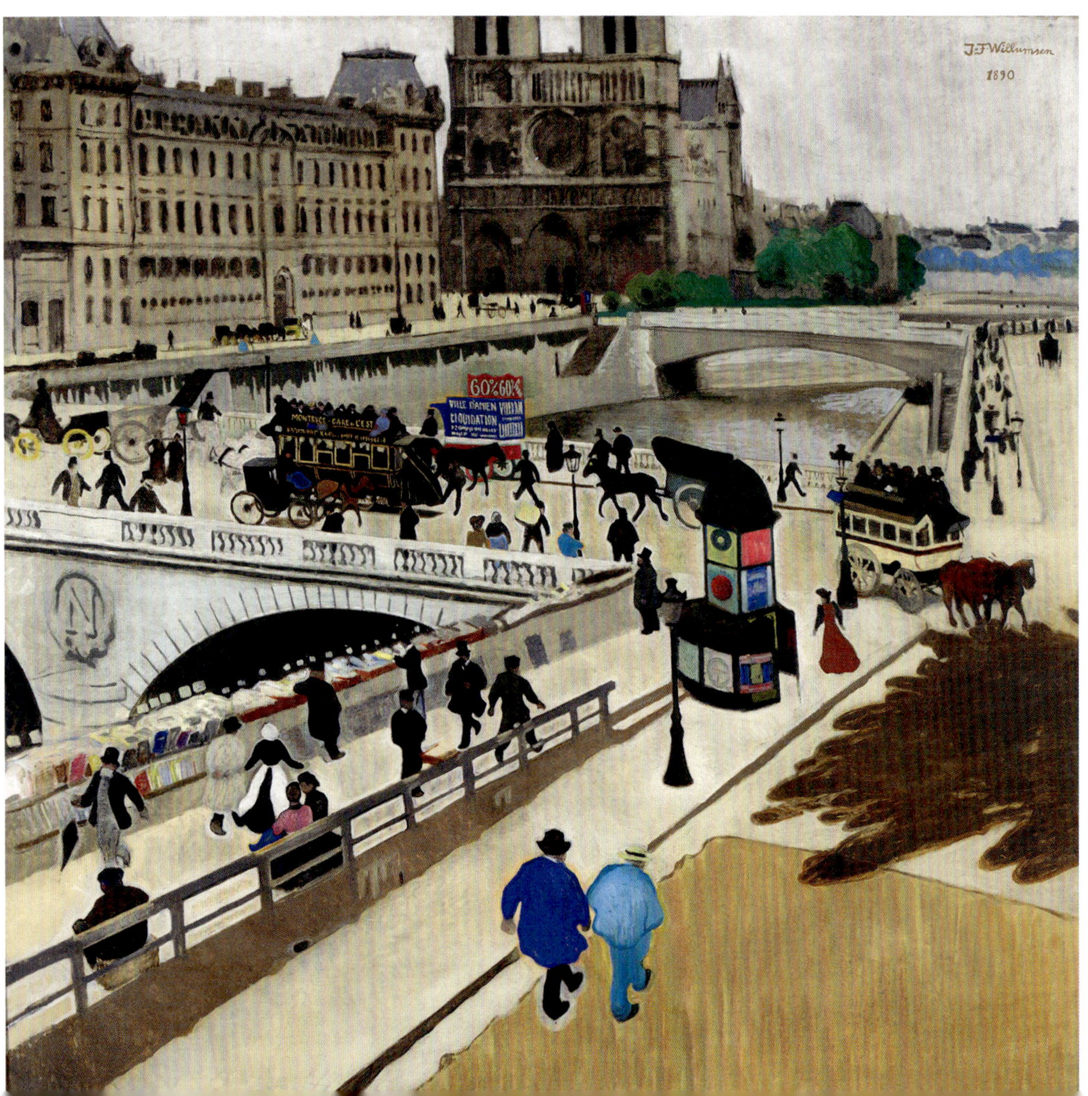

Fig. 8
Ernst Ludwig Kirchner
Leipziger Strasse mit Elektrischer Bahn
(Leipzig Street with Electric Tram), 1914
Oil on canvas, 69.5×79 cm
Museum Folkwang, Essen

Fig. 9
J. F. Willumsen
Billede af livet på Paris' kajer (Life on the Quays of Paris), 1890
Oil on canvas, 150×150.5 cm
Willumsen's Museum, Frederikssund

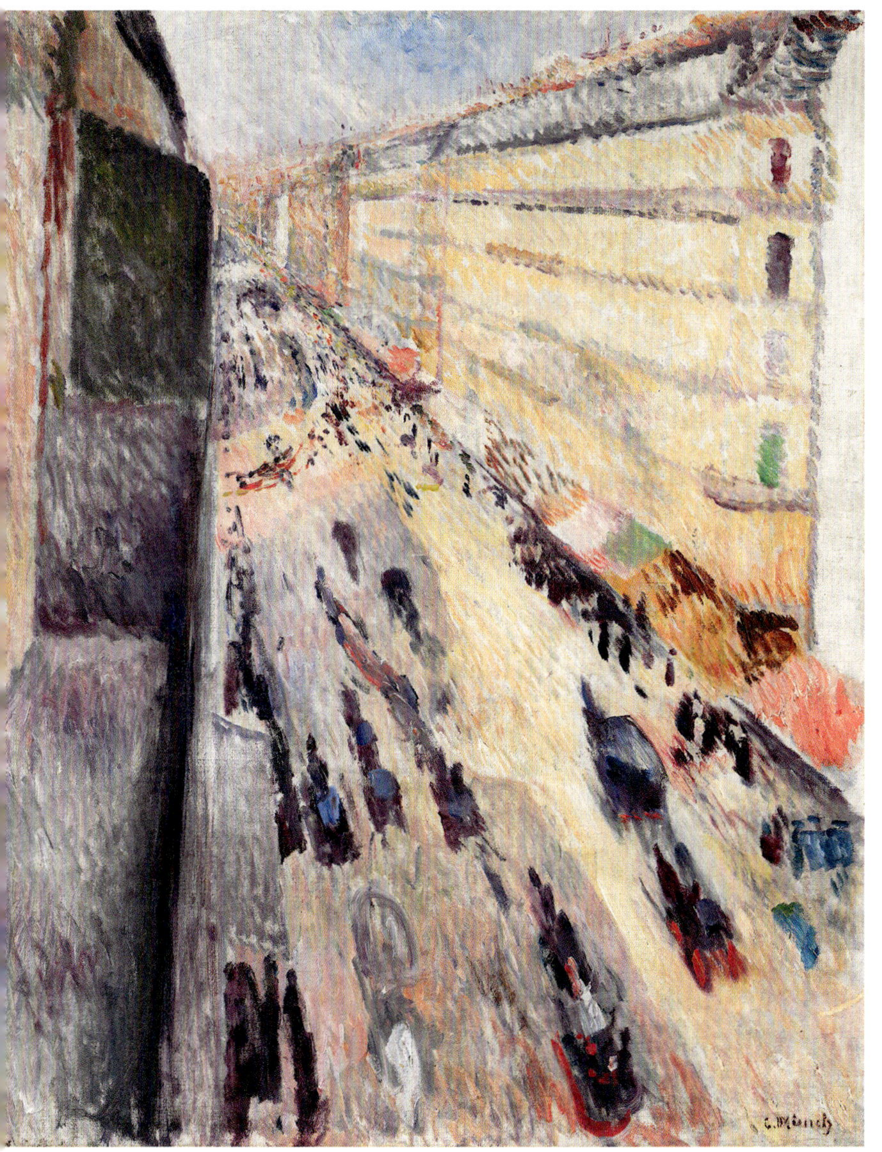

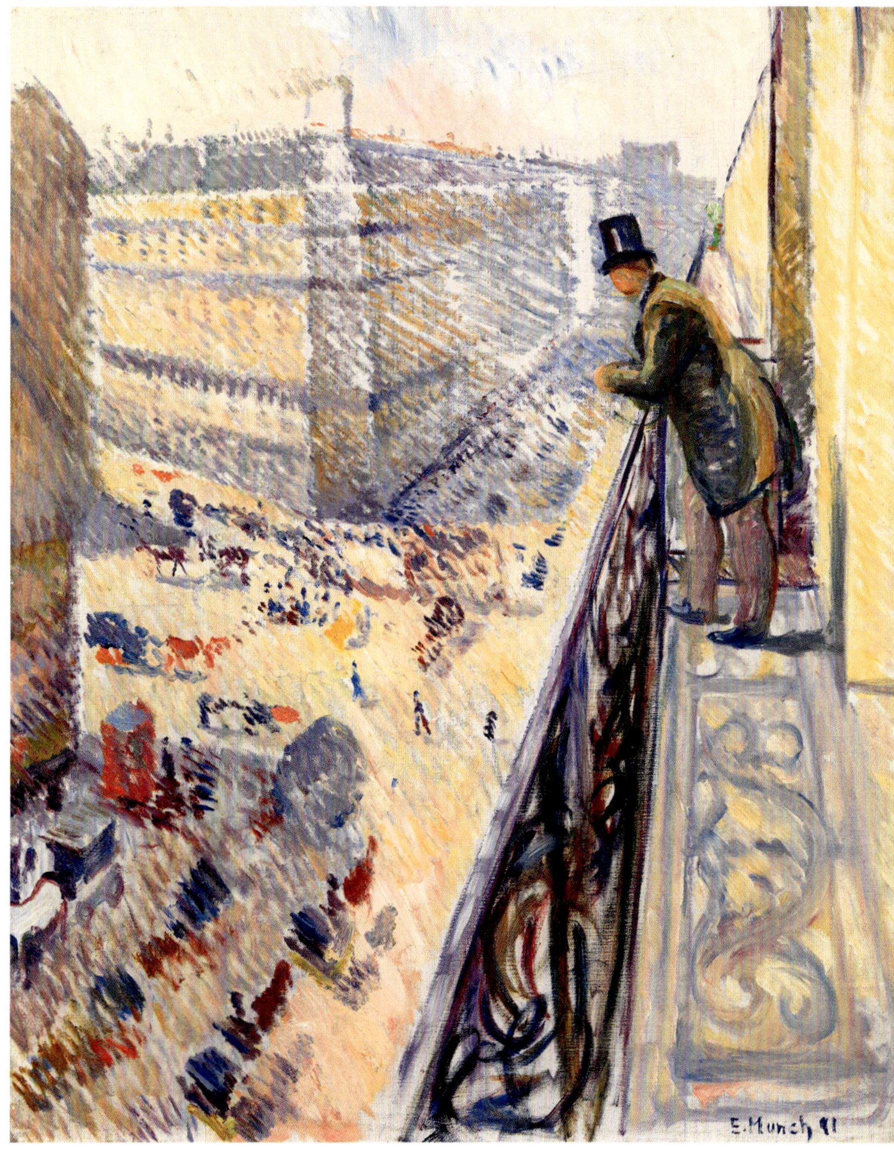

Fig. 10
Edvard Munch
Rue de Rivoli, 1891
Oil on canvas, 81×65.1 cm
Harvard Art Museums/Fogg Museum, gift from Rudolf Serkin, Cambridge

Fig. 11
Edvard Munch
Rue Lafayette, 1891
Oil on canvas, 92×73 cm
The National Museum, Oslo

It was during these years that Kirchner met a number of artists including the author Alfred Döblin, whose novel *Berlin Alexanderplatz* together with works by artist colleagues such as George Grosz have, for an international audience, become the quintessence of the bewitching city and roaring twenties, alongside the dynamic, disconnected montage of Walter Ruttmann's film *Berlin: Die Sinfonie der Grossstadt* (Berlin—Symphony of a Metropolis, 1927). The film's metaphorically orchestrated scene showing the vertigo of a suicidal woman, however, means that despite its spell-binding portrayal of the city and the urban apparatus, the view of the metropolis of Berlin presented in the film is dystopian.

VI.

No cultural philosopher of Kirchner's age has described the lifeworld of the city as precisely as Georg Simmel, who grew up in the heart of Berlin on the corner of Leipziger Strasse and Friedrichstrasse, one of the busiest crossroads next to the city hotspot of Potsdamer Platz. Simmel's social-psychological essay "The Metropolis and Mental Life"[15] addresses the emotions and state of alert also seen in Kirchner's own reaction: the loneliness in the crowd, the blasé attitude, the nervous strain, and the urge to make oneself invisible.

Simmel's influence was considerable. His private lectures were reported in Berlin newspapers, and his private salons in Berlin were attended by artists, writers, and future cultural theorists, such as Ernst Bloch (who later wrote an analysis of Pontoppidan's *Lucky Per*), Siegfried Kracauer, and Walter Benjamin. Simmel corresponded with Henri Bergson, with whom he shares a seismographic receptiveness to city phenomena. Bergson, like Baudelaire, was widely read by French and German artists, as well as by the Italian Futurists, whose obsession with city life and the universal *dinamismo* of mechanization and its transformation of space and time owe much to Bergson.

Like Simmel in his essay, Kirchner in his art—comprised of paintings, pastels and hundreds of sketches—focuses on interactions in public space that give rise to phenomena such as detachment, indifference, distance, and the loss of meaning to be found in the metropolis as a living network of vehicles and the existence of passersby, an agitated anthill of shock receptors. A state that goes hand in hand with an acute, urban, nervous strain. A commonly used stock phrase is the "cocaine nerves" of the metropolis. What many may already know is that Kirchner was a heavy consumer of drugs, sleeping pills, and alcohol. He was at times intoxicated, something that may have contributed to the "hallucinatory" nature of his imagery.[16]

VII.

Above all, like Simmel's essay Kirchner's art provides significant insights regarding perception, the experience of time, and the tempi of city scenes, as well as the strikingly anonymous flow of the masses. At a general level Simmel analyzed money as a connecting link in the new Babylon of Berlin. Like Baudelaire before him, Kirchner sees the prostitute as emblematic of the pecuniary exchanges that permeate the very fiber of economic transactions and physical desire in the metropolis,[17] as portrayed in his famous city scenes of streetwalkers, agitated tumult, and the exchange of stolen glances (fig. 12). It was prohibited for prostitutes in contemporary Berlin to accompany their customers on the street. They were to keep on the move, and were not allowed to stand in front of shop windows. They were also constantly under the surveillance of plain-clothes police officers. In keeping with the ambiguity of the rest of the gallery of characters, these bowler-clad figures in Kirchner's works can also be seen as potential customers.[18]

This flux in the urban environment became more pronounced as it expanded in the face of an exploding population. On the other hand, Simmel, in line with key

15. See Georg Simmel, "The Metropolis and Mental Life," in Gary Bridge and Sophie Watson, eds. *The Blackwell City Reader* (Oxford, 2010), pp. 105–110.
16. This was true before and especially after his breakdown as a soldier during World War I, when he became dependent on morphine and considerable amounts of absinthe.
17. In Berlin contact with prostitutes primarily took place on the streets, unlike in Paris with its many brothels. Willumsen also portrayed prostitution in the city in brothel scenes inspired by the works of Toulouse-Lautrec.
18. See Charles W. Haxthausen, "Motion Pictures: On Kirchner's Berlin Street Scenes," in Sandra Gianfreda, ed., *Vibrant Metropolis / Idyllic Nature: The Berlin Years*, exh. cat. Kunsthaus Zürich (Munich, 2017), p. 22.

Fig. 12
Ernst Ludwig Kirchner
Friedrichstrasse
(Friedrich Street), 1914
Oil on canvas, 125 × 91 cm
Staatsgalerie, Stuttgart

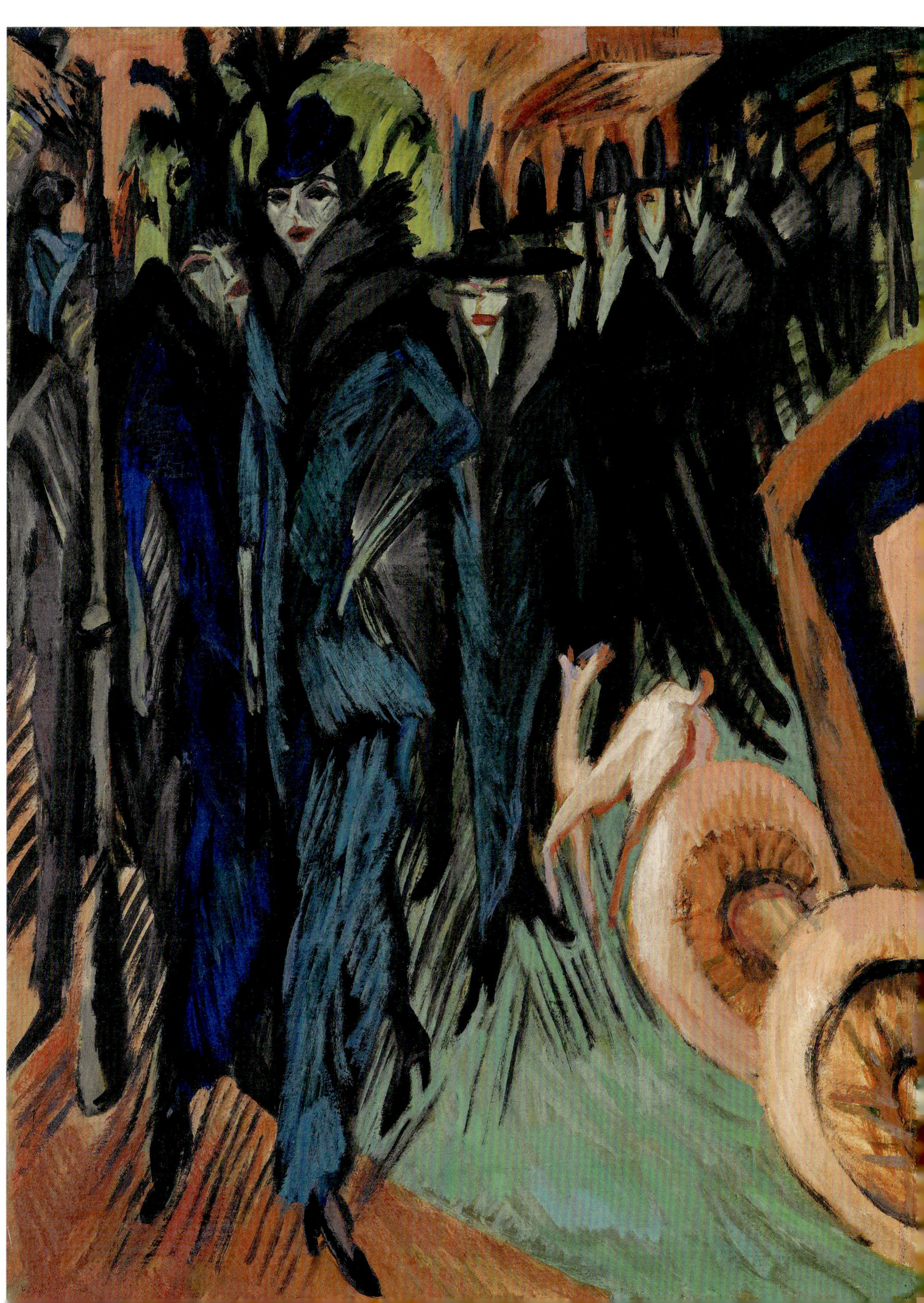

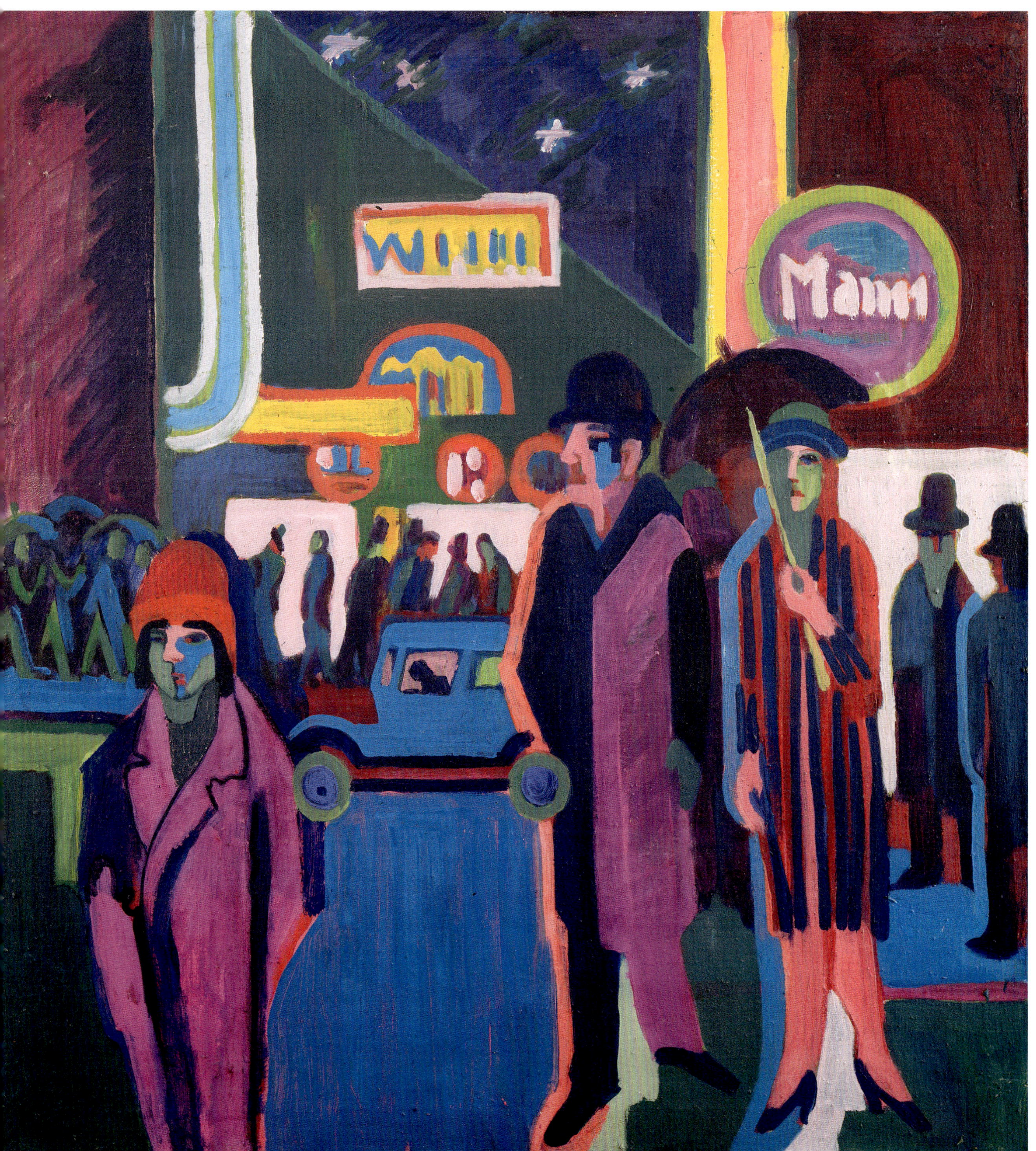

Fig. 13
Ernst Ludwig Kirchner
Strassenszene bei Nacht
(Street Scene at Night), 1925
Oil on canvas, 100×90 cm
Kunsthalle Bremen

Fig. 14
Ernst Ludwig Kirchner
Strasse, Berlin
(Street, Berlin), 1913
Oil on canvas,
120.6×91.1 cm
The Museum of Modern Art,
New York

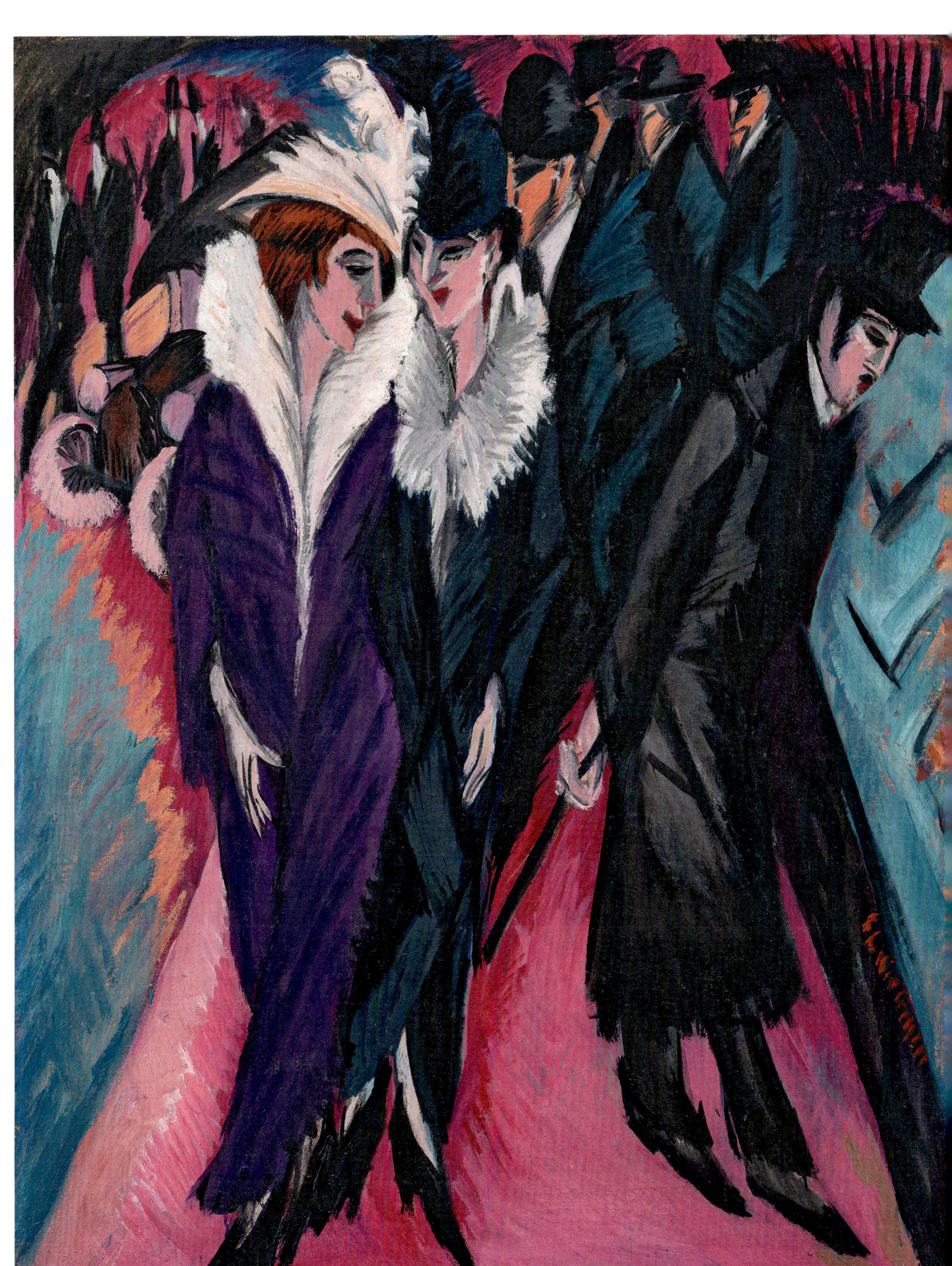

impulses among the Brücke artists and other contemporary circles of German intellectual life, shared the longing for a more "concrete culture" in keeping with *Lebensreform* ideas of local community and rootedness.[19] Something that at first glance would appear to be a contrast to Simmel and Kirchner's striking sensitivity to the city universe. When focusing on new forms of mobility and the city as machine, it is important to remember that during their lifetime these artists were witness not only to the invention of the automobile, but also electric trams, Zeppelins, planes, elevators, the conveyor belt, and arterial roads with a hitherto unknown capacity for traffic. Not to mention film and the medium's dynamic evocation of space. We know that Erich Heckel, Kirchner's Brücke colleague, watched films produced by the Babelsberg Studio starring the Danish actress Asta Nielsen.[20]

Like Kirchner, Simmel was aware of the mental stress caused by the mass accumulation of people in crowds, touching or brushing past each other, yet forced into mental deafness by a sensory bombardment that compelled them to don a facial shield. Apropos Kirchner's observations on keeping people at arm's length and making oneself invisible, he writes:

> [The] jostling crowdedness and the motley disorder of metropolitan communication would simply be unbearable without such psychological distance. Since contemporary urban culture ... forces us to be physically close to an enormous number of people, sensitive and nervous modern people would sink completely into despair if the objectification of social relationships did not bring with it an inner boundary and reserve. The pecuniary character of relationships, either openly or concealed in a thousand forms, places an invisible functional distance between people that is an inner protection and neutralization against the overcrowded proximity and friction of our cultural life.[21]

The nineteen-twenties marked the return of the crowded proximity of city life to Kirchner's art, in works such as *Kaufhaus im Regen* (Department Store in the Rain, 1926–27, fig. 17) and *Strassenszene bei Nacht* (Street Scene at Night, 1925, fig. 13).

In his analysis, Simmel emphasizes detachment as protection against the pressure of pace and sensory bombardment to which inhabitants of the city are subject.[22] Simmel claims that society as such does not exist. Instead, a network of interpersonal relations exists at many levels, from fashion to the role of the newcomer, who through his position as a relative outsider participates in social interaction as a finely tuned observer. Kirchner can be seen as a version of the outsider as participant observer. He shows the streetwalker, despite providing services involving direct physical intercourse, having to distance herself as far as possible from her actual customers, a perfect example of the functional distance Simmel describes as an essential element of metropolitan life.

VIII.

Fascination has an element of attraction as well as repulsion. That which fascinates can be seen in passing vogues, such as the floating hat feathers and low necklines of women's dress in Kirchner's paintings, or the extravagant, closed carriages and facades illuminated by diffuse light sources and neon advertisements, phenomena that create the impression of something piquant, a pleasure-driven ripple, a small frisson of excitement (fig. 14). In a sense that which fascinates is, in all its complexity, the "younger brother" of the sublime.

Among the sublimely overwhelming, on the other hand, is the sight of the arteries of Parisian boulevards seen from above, the moving masses, the high level of complexity of city life or, for example, imagining the area covered by Berlin—an increasingly sprawling city during Kirchner's lifetime—in the face of which the powers of the imagination fall painfully short. Via the intersecting and shattered nature of his motifs, Kirchner's city squares echo this territorial extension. Certain works have a subtle sense of agoraphobia: when coupled with the widespread yet intrinsically omnipresent tendency to crowd together, the city's dimensions and gaps appear threatening (fig. 15).

19. Including the expressionist members of *Die Gläserne Kettei (*The Crystal Chain) who dreamed of a life of purity in the mountains, a *Menschheitsdämmerung* or human twilight in communal houses made of crystal in small communities surrounded by eternal snow. Mountain hiking as deliverance and apotheosis is also the theme of Richard Strauss´ *Alpine Symphony*. Willumsen's famous painting of an emancipated female mountaineer and his monumental Jotunheim painting can be seen to reflect this interest in the mountains and the Alpine region as a route to therapeutic purification of mythical dimensions.

20. It would be interesting to consider the relationship between Kirchner's suite of Berlin paintings and films of the same period. A natural starting point would be Robert Wiene's *The Cabinet of Dr. Caligari*, in which a set of ramps makes the actors appear to move through three dimensions.

21. Georg Simmel, *The Philosophy of Money* [1902]. David Frisby, ed. (London, 1990), p. 477.

22. Søren Christensen et al., ed., *Simmel—sociologiens eventyrer* (Copenhagen, 2019).

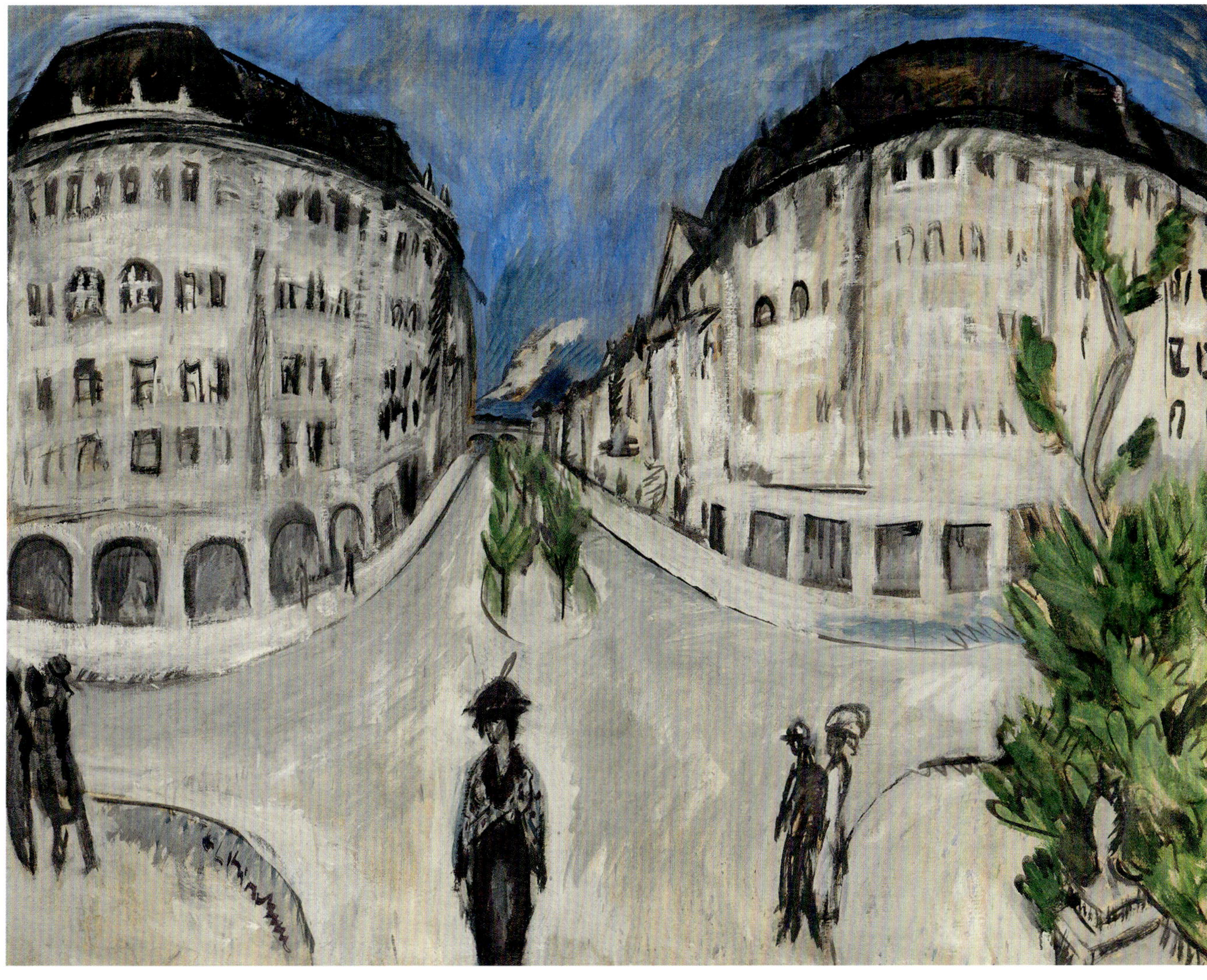

Fig. 15
Ernst Ludwig Kirchner
Strasse am Stadtpark Schöneberg
(Street in Schöneberg City Park), 1912-13
Oil on canvas,
120.97 × 150.81 cm
Gift of Mrs.
Harry Lynde Bradley
Milwaukee Art Museum

Among the affects and emotions Simmel highlights as characteristic of the metropoli is the explosivity within the enervated and overloaded individual in the metropolitan pressure cooker of push and shove. Kirchner's depictions of the city crowd are pervaded by proximity, a latent irritability coupled with indifference and social levelling. Constellations that reach a critical pitch in the metropolis. *Potsdamer Platz* (1914, fig. 16) no longer has the angular, zigzagged contours and large "blotches" of color of the Brücke years. On the other hand, the tilting facades and radical jumps in scale among the black-clad figures in the background create a heavily distorted perspective and spatial dramatization in which the strides of matchstick men add to the nervous, jittery dynamic. On a traffic island in the foreground we see elongated statuesque figures painted with long brushstrokes in a mannerist fashion. The faces are masklike, soulless, and stiff. Optically, the use of complementary red and green makes the station with its red façade and arches jump out.

In the artist's paintings from his second time in Berlin in the nineteen-twenties, such as *Kaufhaus im Regen* (fig. 17), the atmosphere has changed from an insistent dramatization of the scene to colorist harmonization and an emphasis on surface. The elements of figures, shop windows, and neon signs are arranged along strict vertical and horizontal lines. Like the woven tapestries Kirchner designed in Davos, the elements are laid out in an ornamental pattern. The crowd has become texture. Neon light seeps through the cracks. The melancholic atmosphere of a rainy night is like a diverting set design. We are far from the sense of isolation and angst so insistently present in Kirchner's works of the nineteen-tens. *Strasse mit Passanten in Nachtbeleuchtung* (Street with Passers-by under Night Lights, 1926–27, fig. 18)[23] is similarly ornamental and decorative, albeit having more depth and a "phosphorescent" palette reminiscent of Kirchner's mountain paintings of the same year. The vibrant effect of the painting is seen in the unleashing of colors which land after being tossed into the air with an optimized contrasting effect. In terms of atmosphere, the work could be a storyboard for American city films of subsequent decades.

23. At the end of the nineteen-twenties, visitors to Berlin describe the city centre as a sea of light, a reminder of the elated, seductive neon lights and illuminations in the final sequences in Ruttman's 1927 Berlin film. Authors visiting Berlin from abroad experienced Berlin as the Chicago of Europe.

IX.

Willumsen's paintings of Rome and Venice embody a reflection on time, as seen in the night paintings of Venice discussed above. Whereas Kirchner, particularly in the nineteen-tens, engages the viewer with the sudden experience of a snapshot, Willumsen's paintings have a

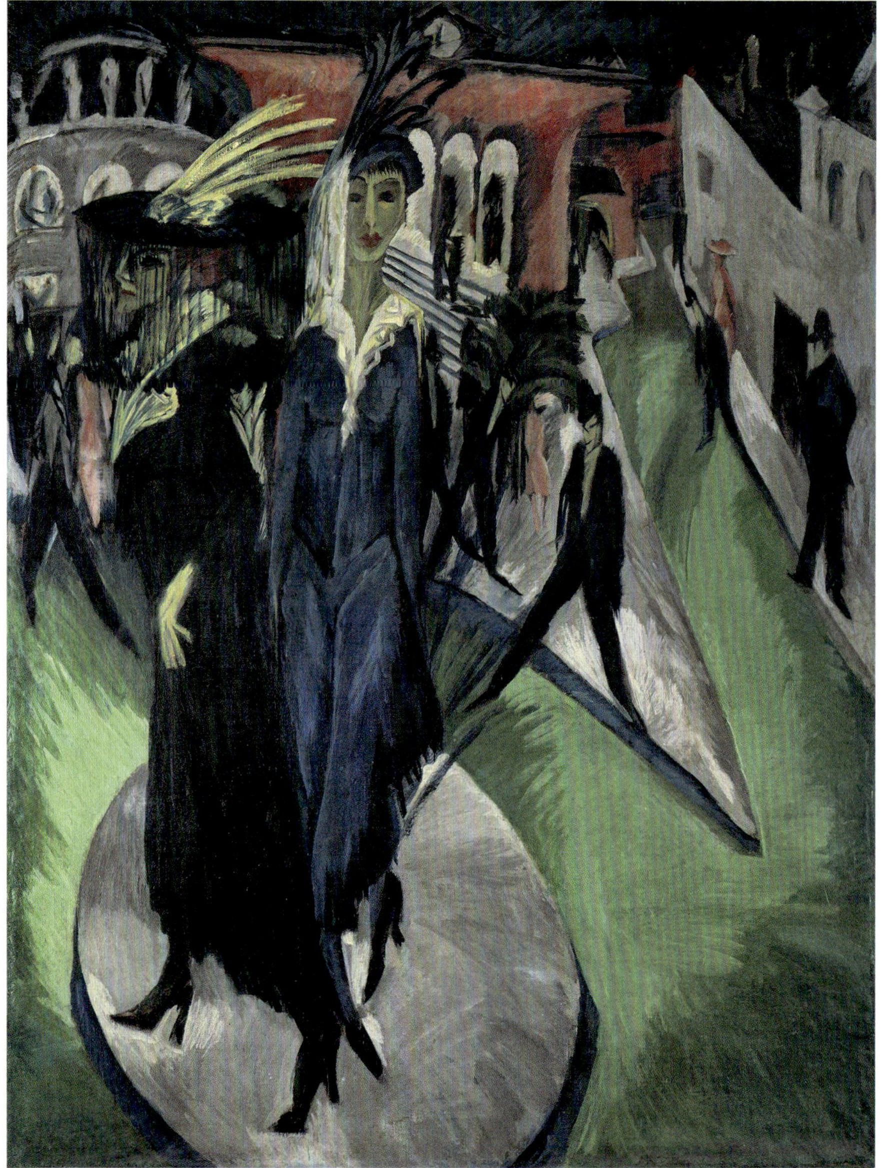

Fig. 16 Ernst Ludwig Kirchner
Potsdamer Platz, 1914
Oil on canvas, 200 × 150 cm
Nationalgalerie – Staatliche Museen, Berlin

Fig. 17
Ernst Ludwig Kirchner
Kaufhaus im Regen
(Department Store in the Rain), 1926–27
Oil on canvas, 65 × 50 cm
Kirchner Museum Davos

Fig. 18
Ernst Ludwig Kirchner
Strasse mit Passanten in Nachtbeleuchtung
(Street with Passersby under Night Lights), 1926–27
Oil on canvas, 87 × 68 cm
Museum Frieder Burda, Baden-Baden

stagnant temporality, a reflection on duration that comes insistently to the fore yet is on the verge of retreat. Willumsen's use of color is distinctive, depicting, for example, a magenta sky above buildings in a piercing, poisonous or greenish yellow. Just as the Brücke artists' euphoric attack had liberated color from academic and scientific chromatology[24] to cast it back at the canvas in powerful, visually stimulating "blotches," Willumsen shakes up the materials of art by experimenting with colorist effects he must have known were beyond the grasp of most. Something made even more remarkable by the fact that he wanted to sell his Rome and Venice paintings to an international audience via galleries in Paris. His densely populated Venice paintings of famous squares often appear as portrayals of high-spirited tourists at night, which is probably accurate. On the other hand, it would appear that Willumsen wanted to free his sparsely populated views from both reportage and any specific temporality. His works with empty gondolas represent a way of painting which, with striking effect, endows the familiar motifs of canals and palaces with Willumsen's recurrent bodily energy, at the same time as creating a classical timelessness through the grandeur of the statuesque male body (fig. 19).

24. As opposed to the Impressionists and Pointillists, who based their use of color on the theories of Michel Eugène Chevreul, among others.

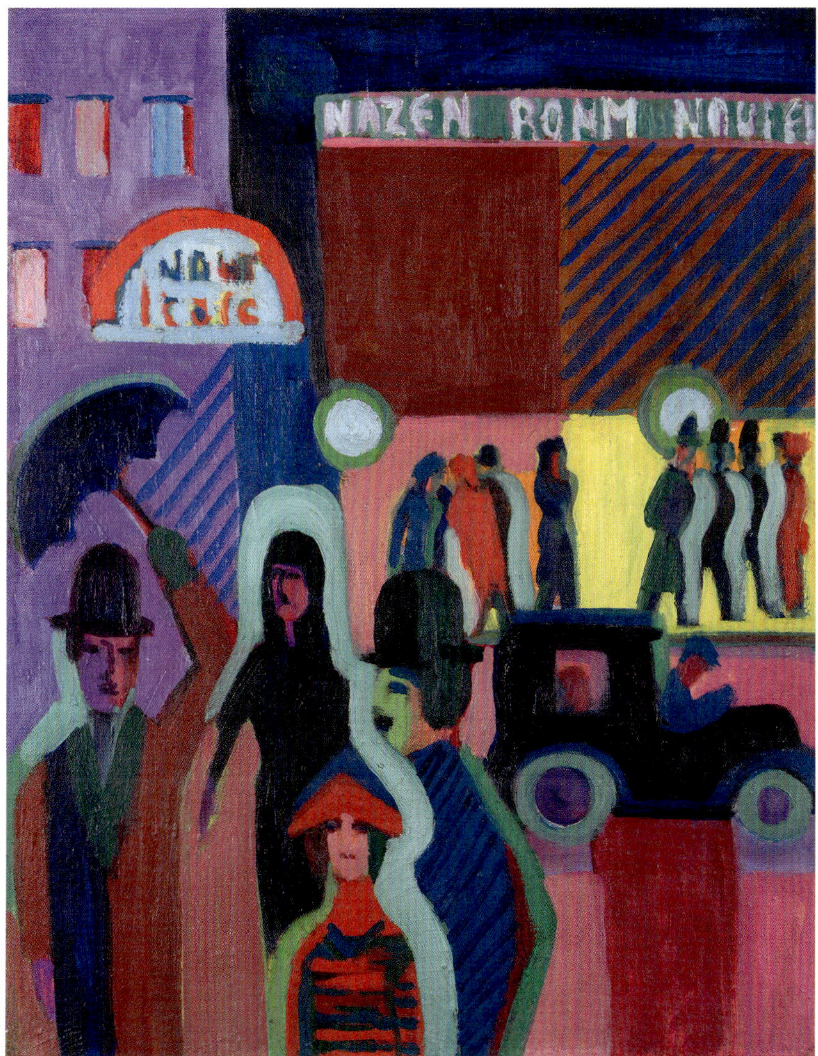

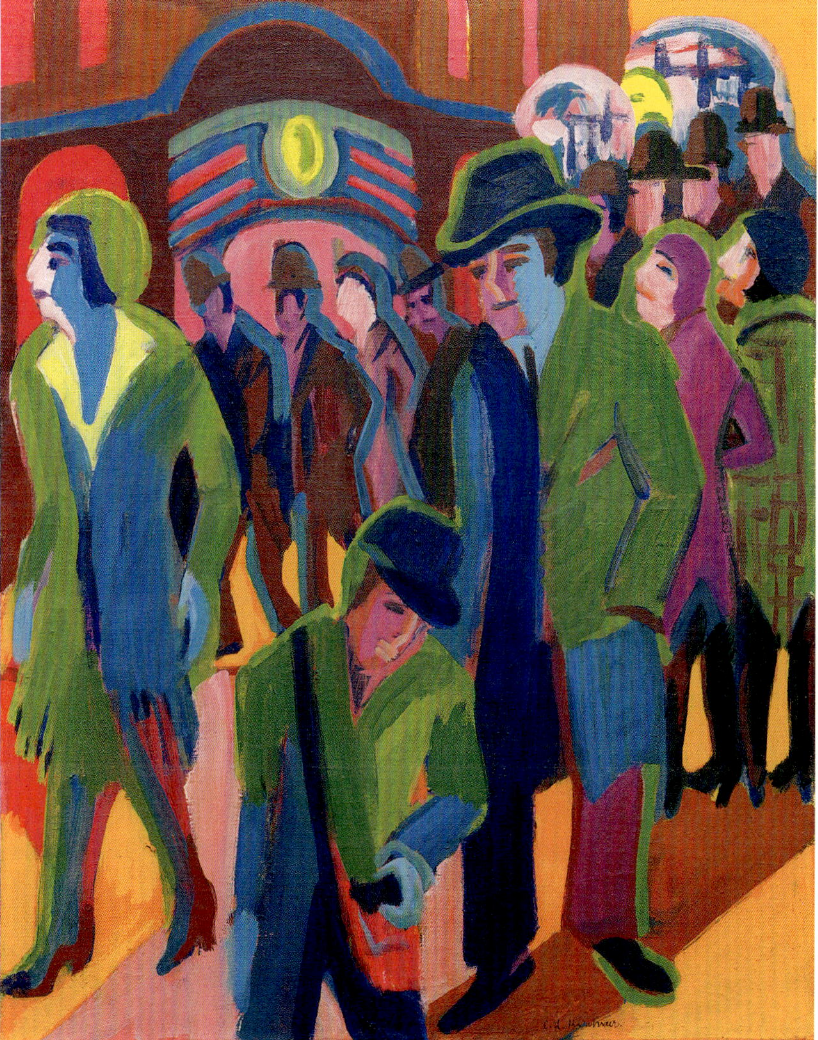

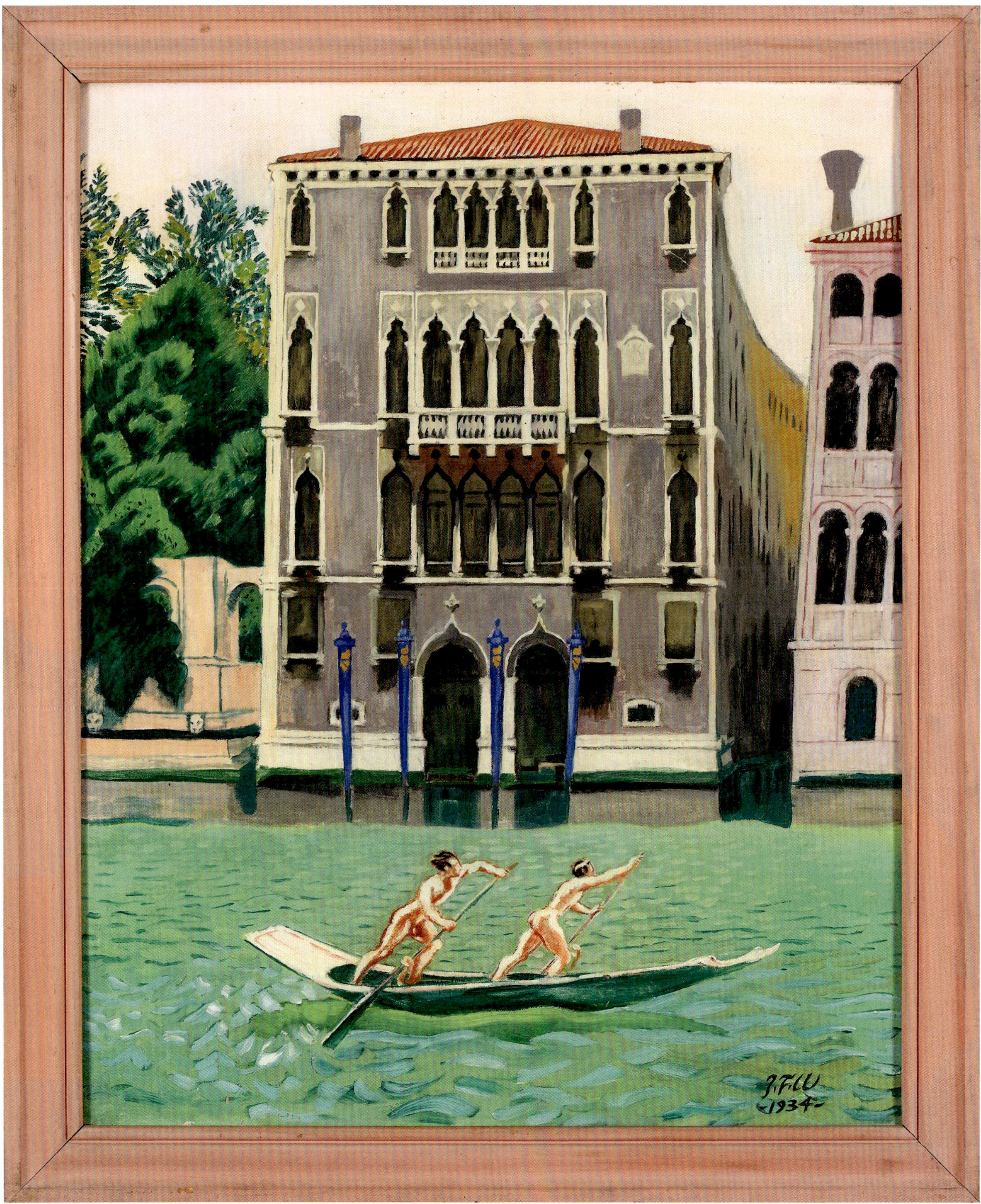

Fig. 19
J. F. Willumsen
Palazzo Morosini ved Canal Grande. En gondol med to nøgne roere (Palazzo Morosini on Canal Grande. A Gondola with Two Naked Rowers), 1934
Oil on canvas, 92 × 73 cm
Willumsen's Museum, Frederikssund

It is well documented that Willumsen's distinctive use of color was influenced by his love of El Greco,[25] whose mannerist, Catholic pathos also appealed to the artist. He may also have found another source of inspiration for his theatrical use of light and colorist canvasses during his visit to Accademia, where Jacopo Tintoretto's large painting of the body of Saint Mark being brought to Venice depicts a night scene in Bengal light accentuated by thunder and lightning. During his time in Italy Willumsen must also have seen works by Giorgio de Chirico, both the Italian artist's metaphysical, godforsaken squares with their accelerated perspective questioning the enigma of classical Antiquity, and his period of intense mannerist and colorist self-portraits.

Regardless of which, the fact remains that with his Italian city paintings Willumsen wanted to go beyond any standard view or Venetian *vedute*. Whereas the disturbing distortions and chilling collusion of the gallery of characters in Kirchner's Berlin works of the nineteen-tens might make them seem *unheimlich*, Willumsen's affinity with the uncanny emerges in his distinctive use of color, light, and an indefinable theatrical atmosphere.[26] Something

25. See Leila Krogh (ed.), *J.F. Willumsen på sporet af El Greco* (Frederikssund, 2005).

26. According to Freud, *Das Unheimliche* is something strange in the ordinary, not something ghastly or actual horror, but a sense of unease in the human psyche. In German, the word *Heimlich* can mean both the concealed, secret, or hidden, or the domestic. Sigmund Freud, *Das Unheimliche* [1919], (Berlin, 2017).

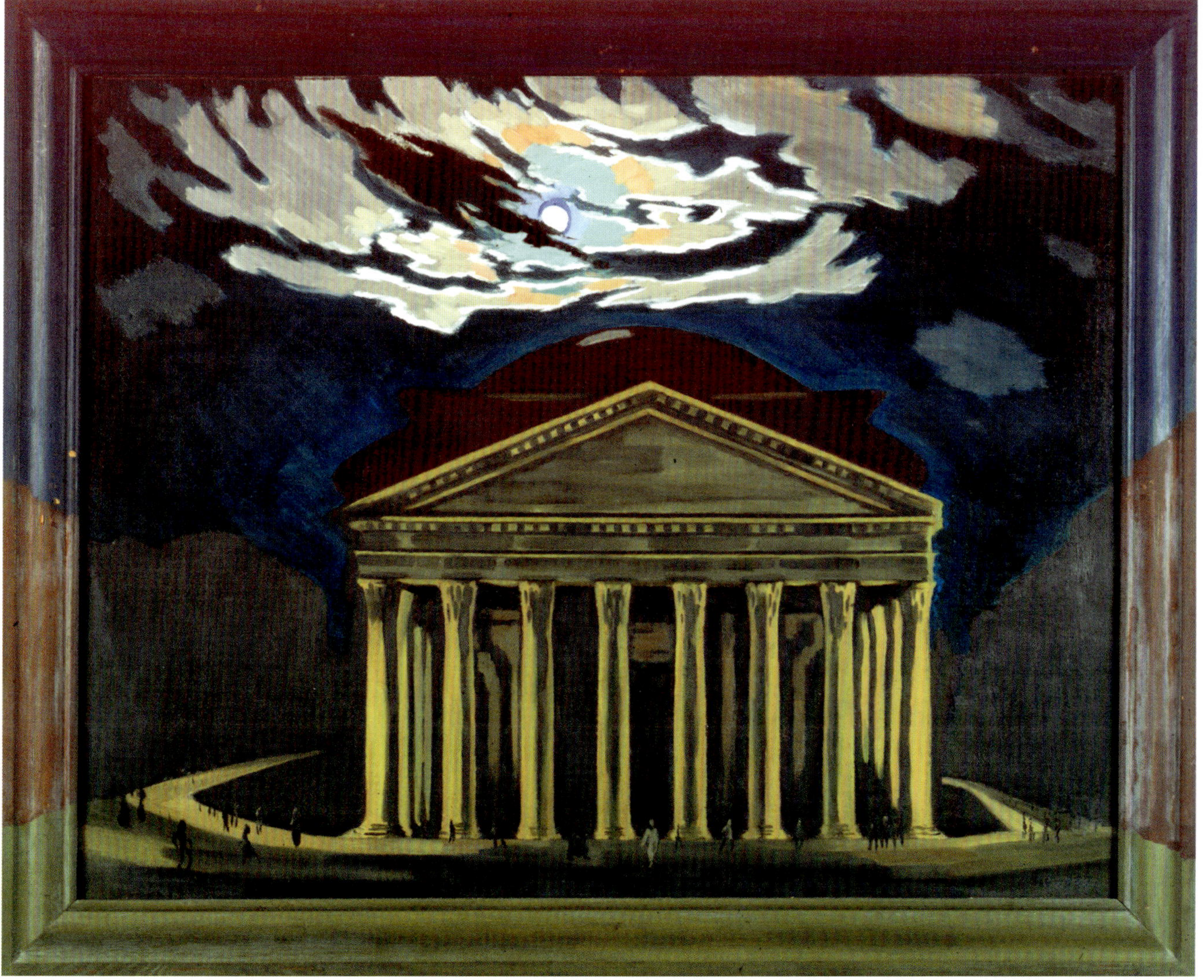

Fig. 20
J. F. Willumsen
Pantheon i Rom. Måneskin
(The Pantheon in Rome. Moonlight), 1937
Oil on canvas, 78 × 92 cm
Willumsen's Museum, Frederikssund

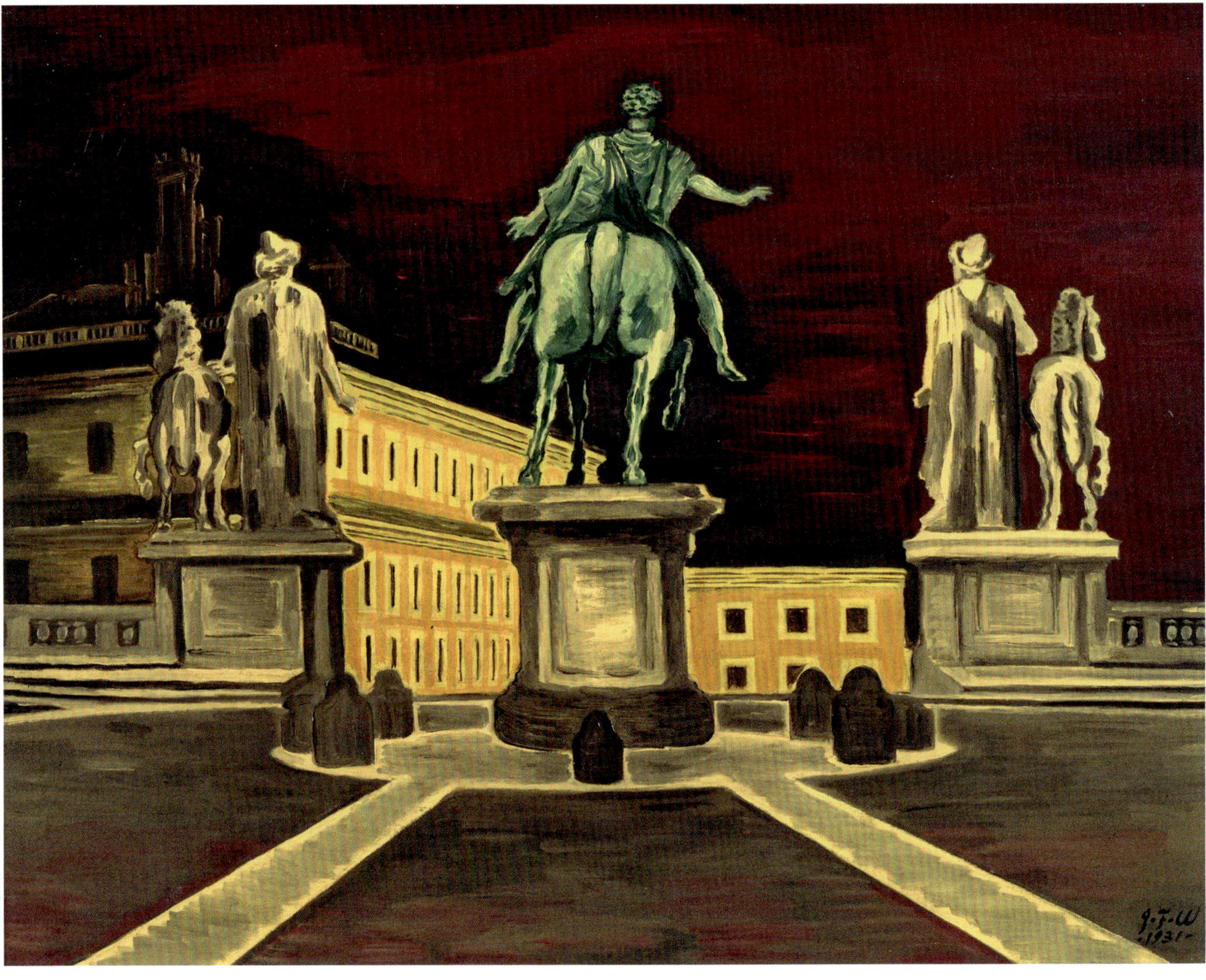

Fig. 21
J. F. Willumsen
Oppe på Campidoglio. Rom (Up on Campidoglio, Rome), 1934
Oil on canvas, 73 × 92 cm
Willumsen's Museum, Frederikssund

unspoken or even repressed comes back to haunt familiar surroundings, something now "homeless." This is akin to the homelessness emanating from the prevailing metaphysical painting's striking emptiness in nineteen-thirties Italy: Giorgio de Chirico's deserted siesta squares with cloaked statues, long shadows, and dark rebuses formed by tailor's dummies and ancient fragments. In Rome, Willumsen paints Piazza Campidoglio by moonlight (fig. 21), deserted yet populated by canonical ancient sculptures or he paints the Pantheon as a solitary backdrop, an eternal, static crystal clamped against something wind-swept and gesticulatory in jagged clouds infused by the glow of the moon (fig. 20).

The color yellow dominates the Venice paintings. Motifs such as Canal San Trovaso and Campo S.S. Giovanni e Paolo are illuminated by night in distorted perspectives (fig. 22 and 23). At night the unfamiliar emerges out of that which is familiar by day. In a letter Willumsen calls it a "mystery." He writes: "But now the light at night was of most interest. The yellow phosphorescence of the moon. The yellow color of mystery, the color of my life, was what I grappled with in these works from Canal

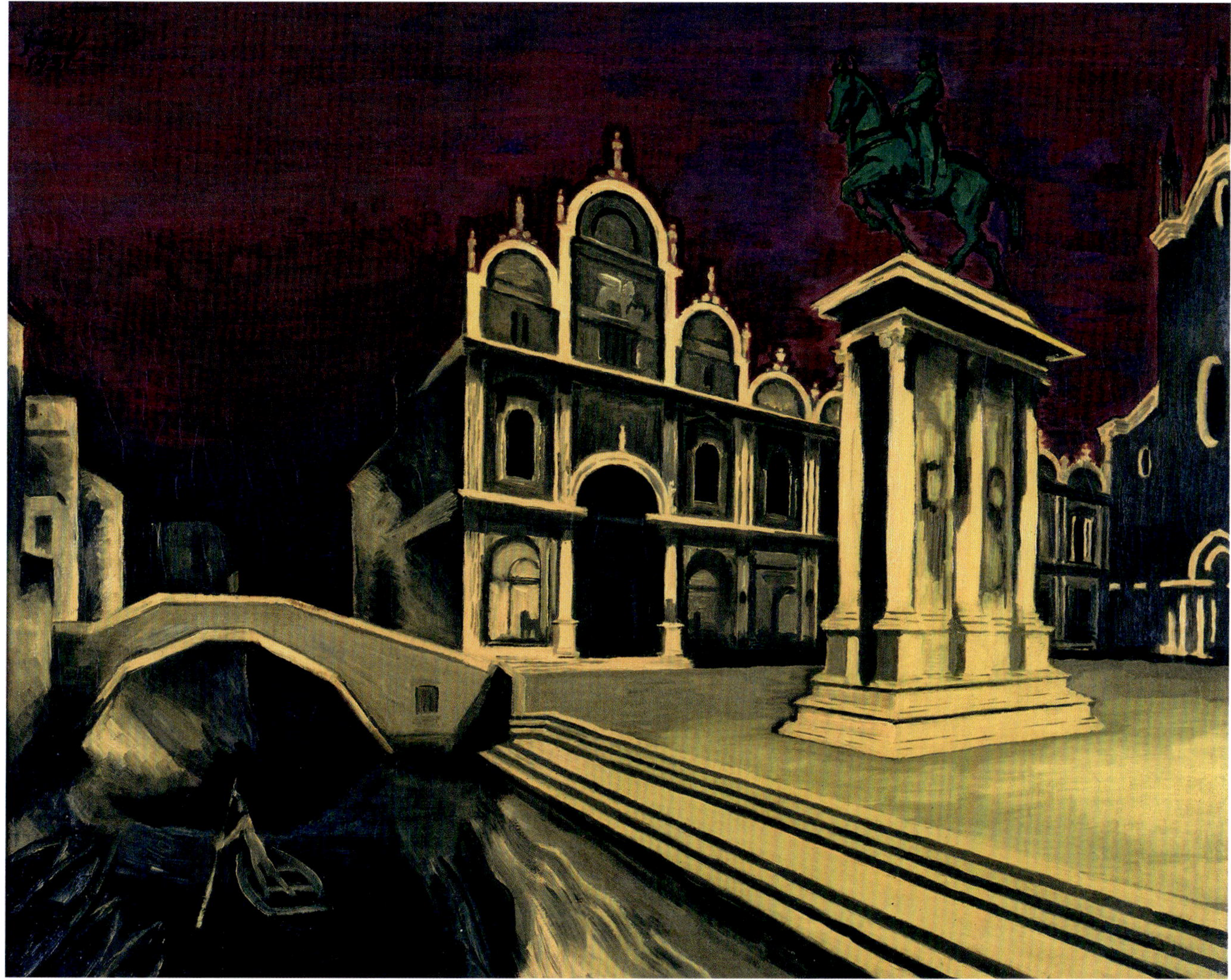

Fig. 22
J. F. Willumsen
Pladsen S.S. Giovanni e Paolo. Nat (Piazza SS. Giovanni e Paulo. Night), 1931
Oil on canvas, 73 × 92 cm
Willumsen's Museum, Frederikssund

Grande ... with romantic gardens and fireworks, with the elegant silhouettes of gondolas."[27]

Willumsen describes the yellowish green color he used as something he invested in both personally and symbolically: "the color of my life." The yellow he uses has a phosphorescence that permeates the city buildings and squares he takes as his motifs. The motifs are both famous and familiar to many, yet few have ever seen them in yellow. This color, together with the unreal perspectives and clouds, creates a sense of something disturbing in Willumsen's Italian works, a static lingering evoking a long tradition of surrendering to a moonlit Venice.[28]

In his most radical works, Willumsen curbs such sentimental abandon, seeming to ask what the monuments mean instead. If the buildings retreat from the modern viewer, do they form a riddle along the lines of the allegories of *pittura metafisica*—the metaphysical painting of Italian art of the same period? Willumsen investigates night as a time when buildings reveal something of their essence and historical fate, their connection to something hidden or forgotten.

27. J. F. Willumsen's memoirs: Ernst Mentze, *J.F. Willumsen. Mine Erindringer fortalt til Ernst Mentze* (Copenhagen, 1953), p. 260.
28. See, for example, Christian Elling, *Den italienske nat* (Copenhagen, 1956).

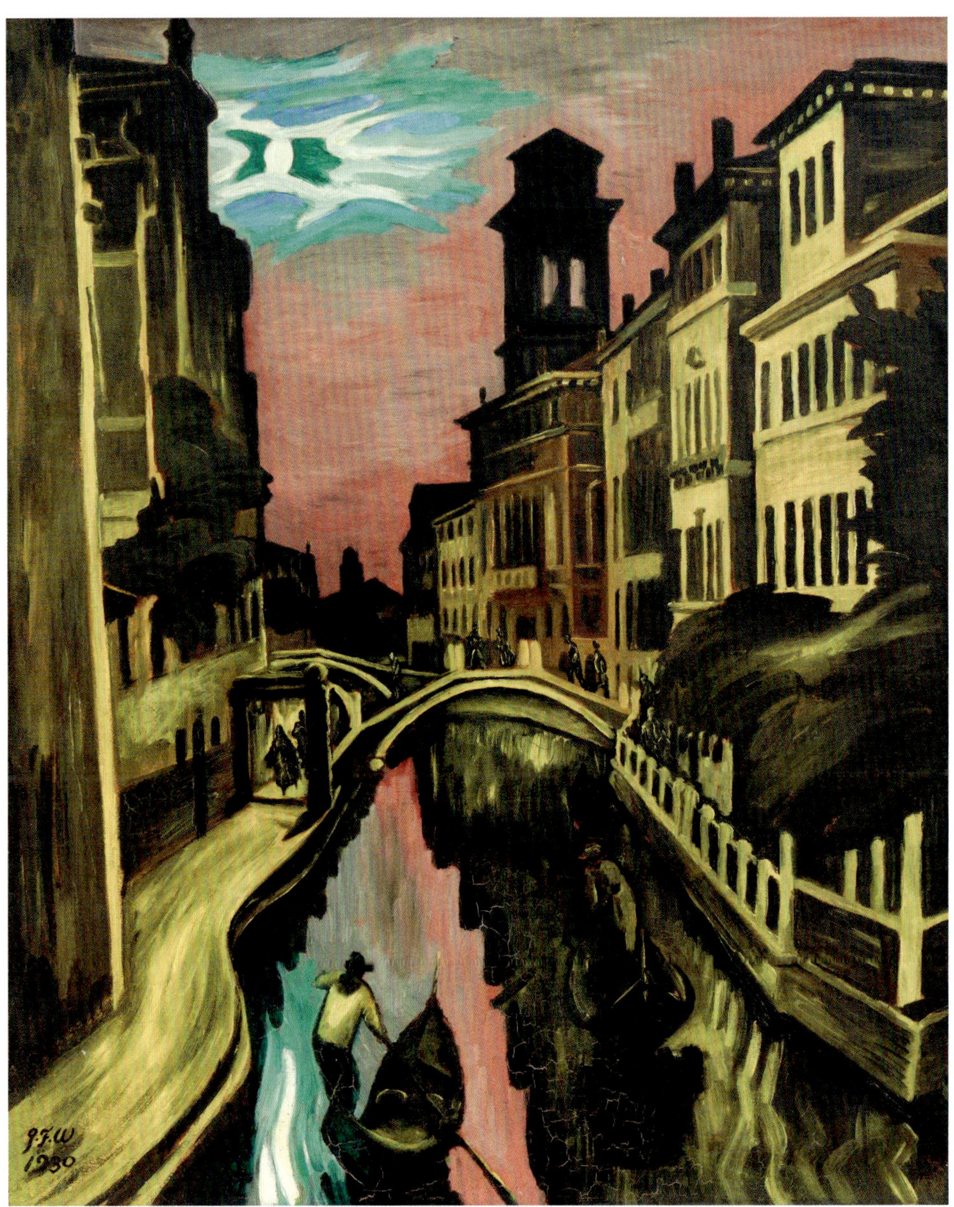

Fig. 23
J.F. Willumsen
San Trovaso Kanalen i Venedig. Måneskin
(The San Trovaso Canal in Venice. Moonlight), 1930
Oil on canvas, 92×73 cm
Willumsen's Museum, Frederikssund

X.

Willumsen uses color to render the city of lagoons in a peculiar light. The resulting representation of the city as partially unreal is something he shares with many artists and visitors. The indistinct clouds in Venetian moonlight, alongside the sound of the distant steps of others or even oneself on the deserted streets at night, create the impression of something ghostlike akin to the reflections in the canals (fig. 24).

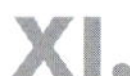

XI.

Willumsen's yellow color adds a certain sense of aura and nobility to a Venice that has become a museum. But it also repels. Beyond his studies of El Greco, his insistence on this specific palette can be seen to stem from a combination of his personal, self-aggrandizing myth of the artist calling for uncompromising wilfulness, as well as an avant-garde gesture aimed at undermining conventional representations. There can be little doubt that Willumsen

Fig. 24
J. F. Willumsen
Uvejr over Venedig, Nat. Palazzo Balbi ved Canal Grande. Nr. 2
(Storm over Venice, Night. Palazzo Balbi on Canal Grande. No. 2), 1934
Oil on canvas, 92 × 73 cm
Willumsen's Museum, Frederikssund

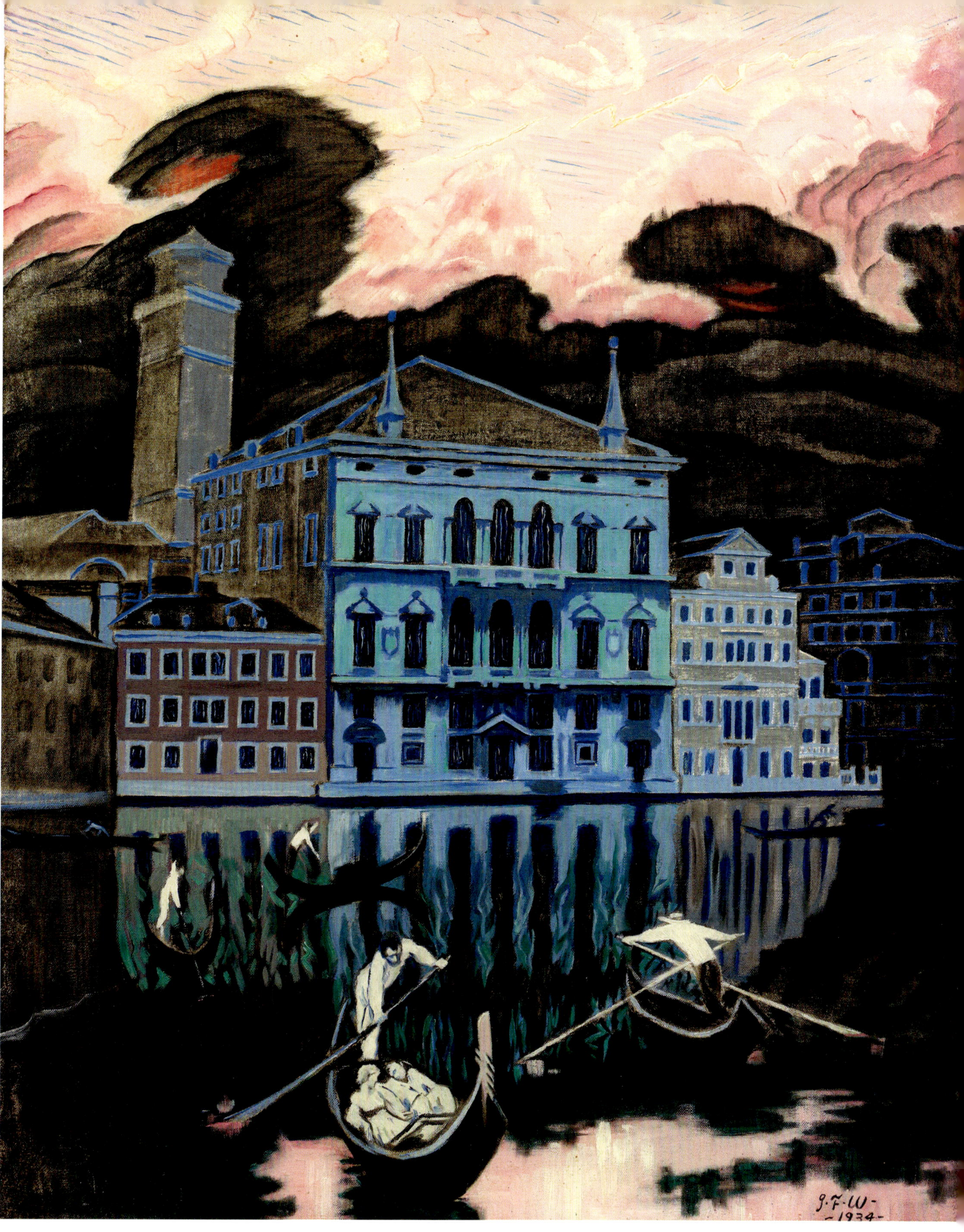

viewed his choice of color as part of a profound quest, the implications of which were as yet unclear. His poetic power of imagination, however, produces an exaggerated theatricality. A directly ominous symbol of moonlight can be seen in the frayed cloud floating past the moon as a flash in the San Trovaso Canal, a cautionary sign.[29]

By the end of the eighteenth century, the lagoon city, which continued to be Willumsen's Italian destination of preference, had ceased to be a European state. During Willumsen's lifetime, in literary works by authors ranging from d'Annunzio to Thomas Mann, the city was associated with labyrinthine and dark desires, fatally drawing people into the labyrinth as the ultimate symbol of dark mystery.[30] One could almost say that art provided a fixed matrix for Venice as a symbolic setting.

The misty, iridescent daylight of Venice has fascinated painters from J. M. W. Turner to the Impressionists, where color becomes pure material, virtually dissolving the subject of the work. The coordinates of time and space collapse. Venice is associated with the evasive in a number of ways.[31] Something that also struck the composer Richard Wagner, who claimed nothing in the city to be contemporary or modern but "a work of art."[32] Willumsen seems to ask in what sense these monuments can be detached from time, given their capacity to establish a mysterious permanence in the dreamlike gleam of night.

At night the palaces in his paintings of Canal Grande become symbols of time, whilst the gondolas and their oars punt ahead, measuring the depth of time. In his novel *De dødes rige* (The Realm of the Dead) Henrik Pontoppidan writes that the moon appears as a powerful god turning its back on mankind. In Willumsen's painting from the Piazzetta, the moon is mid between the columns supporting symbols of Venice—the Lion of Saint Mark and Saint Apollodorus—without any necessary significance beyond the compositional element and use of moonlight as a developing solution and emblem of the city. The strict composition, however, can also be seen as a modest, humorous allegory of Venice as—for Willumsen—the city of moonlight par excellence, a moonlight that creates a hue of mystery.

Late in life Willumsen denied being influenced by German art, which he described as "Teutonic," possibly influenced by public sentiment after World War II.[33] Given his syncretistic approach to his art it is, however, difficult to believe that he had not seen Kirchner's alpine and city paintings on his many travels or in art journals. In his painting of the Pantheon in Rome, for example, the front and raised circle surrounding it look like a piece of Kirchner's scenery. Seen from the perspective of absolute modernity, Kirchner's city paintings reveal his drive to absorb the Zeitgeist and pinpoint it on the basis of "the bustling city" and the forms of perception it generates through the pointed portrayal of a character gallery promenading in the latest fashions. Willumsen, on the other hand, is more driven by a meditation on the permeable boundary between the familiar and the unfamiliar: the city as museum. Part of the process of modernity is an increasing musealization of the world, something these paintings also chart.

29. It is well known that Willumsen was inspired by popular culture, a theme addressed in Margrit Brehm et al. eds., *Café Dolly—Picabia, Schnabel, Willumsen*, exh. cat. Willumsen's Museum, Frederikssund (Ostfildern-Ruit, 2013). This particular painting can be seen to have an affinity with children's book illustrations, as well as anticipating the style of the fantasy genre—neither of which preclude its subtle eeriness.

30. See also Luchino Visconti's film *Senso* (1954).

31. See Carsten Thau, "Venice—Where Reality Wavers" in *The Venice Syndrome—Grandeur and Fall in the Art of Venice*, exh. cat., Gl. Holtegaard (Holte, 2014), pp. 75–103.

32. Ibid., p. 79.

33. See, for example, Chapter 1, "Willumsens forhold til fransk og nordisk kunst" in Ulla Hjorth, *J.F. Willumsen i Europa*. (Frederikssund, 2006).

Bibliography

Baudelaire, Charles. "The Painter of Modern Life." In *The Painter of Modern Life and Other Essays*, edited and translated by Jonathan Mayne. London, 1964.

Bergson, Henri. *L'evolution créatrice.* Paris, 1907.

Café Dolly – Picabia, Schnabel, Willumsen. Edited by Margrit Brehm et al. Exh. cat. Willumsen's Museum, Frederikssund. Ostfildern-Ruit, 2013.

Christensen, Søren et al., eds., *Simmel – sociologiens eventyrer.* Copenhagen, 2019.

Elling, Christian. *Den italienske nat* [1947]. Copenhagen, 2018.

Ernst Ludwig Kirchner – Farbige Druckgraphik. Edited by Günther Gercken and Magdalene Moeller. Exh. cat. Brücke-Museum, Berlin/Museen Böttcherstrass, Bremen. Munich, 2008.

Freud, Sigmund. *Das Unheimliche* [1919]. Berlin, 2017.

Hjorth, Ulla. *J.F. Willumsen i Europa.* Frederikssund, 2006.

J.F. Willumsen – over grænser. Edited by Leila Krogh. Exh. cat. Ordrupgaard, Charlottenlund/ Musée d'Orsay, Paris. Charlottenlund, 2006.

Kandinsky, Wassily, and Franz Marc, eds., *Der Blaue Reiter Almanac.* Munich, 1912

Mentze, Ernst. *J.F. Willumsen. Mine Erindringer fortalt til Ernst Mentze.* Copenhagen, 1953.

Pontoppidan, Henrik. *Lucky Per* [1898-1904]. Translated by Naomi Lebowitz. New York, 2010.

Simmel, Georg. "The Metropolis and Mental Life." In *The Blackwell City Reader.* Edited by Gary Bridge and Sophie Watson. Oxford, 2010.

Simmel, Georg. *The Philosophy of Money* [1902]. Edited by David Frisby. London, 1990.

Thau, Carsten. *Arkitekturen som Tidsmaskine.* Copenhagen, 2001.

Thau, Carsten. "Venice – Where Reality Wavers." In *The Venice Syndrome – Grandeur and Fall in the Art of Venice.* Edited by Maria Gadegaard, exh. cat. Gl. Holtegaard. Holte, 2014.

Vibrant Metropolis / Idyllic Nature. The Berlin Years. Edited by Sandra Gianfreda. Exh. cat. Kunsthaus Zürich. Munich, 2017.

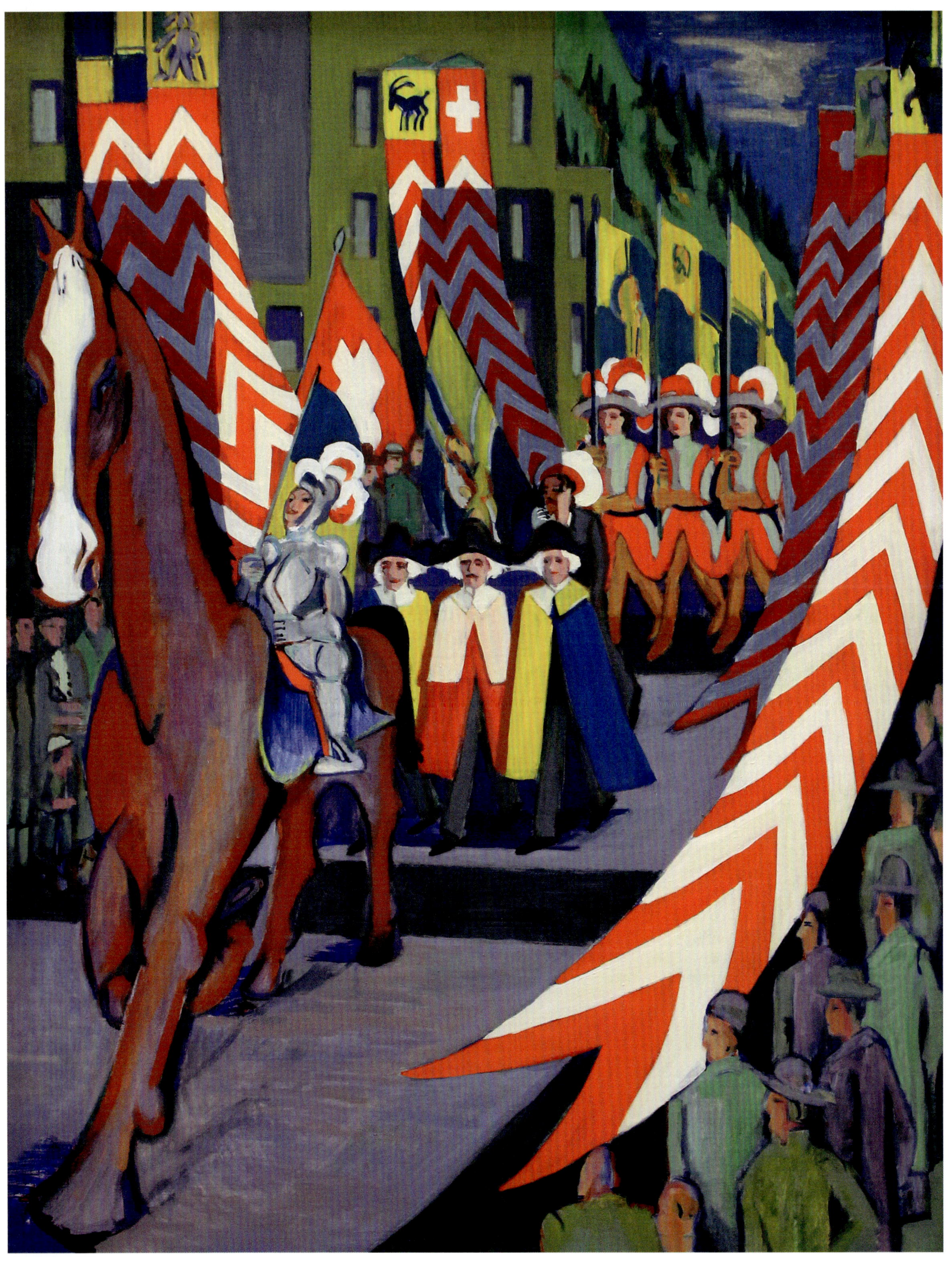

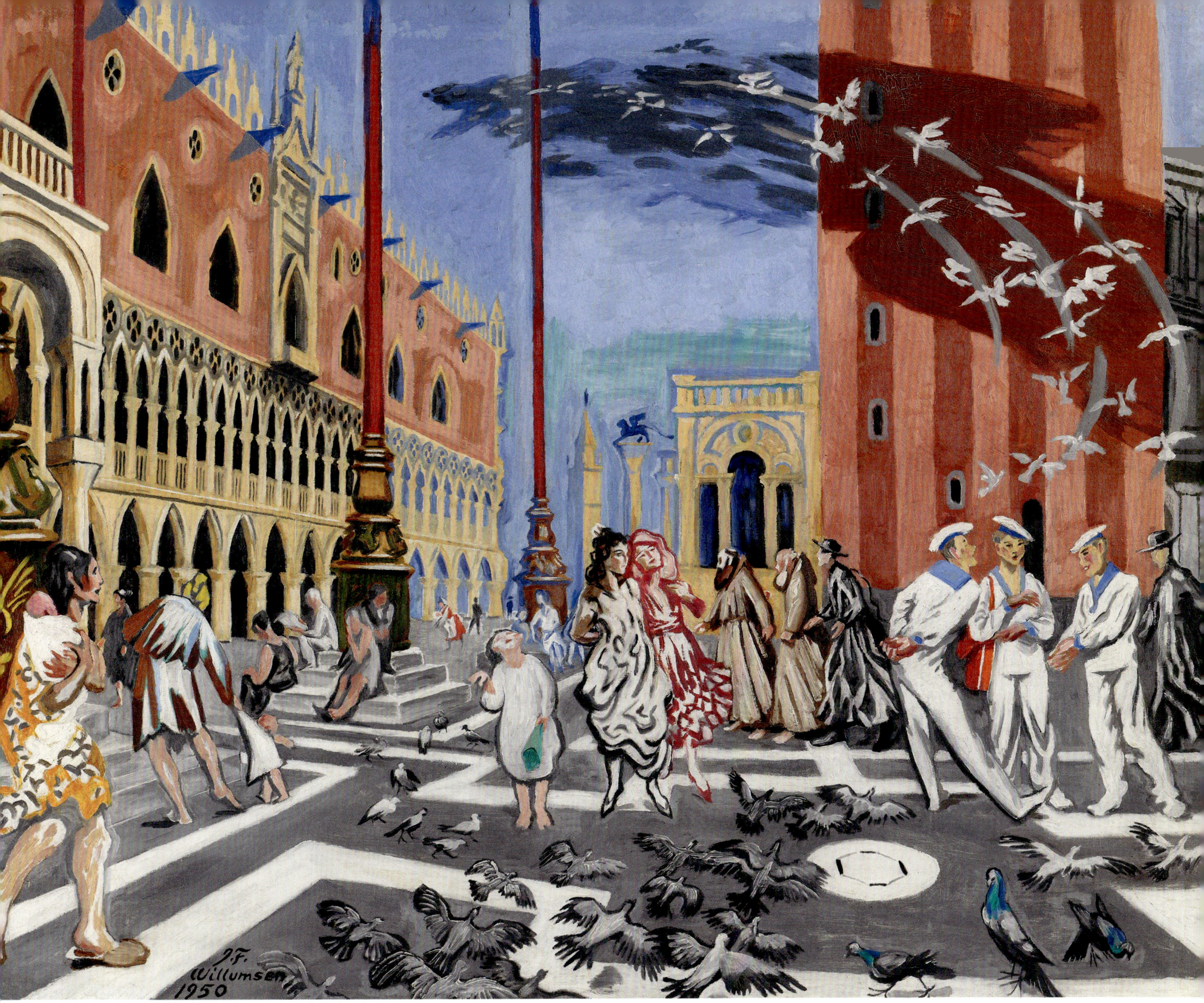

Ernst Ludwig Kirchner
500-Jahrfeier des Zehngerichtebundes
(The 500th Anniversary of the League of the Ten Jurisdictions), 1936
Oil on canvas, 195 × 150 cm
Kirchner Museum Davos

J. F. Willumsen
Markuspladsen i Venedig
(St Mark's Square in Venice), 1950
Oil on canvas, 130 × 164 cm
Willumsen's Museum, Frederikssund

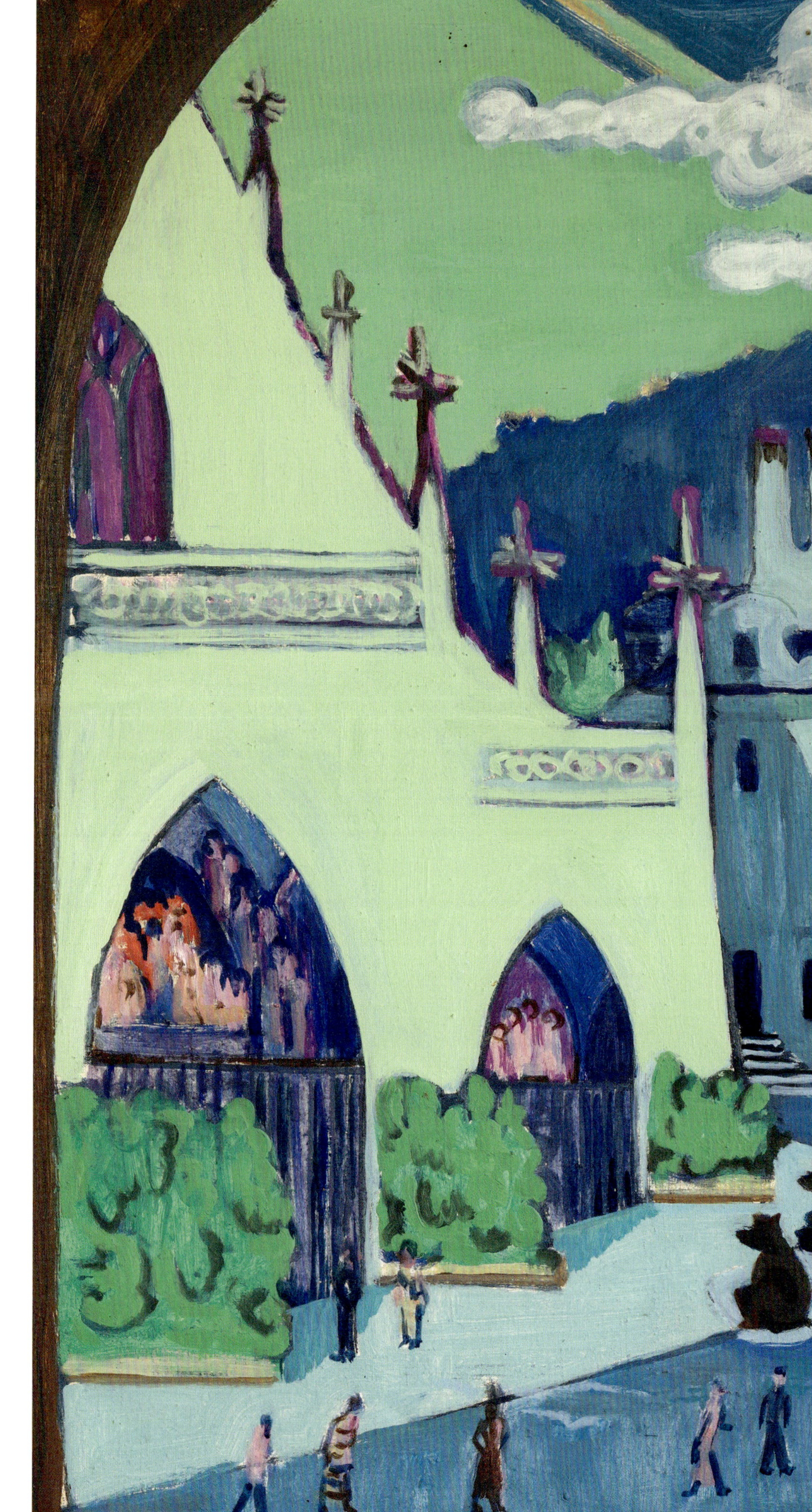

Ernst Ludwig Kirchner
Münsterplatz in Bern (Minster Square in Bern), 1935
Oil on canvas, 113 × 153 cm
Private collection

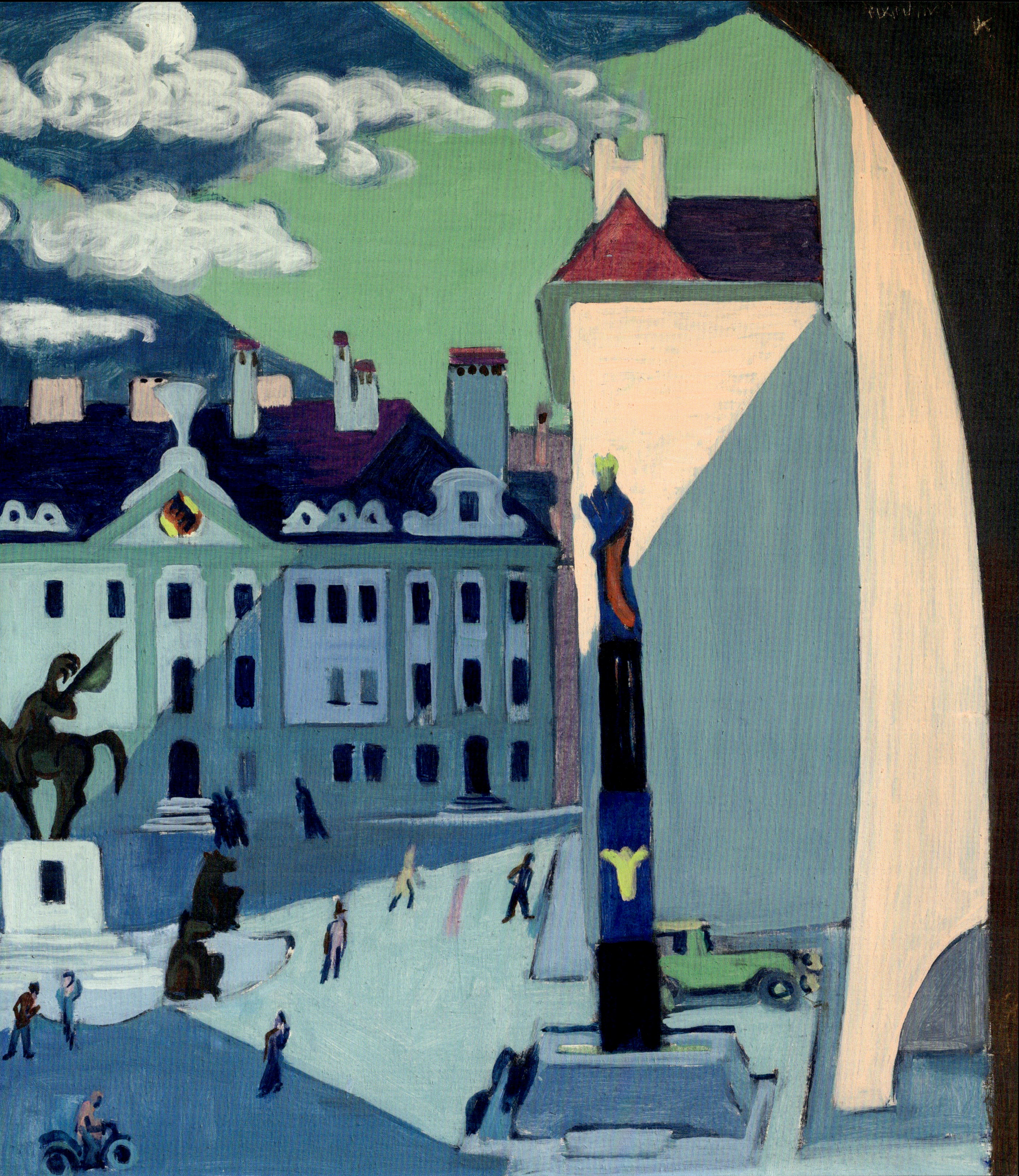

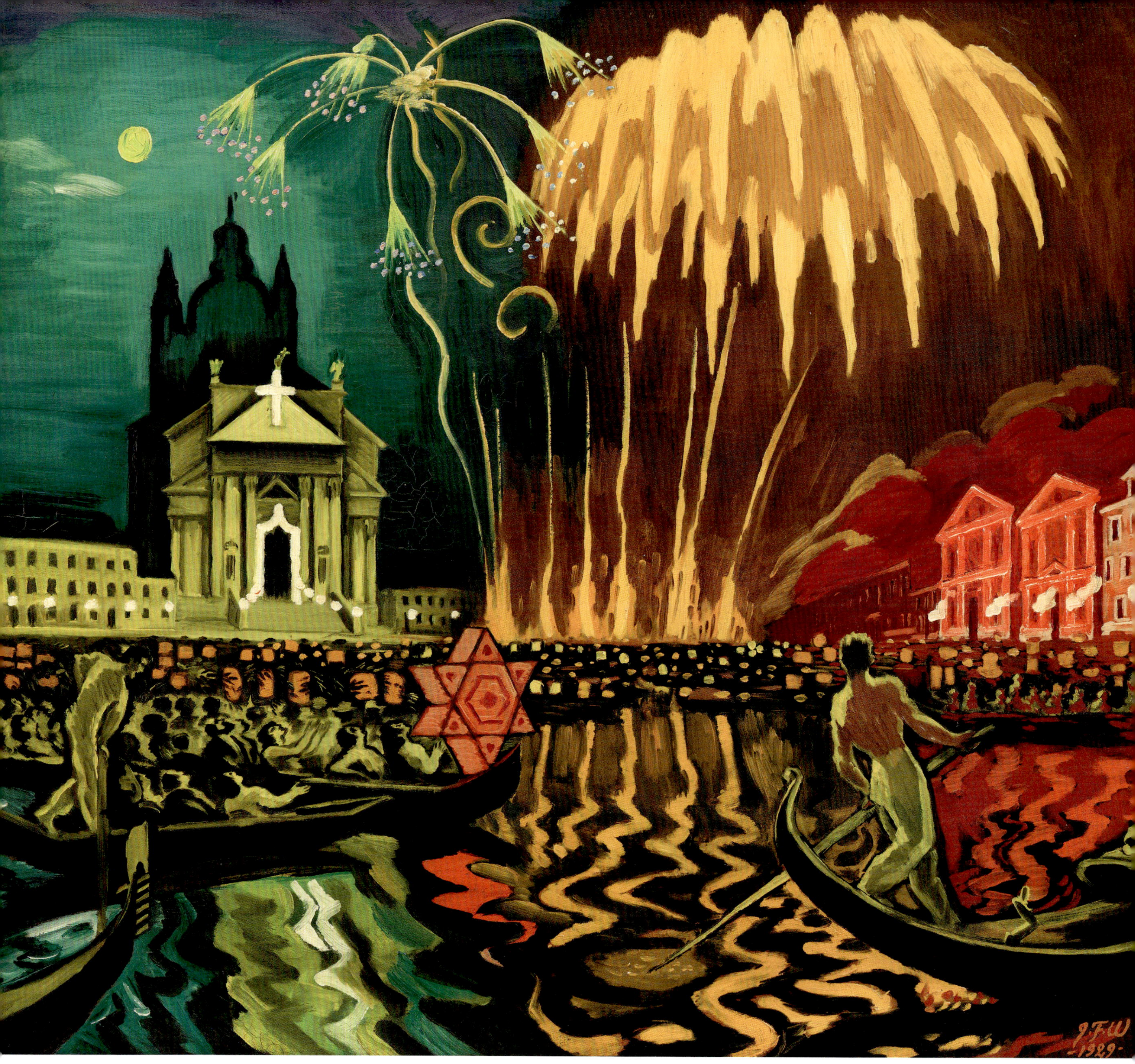

J. F. Willumsen
Redentorefesten i Venedig. Nat. Fyrværkeriet (The Festival of Redentore in Venice), 1929
Oil on canvas, 86.8 × 99 cm
Willumsen's Museum, Frederikssund

J. F. Willumsen
På Piazza Navona
(On Piazza Navona), 1931
Oil on canvas, 92 × 73 cm
Willumsen's Museum, Frederikssund

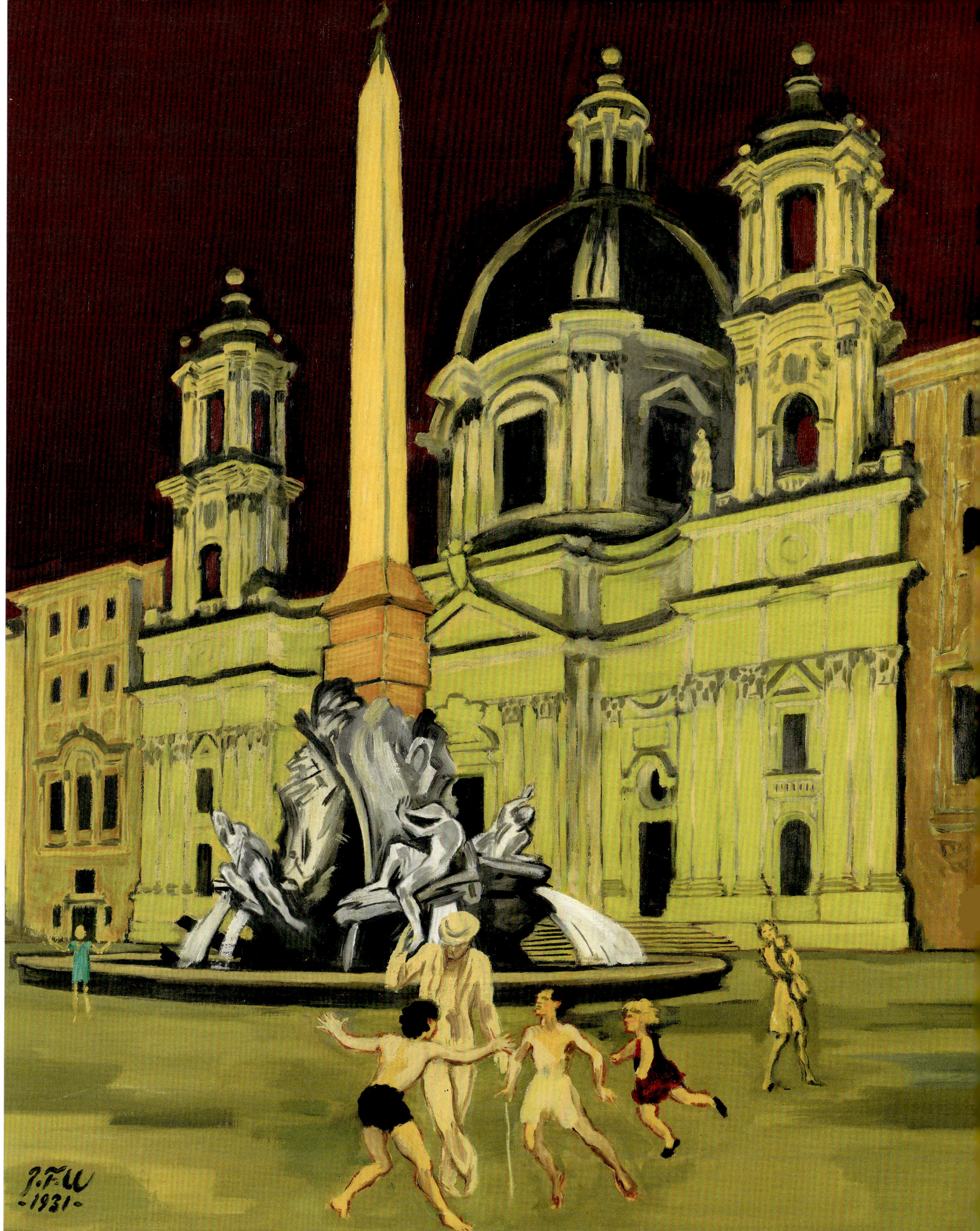
J.F.W
-1931-

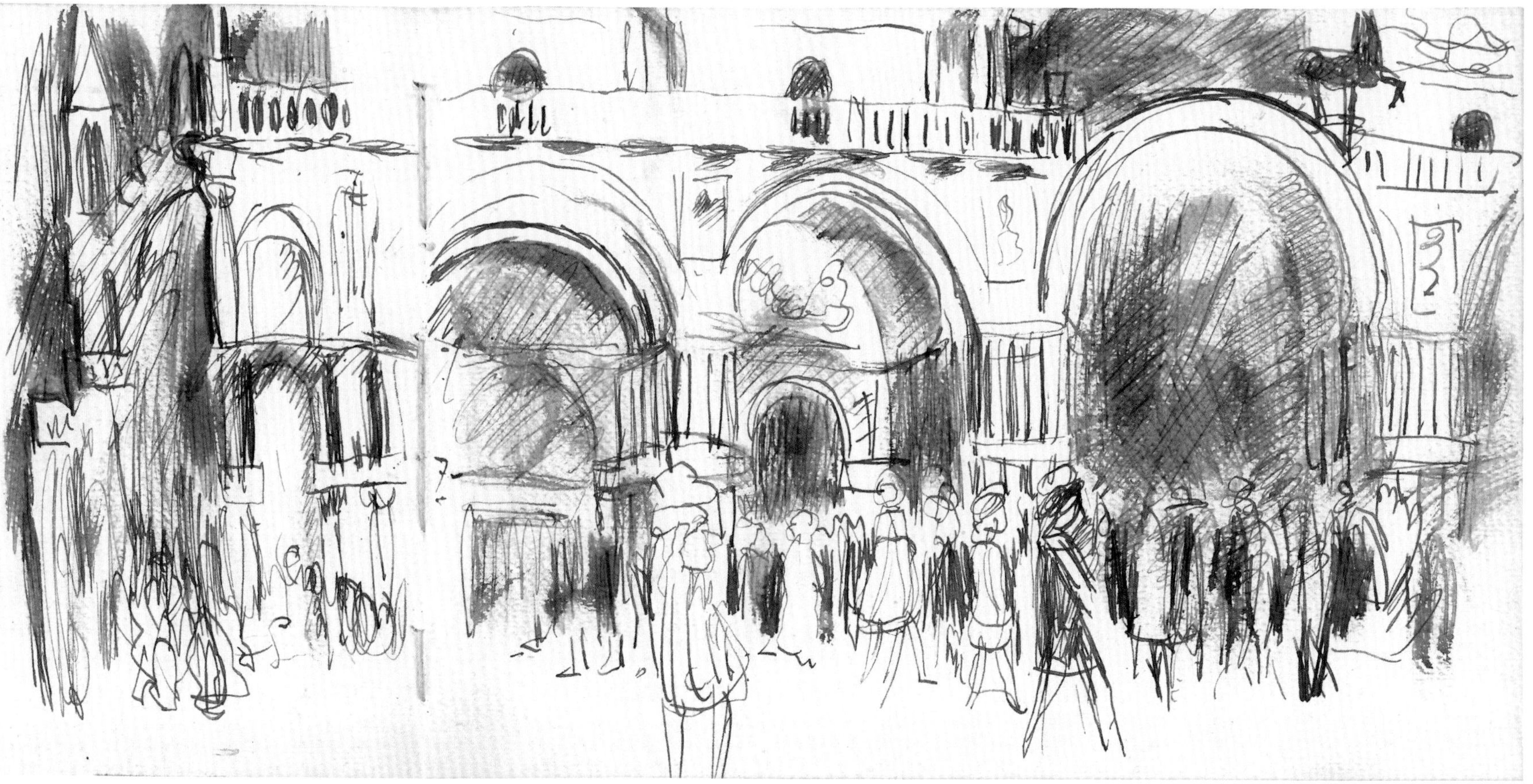

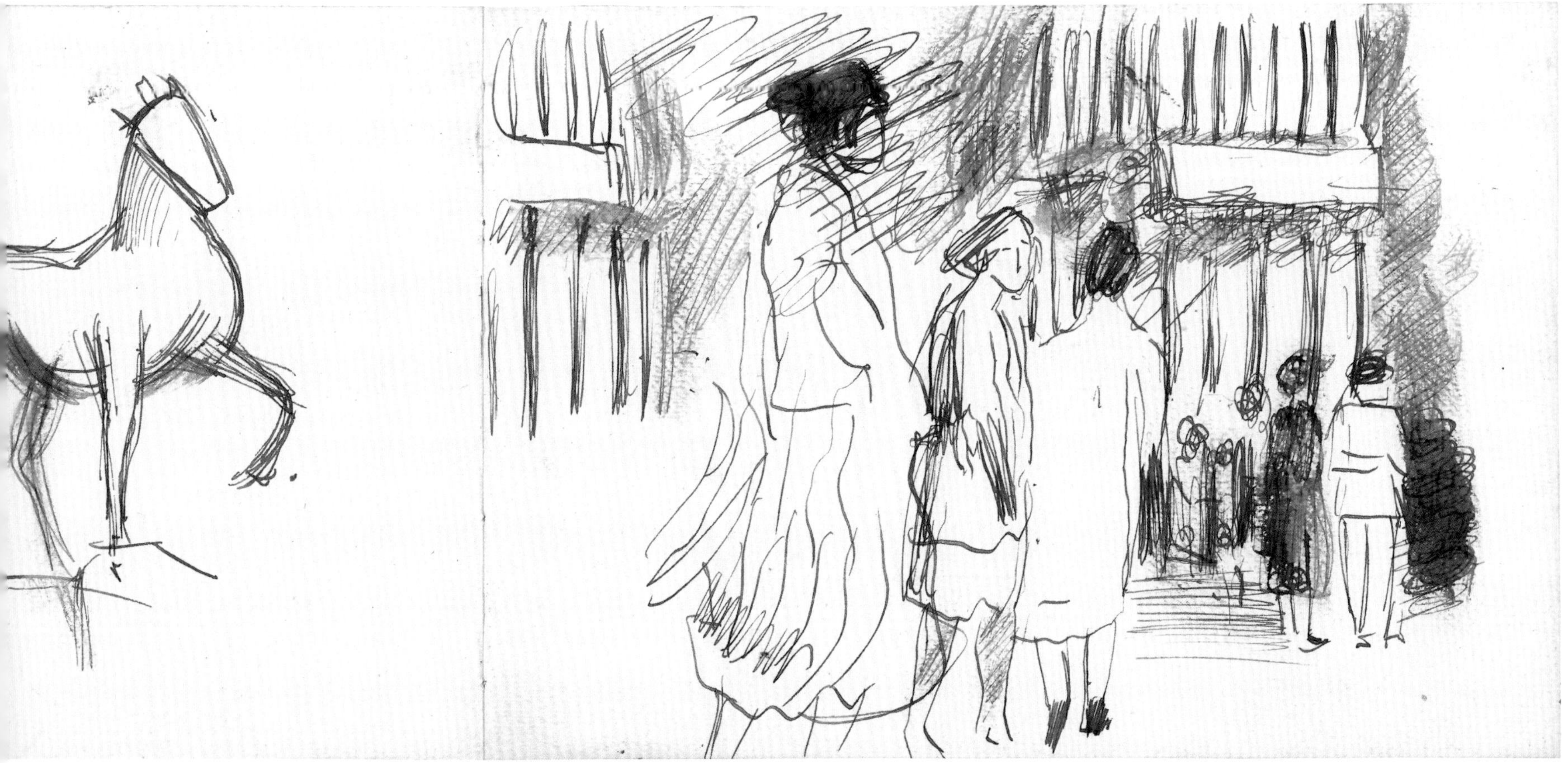

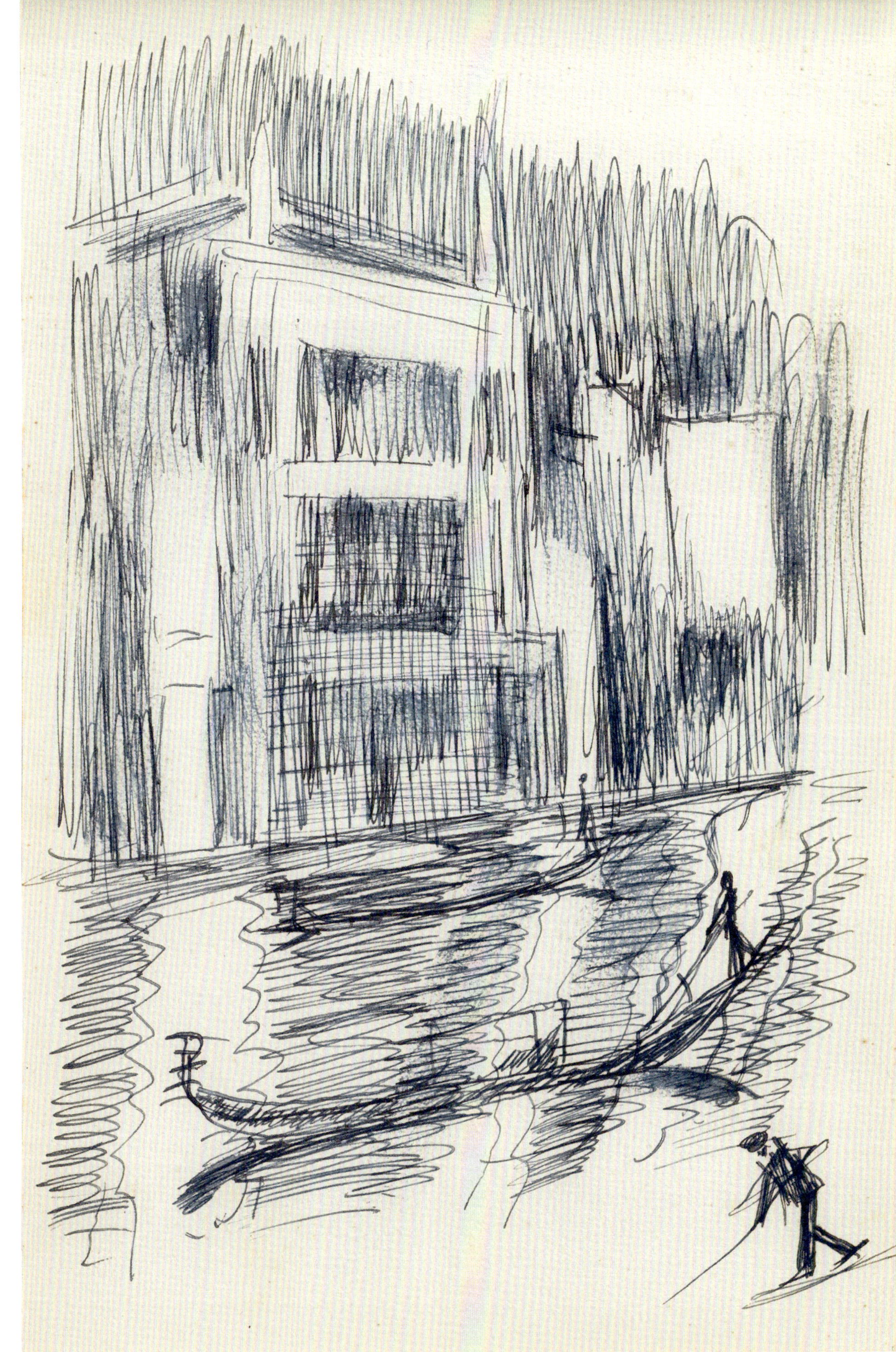

J. F. Willumsen
Two sketchbook pages
from Venice, 1930s
13.5 × 18.5 cm
Willumsen's Museum,
Frederikssund

J. F. Willumsen
Sketchbook page from Venice,
1930s
14.5 × 22.5 cm
Willumsen's Museum,
Frederikssund

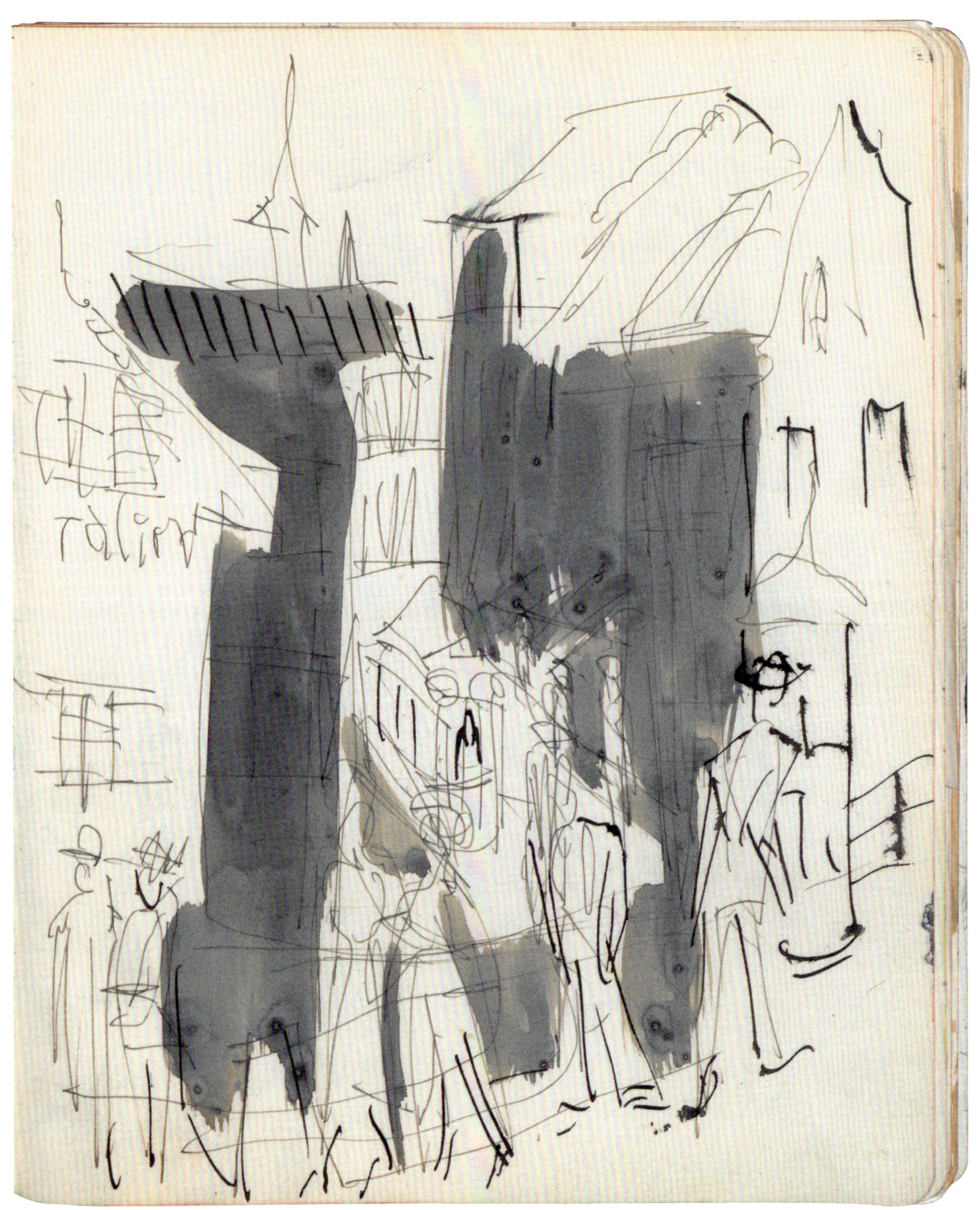

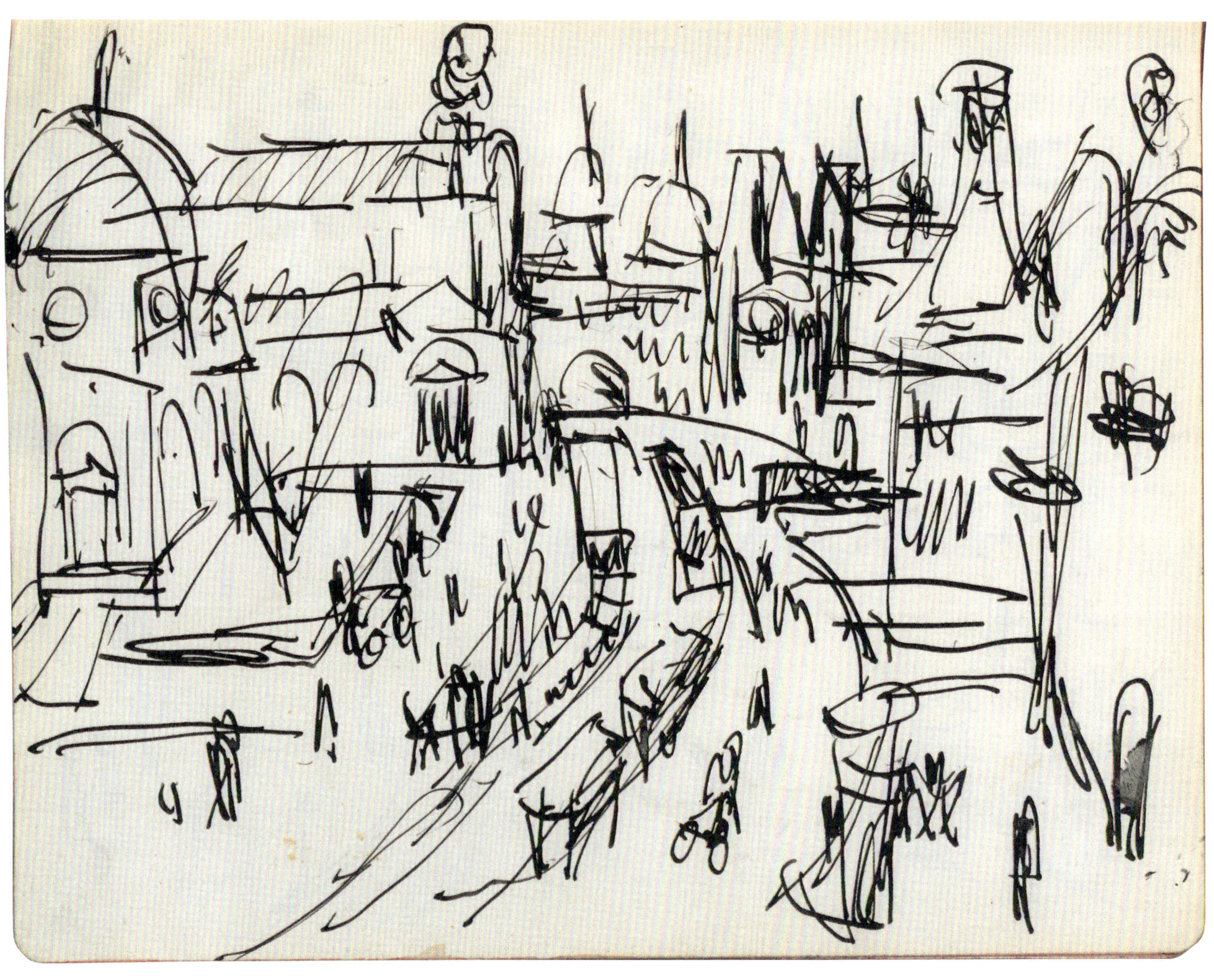

Ernst Ludwig Kirchner
Sketchbook 175,
1935–36, p. 26
21.7 × 17.2 cm
Kirchner Museum Davos

Ernst Ludwig Kirchner
Sketchbook 117, 1925–26, p. 51
20.4 × 16.3 cm
Kirchner Museum Davos

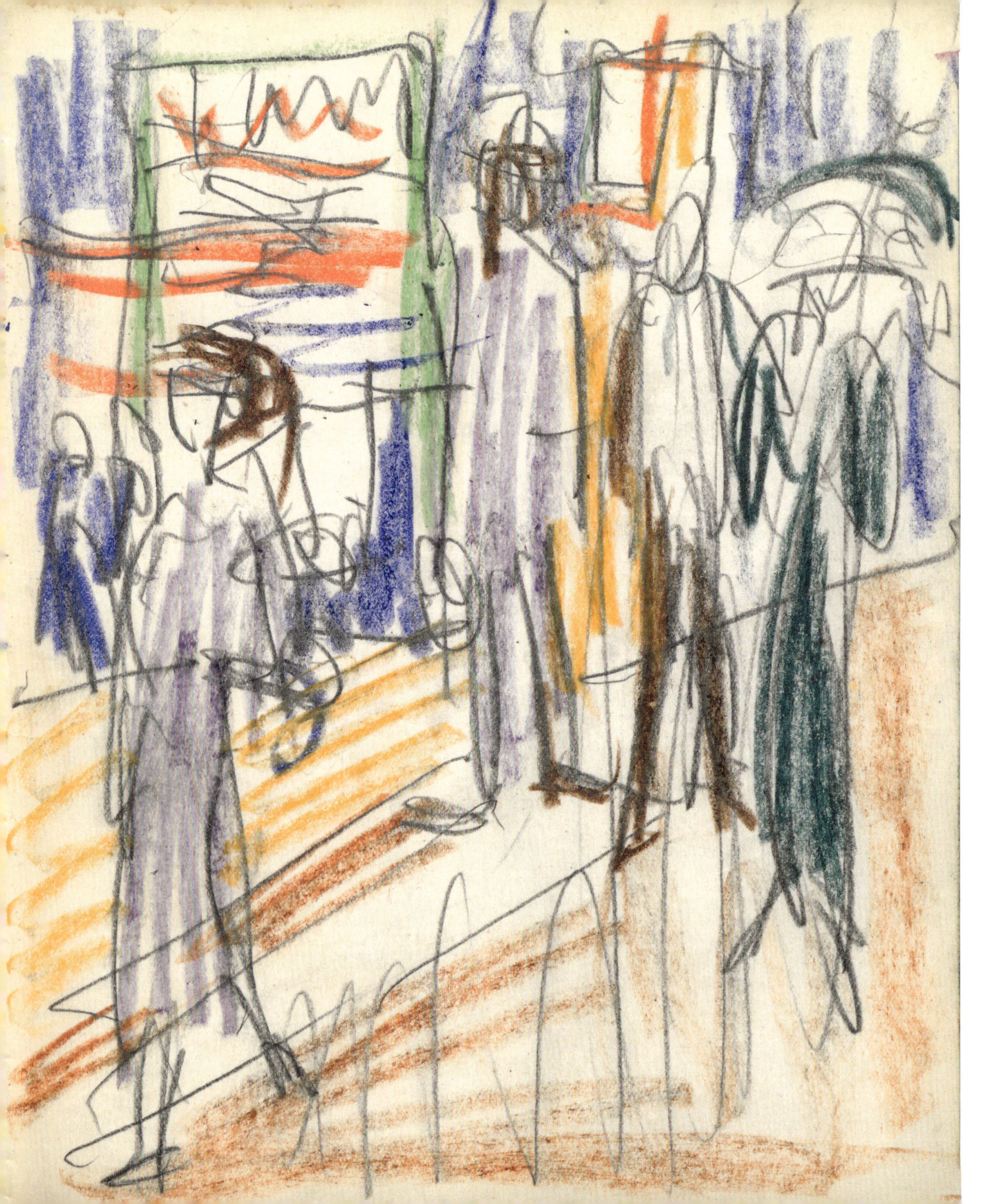

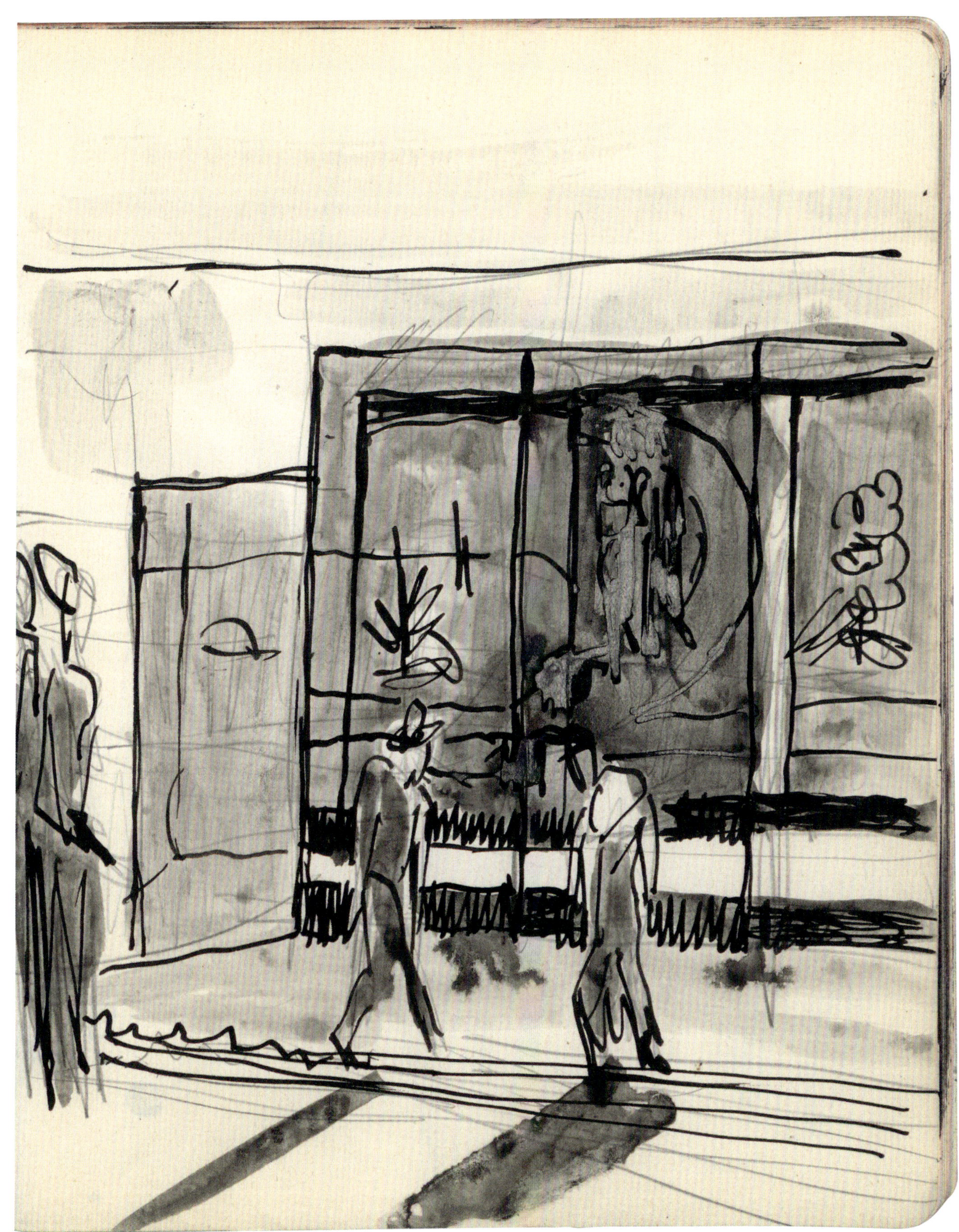

Ernst Ludwig Kirchner
Sketchbook 131,
February 1926, p. 52
20.7 × 17 cm
Kirchner Museum Davos

Ernst Ludwig Kirchner
Sketchbook 076, 1921,
1926–27, p. 31
21.7 × 17.4 cm
Kirchner Museum Davos

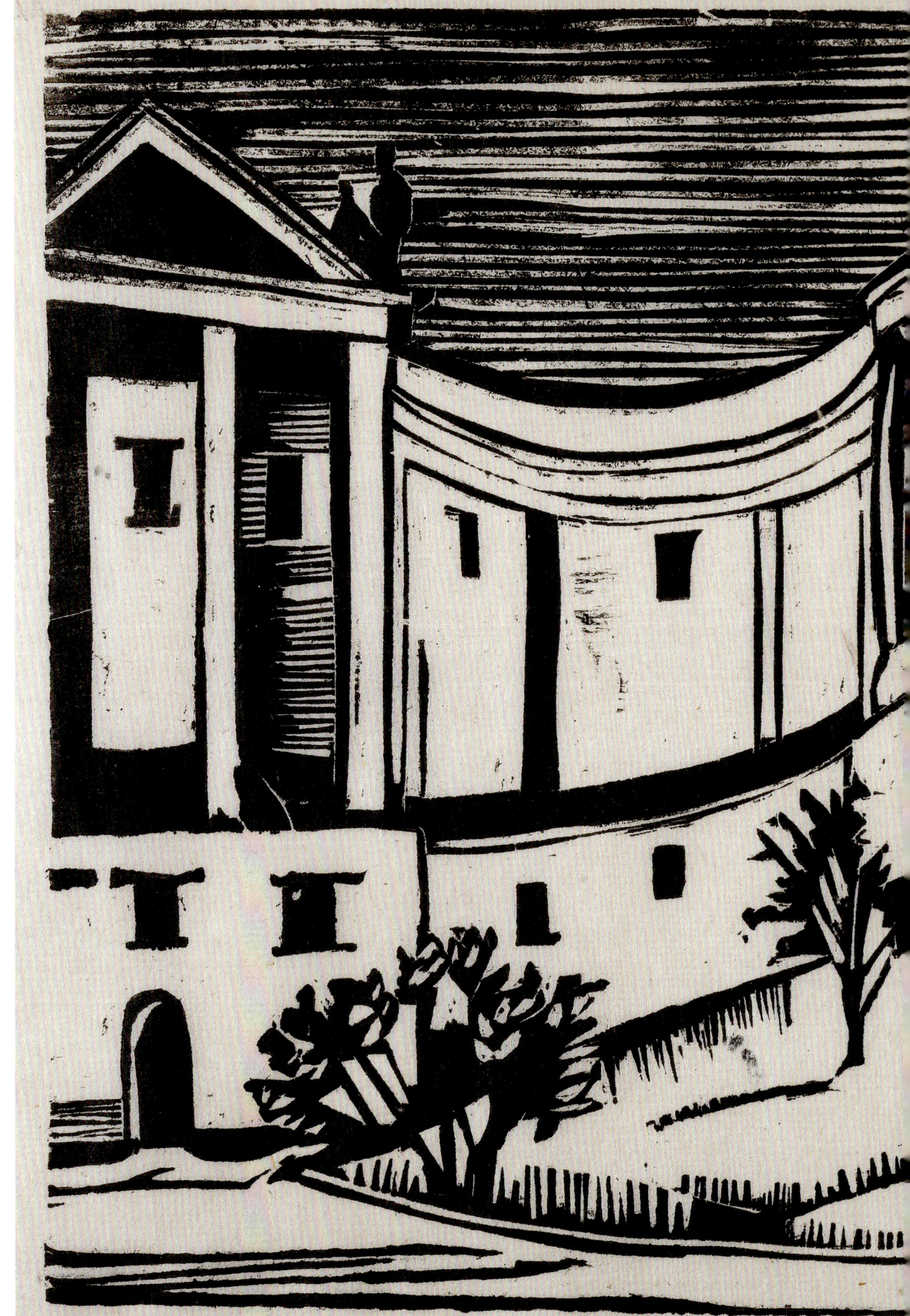

Ernst Ludwig Kirchner
Hedwigskirche Berlin
(St Hedwig's Cathedral Berlin),
1927
Woodcut, 25.7 × 42.2 cm
Kirchner Museum Davos

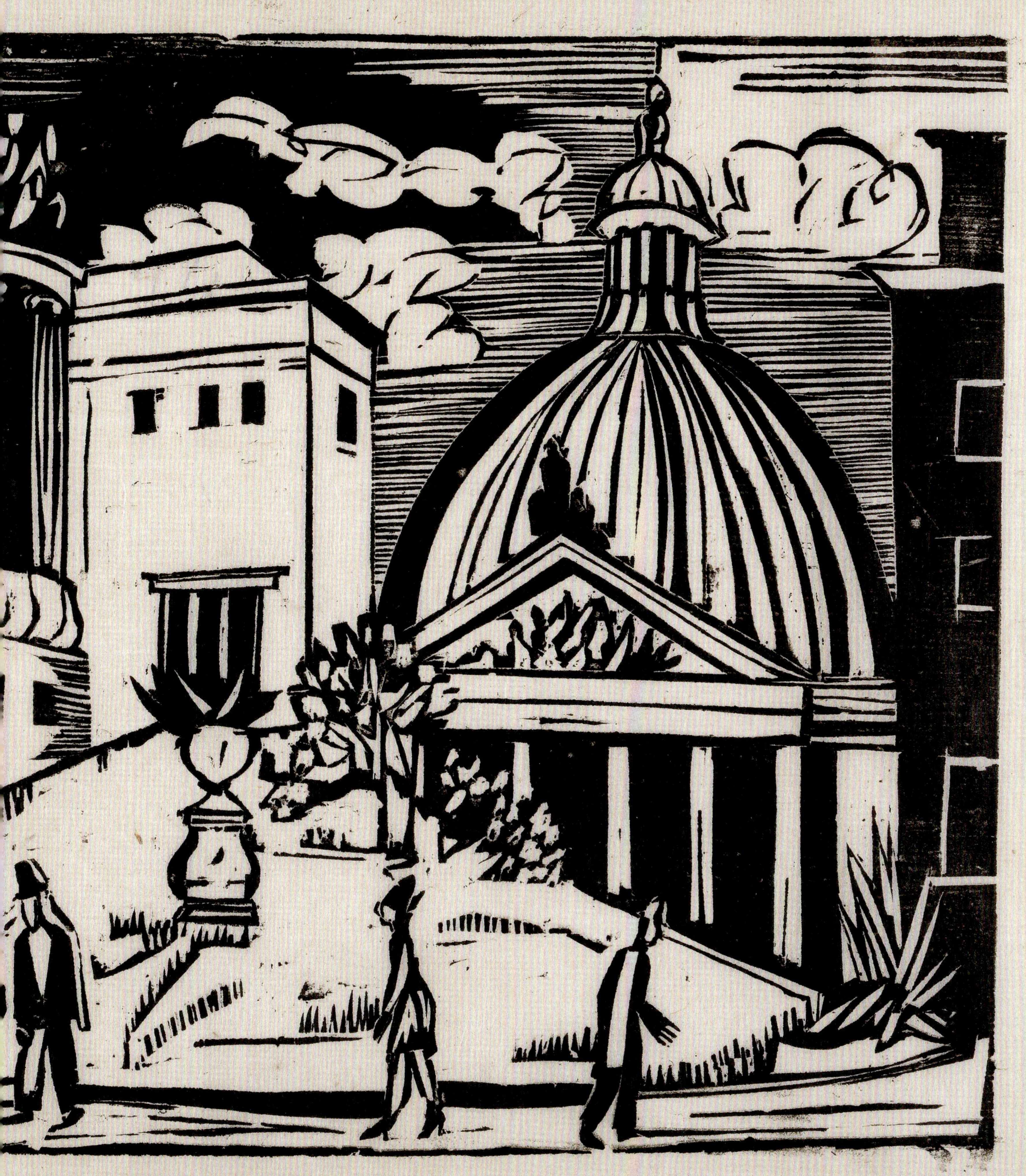

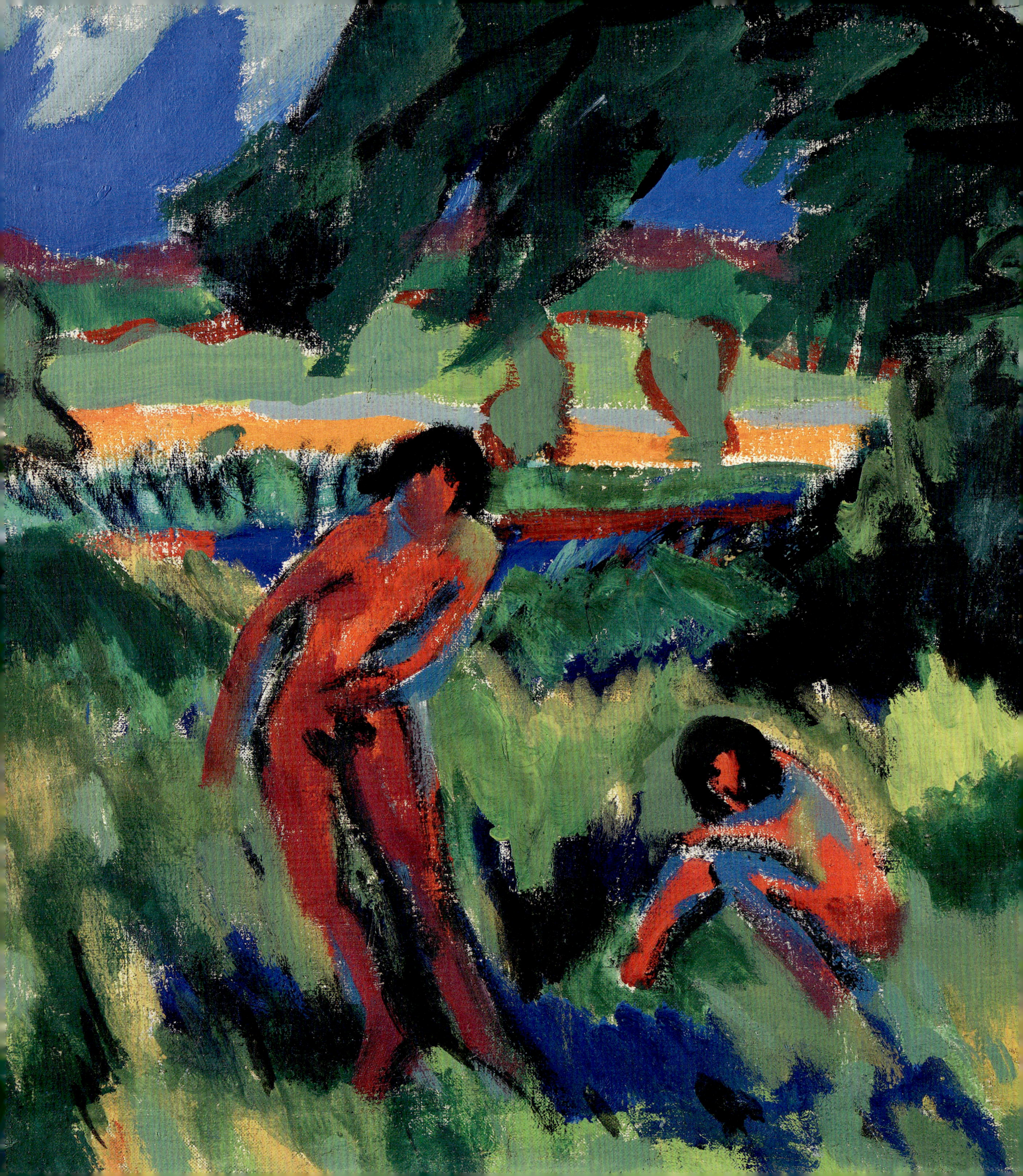

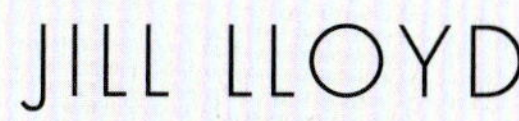
JILL LLOYD

Ernst Ludwig Kirchner: "… there is only the dance."[1]

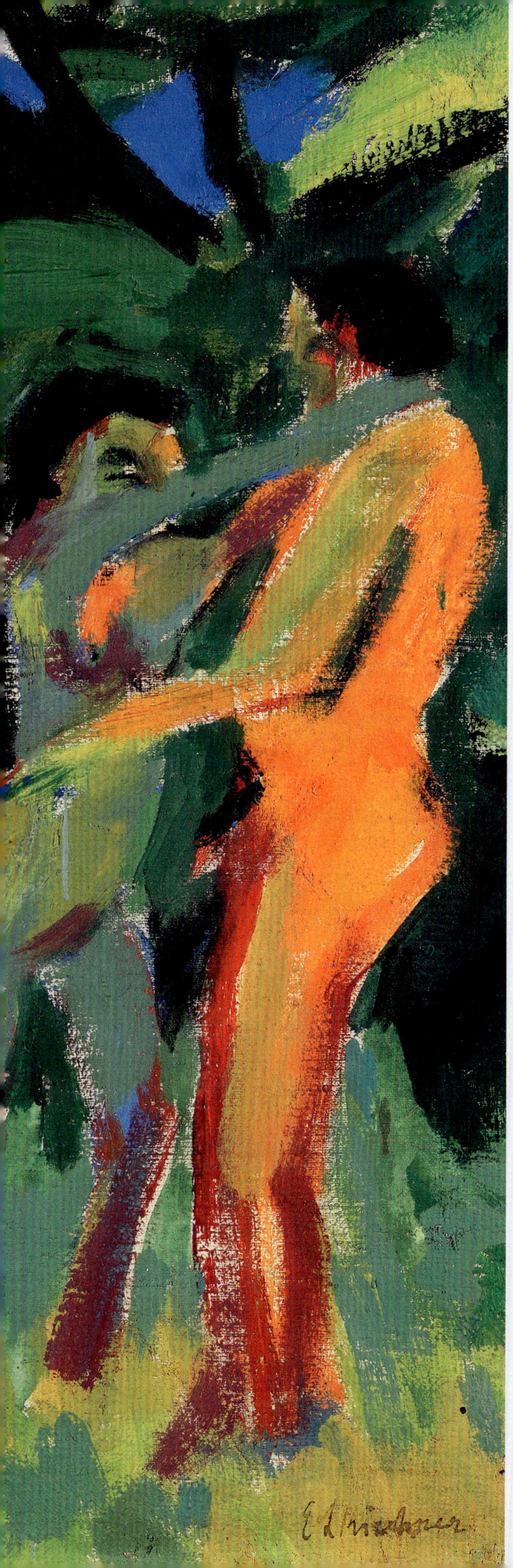

Ernst Ludwig Kirchner
Detail of *Spielende nackte Menschen unter Baum* (Playing Naked People Under the Tree), 1910
Oil on canvas, 77 × 89 cm,
Sammlung Moderne Kunst in der Pinakothek der Moderne,
Munich – Bayerische Staatsgemäldesammlungen

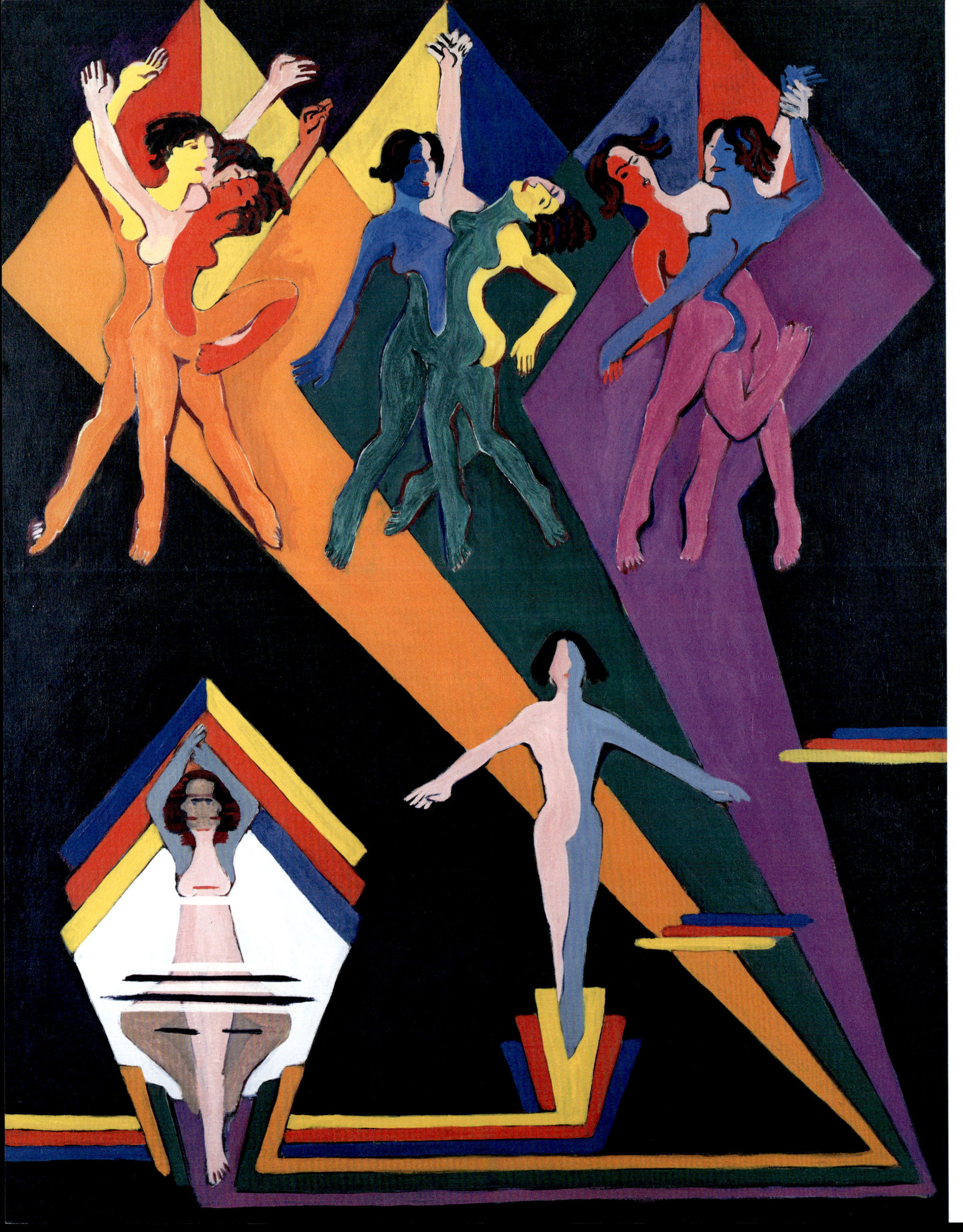

During the last ten years of his life, before he committed suicide in 1938 under the darkening clouds of political crisis in Europe, Ernst Ludwig Kirchner worked obsessively on a composition representing wildly dancing nudes. The artist created numerous variations on this theme in drawings, watercolors, and prints, alongside three major paintings, which he titled *Farbentanz I* (Color Dance I, 1930–32), *Farbentanz II* (Color Dance II, 1932–34), and finally *Tanzende Mädchen in farbigen Strahlen* (Dancing Girls in Rays of Color, 1932–37, fig. 1). Originally conceived as part of a grand scheme of wall decorations for the ceremonial hall of the newly built Folkwang Museum in Essen (a project which also fell victim to the rise of National Socialism in Germany), the dancing figures were to be the crowning glory of Kirchner's designs, positioned on a wall behind the central, altar-like podium in the vast hall. Bathed in rays of colored light emanating from an abstract sun, the three dancing women in *Farbentanz I* and *II* represent the primary colors; red, yellow, and blue. Kirchner's obsessive return to the theme, and his attempts to distil the composition into an increasingly reductive, abstract form, demonstrates the crucial role that dance and the moving body played in his ideas about art and human destiny. At the end of the artist's life, dance was elevated into a quasi-cosmic life force, where human existence became a synthesis of color, light, and movement. How did he arrive at this point? And why did Kirchner so venerate the art of dance? The following essay sets out to explore these questions by tracing Kirchner's transforming attitudes to dance in relation to the historical and philosophical forces that shaped the artist's worldview.[2]

When we look back at Kirchner's origins as a founder member of the Expressionist group Brücke at the beginning of the twentieth century, we find that he had long been fascinated by the relationship between the nude body and the life-affirming light and energy of the sun. The earliest Brücke insignia (fig. 2), a woodcut that Kirchner carved to celebrate the foundation of the group, depicts a nude figure on a bridge throwing up her arms to worship the sun in a gesture known as the *Lichtgebet*, which was popularized by the Jugendstil illustrator Fidus (Hugo Höppener) and became the visual slogan of the nudist movement in Germany at the turn of the twentieth century. The Brücke artists' manifesto underlines the group's sympathy for the wide-sweeping ideals of reformists such as the nudists, who called on youth to challenge outmoded values and to greet the new century in a spirit of rebirth and renewal. "We call together the youth of today," the Brücke manifesto declares, "And, as youths who carry the seed of the future, we intend to obtain for ourselves freedom to move and live in opposition to the older established powers."[3]

Reform ideas

Central to the reformers' aspirations was a new attitude to the human body, which was to be liberated from the shackles of the past—symbolized by the corsets restraining women's bodies, which were cast aside in favor of loose-fitting "reform" dresses. Nudism, vegetarianism, and the free, expressive dance and body exercises developed by dance masters Rudolf Laban and Émile Jaques-Dalcroze, among others, celebrated the liberated body and its new, regenerative relationship with nature. Not only young Expressionists like Kirchner, but a whole generation of artists and reformers were inspired by the writings of Friedrich Nietzsche, who condemned the rational, calculating, "Apollonian" spirit of nineteenth-century society and advocated a reformative "Dionysian" impulse of ecstasy, instinct, and renewal (*Birth of Tragedy*, 1886). The name *Brücke* [Bridge] was inspired by a passage from *Thus Spoke Zarathustra* (1883–85), where Nietzsche described youth as "a new beginning, a sport, a self-propelling wheel, a first motion, a sacred 'yes.'"[4] He continues: "What is great in man is that he is a bridge and not a goal; what can be loved in man is that he is a *going-across* and a *down-going*."[5]

Fig. 1
Ernst Ludwig Kirchner
Tanzende Mädchen in farbigen Strahlen
(Dancing Girls in Rays of Color), 1932–37
Oil on canvas, 195 × 150 cm
Kirchner Museum Davos

1. Quotation from T.S. Eliot's "Burnt Norton," 1935 (*Four Quartets*). See T.S. Eliot, *The Complete Poems and Plays* (London, 1969), p. 173.
2. A number of authors, most recently Sherwin Simmons in his article "The Dancer's revenge: Dance/Pantomime and the Emergence of Ernst Ludwig Kirchner's Fantasy Pictures," *Dance Chronicle* 41:2 (May 2018), have focused on particular dance paintings and groups of paintings by Kirchner. The recent exhibition *Kirchners Kosmos: Der Tanz* (Kirchnerhaus Aschaffenburg 2018) gives an overview of the development of Kirchner's dance motifs. The present essay aims to link Kirchner's representations of dance to *Lebensreform* and his fascination with Nietzsche's philosophical writings, which Kirchner shared with other artists and writers of his generation, including T.S. Eliot and Edvard Munch.
3. The *Brücke Program* was published as a four-page brochure in woodcut form, carved by Kirchner in 1906. For a full exploration of Kirchner's links with the reform movement see Kai Schupke and Daniel J. Schreiber, eds., *Brücke und die Lebensreform*, exh. cat. Buchheim Museum (Bernried, 2016).
4. Friedrich Nietzsche, *Thus Spoke Zarathustra* [1883–85], trans. R. J. Hollingdale, (London, 1969), p. 55.
5. Ibid., p. 44.

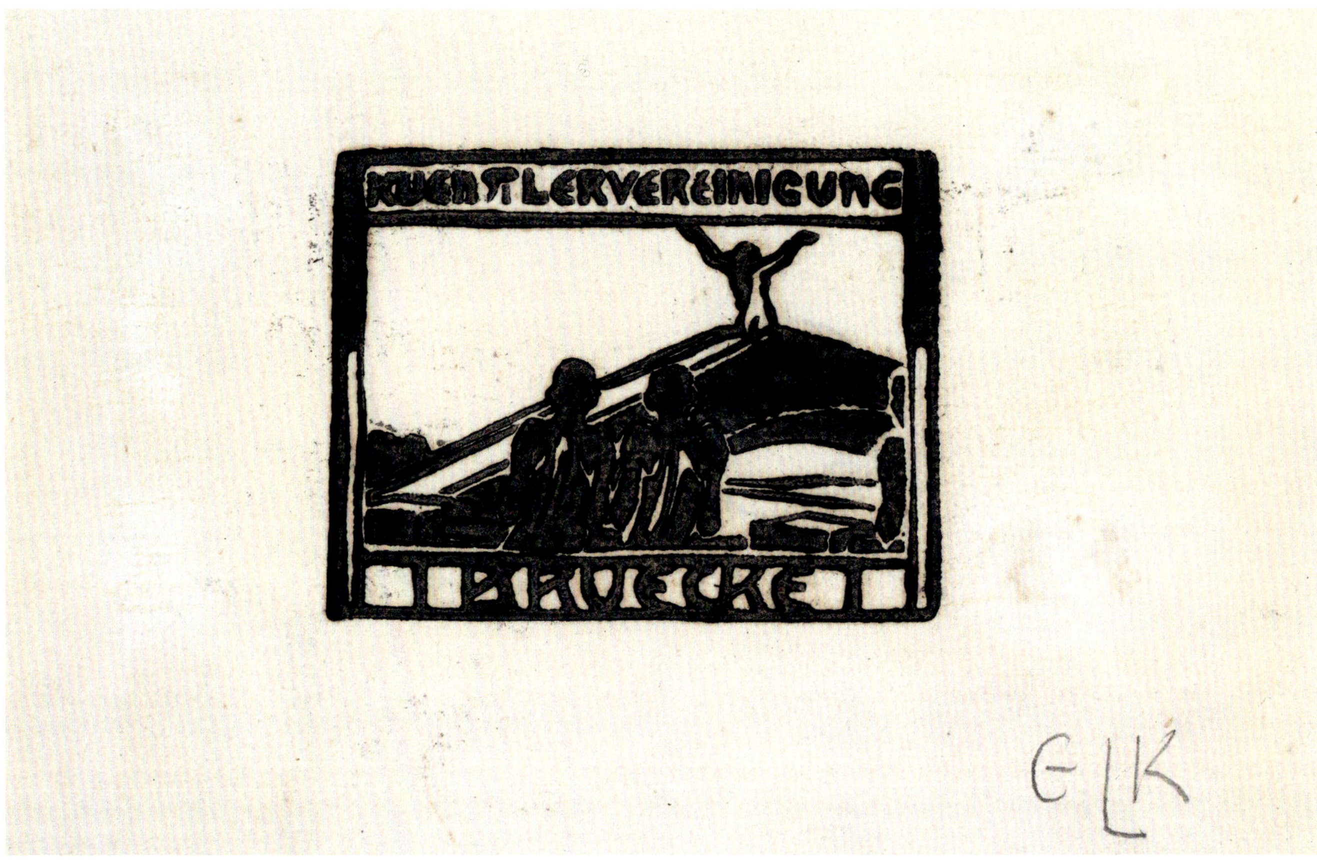

Fig. 2
Ernst Ludwig Kirchner
Künstlervereinigung Brücke
(Artist Association Brücke),
1905
Woodcut, 5 × 6.5 cm
Brücke-Museum, Berlin

Fig. 3
Ernst Ludwig Kirchner
Tanzende (Dancing Woman),
1911
Painted alder-wood,
87 × 35.5 × 27.5 cm
Stedelijk Museum,
Amsterdam

Kirchner was most likely introduced to current reform ideas by his professor for interior design at the Technical University in Dresden, Fritz Schumacher, who was deeply involved in the architectural reform movement that sought to reshape the environment for Nietzsche's "new man." The courses Kirchner attended at the Versuchs- und Lehranstalt für Angewandte und Freie Kunst run by Wilhelm von Debschitz and Hermann Obrist during the semester he spent in Munich in the winter of 1903–04 advocated a new style of drawing that gave visual expression to Nietzschean principles of transformation and "becoming." Students were encouraged to sketch nudes, not in the static academic poses demanded by the art academies, but rather moving freely around the studio. In place of traditional exactitude, they were taught to value qualities of spontaneity, naivety, intuition, and originality in their drawings.[6]

Art and Life

Back in Dresden, Kirchner and the other Brücke artists practiced a similar style of sketching in their so-called "quarter-hour nudes"—speedily executed to capture the essential traits of their moving, bending and turning models. The quick movement of the artist's hand laid the basis for what Kirchner later described as the "ecstasy of first sight" (*Ekstase des ersten Sehens*), a rapturous or ecstatic response to the world through quick, shorthand sketching.[7] Movement, in Kirchner's Expressionist heyday, was thus not simply a question of subject but also style: the *Rausch* or frenzy of the sketch was a quality that he also sought in his paintings, with their spontaneous brushwork and bright colors, and in his woodcuts and sculptures, with their roughly hewn surfaces and boldly twisting compositions (fig. 3).

6. See Henrike Mund, "Bewegung und Ekstase. Ernst Ludwig Kirchner und der moderne Ausdruckstanz," in Jutta Hülsewig-Johnen and Henrike Mund, eds., *Der böse Expressionismus, Trauma und Tabu*, exh. cat. Kunsthalle Bielefeld (Cologne, 2017), p. 156.
7. Lothar Grisebach, ed., *E.L. Kirchners Davoser Tagebuch: Eine Darstellung des Malers und eine Sammlung seiner Schriften* (Cologne, 1968), p. 128. Gerd Pressler's *catalogue raisonné* of Kirchner's sketchbooks, *Ernst Ludwig Kirchner: Die Skizzenbücher* (Karlsruhe, 1996), includes the artist's words; *"Ekstase des ersten Sehens"* as the book's subtitle, highlighting the importance of this concept for all Kirchner's sketching activity.

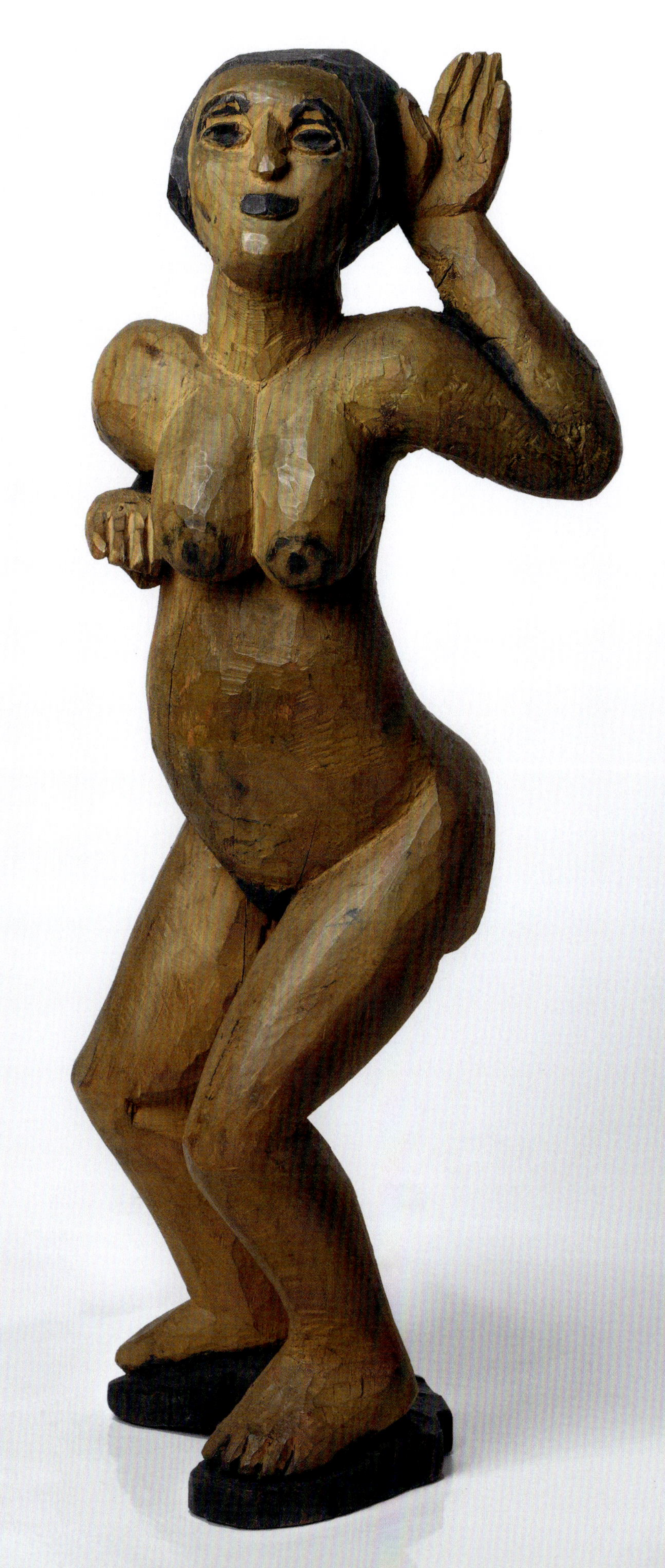

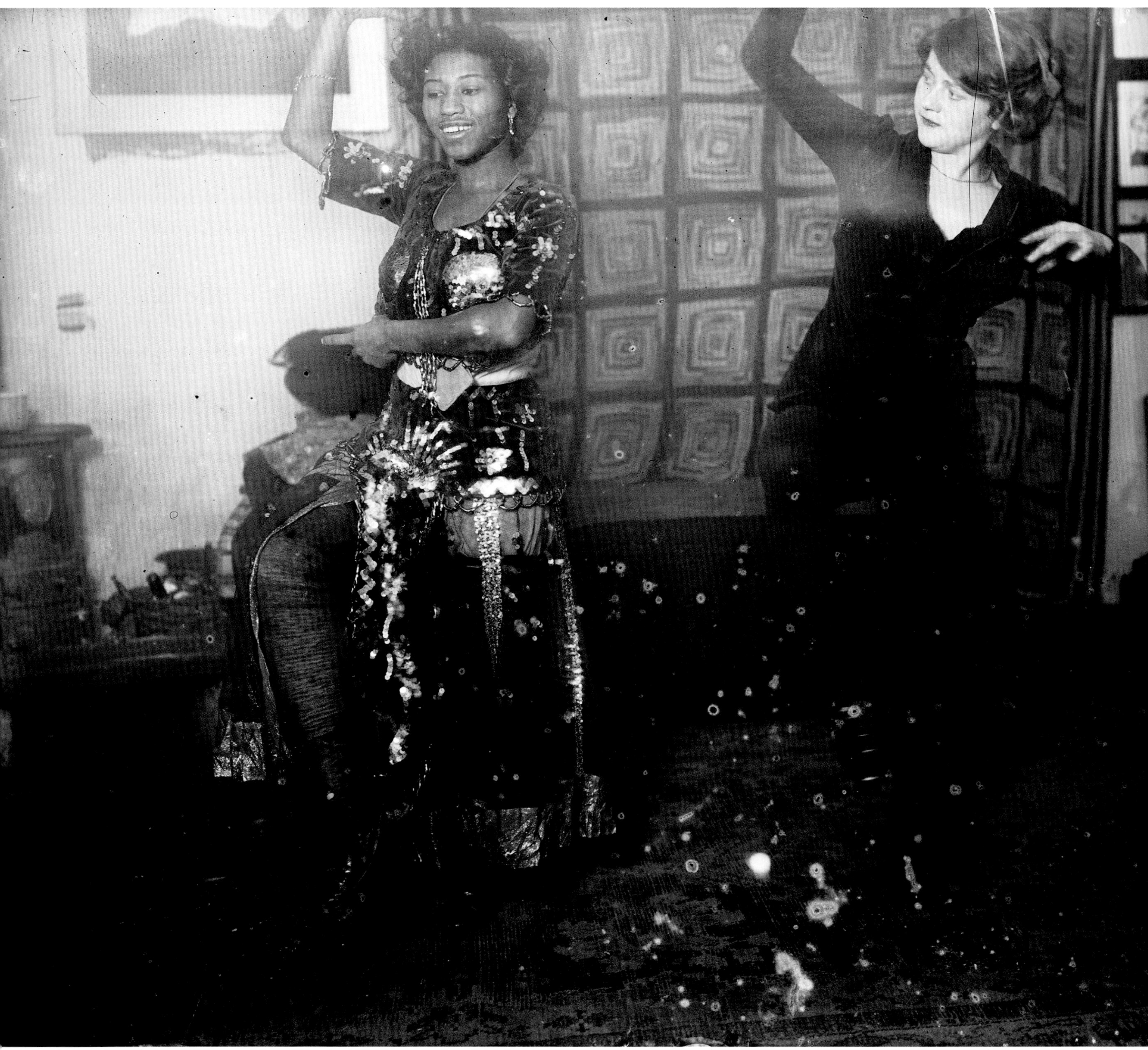

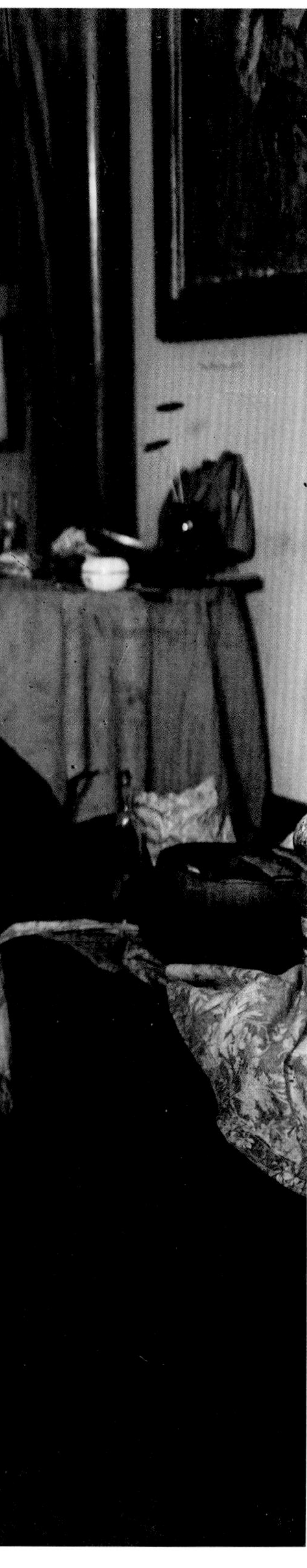

Kirchner's goal was an overarching Nietzschean vitalism that would breathe new life into art and indeed challenge the very boundaries between art and life. In the bohemian, alternative space of the artist's studio, Kirchner's fellow artists and girlfriends are depicted enjoying spontaneous sex, dancing, and brandishing bows and arrows – another Nietzschean reference, as the archer features in *Thus Spoke Zarathustra* as a symbol of becoming and passage towards the future.[8] On occasion adolescent models are implicated in these sexual "games," throwing a dark shadow over the ecstatic mood of the studio. Kirchner's relationships with his child and adolescent models have indeed been revealed as suspect, although such activities were explained at the time as a celebration of Nietzschean forces of renewal associated with the child, and as an attack on bourgeois morality.[9] Kirchner decorated the walls of his studios with boldly painted wall hangings, creating a *Gesamtkunstwerk* or total art environment, which predicts contemporary installation and performance art. In his paintings, drawings, prints, and photographs of the studio, it is difficult to distinguish between art and life: gestures of live models rhyme with the poses struck by figures in wooden sculptures and paintings, bath tubs look like sculptural plinths, and mirrors become indistinguishable from the brightly colored paintings that decorate the studio walls.

Fig. 4
Ernst Ludwig Kirchner
Nelly and Sidi Heckel (Riha), Dancing in Erich Heckel's Studio,
ca. 1910–11
Glass-plate negative, 13 × 18 cm
Kirchner Museum Davos

Nietzschean Dance

Dance played an important role in these Dresden works, not least because several of the young artists' girlfriends and models were drawn from the world of cabaret and circus, which Kirchner and his Brücke friends frequently visited and sketched. This was a world on the margins of society, a popular art form free of bourgeois restrictions where the artists discovered *risqué* acts luridly lit by newly invented spotlights and lime-lights, which had a lasting effect on Kirchner's radiant colors. Handmade postcards with colorful sketches, which the artists exchanged and sent to friends and admirers on a daily basis, depict the exotic acts—Chinese jugglers and snake charmers, acrobats

8. The archer was a frequent motif in Kirchner's work throughout his career, as is evident in several paintings, drawings and photographs included in the exhibition accompanying this publication.
9. See Sherwin Simmons, "'A suggestiveness that can make one crazy': Ernst Ludwig Kirchner's Images of Marzella," *Modernism/Modernity* 22, no. 3 (September 2015).

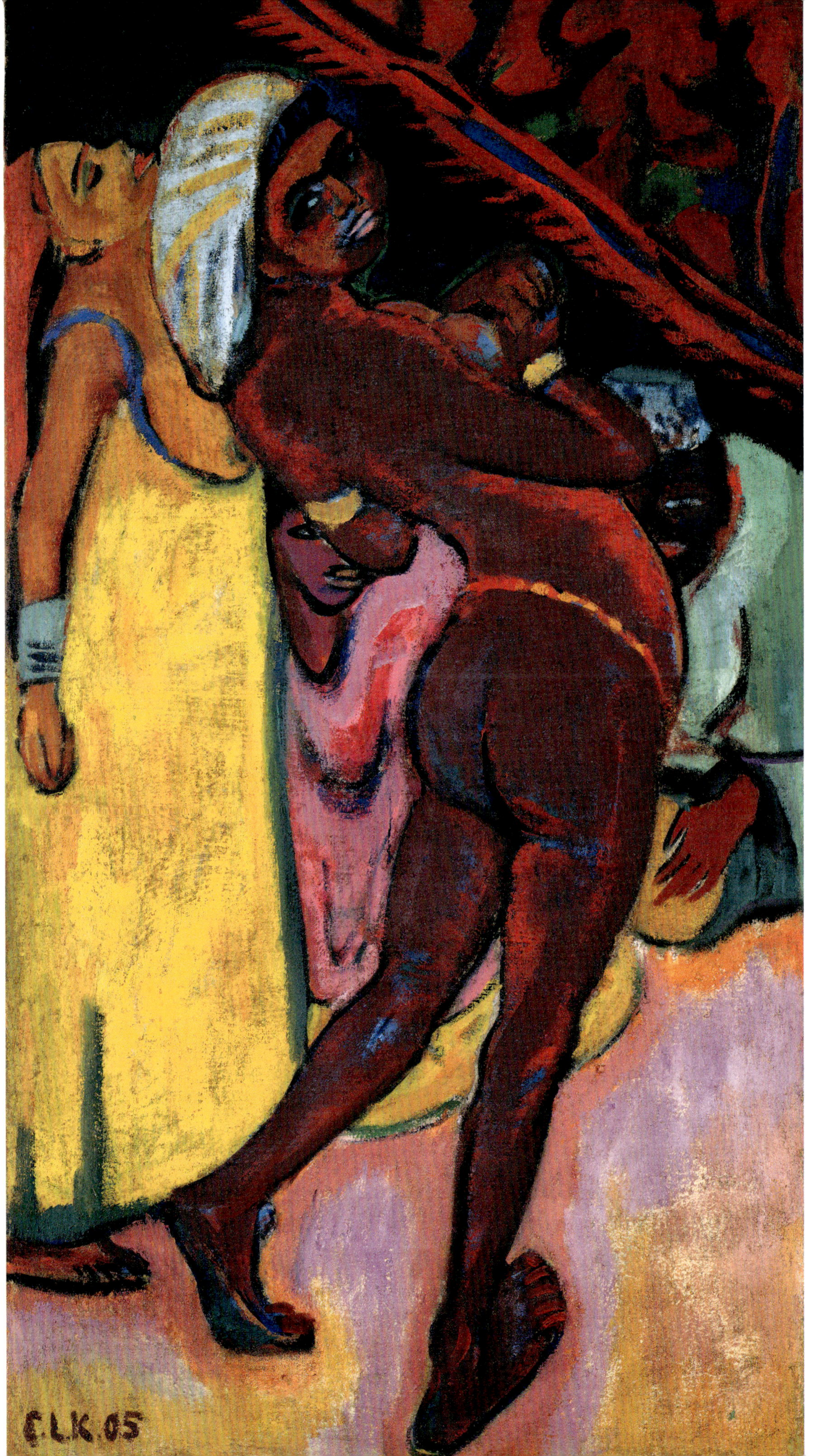
E.L.K.05

and cakewalk dancers—who performed in the makeshift nightclubs and cabarets on the outskirts of the city. Like the archers in Kirchner's studio scenes, the acrobats, tightrope and cancan dancers who appear in his cabaret paintings also refer to images in Nietzsche's *Thus Spoke Zarathustra*: alongside the bridge, Nietzsche uses the daring tightrope dancer as a metaphor of transformation and passage to the future; and in his chapter on "The Higher Man," he writes: "Lift up your hearts my brothers, high! higher! And do not forget your legs! Lift up your legs, too, you fine dancers: and better still, stand on your heads! .... You Higher men, the worst about you is: none of you has learned to dance as a man ought to dance—to dance beyond yourselves!"[10]

Kirchner was attracted above all by exotic acts and black dancers. Viewed at the time as "primitive," tribal societies and art forms offered, in Kirchner's view, a positive, regenerative alternative to decadent Western civilization. In one of Kirchner's experimental photographs we find the young German dancer Sidi Riha (who later married Brücke artist Erich Heckel) imitating movements performed by Nelly, one of the black dancers who joined the Brücke artists' entourage (fig. 4). Kirchner regarded these black dancers —like the tribal art he discovered in the Dresden Ethnographic Museum—as embodiments of his essentially romantic, Nietzschean quest for an instinctive and authentic counter-image to Western society. In the summers of 1909 and 1910 he visited so-called *Völkerschauen*, where whole tribal villages were presented as part of a colonial propaganda campaign within the parameters of Dresden's zoological gardens.[11] Kirchner was particularly captivated by the expressive movements of native Samoans and by dancers in an African village. He recorded his experiences in sketches and colored drawings, using them as the basis for several paintings such as *Negertänzerin* (Black Dancer) from 1909–11/1920 (fig. 5), which shows a nude black dancer, twisting her head and body backwards to meet the male artist's admiring gaze.

Healing and Freedom

Kirchner's essentially naive exoticism (from today's perspective) also led him to create his own "primitive" idyll in the countryside setting of the Moritzburg Lakes outside Dresden. Together with his artist friends, girlfriends, and child models, Kirchner left the city to enjoy nude bathing excursions in the summer months of 1909 and 1910: numerous drawings, prints, and paintings depict the youthful group playing with boomerangs and bows and arrows, and cavorting in the lakes and surrounding forest. *Spielende nackte Menschen unter Baum* (Playing Naked People Under the Tree) from 1910 (fig. 6) shows an embracing couple literally merging with the colors and rhythms of the windblown trees. Once again, there is a Nietzschean impetus behind Kirchner's depiction of liberated nudes in this regenerative, natural setting. In *The Will to Power* (1906), Nietzsche observes that "[t]he domestication (culture) of man does not sink very deep. When it does sink far below the skin it immediately becomes degeneration ... The wild man (or, in moral terminology, the *evil* man) is a reversion to Nature—and, in a certain sense, he represents a recovery, a *cure* from the effects of 'culture.'"[12]

A desire for renewal and recovery from civilization also motivated the nudist movement in turn-of-the-century Germany, which had a strong presence in the Dresden area. A recently established *Lichtluftbad* (a "light and fresh-air bath") close to Moritzburg, and a community nudist resort at one of the Moritzburg ponds were active during the summers that the Brücke artists spent there.[13] Local sanatorium patients, meanwhile, celebrated carnival by dressing up in American Indian costumes and playing natives in the forest.[14] However, the free sexuality in Kirchner's bather scenes clearly distinguishes his radical Expressionism from the prudish attitude of the nudist reformers, who insisted on strict gender segregation. Whereas the ethos and imagery of the broader nudist

Fig. 5
Ernst Ludwig Kirchner
Negertänzerin
(Black Dancer),
1909–11/1920
Oil on canvas, 168 × 93 cm
Sammlung Würth, Künzelsau

10. Nietzsche 1969 (see note 4), p. 305–306.
11. A detailed historical and critical analysis of the colonial and commercial *Völkerschauen* in Germany is provided by Anne Dreesbach, "Colonial Exhibitions, 'Völkerschauen' and the Display of the 'Other,'" *European History Online (EGO)*, May 3, 2012, http://www.ieg-ego.eu/dreesbacha-2012-en (accessed February 20, 2020).
12. Friedrich Nietzsche, *The Will to Power: An Attempted Transvaluation of all Values*, trans. Anthony M. Ludovici, vol. II, Books III and IV (Edinburgh and London, 1913), p. 158.
13. See Jill Lloyd, *German Expressionism, Primitivism and Modernity* (London, 1991), p. 110, note 33.
14. See photograph of carnival at the Weisser Hirsch sanatorium, February 1910, illustrated in ibid., p. 115. Karl May, who was based in nearby Radebeul, had popularized the image of the romantic, noble American Indian in his highly successful Winnetou novels (*Winnetou IV* was published in 1910).

Fig. 6
Ernst Ludwig Kirchner
Spielende nackte Menschen unter Baum
(Playing Naked People Under the Tree), 1910
Oil on canvas, 77 × 89 cm
Sammlung Moderne Kunst in der Pinakothek der Moderne, Munich – Bayerische Staatsgemäldesammlungen

movement was based on the aesthetics of classical Greek art and Greek athleticism, Kirchner was inspired by non-Western, tribal models, which he believed offered a radical alternative to Western civilization. The hunting, fishing, and bathing figures depicted on carved and painted beams from the Micronesian island of Palau, which were on display in the Dresden Ethnographic Museum, directly inspired many of Kirchner's Moritzburg works.[15]

After Kirchner moved from Dresden to Berlin in 1911, he transferred his summer bathing trips to the Baltic island of Fehmarn where he evolved a fluid, experimental style of painting with transparent layers of luminous color to evoke the liberating experience of nude bathers moving in rhythm with the undulating sand dunes, their gestures echoing the waves crashing on the shore and the wind stirring the vegetation.

Dance and the City

Back in the city, however, the vitalistic, celebratory spirit that characterized Kirchner's earlier images of dancers and acrobats in the cabaret and circus was modified by his new contact with big city life. He experienced the city crowds and the competitive atmosphere of the art world in Berlin as a threat to both his sense of individuality and his ideal community of like-minded artists. The close links with other Brücke artists unraveled and Kirchner took a more complicated and reflective approach to familiar subjects.

In Kirchner's cabaret and circus scenes, for example, male observers within his compositions introduce a voyeuristic dimension that increasingly dominates the artist's Berlin work. Performers frequently bear the features of Kirchner's new girlfriend, Erna Schilling, who, together with her sister Gerda, worked as a dancer and probably as a small-time prostitute to scrape together a living.[16] Kirchner became caught in a love triangle between the two women before he eventually decided on Erna, and new tensions arose in his depictions of the relations between the sexes. This is most clearly expressed in a series of works illustrating a pantomime by the literary Expressionist Hans Reimann, entitled *Die Rache der Tänzerin*

15. See illustrations of Palau beams and Greek-inspired athletic motifs in advertisements for the Moritzburg *Lichtluftbad* in ibid., pp. 30 and 110.
16. Simmons 2018 (see note 2), p. 142. In 1912 Erna contracted syphilis and may have tried to commit suicide. See also Kirchner's letter to Gustav Schiefler, January 10, 1930 in *Ernst Ludwig Kirchner: Der gesamte Briefwechsel*, ed. Hans Delfs (Zürich, 2010), pp. 1410–11.

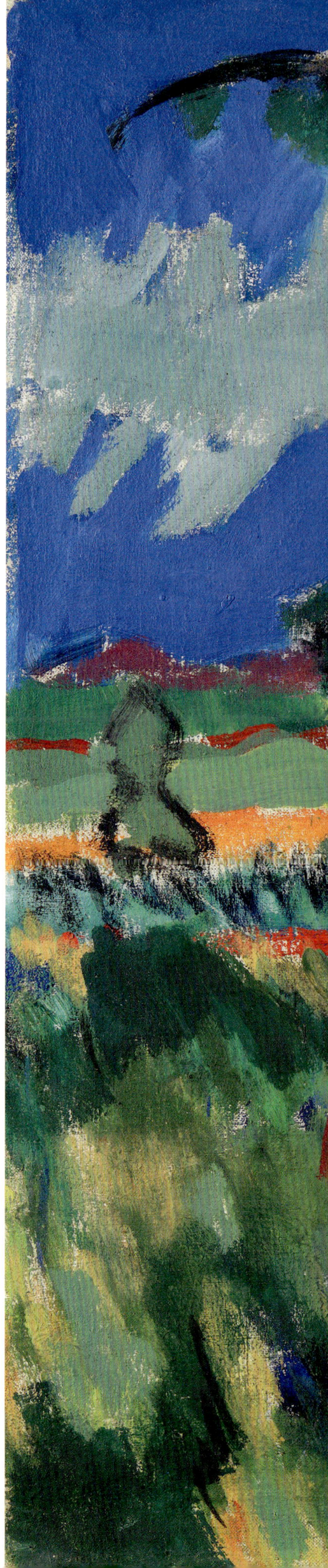

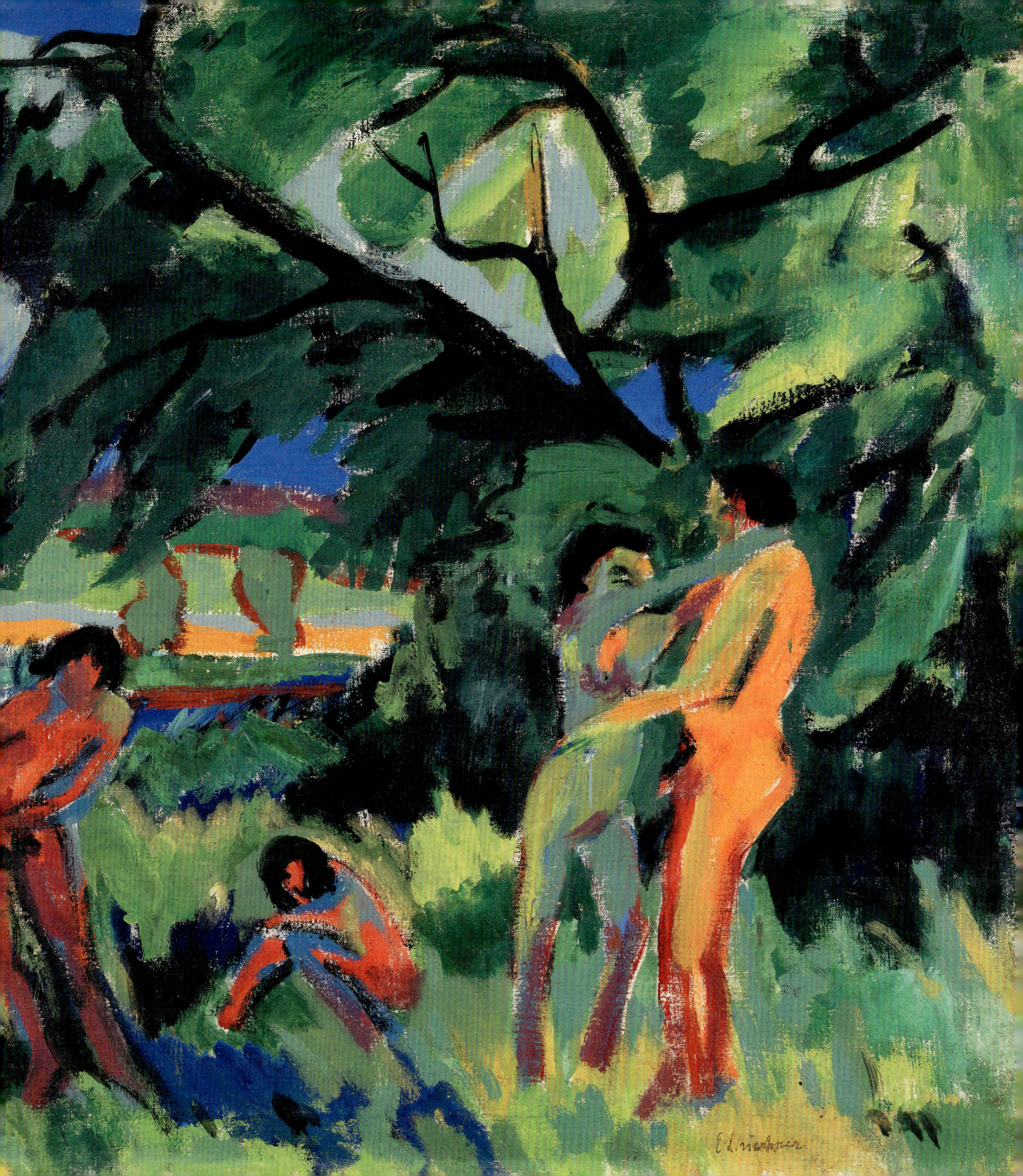

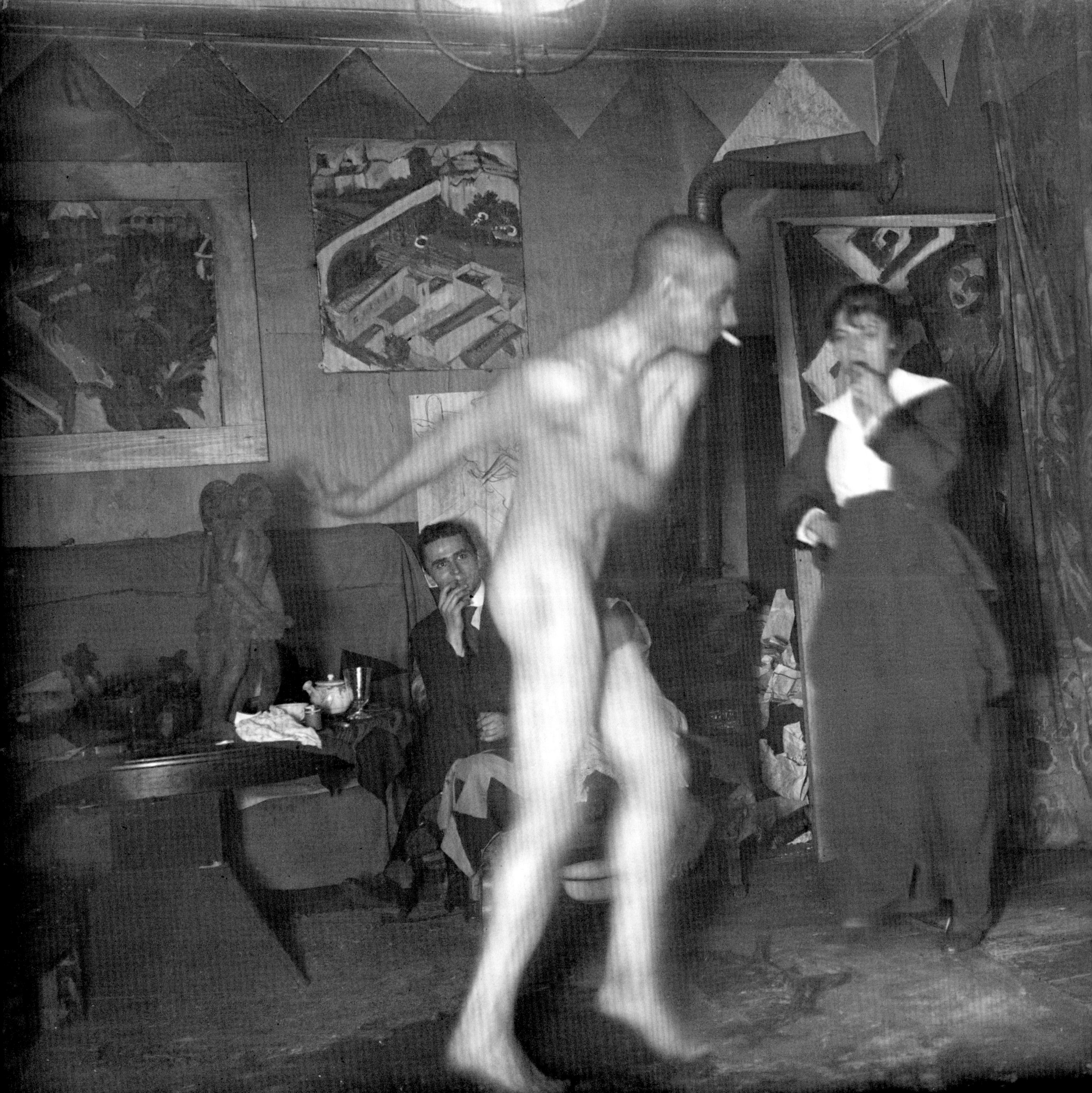

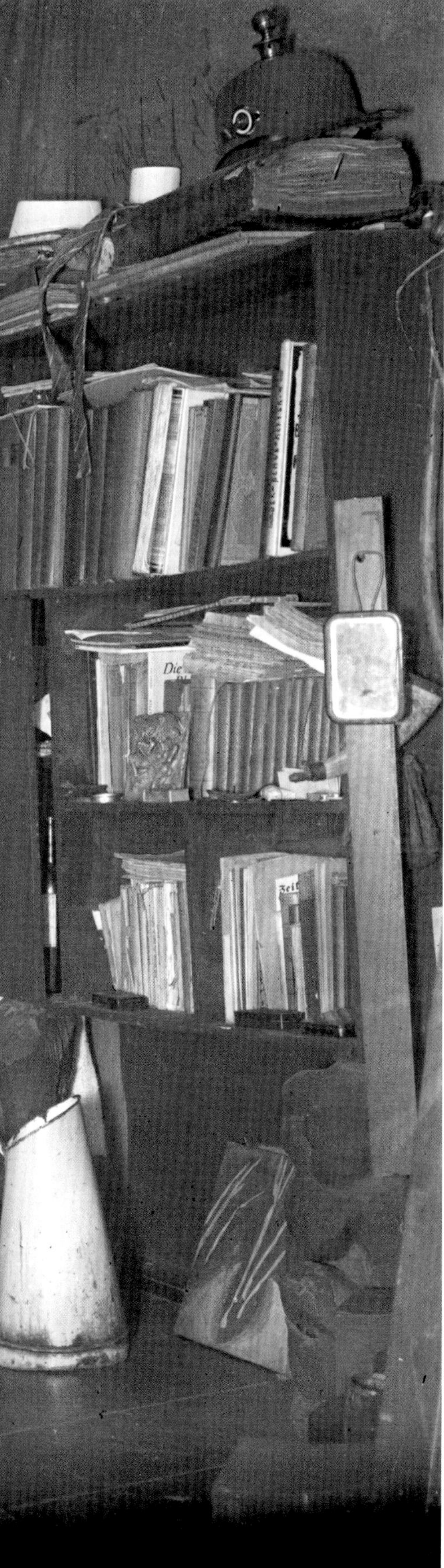

Fig. 7
Ernst Ludwig Kirchner
Werner Gothein, Hugo Biallowons (E. L. Kirchner?), and Erna Schilling in Kirchner's Studio, Körnerstrasse 45, Berlin, 1915
Glass-plate negative, 13 × 18 cm
Kirchner Museum Davos

(The Dancer's Revenge). Kirchner's painting *Pantomime Reimann (Die Rache der Tänzerin)* from 1912 is set in his Berlin studio and depicts Erna in her dancer's costume stamping on the hands and neck of a frock-coated man who prostrates himself at her feet.

Among the most evocative images from this period are photographs that Kirchner took of a bacchanalian studio scene, showing himself (or possibly his friend Hugo Biallowons) wildly dancing in the nude, while Erna, dressed in a fashionable suit-like outfit, coolly looks on (fig. 7). As art historian Sherwin Simmons observes, the inner content of this photo and the related painting—*Der Tanz zwischen den Frauen* (The Dance between Women) from 1915 (fig. 8)—"revolves around the shattering of the secure male gaze through which the male regarded the female dancer as an erotic object."[17] While the "secure male gaze" was clearly evident in works like Kirchner's *Negertänzerin,* the male dancer is now the focus of the woman's attention. Simmons suggests that through his friendship with the classics professor Botho Graef (who was in a relationship with Biallowons), Kirchner became aware that "the male dancer could be associated with instinctual aspects of ancient Greek culture, like the Dionysian satyr – said to be the origins of dance and pantomime—that inspired Nietzsche's figure of Zarathustra."[18] Kirchner's painting, *Der Tanz zwischen den Frauen,* elevates dance beyond the world of the here-and-now, giving it a psychological, symbolic role that signals Kirchner's current sexual dilemmas and his metaphysical state. The disembodied figures—Kirchner depicts an ambiguous dancing male with a single breast between two gesticulating women—take on a transparent, otherworldly appearance. They are outlined in the primary colors; blue, red, and yellow, and gesturing beneath a green arc that suggests the outline of the sun—thus predicting the dancing compositions that recurred in the last decade of the artist's life. Kirchner may well have been referring on a personal level in *Der Tanz zwischen den Frauen* to his conflicting relationships with Erna and Gerda Schilling; but the painting also alludes more generally to the tense and shifting balance of power between the sexes in the lead up to World War I.

17. Simmons 2018 (see note 2), p. 152.
18. Ibid., p. 153.

Fig. 8
Ernst Ludwig Kirchner
Der Tanz zwischen den Frauen (The Dance Between Women), 1915
Oil on canvas, 121.1 × 91.4 cm
Sammlung Moderne Kunst in der Pinakothek der Moderne, Munich – Bayerische Staatsgemäldesammlungen

Metaphysical Dance

The free, expressive movements of the dancers in Kirchner's studio paintings and photographs suggest that the artist had some knowledge of the new dance movement that developed concurrently with his work. He would certainly have had opportunities to see Isadora Duncan, who performed three times in Dresden in 1905–06, or the Wiesenthal sisters, who held many performances in the city from 1908 onwards. Émile Jaques-Dalcroze also became closely linked to Dresden in 1909–10, when he moved his school for eurythmic movement to Hellerau on the outskirts of the city. However, the first concrete evidence of Kirchner's interest in Expressionist dance surfaces after his move from Berlin to Switzerland, following years of mental illness during World War I. In Zurich, Kirchner met the dancer Nina Hard, whom he invited to stay with him and Erna in their house in Davos in the summer of 1921. Nina Hard can be seen posing both dressed and nude in many of Kirchner's works: one photograph presents her in a manly suit, posing confidently with a bohemian cigarette in her hand, while others show her dancing semi-nude on the upper floor of Kirchner's house (fig. 9). In his photographs, like his drawings and paintings, Kirchner developed experimental techniques that reflected his preoccupation with movement and a Nietzschean state of becoming. Double-exposure and photographic blur, such as we see in the photographs of Nina Hard dancing, create expressive effects comparable to the sketchy brushwork and roughly hewn surfaces in Kirchner's paintings and sculptures.

Another sequence of photographs taken in the summer of 1921 show Erna and Nina Hard bathing nude in a mountain stream, a subject that features in many variations in Kirchner's later Swiss works such as *Akt in Orange und Gelb* (Nude in Orange and Yellow, 1929–30, p. 78) and *Ballspielerinnen* (Girls Playing Ball, 1931–32, p. 79). Kirchner began to fuse bather and dancer motifs, photographing a nude girl dancing with expressive gestures in the open air, which he used as one source of inspiration for the dancing nudes in *Farbentanz I* and *II* (1930–34). The local farmers and their families, who enjoyed the barn dances that Kirchner organized from time to time in his house to music played on his much-admired record player, nevertheless considered nude bathing expeditions and the unusual *ménage à trois*, which the artist recreated in Switzerland with Erna and Nina Hard, beyond the pale. After Kirchner designed the set for one of Nina Hard's performances at the Clavadel sanatorium in Zurich in September 1921, the artist and the dancer parted company and his domestic life returned to a more socially acceptable norm.

Kirchner's fascination with expressive dance intensified in the years following his short relationship with Nina Hard. In 1926 he was spellbound by a performance of Mary Wigman's *Dance Macabre II* (*Totentanz II*), which he saw on a visit to Dresden, where he also became acquainted with Gret Palucca's artistic dances. Kirchner made a series of sketches, some highlighted in colored crayon, which follow the expressive movements of Mary Wigman's body in a fluid web of shifting, spontaneous lines (fig. 10).[19] Wigman introduced a new element of psychological intensity to the vocabulary of Expressionist dance—her performances have indeed been described as "dance from the depths of the soul."[20] Wigman's use of the body to express existential states chimed with Kirchner's aim to plumb metaphysical, symbolic, and psychological depths in his *Der Tanz zwischen den Frauen*, and the artist immediately recognized their affinity: "Yes, what we anticipated has become a reality. The new art is there. M.W. uses a lot from modern paintings unconsciously, and the creation of a modern concept of beauty is at work in her dances as well as in my pictures."[21] Indeed, Kirchner believed, like Wigman, that physical movement touched deep levels of human understanding, striking a universal chord: "I believe that all human visual experiences and sensations arise much more from this state of movement and that therefore an art form that is derived from movement speaks much more to the people."[22]

In Kirchner's late dance paintings, which include *Tanz aus dem Narrenspiegel von Laban* (Dance from Laban's Narrenspiegel) from 1927 and *Springende Tänzerin. Gret*

19. Wigman's performance at the *Residenzschloss* in Dresden also inspired Kirchner's large painted, composition *Totentanz der Mary Wigman* (Dance Macabre of Mary Wigman), 1926–28.
20. Mund 2017 (see note 6), p. 159, note 50.
21. Translated by the author. Original citation: "Ja, das was wir geahnt haben, das ist doch Wirklichkeit geworden. Die neue Kunst ist da. M.W. benutzt vieles aus den modernen Bilder unbewusst, und das Schaffen eines modernen Schönheitsbegriffs ist ebenso in ihren Tänzen am Werke wie in meinen Bildern." Ernst Ludwig Kirchner, January 16, 1926, in Lothar Grisebach, ed., *Kirchners Davoser Tagebuch* (Ostfildern-Ruit, 1997), p. 126.
22. Translated by the author. Original citation: "Ich meine dass alle Seh- und Empfindungerfahrungen der Menschen sehr viel mehr aus diesem Zustand der Bewegung kommen und dass deshalb eine Form, die aus der Bewegung abgeleitet wurde, sehr viel mehr zu den Menschen spricht." Eberhard W. Kornfeld, *Ernst Ludwig Kirchner: Nachzeichnungen seines Lebens*, exh. cat. Kunstmuseum Basel (Bern, 1979), p. 341, quoted by Mund 2017 (see note 6), p. 157, note 30.

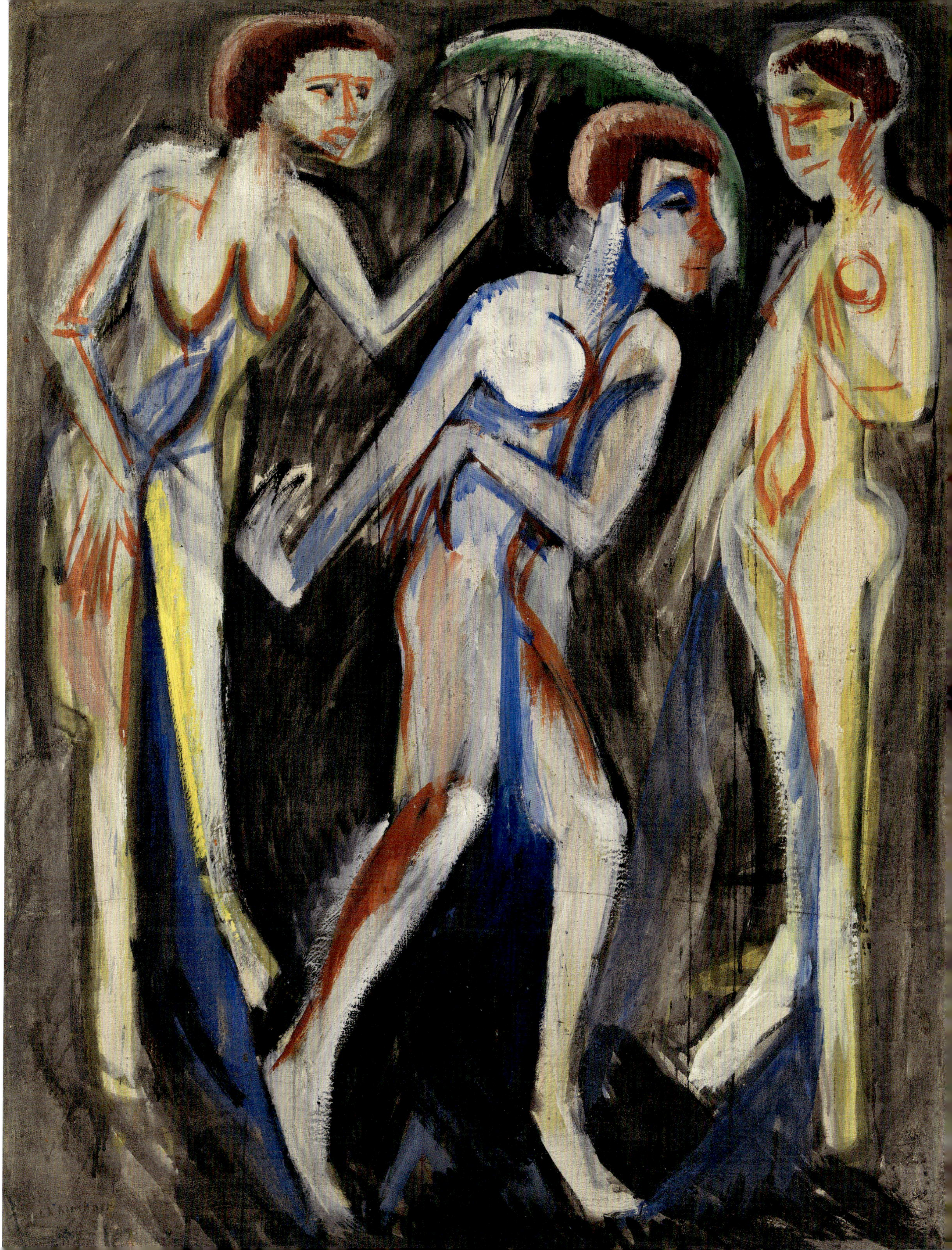

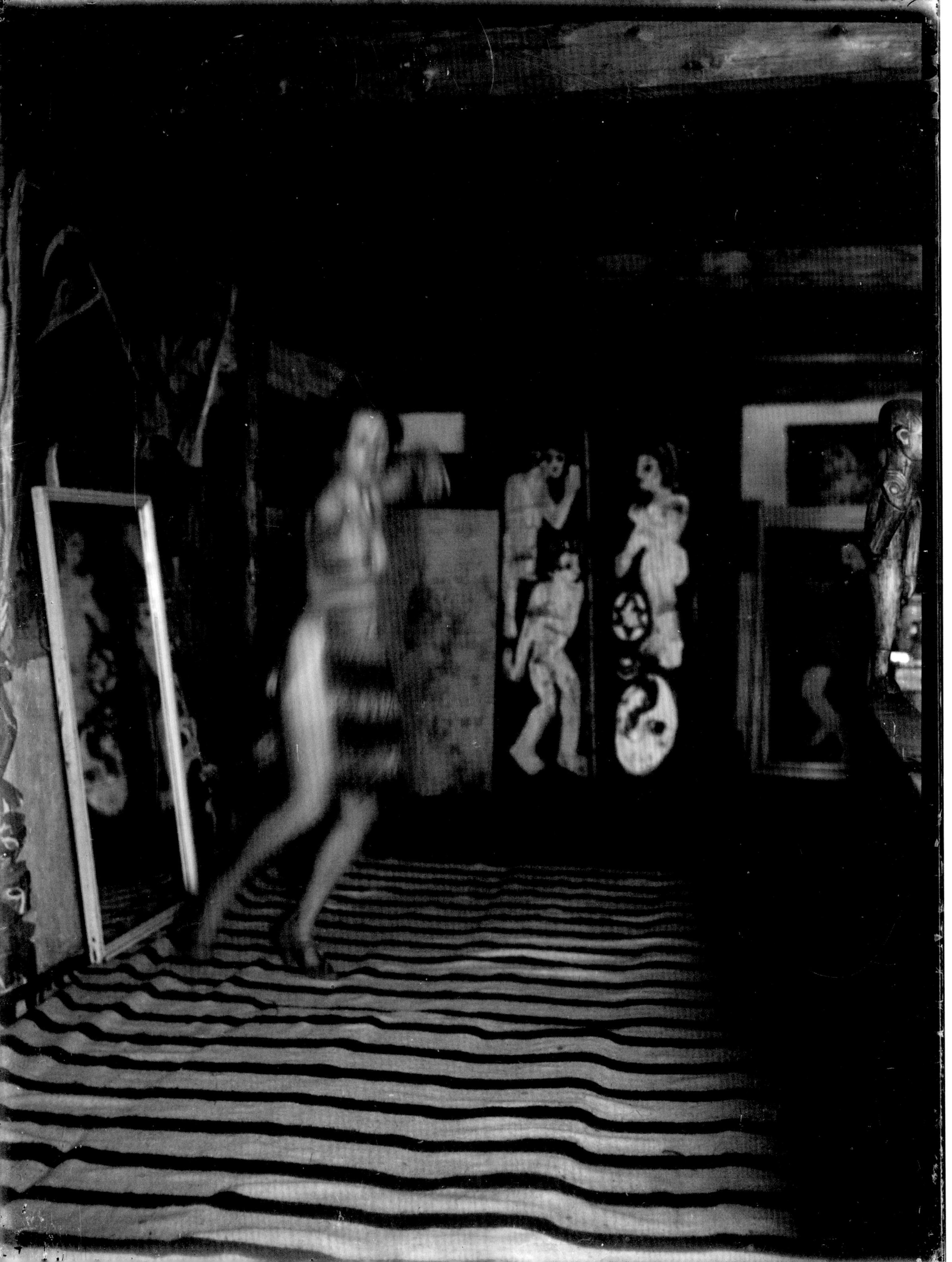

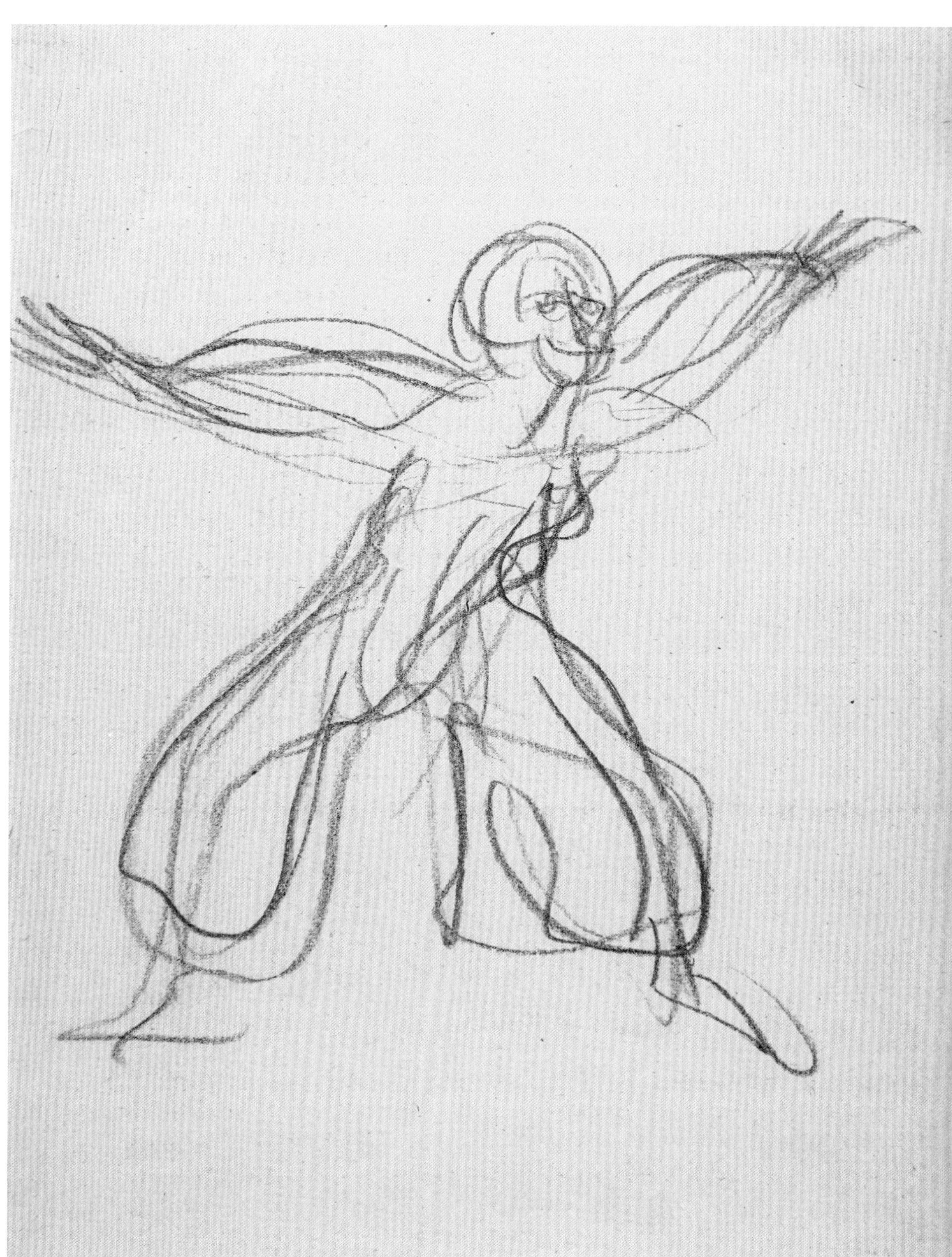

Fig. 9
Ernst Ludwig Kirchner
Nina Hard (Engelhard), Dancing in the Upper Floor of the House "In den Lärchen", 1921
Glass-plate negative, 24 × 18 cm
Kirchner Museum Davos

Fig. 10
Ernst Ludwig Kirchner
Totentanz, Mary Wigman (Dance of Death, Mary Wigman), 1926
Black crayon on paper, 47 × 37 cm
Galerie Henze & Ketterer, Bern

Palucca (Rushing Dancer Gret Palucca) from 1931–32, as well as *Farbentanz I* and *II*, and *Tanzende Mädchen in farbigen Strahlen* (fig. 1), the artist was less interested in capturing reality on the wing in a state of Nietzschean becoming than in representing a synthetic, metaphysical, and universal vision of human experience. This is indeed a development we see in all Kirchner's later Swiss paintings, but it perhaps reaches a climax in his planned decorations for the Folkwang Museum's ceremonial hall.[23] Rather like Edvard Munch's murals for the aula at the university of Oslo, Kirchner's Folkwang decorations represented a visionary synthesis of his ideas about art and life. Indeed, both artists based their decorative schemes around a paean to the sun. While Kirchner's original plans for the Folkwang decorations involved a panoramic survey of human life against a landscape background, he gradually developed a more metaphysical perspective: one wall should display a triptych comprising *Lebsensweg. Weisheit und Gesellschaft des Reinsten* (The Path of Life. Wisdom and Society of the Purest) and *Genius* (Genius), while another wall was to be decorated with two giant heads representing *Vergangenheit* and *Zukunft* (Past and Future).[24] The idea of a large dance composition for the podium wall existed from the beginning, but in Kirchner's developing sketches, the dancing nudes often merged with the idea of "the ascending one" (Aufsteigender), who rises up "from the dark earth into a sun-filled existence."[25] The ultimate goal of man's striving through "battle and love" (Kampf und Liebe)[26] is to reach the higher state of consciousness that Kirchner—like Nietzsche—associated with dance.

Just as the primary and secondary colors on Kirchner's palette merge in white light, so too do the moving, gesticulating, living dancers gradually achieve a state of revolving stasis in the unifying white light of the sun. This state of immanence, represented by the pirouetting dancer in the bottom left of Kirchner's *Tanzende Mädchen in farbigen Strahlen,* corresponds to T.S. Eliot's "still point of the turning world" in his poem "Burnt Norton" (1935), where "past and future are gathered" in an eternal present in which dance rules supreme. "Except for the point, the still point," Eliot writes, "there would be no dance, and there is only the dance."[27] Threatened again by the darkening clouds of world war, Kirchner returned in his final dance paintings to his early Nietzschean motifs with a new intensity of vision. In his Dresden years Kirchner had focused on movement and dance as a source of vitality and renewal, while in Berlin his dance motifs took on a symbolic dimension, often referring to his own psychological state and shifts in the relationship between the sexes under the pressures of modern living. In Switzerland Kirchner introduced a spiritual, cosmic aspect to his representations of dance, using moving figures dancing in the prismic light of the sun to evoke man's universal destiny and the highest aspirations of humankind.

23. Kirchner's shift to an increasingly cosmic world view in his Swiss work is analysed by Roland Scotti in "Realität—Abstraktion—Surrealität," in Mario-Andreas von Lüttichau and Roland Scotti, eds., *Ernst Ludwig Kirchner: Das innere Bild. "Farbe sind die Freude des Lebens,"* exh. cat. Kirchner Museum Davos, Museum Folkwang Essen (Ostfildern, 1999).

24. See Hubertus Froning, "Krone und Vollendung," in ibid., pp. 80–111.

25. Kirchner to Luise Schiefler, July 29, 1937, quoted by Roland Scotti in "Realität—Abstraktion—Surrealität," in ibid., p. 142, note 49.

26. Quoted by Froning in ibid., p. 108, note 23.

27. It is unlikely that Kirchner had any direct knowledge of Eliot's poetry, although the similar time frame of Eliot's *Four Quartets* and Kirchner's late dance paintings is intriguing. The most likely explanation for any similarities of vision lies in the influence that Nietzsche exerted over both artists' imaginations.

Bibliography

Dreesbach, Anne. "Colonial Exhibitions, 'Völkerschauen' and the Display of the 'Other.'" *European History Online (EGO)* (May 3, 2012).

Eliot, T.S. *The Complete Poems and Plays.* London, 1969.

Ernst Ludwig Kirchner: Das innere Bild. "Farbe sind die Freude des Lebens." Edited by Mario Andreas von Lüttichau and Roland Scotti. Exh. cat. Kirchner Museum Davos, Museum Folkwang Essen. Ostfildern, 1999.

Grisebach, Lothar, ed. *E.L. Kirchners Davoser Tagebuch: Eine Darstellung des Malers und eine Sammlung seiner Schriften.* Cologne, 1968.

Grisebach, Lothar, ed. *E.L. Kirchners Davoser Tagebuch: Eine Darstellung des Malers und eine Sammlung seiner Schriften.* New edition supervised by Lucius Grisebach. Ostfildern-Ruit, 1997.

Der böse Expressionismus, Trauma und Tabu. Edited by Jutta Hülsewig-Johnen and Henrike Mund. Exh. cat. Kunsthalle Bielefeld. Cologne, 2017.

Kirchner, Ernst Ludwig. *Ernst Ludwig Kirchner: Der gesamte Briefwechsel,* edited by Hans Delfs. Zürich, 2010.

Nietzsche, Friedrich. *Der Wille zur Macht.* Stuttgart, 1964.

Nietzche, Friedrich. *Nietzsche Werke: Kritische Gesamtausgabe.* Vol. VI. Edited by Giorgio Colli and Mazzino Montinari. Berlin, 1968.

Nietzsche, Friedrich. *Thus Spoke Zarathustra.* Translated by R. J. Hollingdale. London, 1969

Nietzsche, Friedrich. *The Will to Power, An Attempted Transvaluation of all Values.* Translated by Anthony M. Ludovici, vol. II, Books III and IV. Edinburgh and London, 1913

Pressler, Gerd. *Ernst Ludwig Kirchner: Die Skizzenbücher.* Karlsruhe, 1996.

Brücke und die Lebensreform. Edited by Kai Schupke and Daniel J. Schreiber. Exh. cat. Buchheim Museum. Bernried, 2016.

Simmons, Sherwin. "'A suggestiveness that can make one crazy': Ernst Ludwig Kirchner's Images of Marzella." *Modernism/Modernity* 22, 3 (September 2015).

Simmons, Sherwin. "The Dancer's revenge: Dance/Pantomime and the Emergence of Ernst Ludwig Kirchner's Fantasy Pictures." *Dance Chronicle* 41:2 (May 2018).

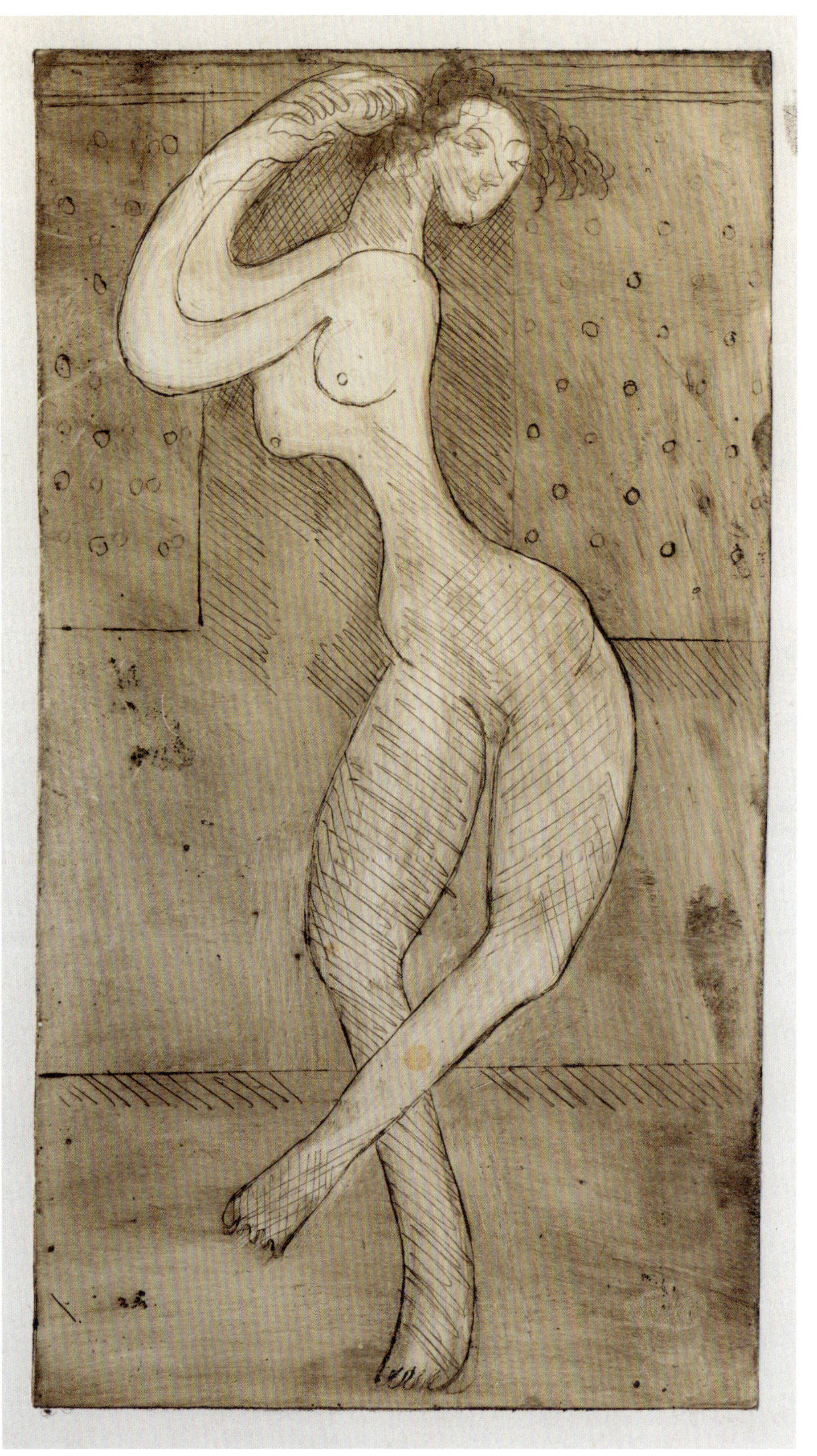

Ernst Ludwig Kirchner
Nackte Tänzerin
(Naked Dancer), 1934
Etching, 38 × 20.4 cm
Kirchner Museum Davos

Pp. 75–77
Ernst Ludwig Kirchner
Dancer in the Forest, ca. 1929
Cellulose nitrate negative,
14.5×9 cm
Brücke-Museum Berlin,
courtesy Kirchner Museum Davos

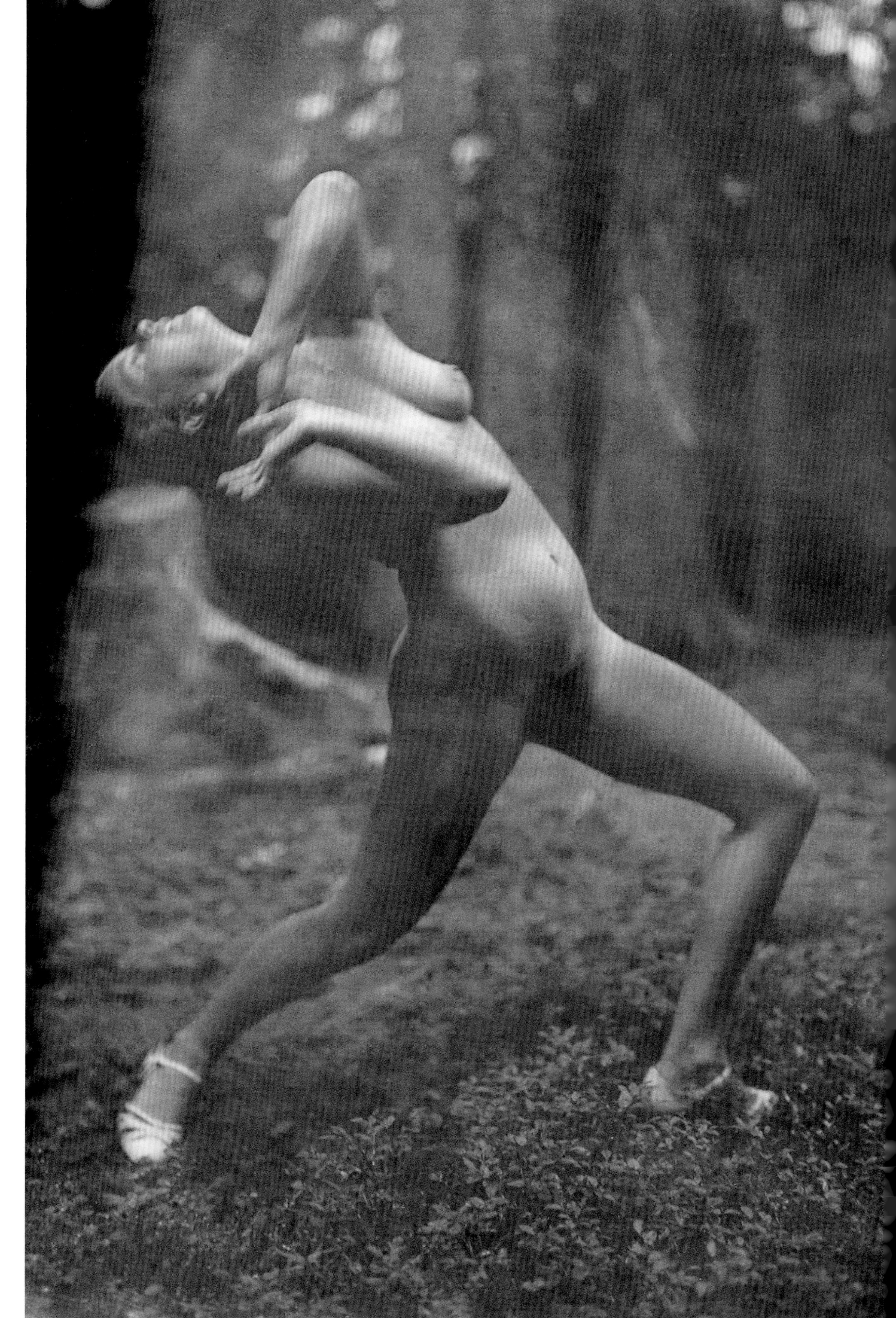

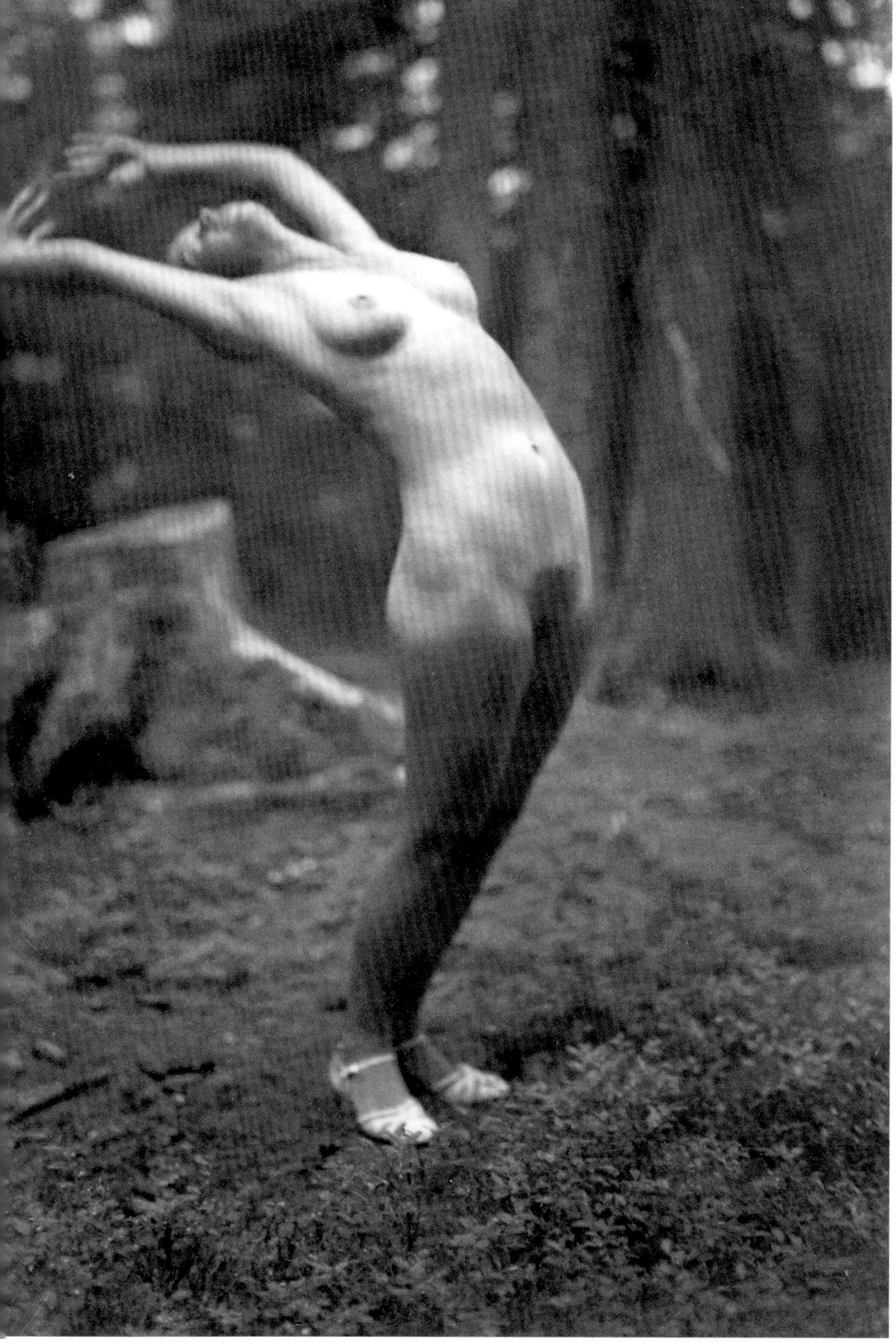

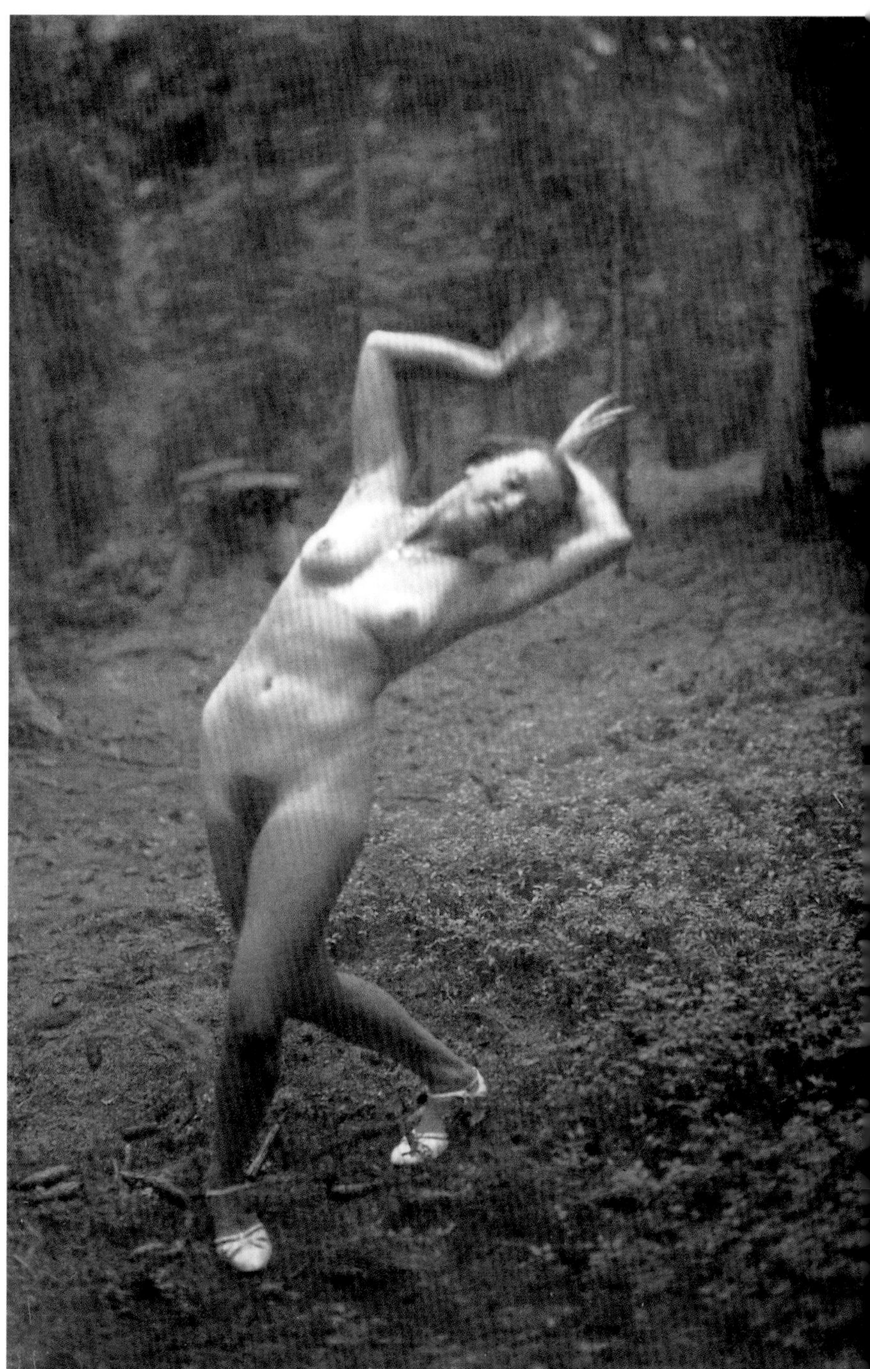

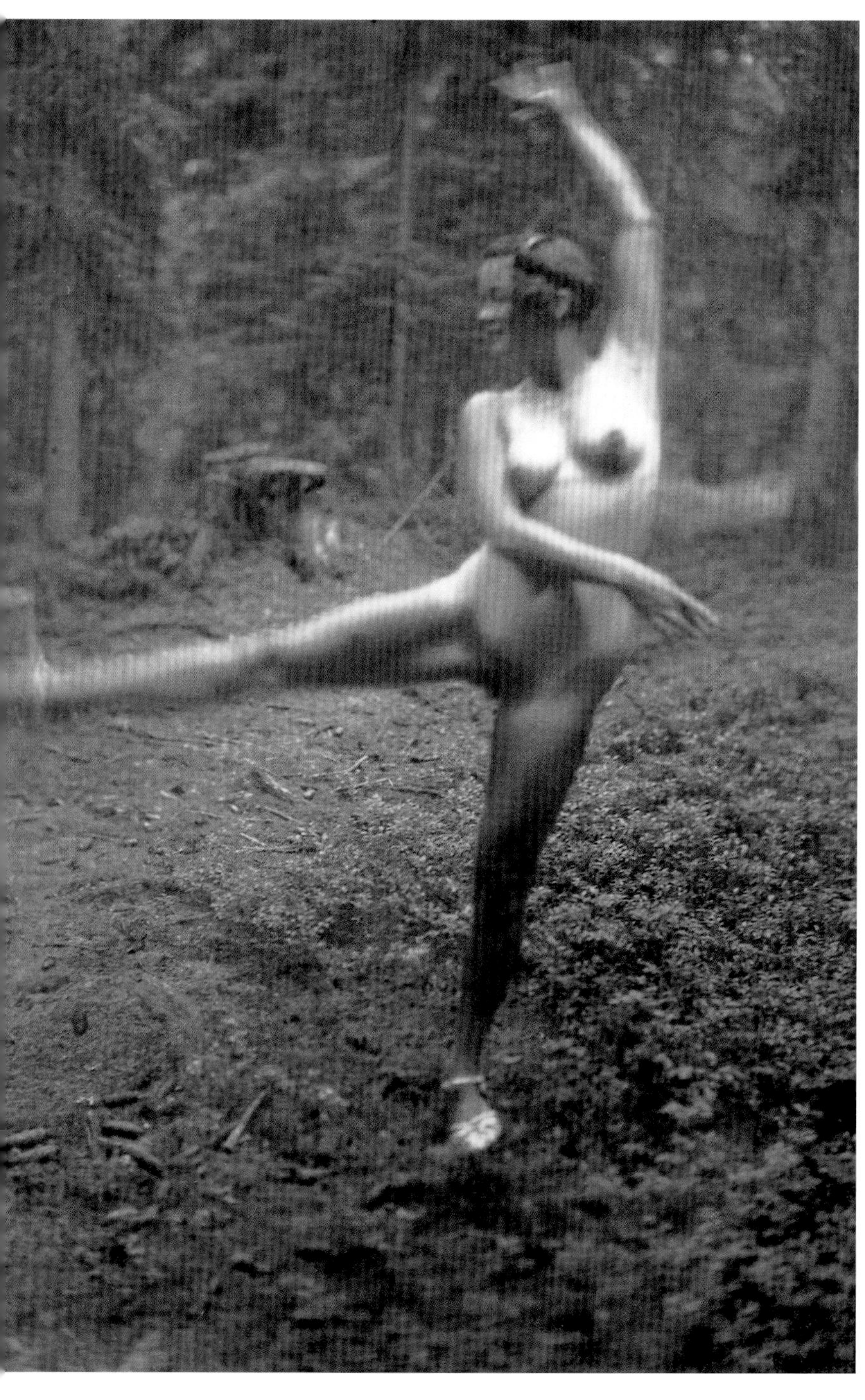
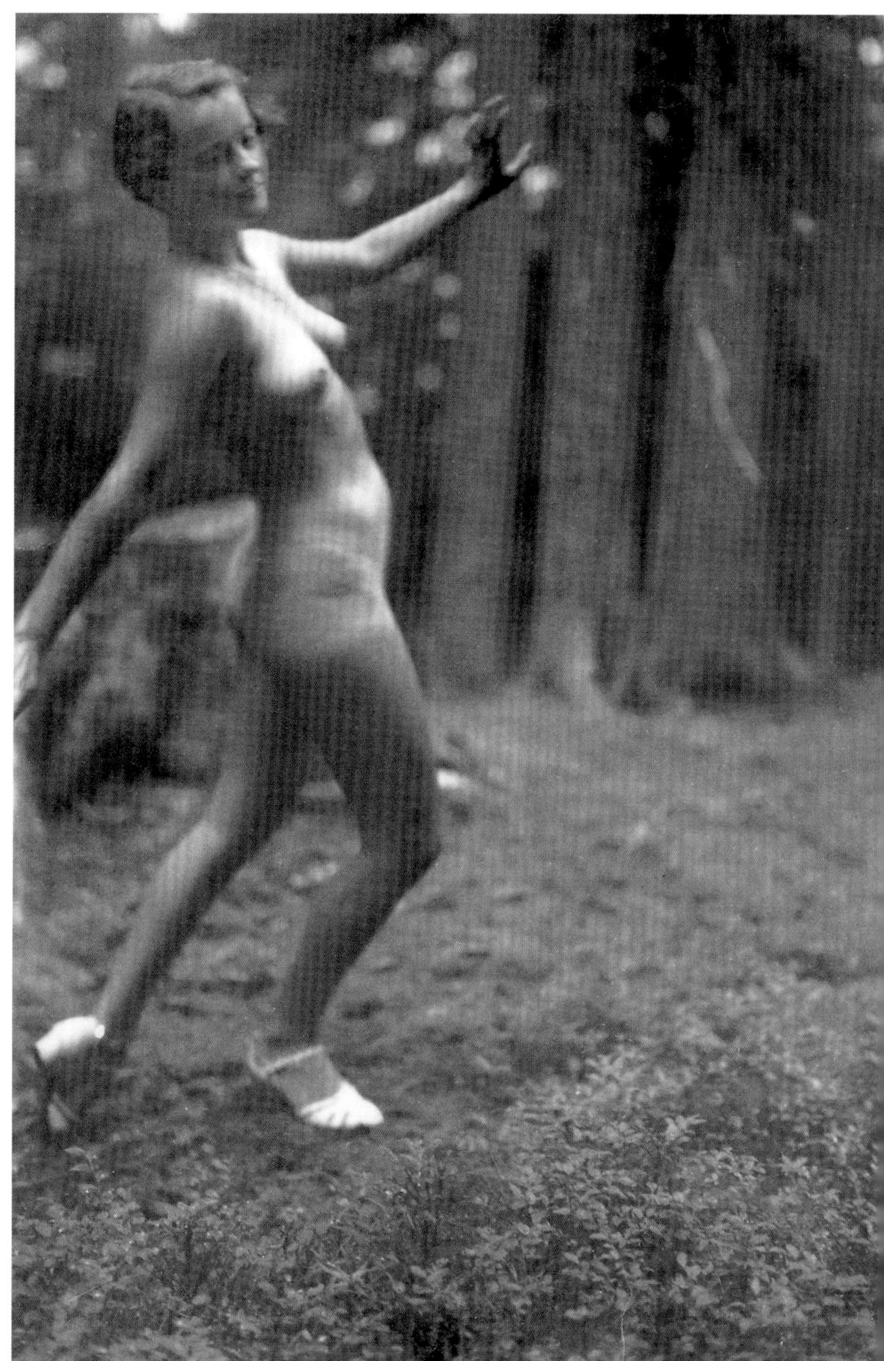

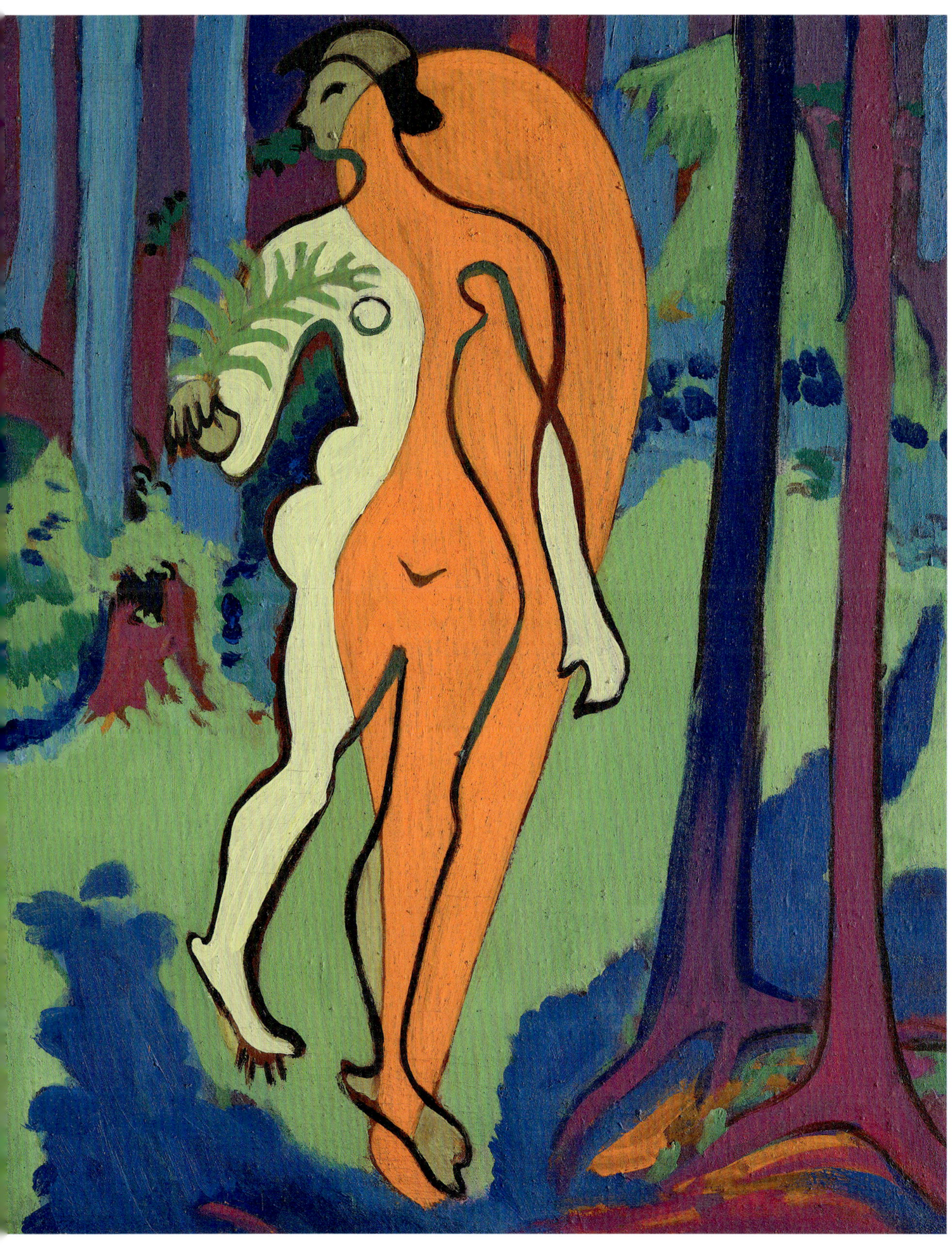

Ernst Ludwig Kirchner
Akt in Orange und Gelb
(Nude in Orange and Yellow),
1929–30
Oil on canvas, 91 × 71 cm
Kirchner Museum Davos

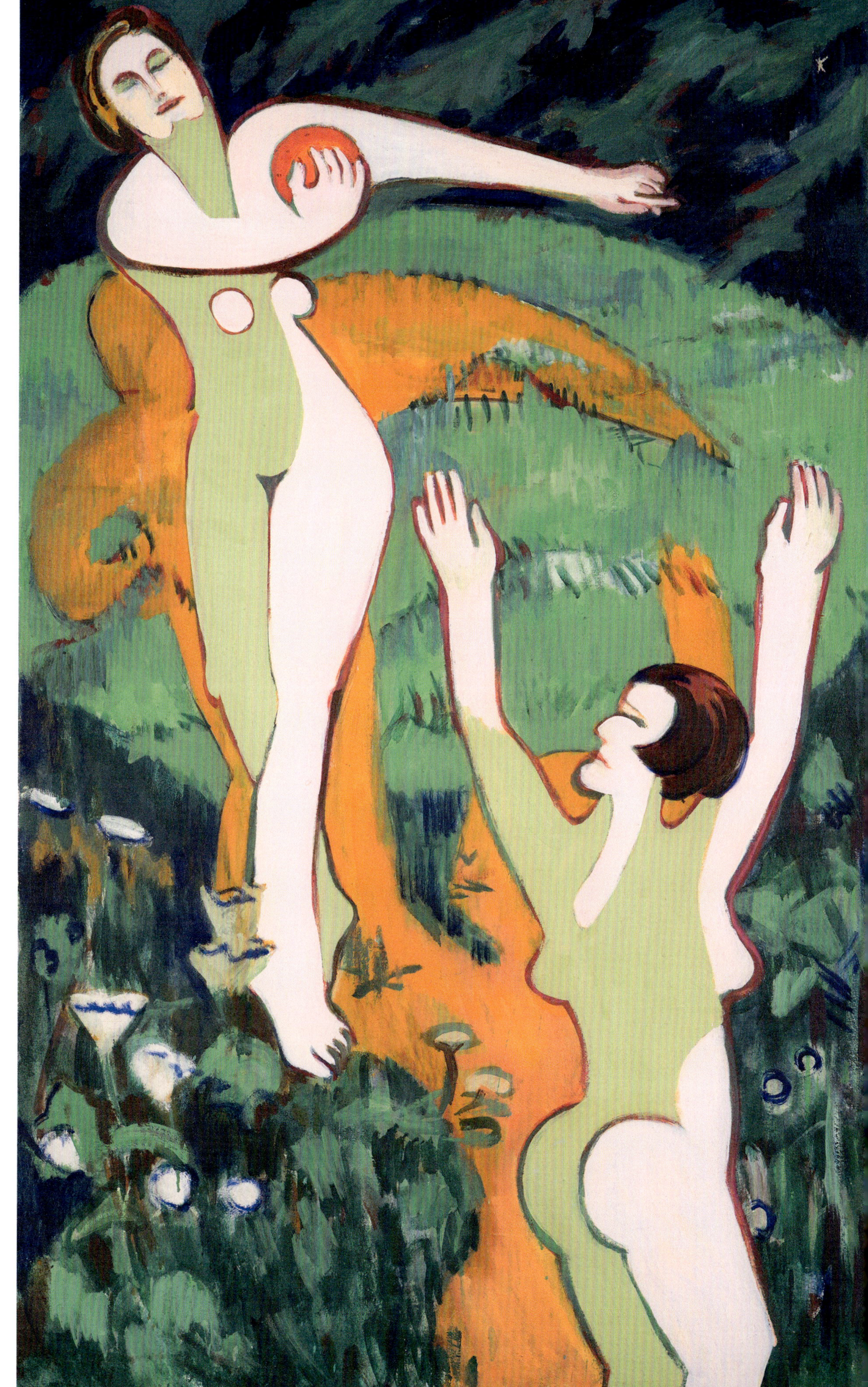

Ernst Ludwig Kirchner
Ballspielerinnen
(Girls Playing Ball),
1931–32
Oil on canvas, 152 × 89.5 cm
Kirchner Museum Davos

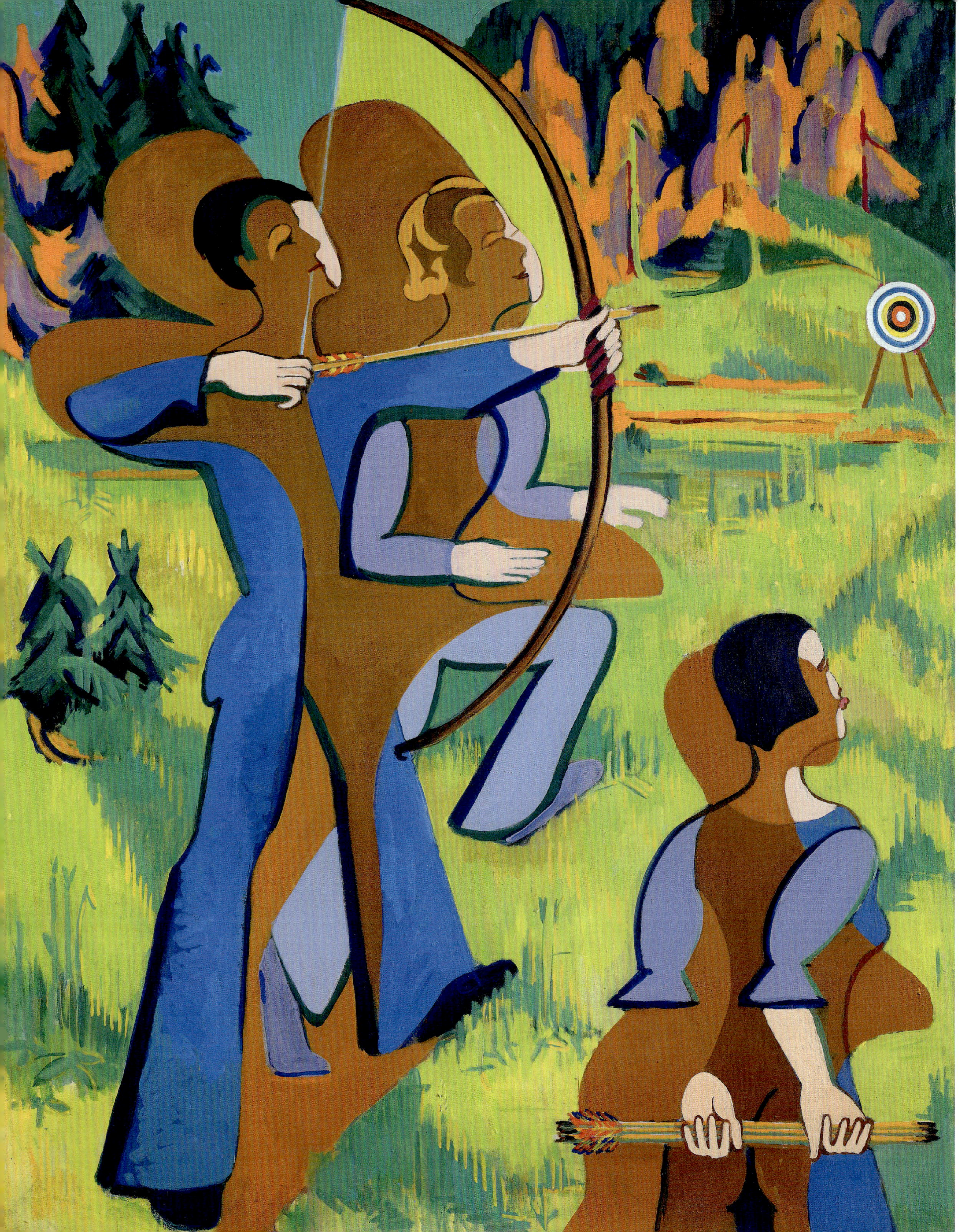

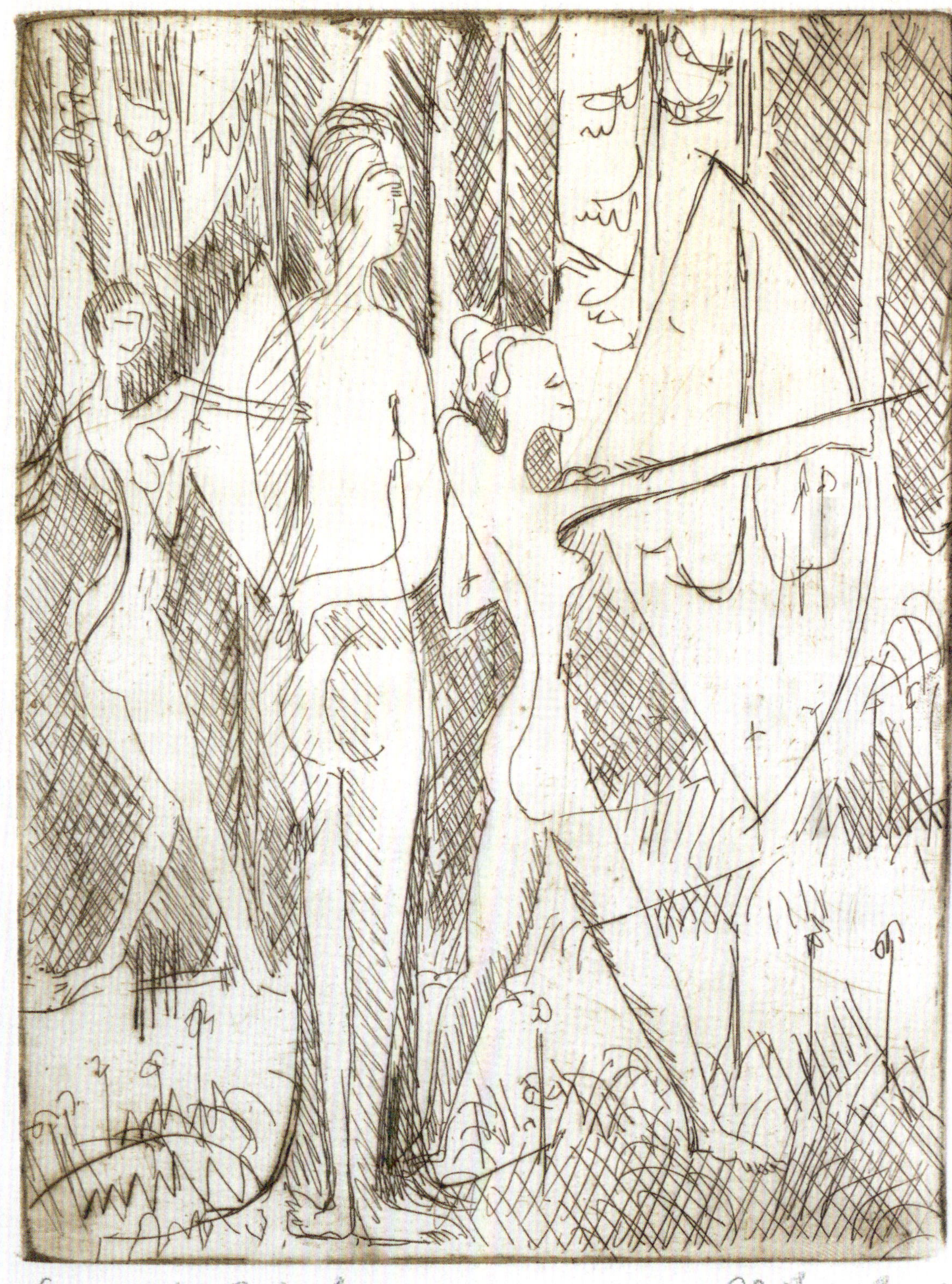

Ernst Ludwig Kirchner
Bogenschützen (Archers),
1935–37
Oil on canvas, 195 × 150 cm
Kirchner Museum Davos

Ernst Ludwig Kirchner
Bogenschiessende Mädchen im Walde (Female Archers in the Forest), 1934
Etching, 20 × 14.6 cm
Kirchner Museum Davos

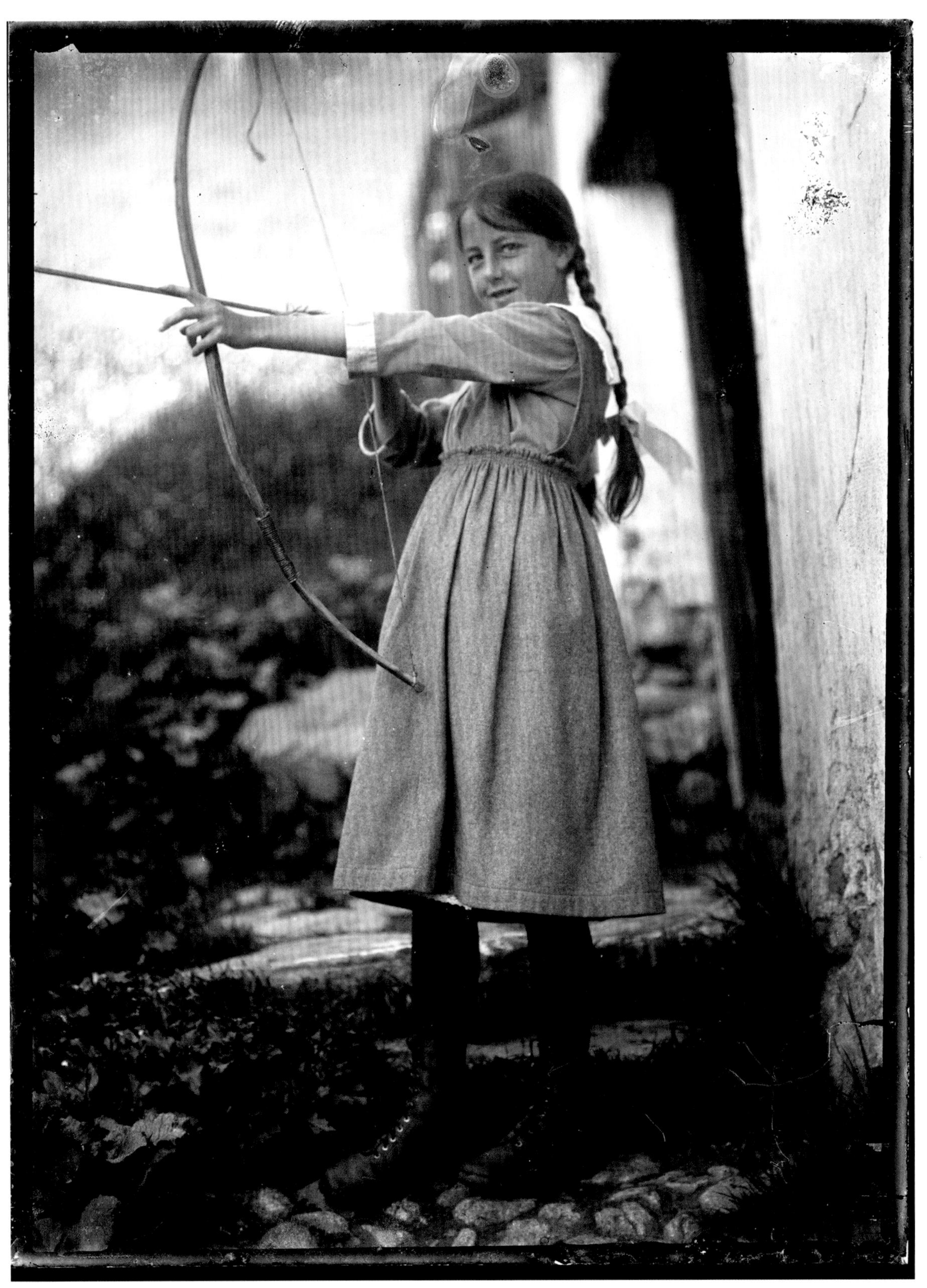

Ernst Ludwig Kirchner
Country Girl Practicing Archery in Front of the House "In den Lärchen", ca. 1919–23
Glass-plate negative, 18 × 13 cm
Kirchner Museum Davos

Ernst Ludwig Kirchner
Bogenschützinnen (Female Archers), 1935
Etching, 25.5 × 25.3 cm
Kirchner Museum Davos

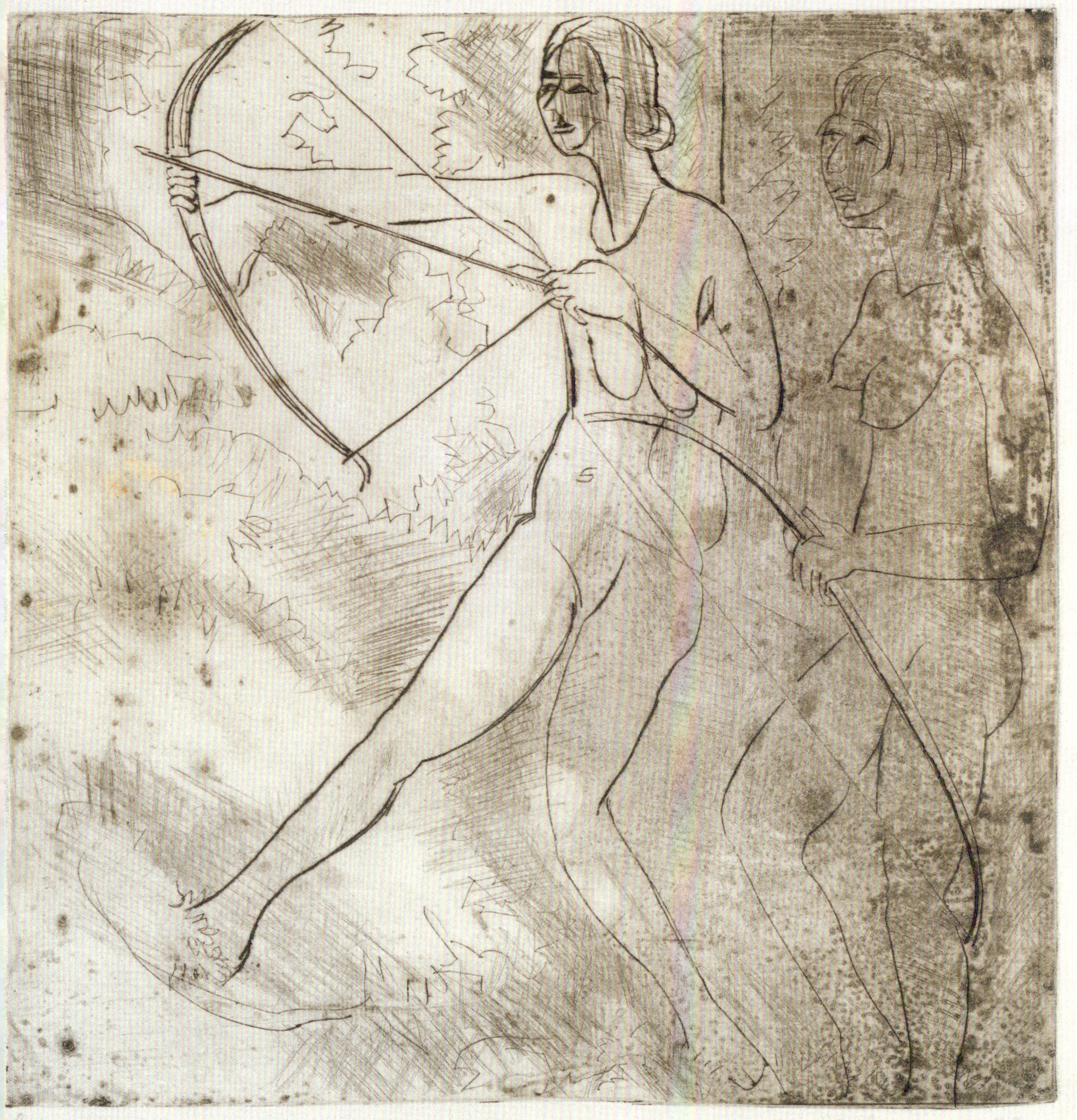

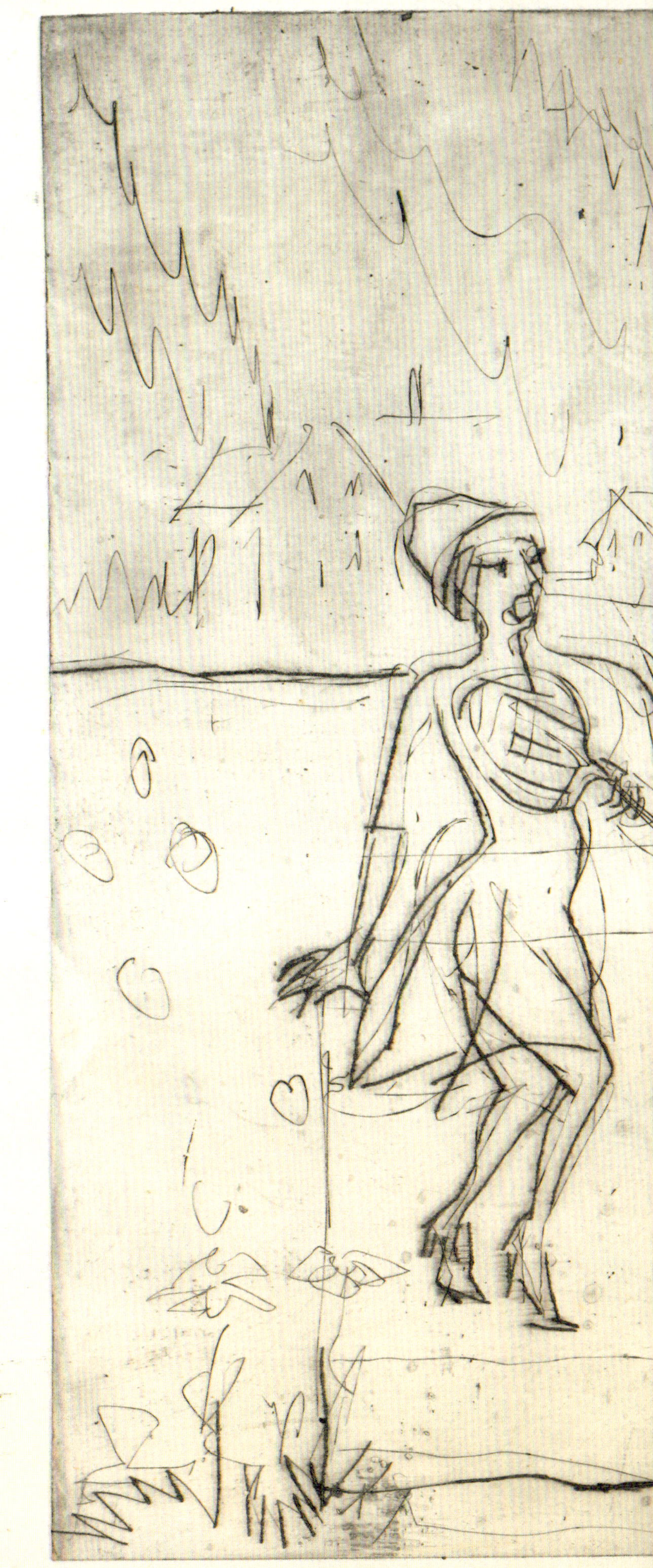

Ernst Ludwig Kirchner
Tennisspiel (Tennis Match), 1927
Etching, 24.8 × 30.9 cm
Kirchner Museum Davos

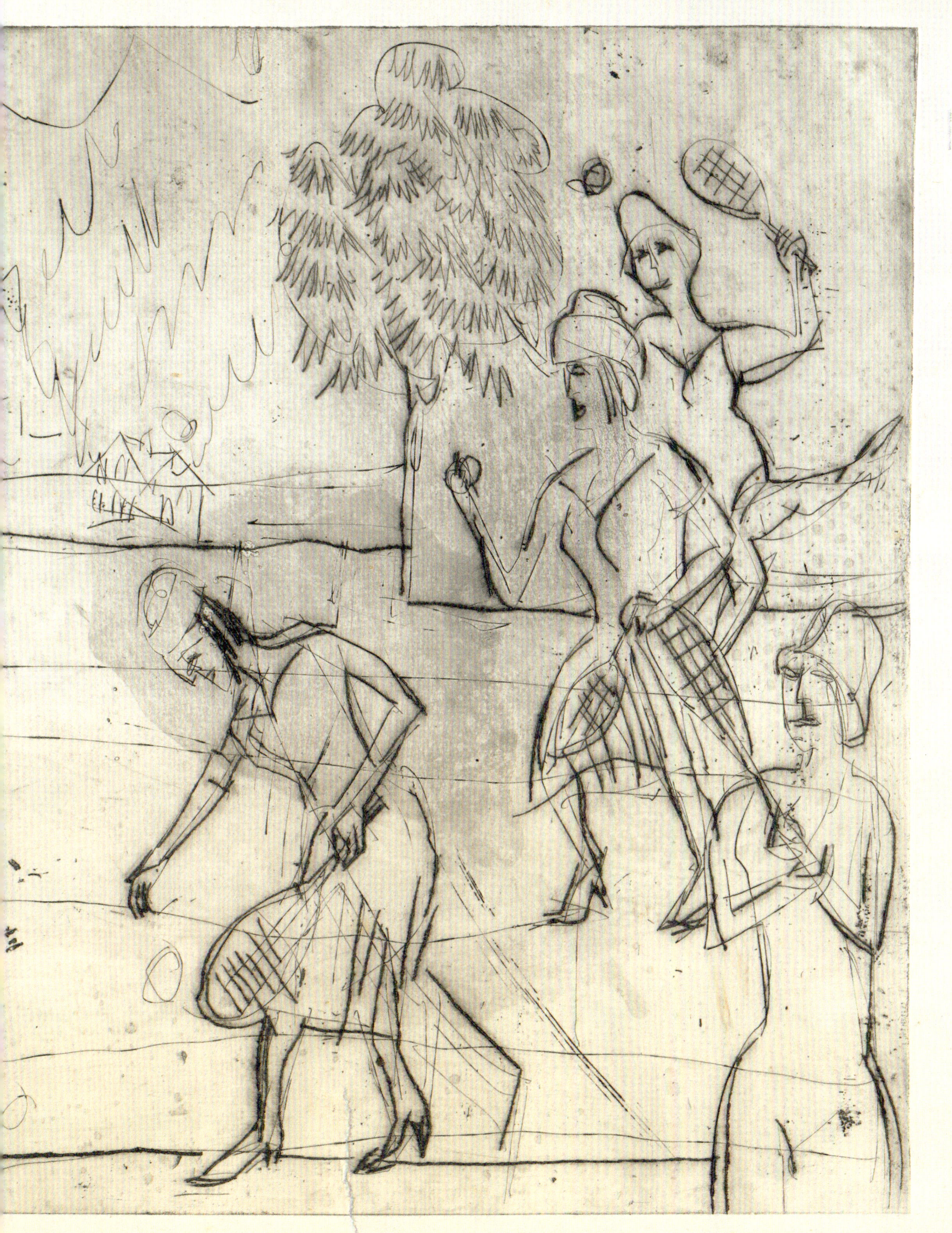

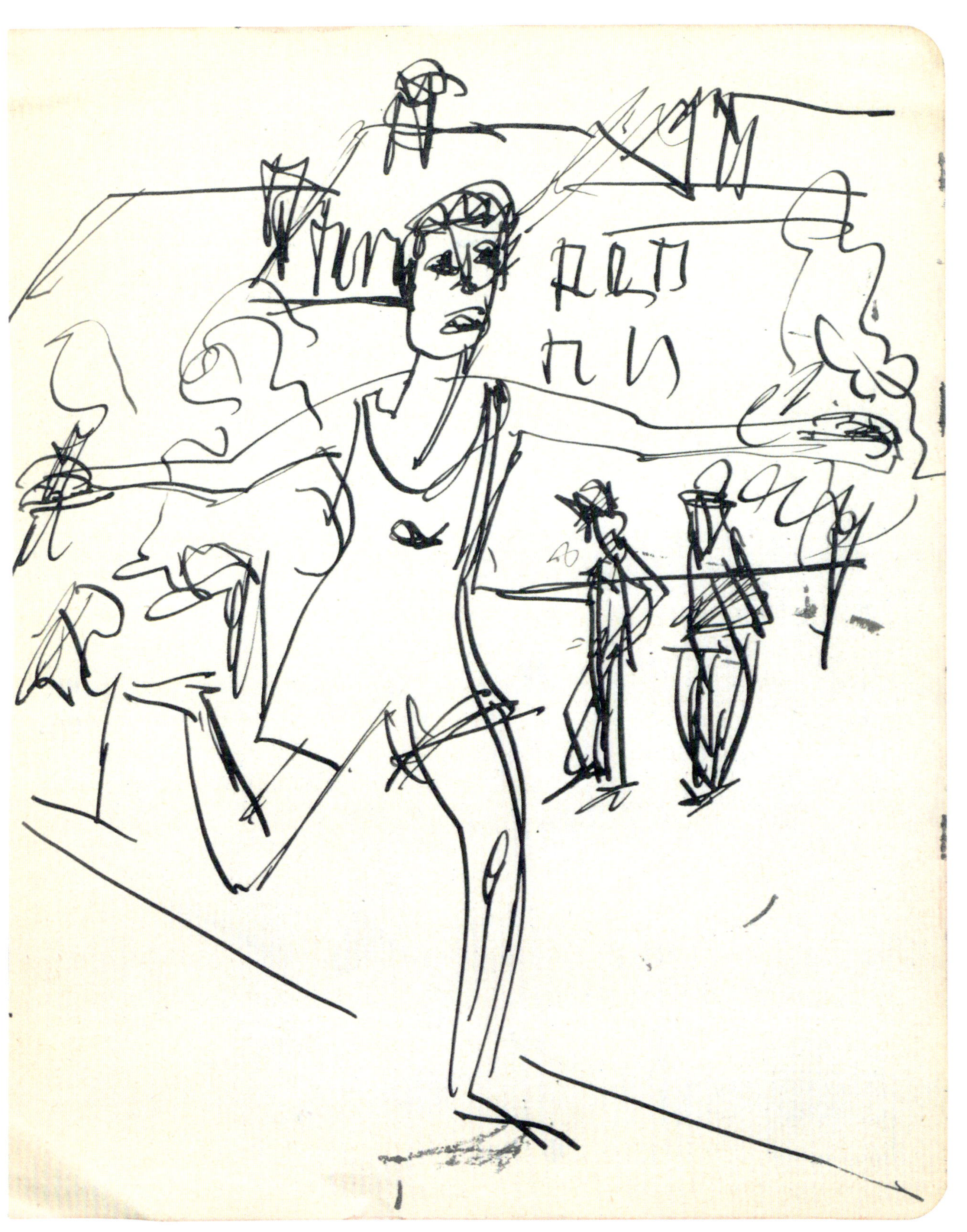

Ernst Ludwig Kirchner
Sieger im Wettlauf
(Race Winner), 1926–27
Pen and ink on paper,
21.8 × 17.2 cm
Kirchner Museum Davos

Ernst Ludwig Kirchner
Radfahrerin (Cyclist), 1934
Lithograph, 32.6 × 27.3 cm
Kirchner Museum Davos

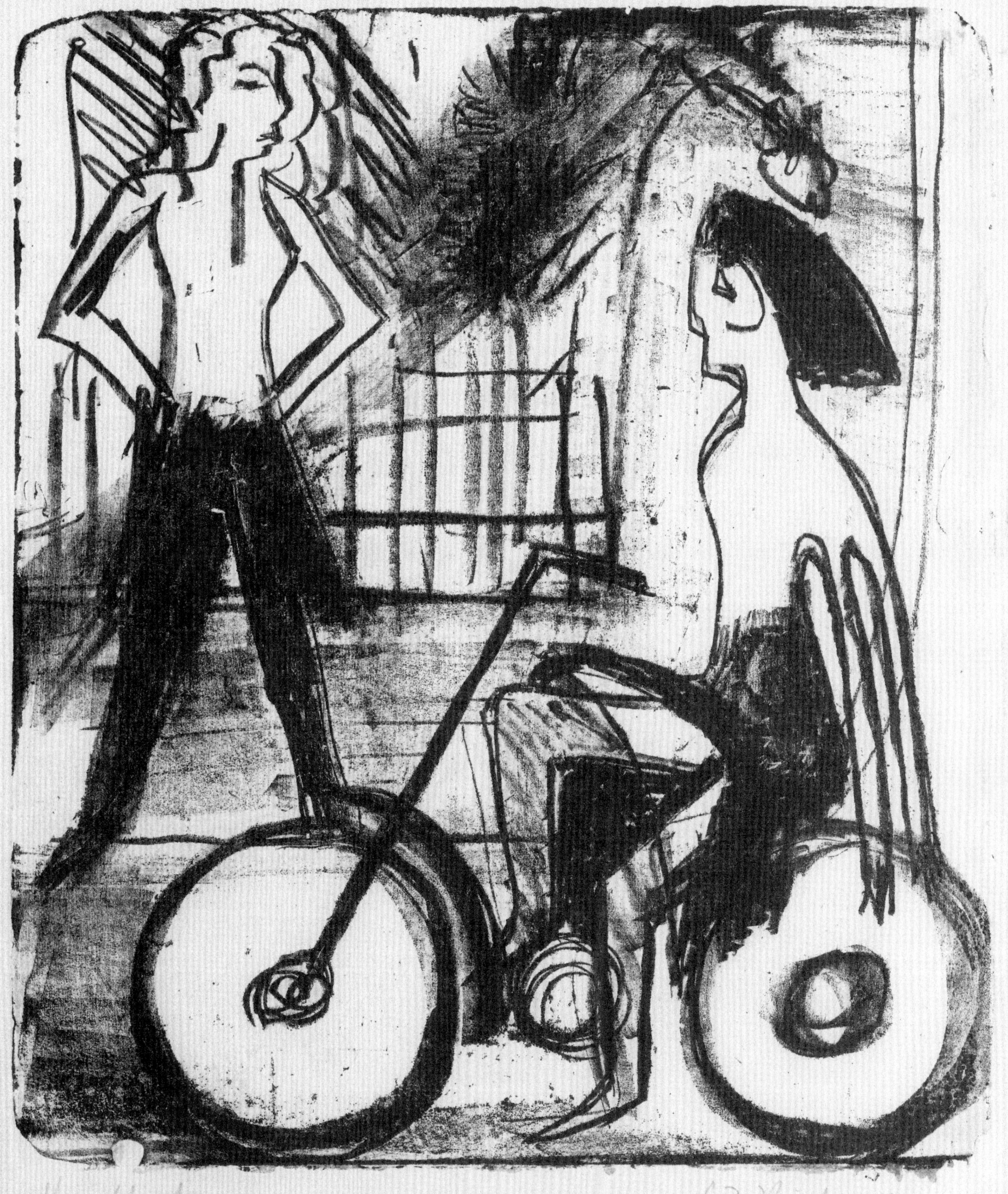

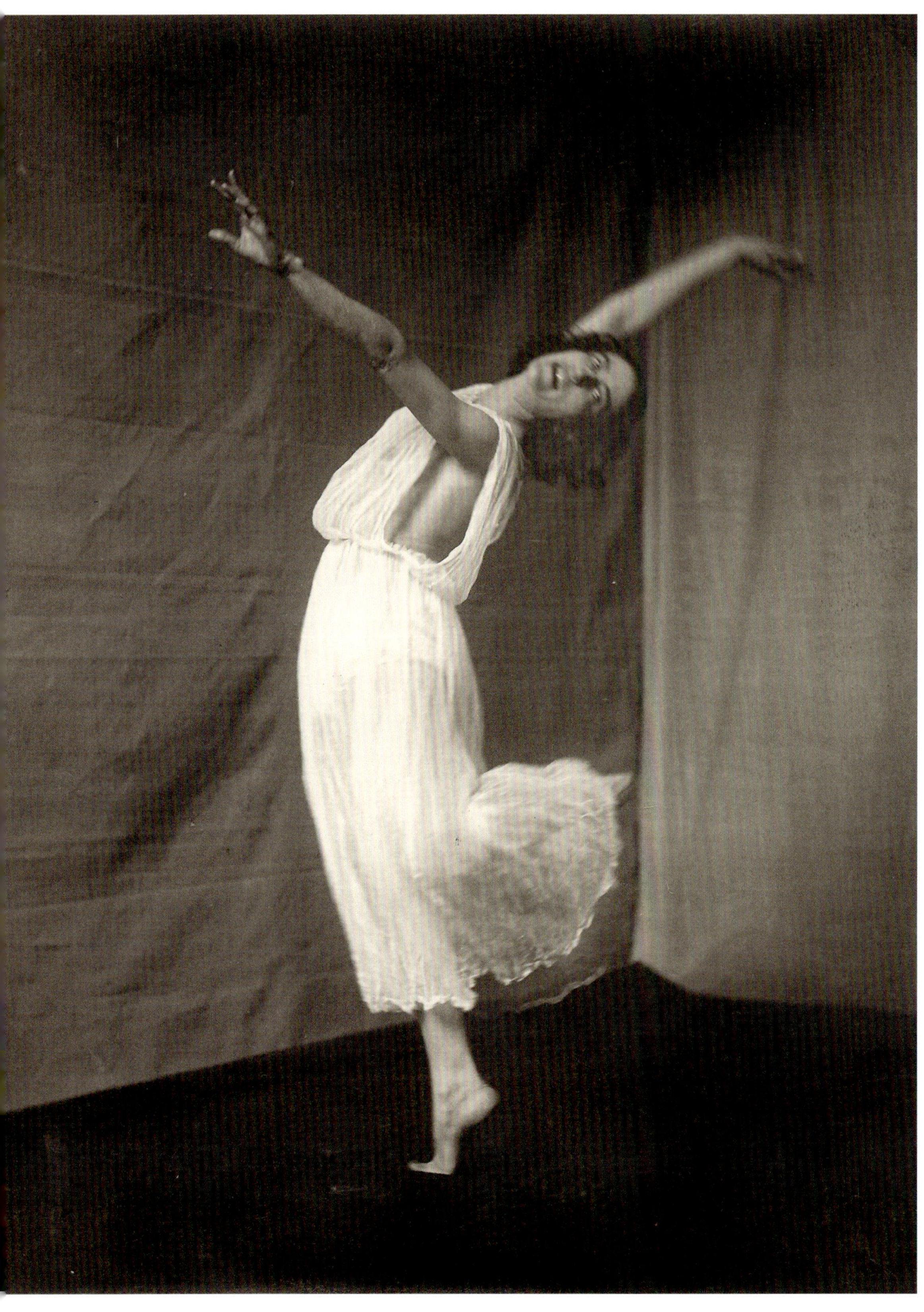

J. F. Willumsen
Michelle Bourret in Dance Position Inspired by Sergei Diaghilev's "Les Ballet Russes," ca. 1934–35
Photo, 17.7 × 12.7 cm
Willumsen's Museum, Frederikssund

J. F. Willumsen
Lola danser (Lola Dances), 1921
Oil on canvas, 155 × 135 cm
Willumsen's Museum, Frederikssund

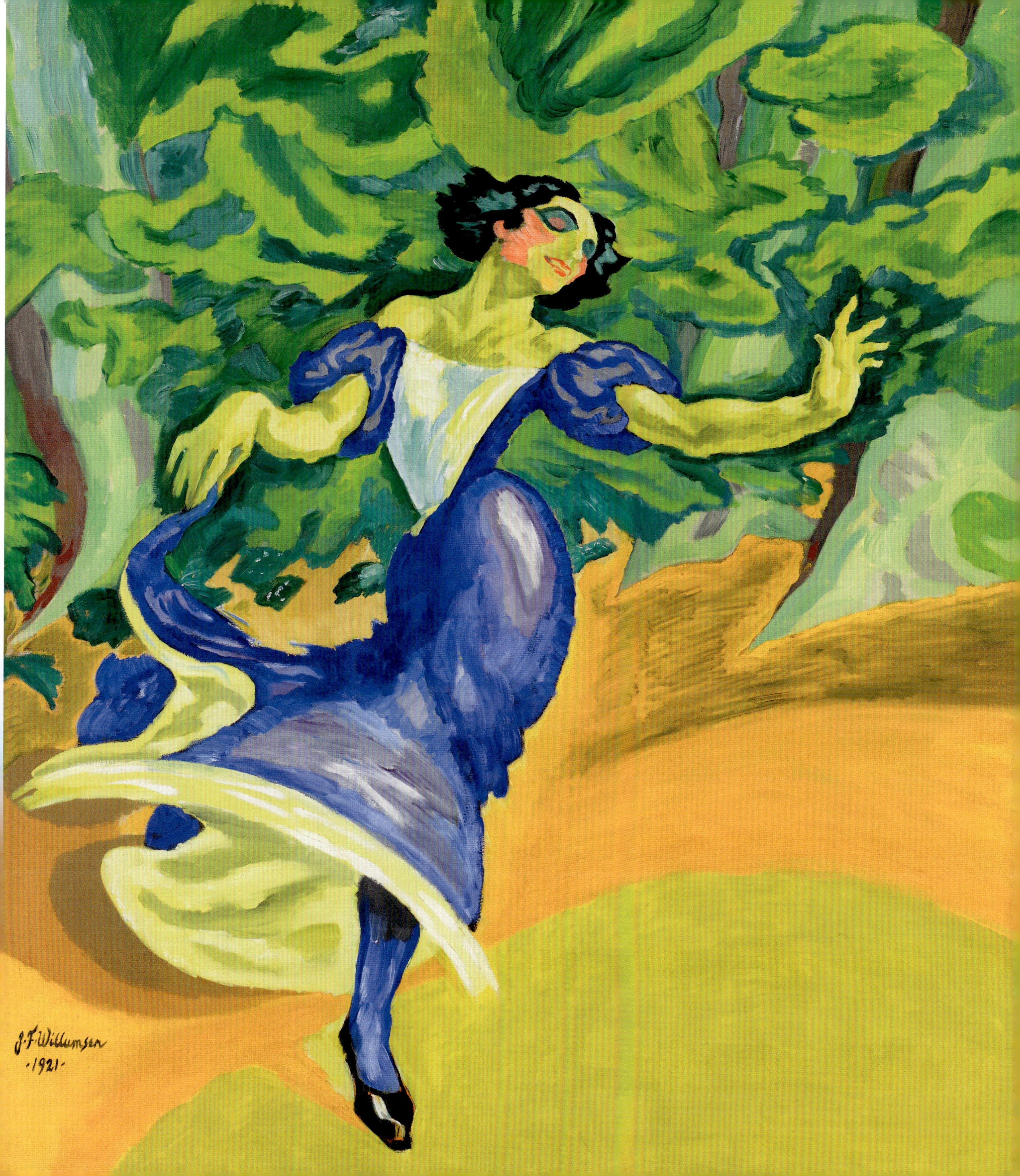
J.F. Willumsen
·1921·

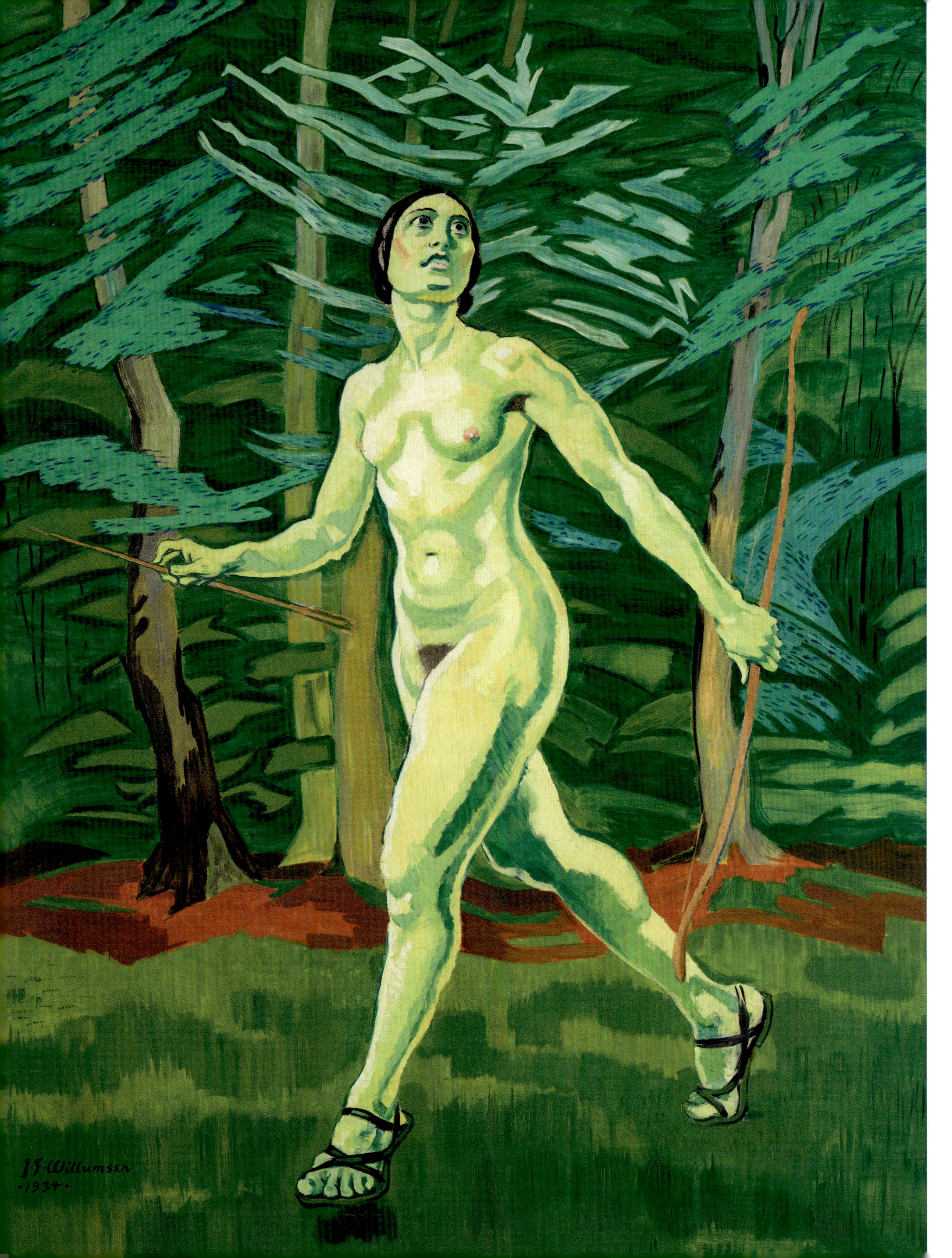
J.F. Willumsen
·1934·

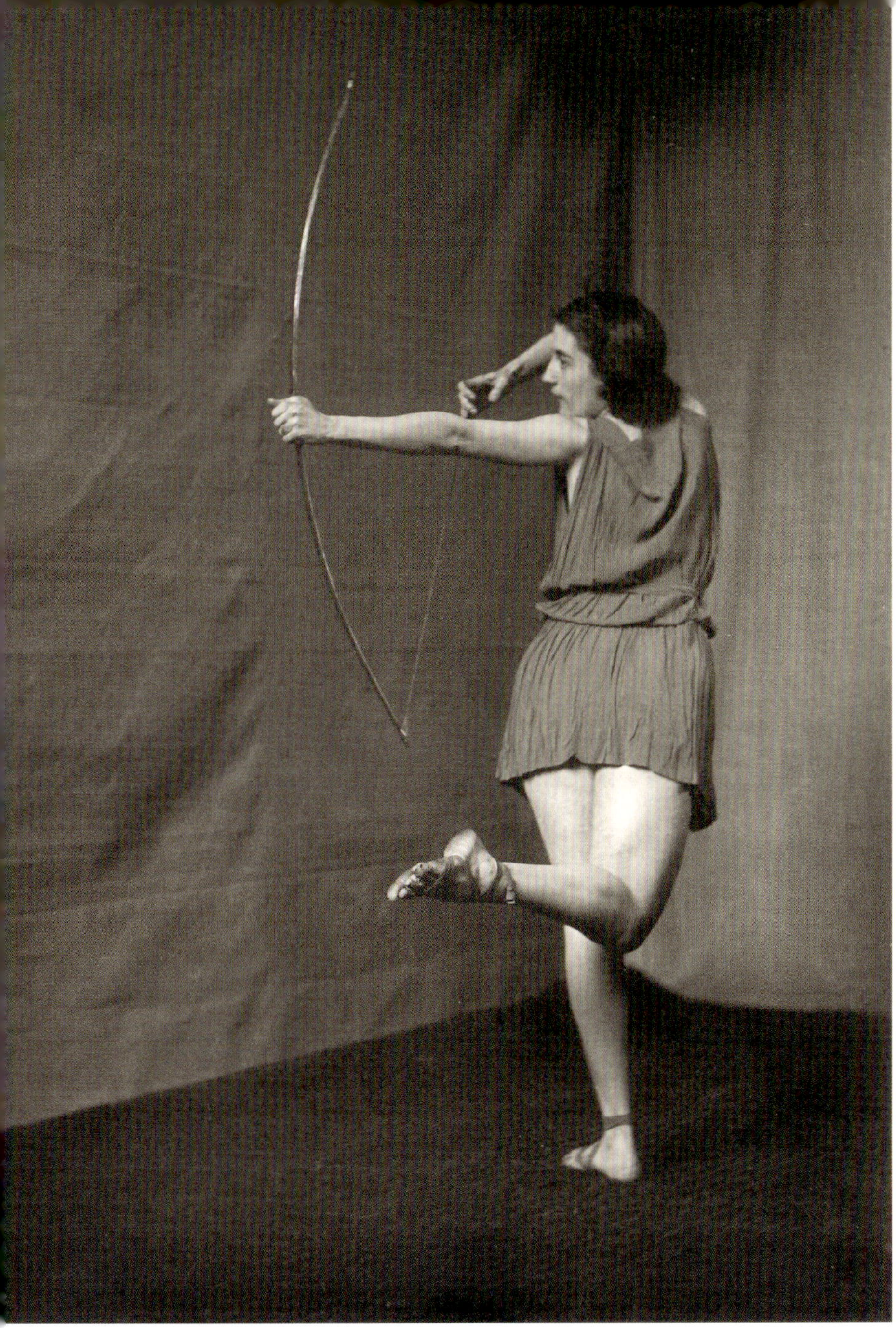

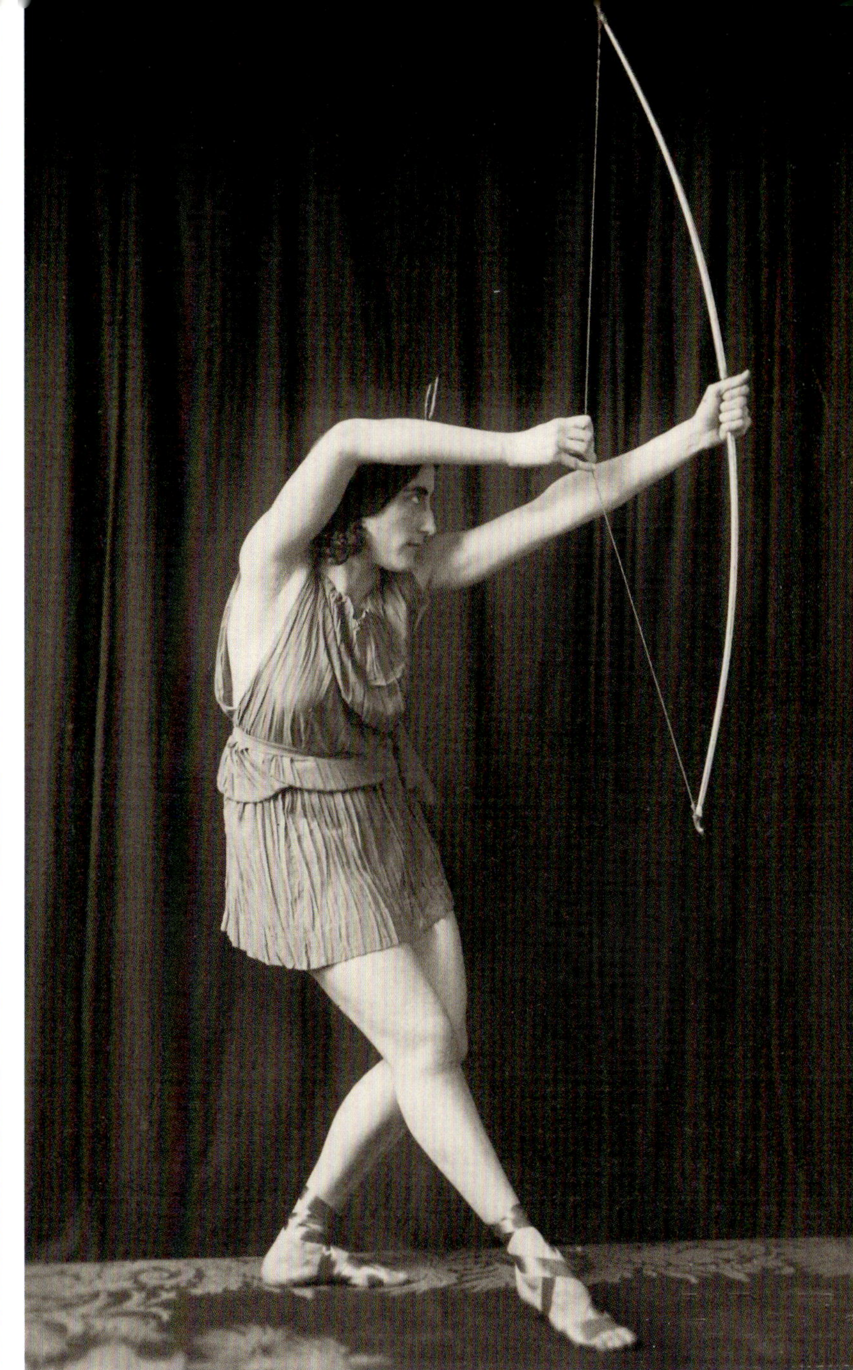

J. F. Willumsen
Jægerpige i skoven
(Huntress in the Forest), 1934
Oil on canvas, 190 × 141 cm
Willumsen's Museum,
Frederikssund

J. F. Willumsen
Michelle Bourret
as Huntress, 1932
Photo, 18 × 12.8 cm
Willumsen's Museum,
Frederikssund

J. F. Willumsen
Michelle Bourret
as Huntress, 1932
Photo, 14 × 9 cm
Willumsen's Museum,
Frederikssund

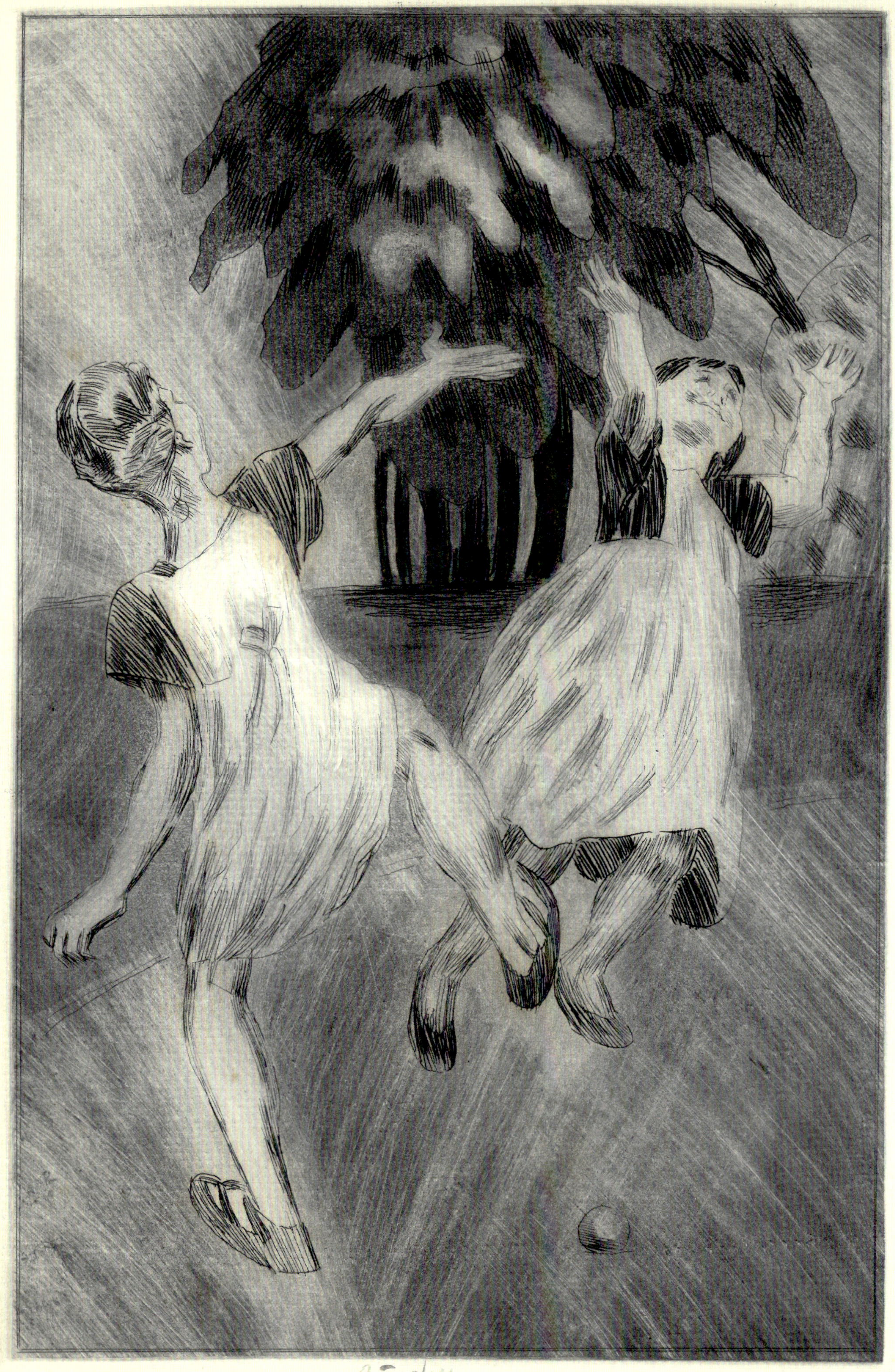

J. F. Willumsen
De to boldspillende småpiger (Two Young Girls Playing Ball), 1916
Etching, 32.5×21 cm
Willumsen's Museum, Frederikssund

J. F. Willumsen
To atleter (Two Athletes), 1916
Etching, 23.7×17.4 cm
Willumsen's Museum, Frederikssund

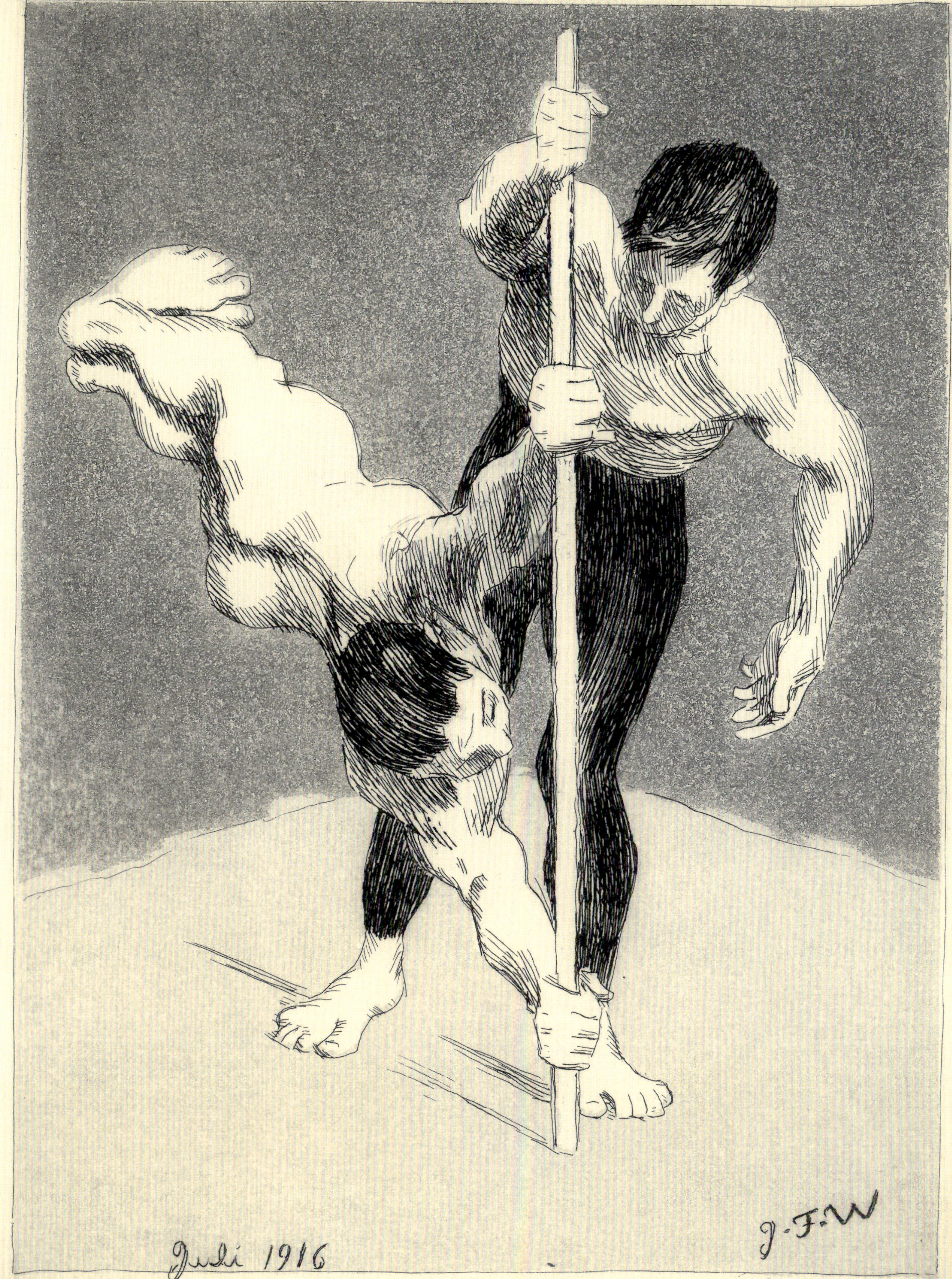
Juli 1916
J·F·W

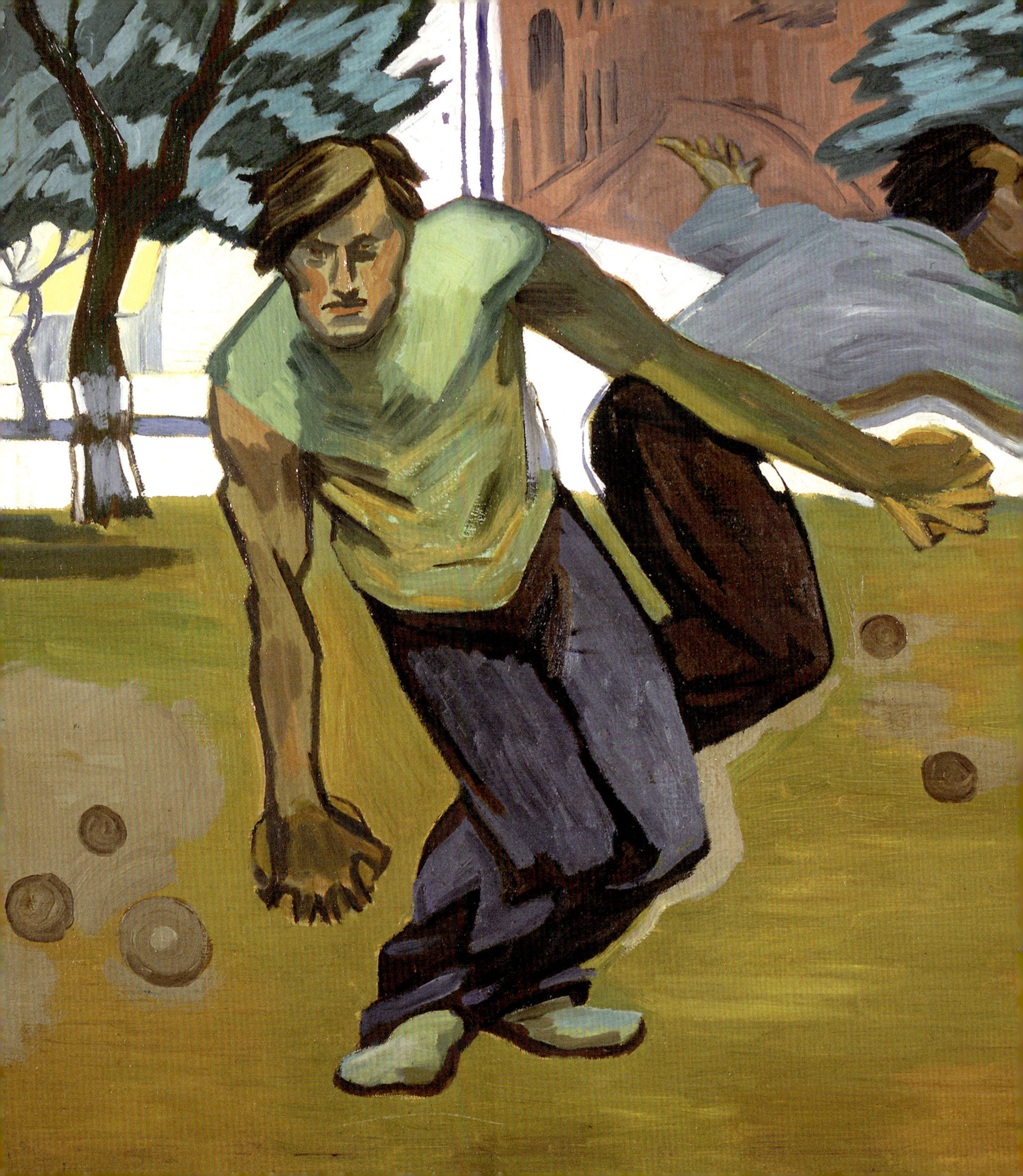

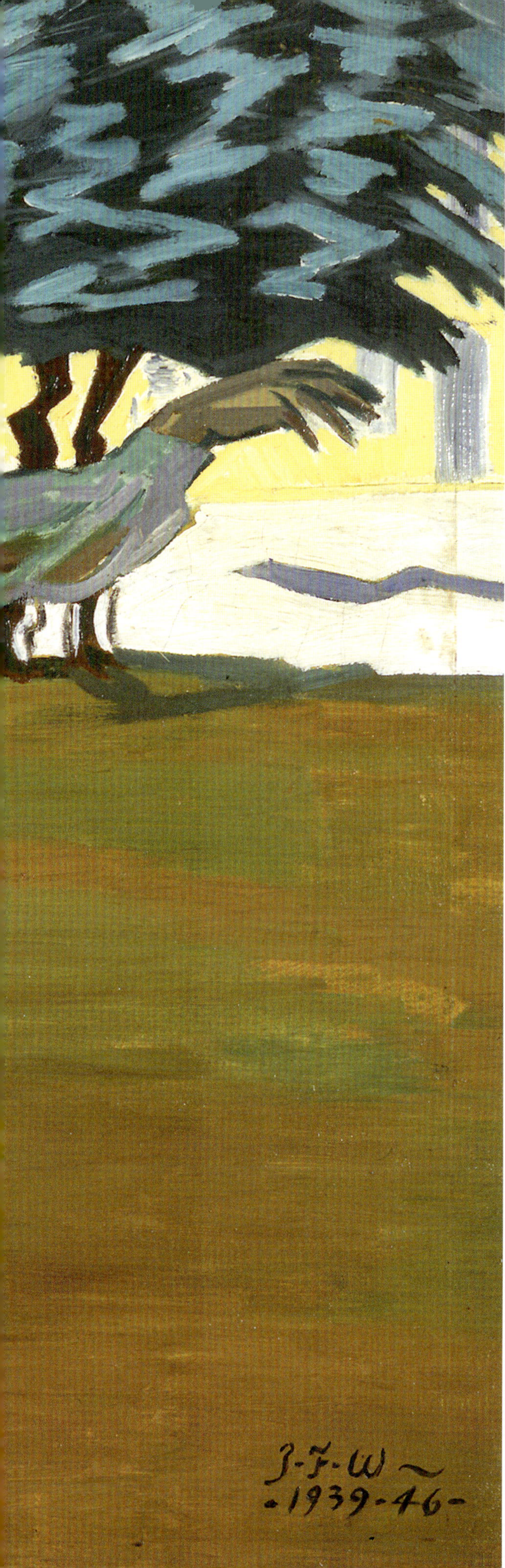

J. F. Willumsen
Kuglespillere. Provence
(Ball Players. Provence), 1939–46
Oil on canvas, 74×91.5 cm
Willumsen's Museum, Frederikssund

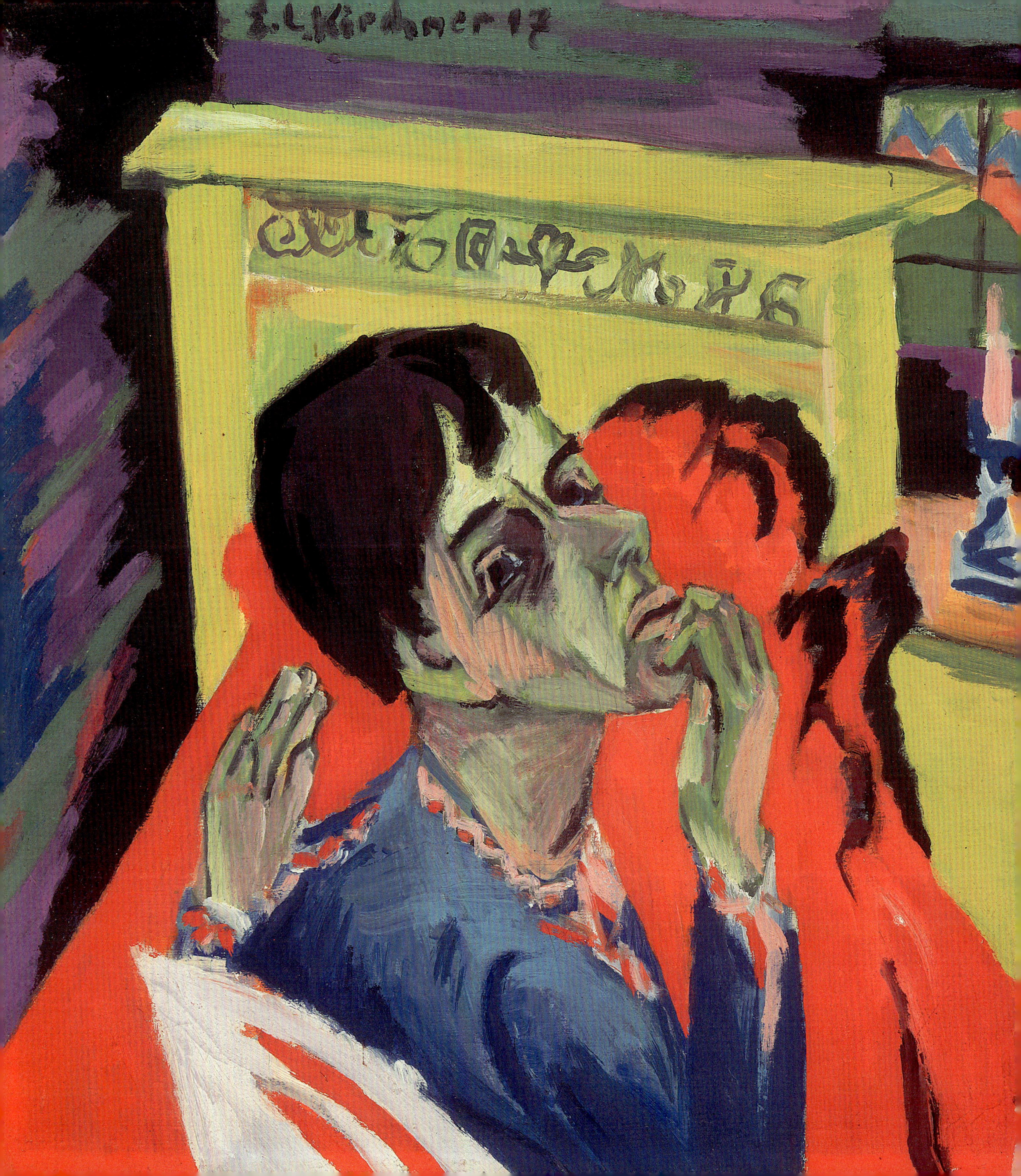
E.L.Kirchner 17

ANNE GREGERSEN

Self-Mythologizing and Control of Reception by J. F. Willumsen and Ernst Ludwig Kirchner

Ernst Ludwig Kirchner
Selbstbildnis als Kranker (Self-Portrait as a Sick Man), 1918–30
Oil on canvas, 59 × 69.3 cm
Bayerische Staatsgemäldesammlungen, Munich

J.F. Willumsen (1863–1958) and Ernst Ludwig Kirchner (1880–1938) elected almost simultaneously to pursue their own individualistic projects and disassociate themselves from contemporary art movements. From 1917 the mountains of Switzerland became a refuge for Kirchner after a mental breakdown, whereas Willumsen moved to the South of France in 1916, where he "settled down," as he put it many years later.[1] Neither of them returned to their respective home countries, choosing instead to devote the rest of their lives to the pursuit of a personal, artistic vision in self-imposed exile. They did, however, make every effort to control the reception of their art and mythologize themselves as artists in the homelands they had left. Both artists had suffered decades of mixed critical responses to their work, and a lack of recognition of what they saw as the originality and universal power of their art. Living abroad provided them with the opportunity—through strategic skill, a self-assertive attitude, and cultural awareness—to rethink and construct an art-historical narrative they wanted to be part of. The goal was nothing less than securing their position among the pantheon of master painters. Both artists used remarkably similar means to sustain the narrative they desired, achieving in some respects the same results. Yet despite Kirchner and Willumsen's persistent efforts to control the reception of their works and create connections between the personality of the artist and the art they produced, towards the end of their lives they were classified as outsiders rather than unique geniuses. Whilst they themselves saw their late period as expressing the full force of their maturation as artists, it was their early works pre-dating their self-imposed exile that secured them the position they coveted in art history. Not until long after their deaths did any serious interest in their later works emerge.

Kirchner's strategic self-promotion is often highlighted, and has also been the subject of detailed analysis.[2] Willumsen has often been depicted as highly individualistic and as staging his persona as such.[3] This self-mythologizing by the Danish artist has not, however, previously been analyzed as a series of tactical choices made in a specific historical context, or as comparable to the strategies of other artists of his time. Instead, his self-mythologizing is usually viewed as incidental and possibly pathological, a symptom of his psychobiographical circumstances. Comparing Kirchner and Willumsen, however, provides us with an opportunity to probe the reasons and ways in which they deliberately positioned themselves as individualists, and to try to understand the path they took in rejecting contemporary art movements. To what extent can their strategies of self-mythologization be connected to conditions on the art market and competition in the art world? How did they initially participate in and then reject strategic networking to fulfill their ambitions? What role did the art of the past play in their self-image? And what means did they use to create a narrative in which they played a starring role? Through a parallel reading and contextualization of Kirchner and Willumsen's strategies of self-mythologizing, and the ways in which they tried to control the reception of their works, this article discusses and presents a framework for understanding the path the two artists took to achieve an individualistic position as a deliberate strategy —a position that drove their work as artists, and which they also promoted shamelessly. The article draws on analyses of the art market during the first decades of the twentieth century, and the opportunities artists had to assume a position on the art scene through performative self-presentation.

The Empowered yet Marginalized Artist

Willumsen and Kirchner tried to position themselves on the art scene in the nineteenth century and the first decades of the twentieth respectively, a period during which industrialization and the international market economy developed explosively. The art market expanded and became increasingly professionalized, and self-promotion and networking emerged as key to success. Modern artists who wanted to sell work and gain recognition therefore had to consider how to promote their artistic vision and originality, but also how to build alliances with influential critics, gallery owners, and collectors, as well as develop an international network.[4] Around the turn of the

1. Ernst Mentze, *J.F. Willumsen: Mine erindringer fortalt til Ernst Mentze* (Copenhagen, 1953), p. 214.
2. See Christian Weikop, "Ernst Ludwig Kirchner as his Own Critic: The Artist's Statements as Stratagems of Self-Promotion," *Forum for Modern Language Studies* vol. 48, no. 4, September 26, 2012.
3. See Henrik Wivel, *J.F. Willumsen* (Copenhagen, 2005) and *Ny dansk kunsthistorie bind 5: Symbolisme og impressionisme* (Copenhagen, 1994).
4. See Robert Jensen, *Marketing Modernism in Fin-de-Siècle Europe* (Princeton, 1994) and Sylvie Patry, *Inventing Impressionism: Paul Durand-Ruel and the Modern Art Market* (New Haven, 2015).
5. Julius Meier-Graefe, *Entwicklungsgeschichte der modernen Kunst* (vol. 1 published in 1904, vols. 2 & 3 in 1914–24). Richard Muther, *A History of Modern Painting* (New York, 1896).

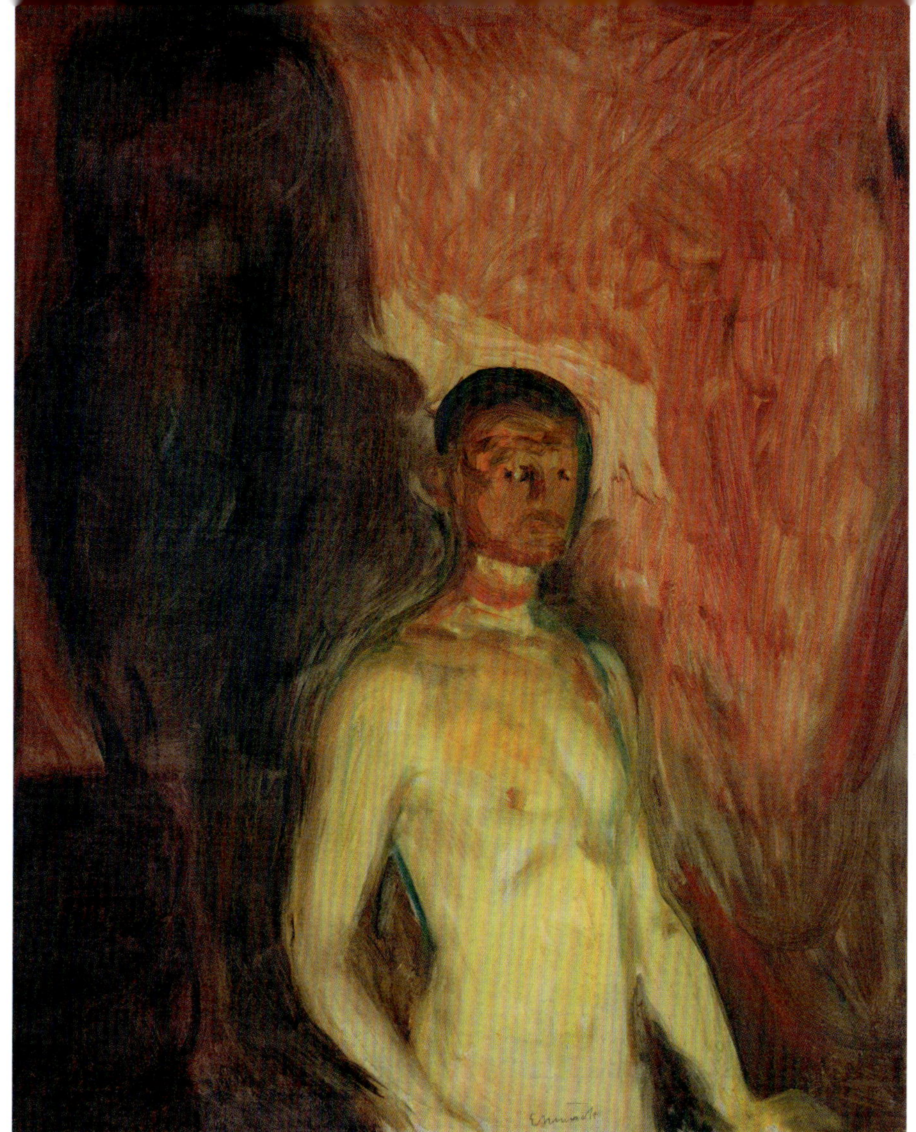

Fig. 1
Edvard Munch
Selvportrett i helvete
(Self-Portrait in Hell), 1903
Oil on canvas, 82 × 66 cm
The Munch Museum, Oslo

century there were various initiatives aimed at embedding new, modern art in the writing of art history, and therefore also, for the first time, understanding contemporary art in a historical context. This took place through books on art history by leading advocates of modern art such as Julius Meier-Graefe and Richard Muther,[5] as well as through major retrospective exhibitions in a number of European capitals that presented French Impressionism, Neo-Impressionism, and contemporary modern art as part of a linear narrative of development. Gradually, as academic art was downgraded and the previously scandal-ridden new art canonized, it became obvious that the battle to define and write art history gave rise to new paradigms. A new, evolutionary narrative emerged in which the maladjusted, alienated, yet highly original artist was seen as pivotal to the triumph of modern art.[6] As Robert Jensen has demonstrated, by the beginning of the twentieth century the role of the outsider was an artistic and commercial plus, used consciously and strategically by artists such as Egon Schiele.[7] Edvard Munch also managed to assume the role of the mad and misunderstood genius, at the same time as aiming directly for artistic fame and fortune (fig. 1).[8]

This new artist's role is clearly represented in an equally new style of self-portraiture depicting the artist as simultaneously empowered and marginal, a visual topos that was to prove popular throughout most of the twentieth century. Whereas historically the genre of the self-portrait had been associated with presenting the (exclusively) male artist as a high-minded, creative individual

6. Jensen, 1994 (see note 4), p. 8. See also Robert Jensen, "Selling Martyrdom," *Art in America* 80, April 1992, and Oskar Bätschmann, *The Artist in the Modern World: The Conflict Between Market and Self-Expression*, translated by Eileen Martin (Cologne, 1997).
7. Robert Jensen, "A Matter of Professionalism: Marketing Identity in Fin-de-Siècle Vienna," in Steven Beller, ed., *Rethinking Vienna 1900* (New York, 2001), p. 203.
8. This is an analysis presented in various contexts. Patricia G. Berman addresses it in "The Business of Being Edvard Munch," in Gary Garrels et al., eds., *Edvard Munch: Between the Clock and the Bed*, exh. cat. The Metropolitan Museum of Art (New York, 2017).

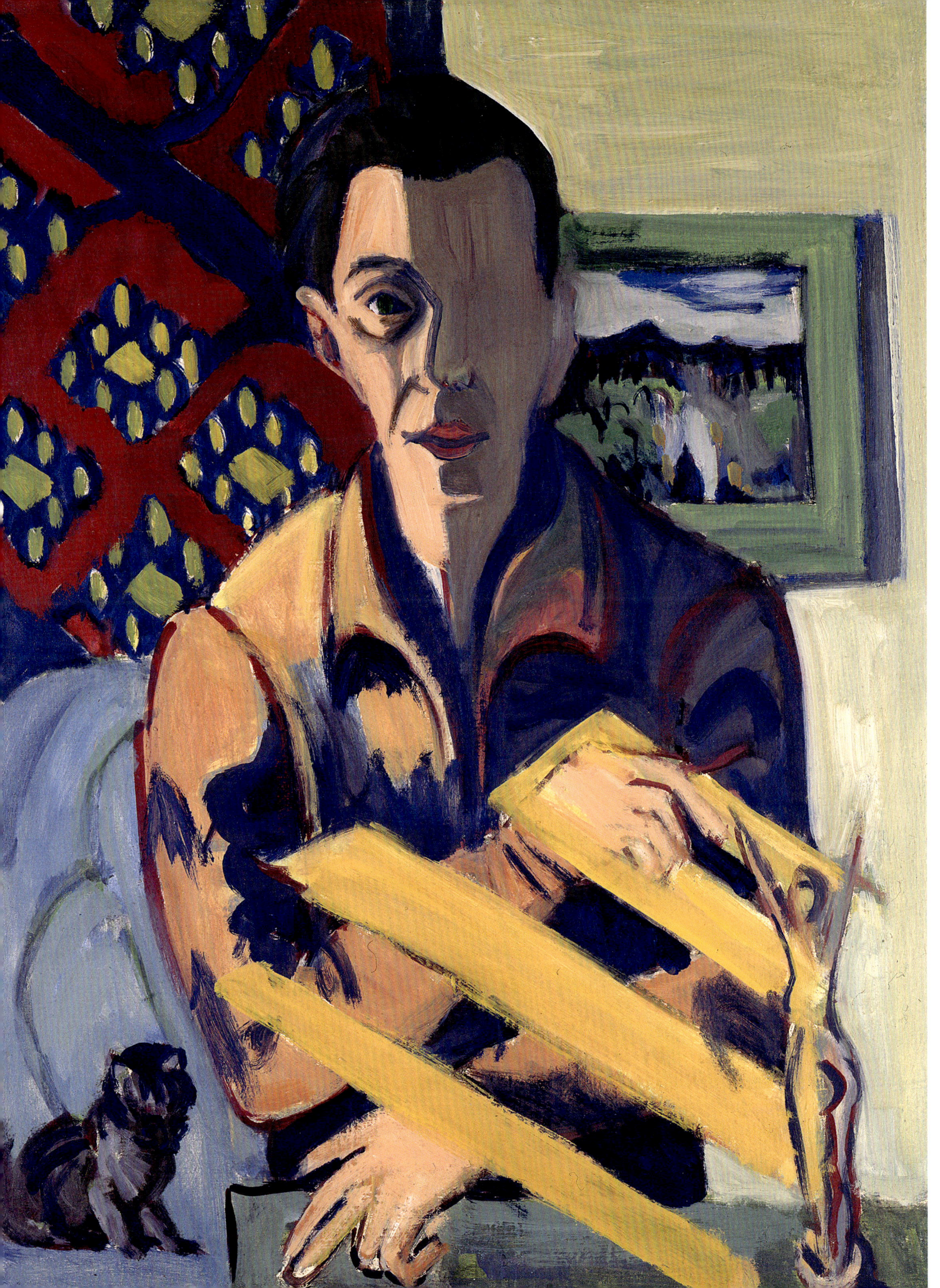

Fig. 2:
Ernst Ludwig Kirchner
Selbstbildnis
(Self-Portrait), 1934–37
Oil on canvas,
84×61 cm
Bünder Kunstmuseum
Chur

with the status of authenticity, around 1900 the martyred (still male) genius became a new and potentially ambivalent role for artists.[9] Several of Kirchner and Willumsen's self-representations, which were of course both exhibited and for sale, reveal their identification with precisely this role. Thirsting for success and suffering, they insisted on staging the privileged position of the artist as ambivalent and tragic.

Here, two late self-portraits can serve as examples (figs. 2 and 3), examples that can perhaps also be seen to cross the line between the performatively martyred genius and woeful defeat. In both works the artist looks intensely and directly at the viewer with a grave, confrontational gaze. Kirchner faces the viewer, whereas Willumsen turns away from the canvas and act of painting. Both paintings are composed of contrasts between figuration and abstraction, light and darkness, power and passivity, memory and *tabula rasa*. In Willumsen's self-portrait we see an empty canvas, which appears as an abstract form, whereas in Kirchner's part of his face is wreathed in shadow and erased. Whereas the canvas can be interpreted as the finest attribute of the omnipotent painter, in Willumsen's painting it exists as an empty reference—as if we have yet to see any evidence of his talent. In Kirchner's work on the other hand, the mountain painting in the background and statuette of a naked woman with arms extended in a gesture of tribute represent the demonstrable results of his creative powers. But the (paradoxically) illuminated right hand, holding what looks like a cigarillo, is trapped by the yellow, diagonal lines extending across the surface of the painting in an abstract pattern. As in several other works by Kirchner, the movement of his hands and arms is restricted. The painting, considered to be his last self-portrait, implies that Kirchner's ability to create in the future is also challenged. The tapestry in the background, with its swastika-like form, becomes a threatening element. In the works of both artists, the use of shadows is symbolic. Willumsen is surrounded by a dark shadow, whereas Kirchner uses darkness to divide his figure into two and obliterate one of his eyes. Given what we know about how the lives of both artists ended—Kirchner, who struggled mentally, committed suicide in 1938 after his works were stamped as *Entartete Kunst* (degenerate art) by the Nazis, and Willumsen died bitter, isolated, and largely ridiculed by his compatriots in 1958—these portraits can also be seen as melancholic admissions of defeat.

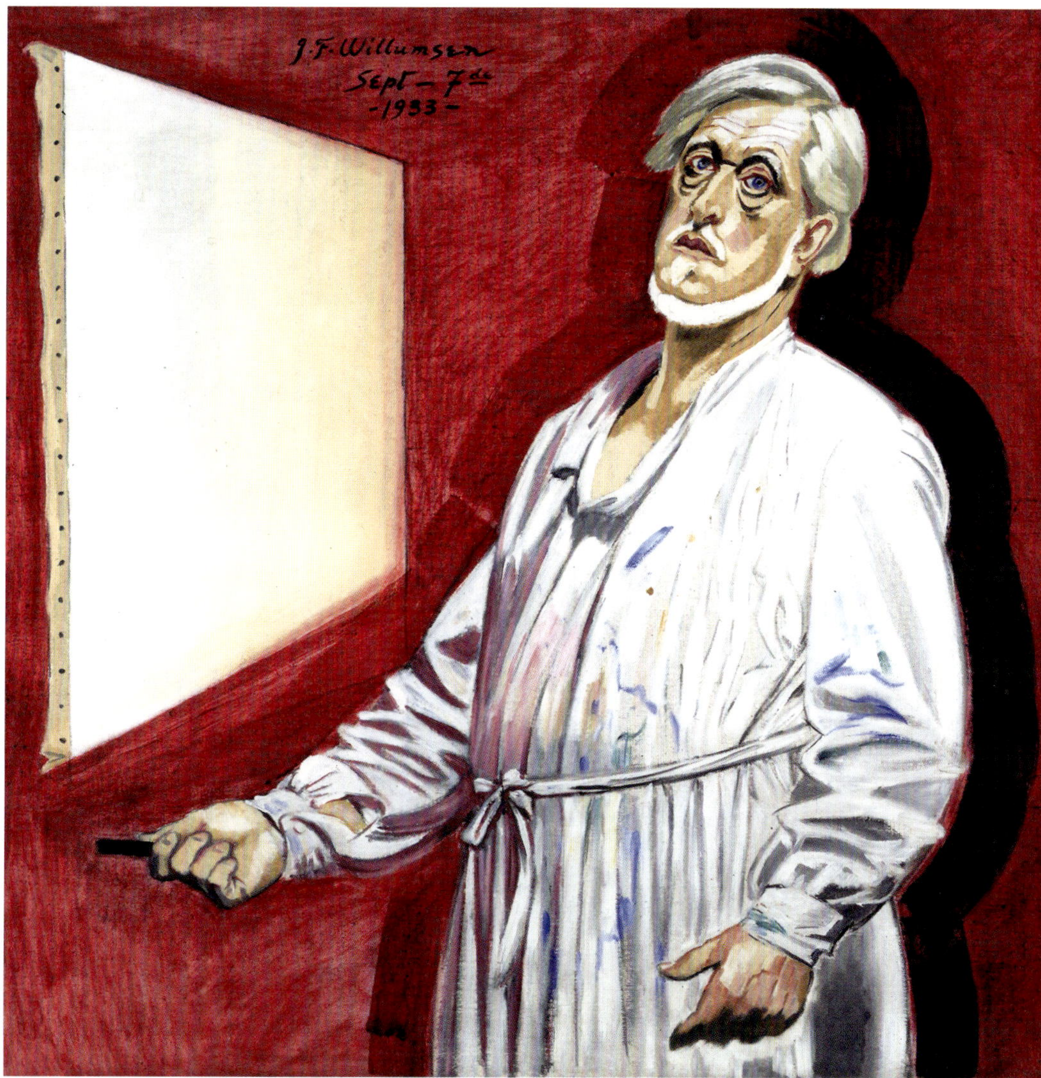

Fig. 3
J. F. Willumsen
Selvportræt i malerbluse
(Self-Portrait in Painter's Smock), 1933
Oil on canvas, 119 × 117 cm
Willumsen's Museum, Frederikssund

9. Marsha Meskimmon, *The Art of Reflection: Women Artists' Self-Portraiture in the Twentieth Century* (London, 1996), pp. 22–24. Kirchner is one of Meskimmon's examples. In her feminist reading Meskimmon emphasizes that even though the marginalized position has traditionally belonged to women, it is the male artist's privilege to turn this position into a dominant norm. See also Amelia Jones, "'Clothes Make the Man': The Male Artist as a Performative Function," *Oxford Art Journal*, vol. 18, no. 2, 1995, pp. 18–32 for a feminist analysis of the male artist's performative creation of identity.

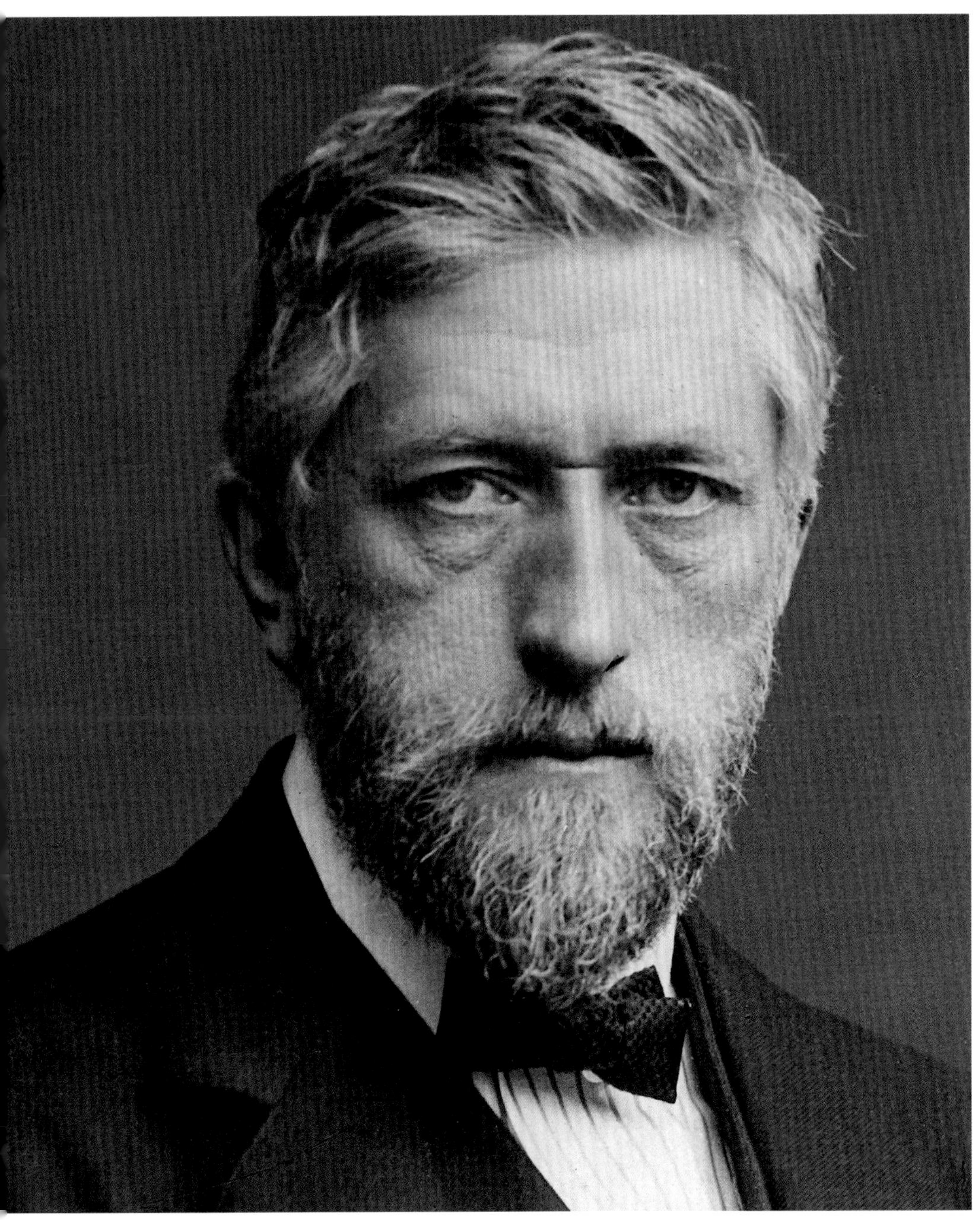

Fig. 4
Harald Perch, *Portrait of J. F. Willumsen*, ca. 1917
Photo, 27.8 × 20 cm, Willumsen's Museum, Frederikssund

Individualism and Strategic Networks

Kirchner and Willumsen are both examples of the modern artist's simultaneous cultivation of an individualistic outsider role and strategic use of contacts, artist groups, and connections that bridged generations artistically. The artist communities that emerged in different parts of Europe from the eighteen-nineties to the early twentieth century were rooted in idealism, but were also equally important as a means of self-promotion and key positioning platform in the art world. Both Willumsen and Kirchner were active members of artist communities and co-founded artist associations, at the same time as being highly conscious of presenting themselves as outsiders with their own unique artistic agendas.

Willumsen (figs. 4 and 5) was one of the founders of Den Frie Exhibition in Copenhagen in 1891, and in the early twentieth century collaborated with the German art historian and art dealer Julius Meier-Graefe on the creation of a *Salon des Étrangers* for foreign artists in Paris. For Willumsen this was an ambitious attempt to establish a position among the most important international developments in the art world, and Meier-Graefe was a key figure. Due to his status and influence in the art world, he was central in legitimizing the standing of young, foreign artists on the art scene and art market. In 1903, the same year Willumsen's plans were taking shape, Meier-Graefe was the primus motor behind an exhibition with the artists of the Vienna Secession, locating the very latest French art in a genealogy going back to the Impressionism of the previous generation, as well as selected older artists. Willumsen understood the role of such exhibition-generated genealogies in artistic success. The *Salon des Étrangers* was to bring together a broad range of contemporary artists from Northern Europe, Central Europe, and the US. Willumsen's list of artists included a number of his Danish contemporaries, as well as artists such as Ferdinand Hodler, Félix Vallotton, Fernand Knopff, Henry van der Velde, Max Klinger, Lovis Corinth, Gustav Klimt, Akseli Gallén-Kallela, and Edvard Munch. The idea was that these non-French artists should exhibit with French artists, including Auguste Rodin, Maurice Denis, Édouard Vuillard, and Pierre Bonnard, as well as the established French Impressionists Claude Monet and Pierre-Auguste Renoir.[10] This would give foreign artists having difficulty making a name for themselves in Paris an exhibition platform and connection to French art. Rather than creating a forum for a different kind of "foreign" art, the strategy was to make the Northern European artists part of an international art-historical narrative (in which Monet and Willumsen, interestingly, were to hang side by side). As Ulla Hjorth writes, the inclusion of Renoir and Monet might seem surprising given Willumsen's rejection of Impressionism,[11] yet it was during these very years that Impressionism went from being an "obscure avant-garde movement" to become—for a brief period—synonymous with modern art and life.[12]

Meier-Graefe and Willumsen corresponded about the *Salon des Étrangers* throughout 1904, and the exhibition plans also featured in the Danish press during that summer, but communication between the two gradually ebbed out, and the project came to nothing. In 1905 Willumsen moved back to Denmark after living abroad since 1900. After his return, his ambition of securing an international breakthrough via joint artistic projects apparently declined, although he continued to network and exhibit abroad, particularly in Germany where he felt a much stronger connection with the art and culture than he had in France.[13] He exhibited eight works at the Berlin Secession in 1906, after which he was invited via Emil Nolde to participate in one of the Brücke artists' exhibitions. That his networking can be seen as carefully and strategically planned is supported by Willumsen declining this invitation. As Loa Haagen Pictet has suggested, Willumsen turning down the offer was probably based on his lack of interest in the woodcut theme of the exhibition—woodcuts being a medium he did not turn to until late in life—and that he regarded the primarily young Brücke artists as insignificant and therefore of little use in terms of an international breakthrough.[14] When he also failed to have any kind of breakthrough on the German contemporary

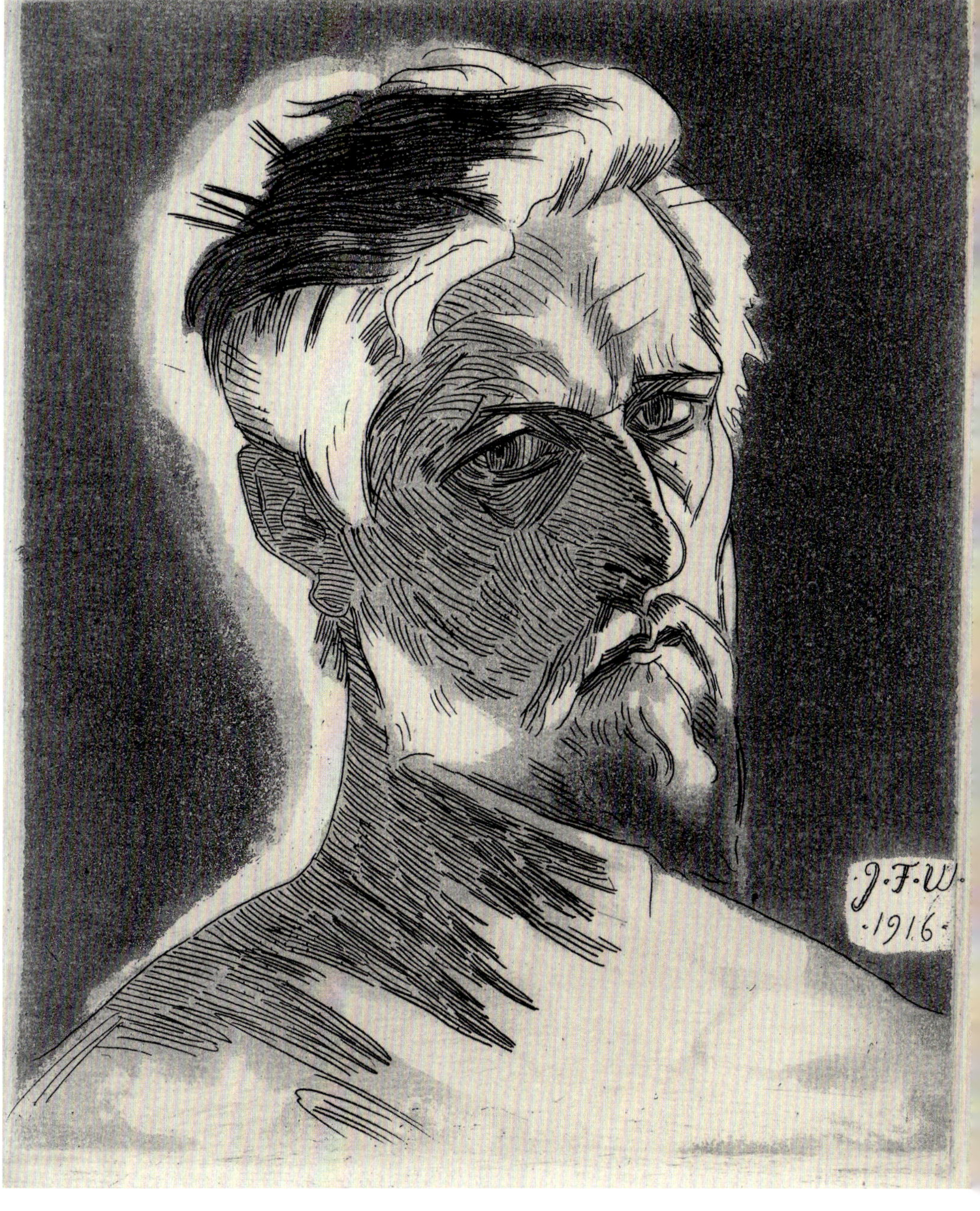

Fig. 5
J. F. Willumsen
Også et selvportræt
(Also a Self-Portrait), 1916
Etching, 23.7 × 19.3
Willumsen's Museum, Frederikssund

10. Ulla Hjorth, *J.F. Willumsen i Europa* (Frederikssund, 2006), pp. 20–21 and Vibeke Petersen, "J.F. Willumsen og Tyskland omkring århundredskiftet," *Konsthistorisk tidskrift/Journal of Art History*, 63:3–4, (1994), DOI: 10.1080/00233609408604364, pp. 218–19.
11. Hjorth 2006 (see note 10), p. 22.
12. Jensen 1992 (see note 6), p. 143.
13. Regarding Willumsen's relationship to Germany, see Loa Haagen Pictet's illuminating article "Europæeren J.F. Willumsen," in Peter Nørgaard Larsen, ed., *Sjælebilleder: Symbolismen i dansk og europæisk maleri 1870–1910*, exh. cat. The National Gallery of Denmark (Copenhagen, 2000).
14. Ibid., pp. 211–12.

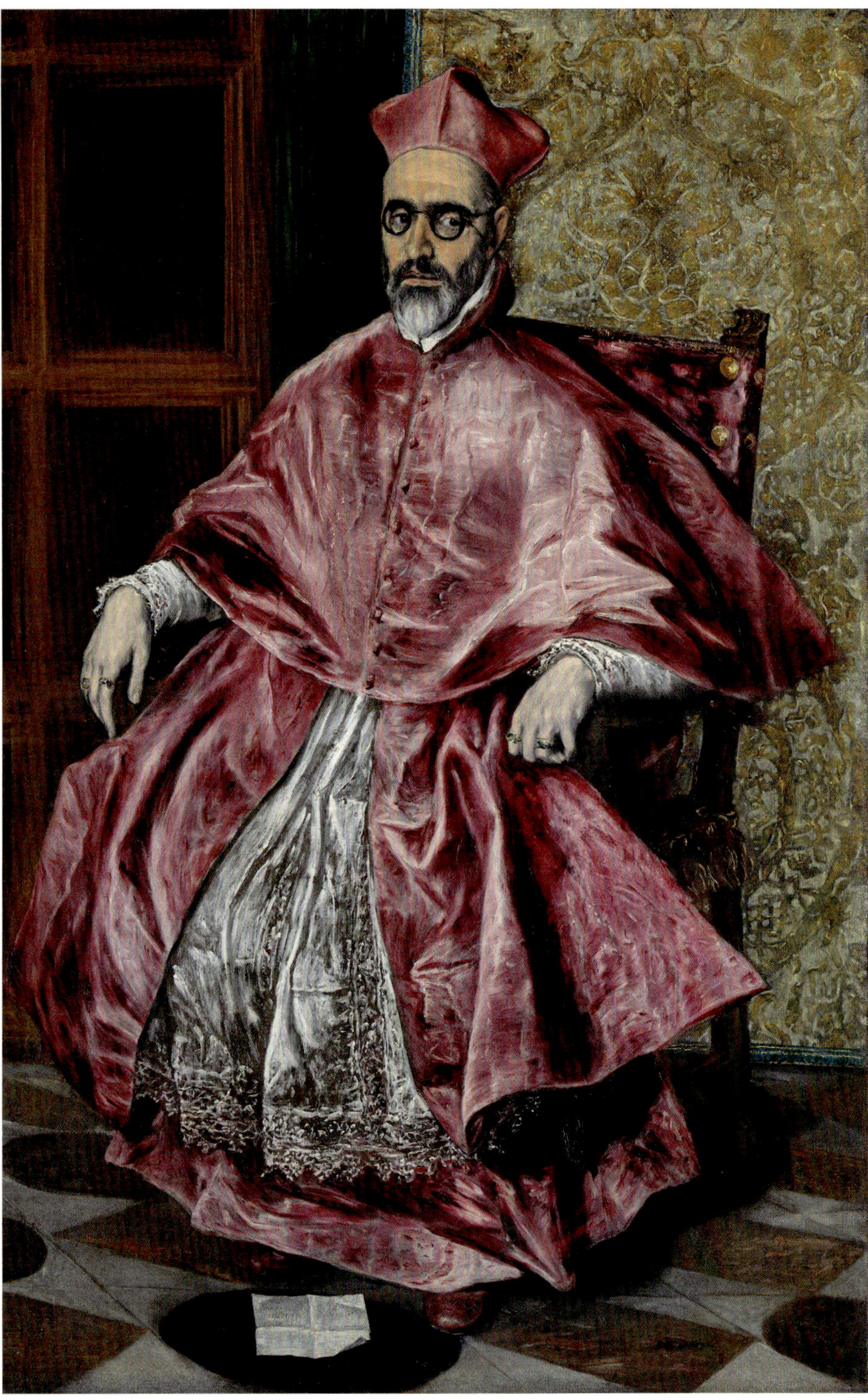

Fig. 6
El Greco (Domenikos Theotokopoulos)
Cardinal Fernando Niño de Guevara (1541–1609), ca. 1600
Oil on canvas, 170.8 × 108 cm, The Metropolitan Museum of Art, New York

art scene, Willumsen started to invest more heavily in a new strategy focusing on older art and creating links between himself as a modern art genius and the Greek-Spanish Late Renaissance painter El Greco, for example (fig. 6).[15] It is worth noting that Willumsen did so at a time when El Greco was being positioned as the father of modern art in books and exhibitions alike by Meier-Graefe and others.[16] From the nineteen-tens onwards, Willumsen's cultivation of older art started to supersede his attempts to position himself in a contemporary art context. He did not, however, abandon all hope of an international breakthrough, and in 1926 even suggested creating a "Propaganda Agency" for the promotion of Danish art abroad to the Danish Minister of Culture.[17]

Kirchner pursued a similar strategy of joint activities, especially in connection with the creation of the Brücke artist group in 1905, which particularly after its disbandment in 1913 was an important element in Kirchner's own art-historical narrative. The group was started by four German architecture students: Fritz Bleyl, Erich Heckel, Karl Schmidt-Rottluff, and Kirchner himself, supplemented during briefer periods by artists like Emil Nolde, Max Pechstein, and Otto Mueller. The name "Brücke" (Bridge) was a metaphor from Friedrich Nietzsche's novel *Thus Spoke Zarathustra* (1883–85), but also for the artists' goal of building bridges between the past and the present—between older German art and their own experiments in modern art. The group highlighted the importance of Lucas Cranach the Elder, Albrecht Dürer, and Matthias Grünewald—as well as Rembrandt, who many at the time regarded as

15. Regarding El Greco and modernism see Beat Wismer et al., eds., *El Greco and Modernism*, exh. cat. Museum KunstPalast, Düsseldorf (Ostfildern, 2012). Regarding Willumsen and El Greco see Leila Krogh, *J.F. Willumsen på sporet af El Greco* (Frederikssund, 2005) and Yannis Hadjinicolau, "J.F. Willumsen and El Greco: Collecting, Theory and Practice," in Anne Gregersen, ed., *Echo Room: Thorvaldsen, Willumsen, Jorn and Their Collections*, exh. cat. Willumsen's Museum, Frederikssund (Berlin, 2018).

16. With the publication of *Spanische Reise* in 1910 Julius Meier-Graefe also played a central role here. The artist group Der Blaue Reiter (The Blue Rider) included El Greco in their 1912 almanac to demonstrate the similarities between his painting and modern art.

17. Draft letter from Edith Willumsen to Nina Bang, February 17, 1926, and from J. F. Willumsen to Erick Struckmann, March 22, 1926. The Willumsen Museum Archive, available in Danish at www.ktdk.dk.

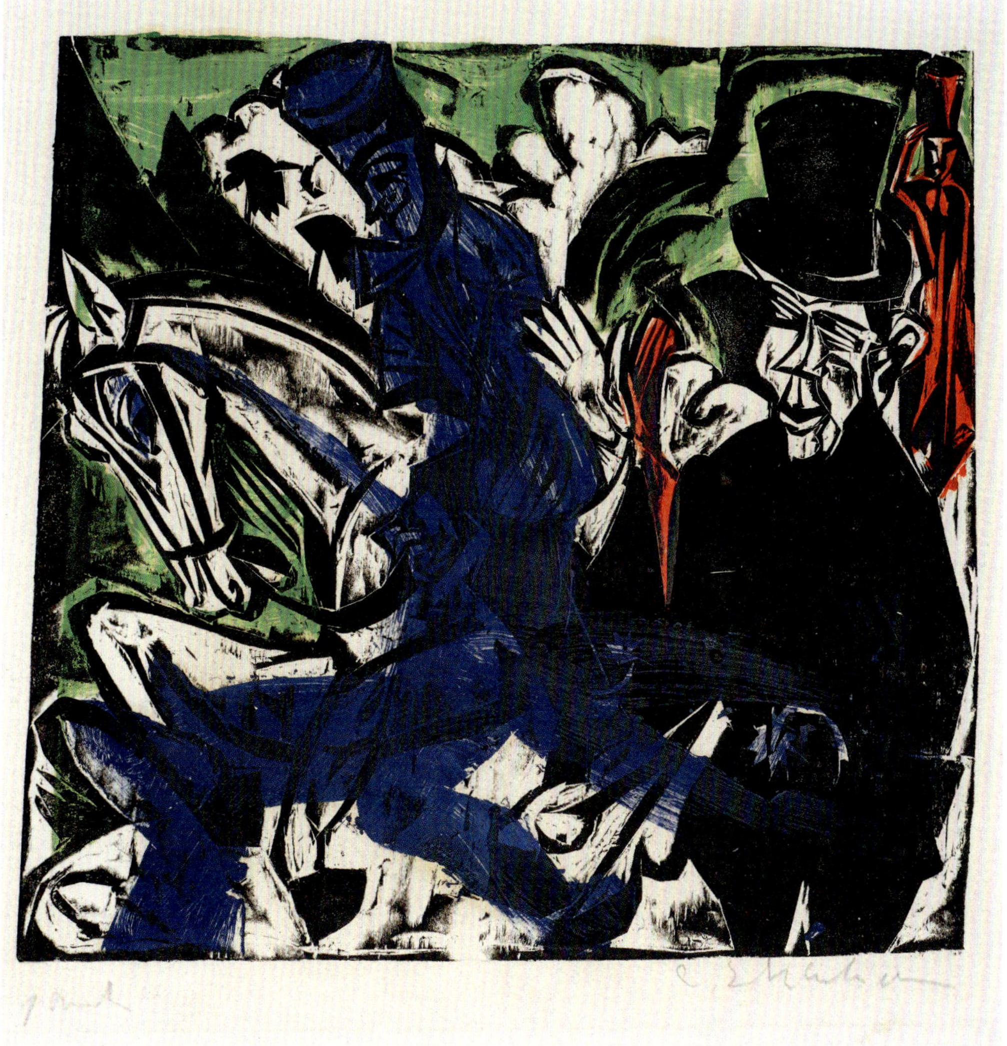

Fig. 7
Ernst Ludwig Kirchner
Schlemihl mit dem grauen Männlein auf der Landstrasse (Schlemihl's Encounter with the Little Gray Man on the Highway), 1915
Color woodcut, composition 30 × 31 cm
Museum Folkwang, Essen

quasi-German—as the true representatives of a German art to which they saw themselves as successors. By claiming his woodcuts to be directly based on old prints from Nuremberg, Kirchner promoted himself as a new Dürer, bringing the core of German art into the present (fig. 7).

As Norman Rosenthal has emphasized in relationship to Kirchner, the beginning of the twentieth century was a period of new philosophical and scientific ideas, which simultaneously and paradoxically focused on the centrality of the individual and the importance of community,[18] something reflected in the contemporary focus on the significance of the individual artist on the one hand, and the cultivation of artist groups and associations on the other. Artists' unions, associations, and communities started to flourish, at the same time as the art market was internationalized and commercial galleries gained power. While people read Nietzsche[19] and identified with his solitary prophet and mountain hiker Zarathustra, artists—motivated by idealism as well as practicalities—came together to create a future that would secure them a place in an evolutionary history of art defined by new departures and the original contributions of individual artists. The art market was invested in supporting this narrative, and artists acknowledged the need to legitimize their individual importance in order to succeed on an increasingly competitive art market.

18. Norman Rosenthal, "Ernst Ludwig Kirchner, Expressionist," in Jill Lloyd and Magdalena M. Moeller, eds., *Ernst Ludwig Kirchner, 1880–1938*, exh. cat. National Gallery of Art (Washington D.C., 2003), p. 9. Rosenthal calls this paradox Kirchner's "driving obsession."
19. Friedrich Nietzsche published his philosophical novel *Also sprach Zarathustra: Ein Buch für Alle und Keinen* in 1883–85. The first English translation, *Thus Spoke Zarathustra: A Book for All and None*, was published in 1896. Regarding the influence of Nietzsche on Kirchner see, for example, Sharon Jordan "'He is a Bridge': The Importance of Friedrich Nietzsche for Ernst Ludwig Kirchner," in Jill Lloyd and Janis Staggs, eds., *Ernst Ludwig Kirchner*, exh. cat. Neue Galerie (New York, 2019).

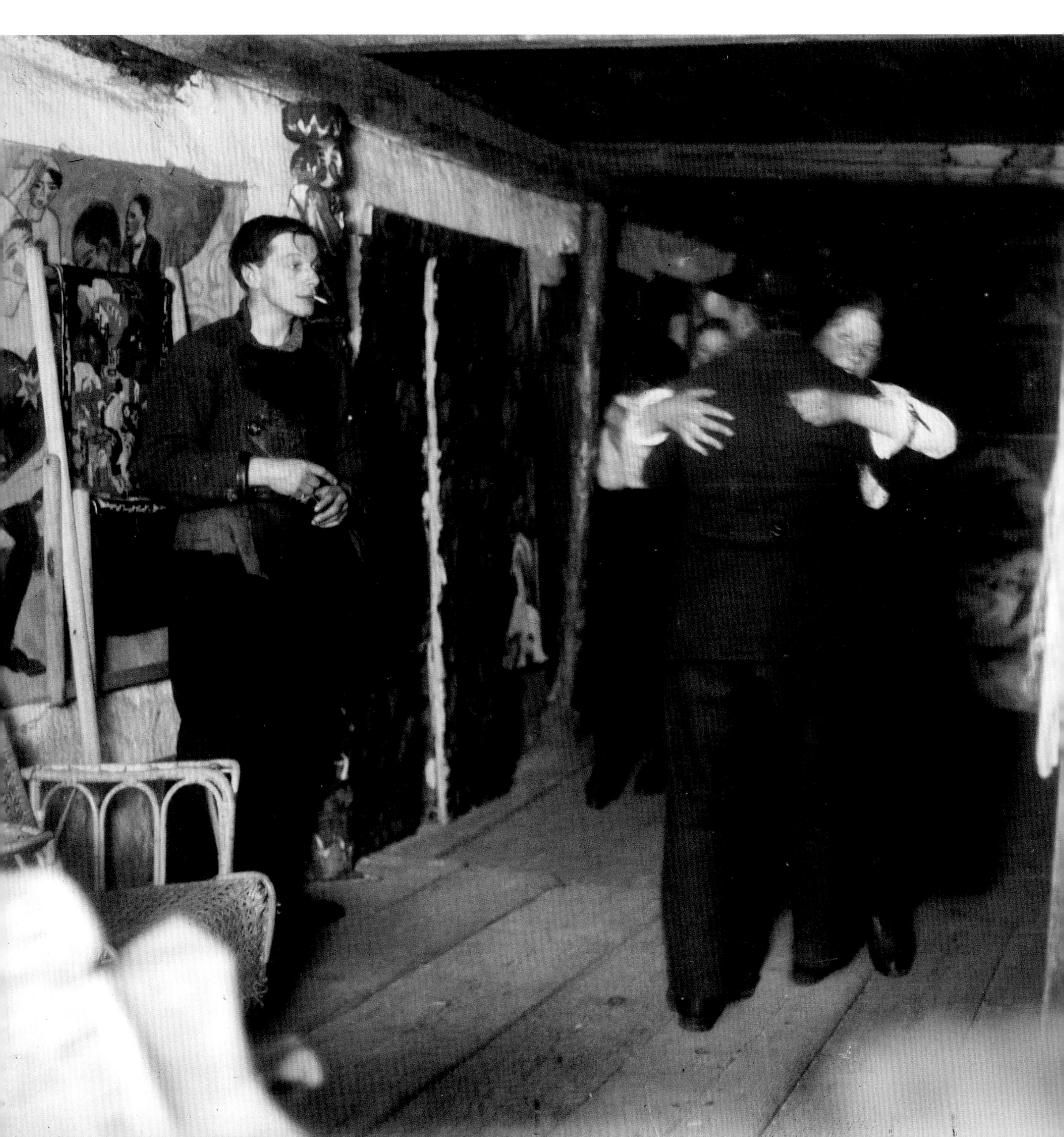

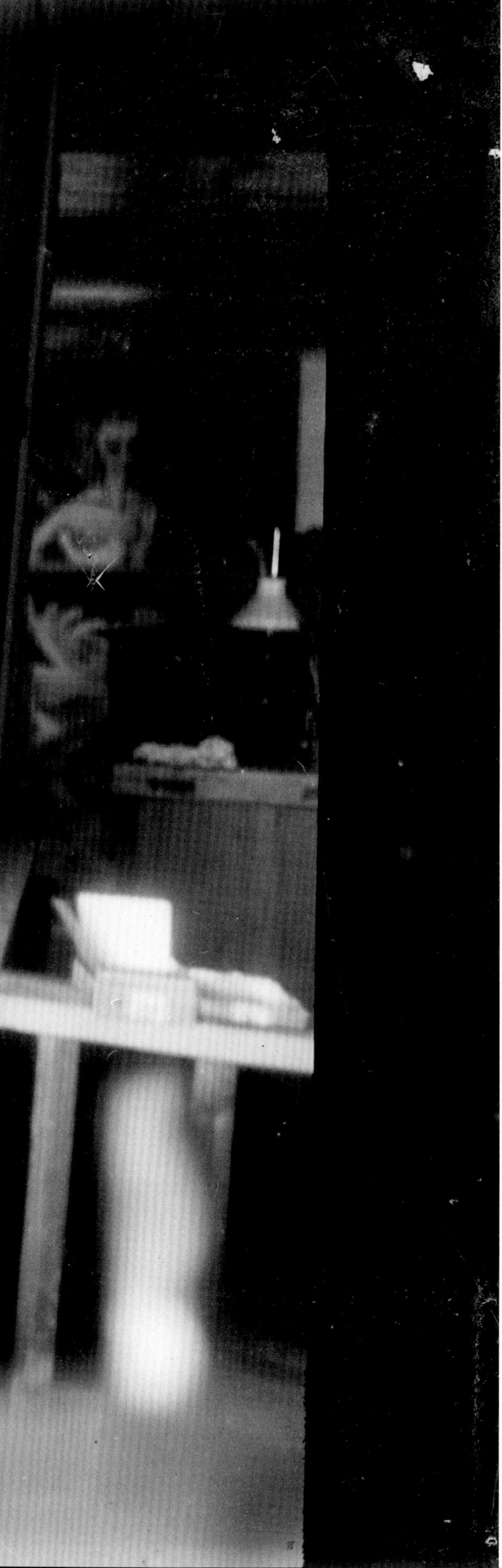

Fig. 8
Ernst Ludwig Kirchner
Barn Dance on the Upper Floor of the house "In den Lärchen" with Self-Portrait at the Left, 1919–20
Glass-plate negative, 18 × 24 cm
Kirchner Museum Davos

The Brücke group was a joint project with no leader, but this was not the message sent by Kirchner's *Chronik der Künstlergruppe Brücke*, which he wrote in 1913. Kirchner presented himself as the principal figure of the Brücke group, underplaying the importance of the other members. They rejected Kirchner's self-promoting interpretation, which contributed to the disbandment of the group.[20] Later Kirchner distanced himself entirely from the group and from being categorized as an Expressionist, at the same time as trying to develop his own unique form of visual expression. That Kirchner was given the opportunity to hold a solo exhibition in 1912 at Kunstsalon Fritz Gurlitt, one of Berlin's most important galleries, must have reinforced his belief that he was on the verge of a major breakthrough. During these years, however, Kirchner was also plagued by mental health issues and drug and alcohol abuse, which in 1917 led to a nervous breakdown and physical paralysis. He was admitted to Bellevue Sanatorium on Lake Constance in Switzerland, and later decided to settle in the Swiss Alps. Even though in doing so Kirchner distanced himself from the art center of Berlin, he did not stop trying to exert influence and consciously promote himself. On the contrary, life in self-imposed exile gave him the opportunity to cultivate the individualistic position he sought. He felt he had come full circle artistically, returning to the imaginative, spontaneous, and universal imagery of his early years, now in harmony with the crystalline mountain landscape.

In the Alps, Kirchner staged himself as part of local folk life. He started to live like a villager, dress like a villager, and take on the role of "bohemian peasant" (fig. 8). From being a city artist depicting the life and figures of the streets, including prostitutes, their customers, cabarets, the circus, and cafés, Kirchner now started to aestheticize local life in Davos (fig. 9).[21] He moved into a cabin, had a peasant's outfit made, designed furniture, textiles, and sets for local

20. Weikop 2012 (see note 2), pp. 407–9.

21. Kirchner also depicted nature during his early career as an artist, especially the lakes where he and his art circle and their models bathed and cultivated a Vitalist view of nature in keeping with the contemporary *zeitgeist*.

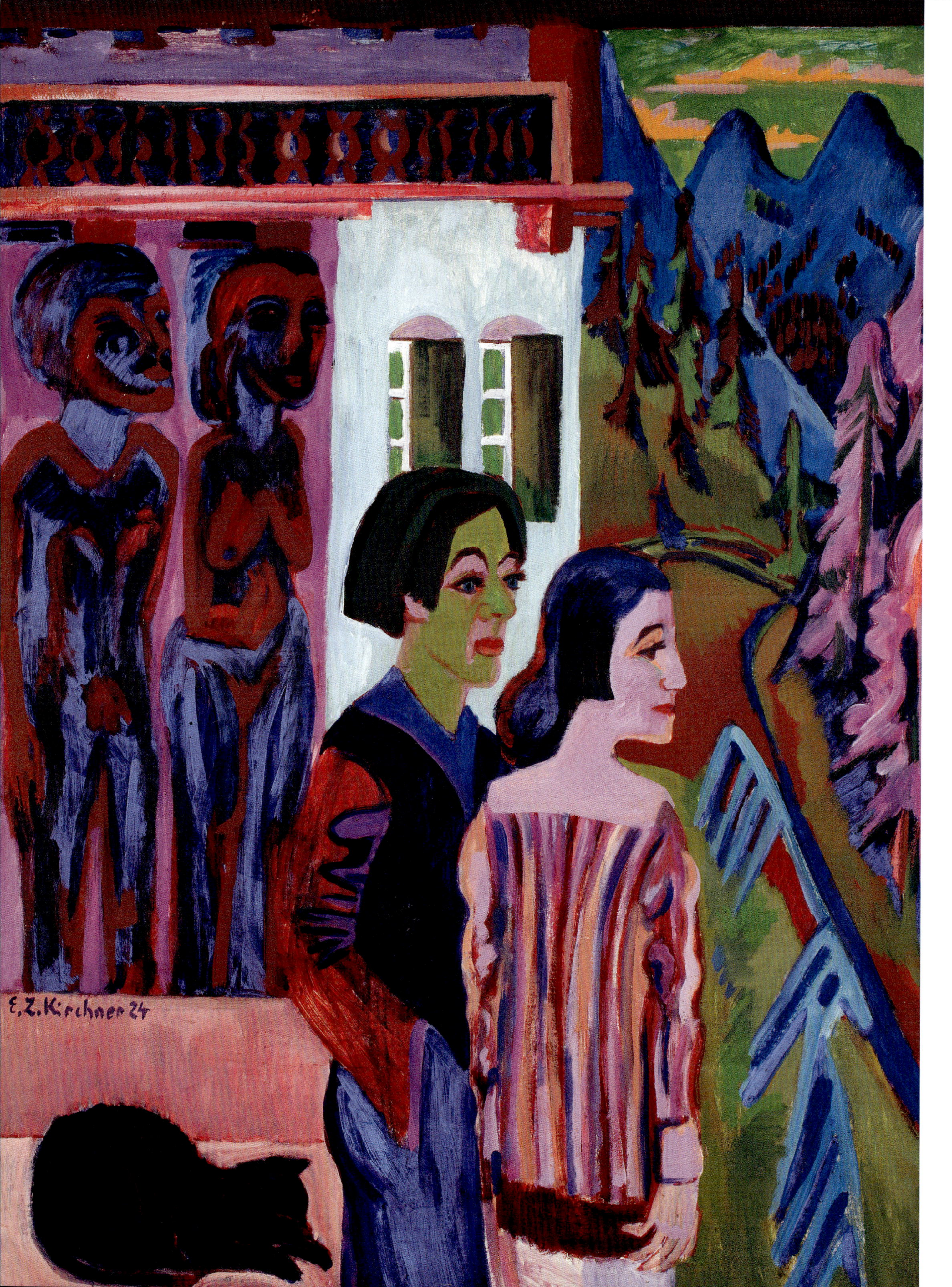
E.L.Kirchner 24

amateur theatrics, carved wooden sculptures and other decorative items, and painted panoramic alpine landscapes—all at the same time as exhibiting extensively in Switzerland and Germany. That he kept up to date with the latest art trends and kept an eye on the contemporary art scene can, for example, be seen in his visit to the 1925 Internationale Kunstausstellung in Zürich and his interest in Pablo Picasso, who he compared himself to. During these years he was also in active dialogue with the Basel-based Rot-Blau group, founded by three young Kirchner "devotees" who he mentored and promoted for a short period of time.

Alongside developing a new mode of expression, during the clearance of his Berlin studio from 1919–21 Kirchner started restoring, repainting, and ante-dating earlier works. At the beginning of the nineteen-thirties he also restored and completed earlier works in preparation for his largest retrospective exhibition to date, held in Bern in 1933.[22] These activities show that he continued to believe in his ability to establish his position as an artist in both the present and posterity. He staged himself as an outsider, an artist in voluntary exile, who was both ambitious and assertive in creating the identity of a solitary genius in the mountains. As Thorsten Sadowsky writes: "Kirchner's transformation from a hyper-nervous urban dweller into a Rousseausque existence in a rural environment should not blind us to the fact that we are talking about an eminently well-informed, very widely-read artist who was also a prolific art critic. Kirchner's attempts at repositioning his art were characterized by remarkable strategic skills."[23] Sadowsky sees Kirchner's path to individualism as a strategic choice at a point when Bauhaus aesthetics had taken over the role of Expressionism in Germany, and when other new avant-garde movements did not appeal to him. By inscribing his art in an independent narrative, in which he invented the concepts and emphasized its roots in spontaneity, he carved out a role for himself on the art scene as an original outsider and important contributor to the rejuvenation of modern art.

Control of Reception and Legacy

Self-promotion and the cultivation of a public image became more and more common among artists during the first decades of the twentieth century. This only increased with the professionalization of the art market, even among modernist artists pursuing the impersonal or even anti-personal as an aesthetic ideal. In the context of the literary world, Rod Rosenquist writes: "[T]he rising tide of impersonality in the late 1910s and early 1920s gave way to a counter current of authorial personality, notably in memoirs written during the late 1920s and 1930s."[24] Such memoirs were aimed at a broad market, and went hand in hand with the rise of celebrity culture to which elitist "fine" culture was far from exempt.[25]

Willumsen was also aware of the potential represented by the memoir. In the early twentieth century, in his late thirties, Willumsen started to write in detail about his family history and memories up until 1900. His autobiography was completed in 1939–45, and together with interviews with the then ninety-year-old Willumsen in his home in Cannes (fig. 10)[26] provided the basis for Ernst Mentze's biography of Willumsen, published in 1953. The biography is full of both Willumsen and Mentze's sense for staging the artist as an outsider in the face of opposition, an outsider described in the epilogue as a mythological figure for his generation.[27] It is easy to imagine Mentze drawing inspiration from the style of other artist biographies, such as Rolf E. Stenersen's 1945 Munch biography *Close-Up of a Genius*, Irving Stone's 1934 biographical novel based on the life of Vincent van Gogh, or other simultaneously heroizing and psychoanalytical artist portraits for which Sigmund Freud indirectly set a precedent with his 1910 text on Leonardo da Vinci. The increasing number of autobiographies by artists, such as that by Lovis Corinth from 1926 (illustrated with thirty self-portraits) may also have provided inspiration for Willumsen's memoirs.

Fig. 9
Ernst Ludwig Kirchner
Vor Sonnenaufgang
(Before Sunrise), 1925–26
Oil on canvas, 168 × 120 cm
Sammlung Glarner Kunstverein, Glarus

22. Donald E. Gordon, *Ernst Ludwig Kirchner* (Cambridge, 1968), p. 136.
23. Thorsten Sadowsky, "Flatland: The Late Work of Ernst Ludwig Kirchner," in Katharina Beisiegel, ed., *Ernst Ludwig Kirchner: Imaginary Travels*, exh. cat. Kunst und Austellungshalle der Bundesrepublik Deutschland, Bonn (Munich, London, New York, 2018), p. 324.
24. Rod Rosenquist, "Trusting Personality: Modernist Memoir and its Audience," in John Attridge and Rod Rosenquist, eds., *Incredible Modernism: Literature, Trust and Deception* (Farnham, 2013), p. 38.
25. Rod Rosenquist, "Modernism, Celebrity and the Public Persona," *Literature Compas* 10/5 (2013), pp. 438–39.
26. During these conversations Willumsen broached the possibility that he was the illegitimate son of the Danish sculptor J. A. Jerichau, for whom his mother had modelled. Despite this fitting perfectly with Willumsen's self-image, it was a theory he later abandoned. Mentze 1953 (see note 1), pp. 4–5.
27. Ibid., p. 320.

Fig. 10
J. F. Willumsen in Cannes, 1947
Photo, 18.3 × 23.6 cm
Willumsen's Museum, Frederikssund

Fig. 11a–d
Pages from Hjalmar Öhman's monograph on Willumsen, published in Copenhagen, 1921

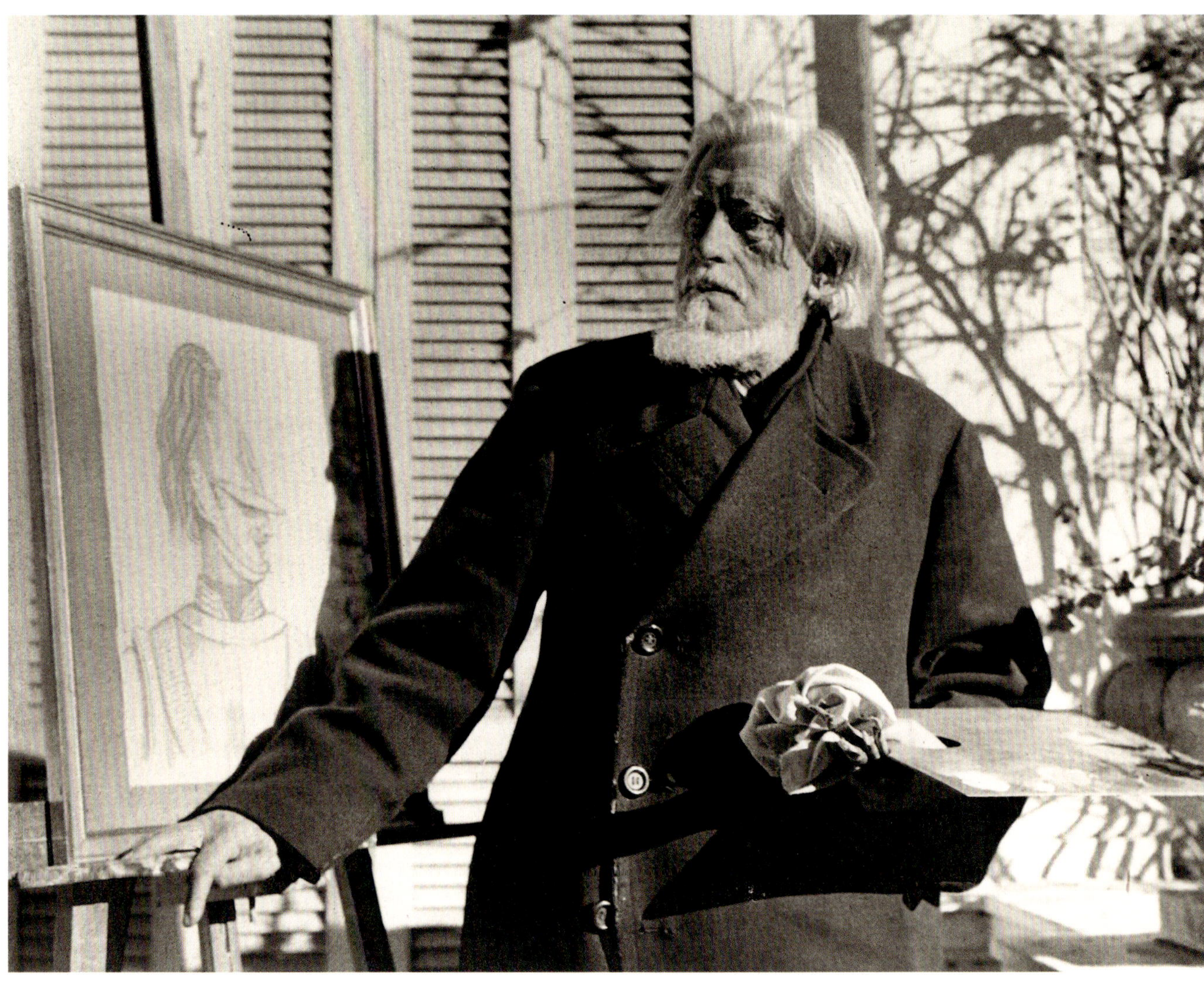

Many articles and monographs on Willumsen were published over the years. Among the monographs we find a highly unusual and unorthodox large-format book published in 1921 by the young Finnish art historian Hjalmar Öhman.[28] Despite the highly original form and design of the book, as well as its importance in Willumsen's construction of an autobiographical narrative, it has rarely been referred to in analyses of the artist. The monograph was a gushing tribute to Willumsen's genius and "revolutionary achievements," with statements such as: "It looks as if he, the denounced, has now reached the point where all taunting falls silent, and arms extend in rapture towards the glorious new standards of beauty he has created."[29] The monograph consisted of Öhman's descriptions of Willumsen's life, development as an artist, and works. Highly unusually, however, the book contained not only Öhman's views, but also Willumsen's own corrections and additions as decorative footnotes in lettering of the same size and type (figs. 11a–d). Öhman's foreword makes it clear that it was Willumsen's own radical idea to include a commentary "printed as footnotes in the context of my text."[30] Willumsen used the footnotes to make comments, correct misunderstandings, expand upon points, and add his own interpretations, but most of all he used them to

28. Hjalmar Öhman, *J.F. Willumsen: Med kommentarer af J.F. Willumsen* (Copenhagen, 1921). The manuscript and Willumsen's notes were completed in 1918, but the monograph was not published until 1921.
29. Ibid., unpaginated (p. 9).
30. Ibid., unpaginated (p. 5).

sig selv, det vil sige, bare at arbejde væk, og paa den Maade man havde Trang til, selv om det gik stik imod alle Vedtægter. Man har altid talt mest om den Indflydelse, som Gauguins Kunst havde paa min, og dog er den maaske mindre end flere andres. Jeg nævner blandt disse Raffaellis. Bretagnekonerne, der er malet før jeg gjorde Gauguins Bekendtskab, og førend jeg kendte hans Kunst, har saaledes ingen Lighed med hans. Han brugte ikke saadanne Farvetoner og malede ikke Bevægelser. Der er anden Kunst, som dengang havde stor Virkning paa mig, det var den assyriske og den ægyptiske, som jeg gjorde flere Kopier af. Det var disse, som lærte mig Simplificeringen eller Stiliseringen, baade Farvens, Linjens og Formens. Det er ogsaa dem, jeg skylder min Elskov til Keramiken og de straalende Glasurer. Endelig maa jeg ikke forbigaa den kinesiske Kunst, den japanske interesserer mig mindre. Det gaar forøvrigt saaledes med Paavirkninger, at de har ingen Magt over En, før man er naaet i Udvikling op paa Siden af det, som paavirker, man skal allerede eje en beslægtet Kunst. Det, som ligger fjærnt fra En, paavirker ikke. Gauguins Kunst var begyndt at blive noget fremmedagtig, der var allerede kommet noget afrikansk over den.

ligesaa bemalet og sminket, og Tegningen ligesaa snoet, som de jagende Kokotter. De to grønne Linjer foroven betegner Linjevirkningen af en Rutschebane, som strækker sig over hele Salen. I Midten sidder en Mand, hvis Tilbøjelighed for Kokotten ved hans Side fremstilles synlig ved ligesom at lade ham blive suget hen imod hende."

Man maa i Sandhed have en mere end almindelig Fantasi for at fremstille saadan en Buket af forsoldede Mands- og Kvindetyper som paa dette Billede, og for at udfinde en Farveskala, som saa fortræffeligt smelter sammen med Emnet, og som dannes af de mærkeligste Dissonnanser mellem graaviolette og mørkeblaa, sorte og matrøde, eller brune og graa Farver. Behandlingsmaaden minder i sin Primitivitet om Gauguins Billeder fra Tahiti. ⟨8⟩ Gauguin havde endnu

Men Willumsen nøjes ikke alene med at lade Farverne tale. Han udformer ogsaa sine Ideer i flad Træskulptur, maler dem i de bizarreste Farver og lader Fremstillingen løbe ud i Rammen, saa at denne virker med i Helheden. Bestræbelsen for at komme bort fra de forgyldte Gibsrammers Mangel paa Stil er karakteristisk for Tiden. Blandt finske Kunstnere gaar Gallén i Spidsen for Bevægelsen. Allerede til sine to Billeder fra 1880 „Paa Vej til Dødsriget" og „Triptykon af Aïnomythen" har han selv tegnet, skaaret og malet Rammerne.

To af Willumsens polykrome Træskulpturer „Kokotte paa Jagt" ⟨9⟩ Her er samt „De trællende Mennesker og den fri Dyreverden" er i Grosserer Levinsens Besiddelse, den tredie, „Jotunhejmen", eller „Ultima Thule" ⟨10⟩ Ligesom de ejes af Fru Willumsen født Meyer. Førstnævnte, „Kokotte paa Jagt", forestiller atter en Scene fra det berømte „Montagnes-russes", hvor der iblandt andre Seværdigheder ogsaa engang forevistes en Høne med fire Ben. Willumsen gengiver en af de kvindelige Stamgæster siddende ved et lille Bord med Absinthglasset foran sig og ligesom Edderkoppen i sit Net lurende paa Rov. Hendes Dragt er karakteristisk i sin tarvelige Væren paa Mode, og omkring hendes Mund og Øjne spiller et ubeskriveligt bittert Smil. Øverst i

⟨8⟩ Gauguin havde endnu ikke været paa Tahiti, da det Billede blev malet; han havde derimod set Billedet flere Gange hjemme hos mig og paa Indépendant-Udstillingen, før han rejste. Men dermed vil jeg ikke sige, at Gauguin har lært noget af mit Billede, for det ved jeg ikke. Kan det i det Hele taget tænkes, at en fransk Maler kan have lært noget af en dansk? Umuligt! Da skal Solen først have gaaet den gale Vej i nogen Tid.

⟨9⟩ Her er netop et Eksempel paa den praktiske Indflydelse, som Gauguins Kunst havde paa mig. Jeg fik nemlig Lyst til at skære et af mine Motiver i Træ, fordi at jeg hos Gauguin havde set to Relieffer, som han havde skaaret og malet. Men Emnet og Stilen er ganske ulig Gauguins.

Relieffet ser man ornamentale Fremstillinger af elektriske Glødelamper og en Buelampe.

„De trællende Mennesker og den frie Dyreverden" (Tavle VI) ⟨11⟩ Billedet viser i stærkt stiliseret Fremstilling fire Mænd, som hugger og transporterer Sten. Landskabet antydes ved stiliserede Grupper af Træer og Buske. Paa en forgyldt Sten staar en bevinget, ligeledes forgyldt Gemse. Bemalingen er gjort med stærke grelle Farver. Mændene mørkebrune med hvide Skjorter. Grønsværet af en dyb saftig Farve, hvis grønne Tone staar brutalt imod Bjærgets monotone Stenfarver. En tropisk Sol straaler over de trællende Mænd, og Virkningen heraf forøges yderligere igennem Gemsens Forgyldning. ⟨12⟩ Jeg har ikke Willumsen karakteriserer selv Værket saaledes: „Mænd bryde Sten af et Bjærg, dækket af en frodig Vegetation. De maa slide haardt for at tjene Føden, medens den paa Bjærget fritlevende Dyreverden let finder sin Føde i den rige Vege-

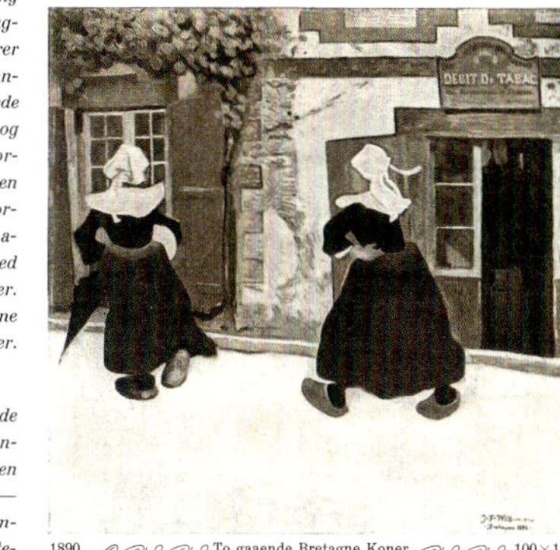
1890 To gaaende Bretagne Koner 100×100

⟨10⟩ Ligesom de andre Billeder fra den Periode, havde det ingen Titel i Udstillingskatalogerne, men en forklarende og suggestionerende Tekst. — Men imellem Vennerne blev det, for Nemheds Skyld, kaldt „Jotunhejmen" efter Stedet, hvorfra jeg hentede Motivet. Jeg tror, at det var den, som skrev Kataloget til Verdensudstillingen 1900, der gav det Titlen „Ultima Thule". Den forklarende Tekst lød saaledes:

„. . . Skyerne drev bort, og jeg befandt mig ved Randen af en Afgrund, og saa ud over et bjærgfuldt Landskab i det høje Nord, alvorligt og brutalt, dækket med evig Is og Sne, en Verden, ubeboelig for Mennesker. Under Indtrykket af denne Stemning af Alvor formede sig Sindbillederne i Relieffene. Figurerne paa Relieffet til venstre repræsenterer dem, som med fast Vilje søge ved Lærdom og Forstand at finde Forbindelsen mellem det uendeligt Store og det uendeligt Smaa. Det uendeligt Store er fremstillet ved en Stjærnetaage, det uendeligt Smaa ved nogle Mikrober. Figuren forneden er under Inspiration; Figuren foroven føler sig overbevist om det rigtige Resultat af sin Forskning. Relieffet til højre repræsenterer en Modsætning til Relieffet til venstre: det Hensigtsløse. Forneden to Mænd, af hvilke den ene fletter paa et Fletværk, som den anden løser lige saa hurtigt op. I Midten en Gruppe Indifferente. Foroven en Figur, der forestiller den kimæriske Drøm. Rammen bærer øverst en dekorativ Fremstilling af en Bjærgkæde, udført i Emalje paa Kobber."

⟨11⟩ Billedet kaldes, for Nemheds Skyld, „Den forgyldte Gemse". Og nu efter at jeg har malet et nyt Billede, der ogsaa har sit Motiv fra et Stenbrud, tillige „Stenbrud Nr. 1".

⟨12⟩ Jeg har ikke tænkt paa at ville male Solskin i dette Billede; Kunstformen egner sig ikke dertil. Det er Plastik malet med Lokalfarver. Pointen skulde ligge i Modsætningen mellem de materielle Farver, om saadant kan siges, og Guldglansen, der symboliserer en Slags Glæde. Dette Relief er et godt Eksempel paa den ægyptiske Kunst's Indflydelse.

fuldt Orkester.

Et Interiør med Lys og Farver af enestaaende Glans og Skønhed er „Sophus Clausen læser sit Digt Imperia", 1915, Levinsens Samling (Tavle XLV). Digteren, Sophus Clausen, sidder paa en Stol midt i Værelset og læser højt for sine Venner, Helge Rode og den i Baggrunden paa en Divan siddende Willumsen. Den læsende har glemt Tid og Rum. Som han sidder der og med aaben Mund deklamerer sine Digte, virker han i Stilling og Ansigtsudtryk som den, der fuldstændigt er revet hen i den Verden af Tanker og Følelser, han opruller for sine Venner. Helge Rode har drømmende kastet Hovedet bagover. Ogsaa hans Udtryk vidner om en til det komiske grænsende Interesse. Hos den i Baggrunden siddende Mester giver denne Interesse sig Udtryk i et Smil, nærmest som hos en Tryllekunstner, der har arrangeret en Effekt og afventer Resultatet. Den elskværdige Humor, som gennemsyrer hele Fremstillingen, er yderligere understreget f. Eks. i Modelleringen af Rodes Ben og Sko. Det hele virker som et muntert Indfald, der har revet Fortællertalentet med sig. Men ud fra Billedet straaler ogsaa en Varme og Sympati, som ikke er til at tage fejl af. Den lyser i den pragtfulde, herlige Farve og den glimrende Belysning. Det stærke, gule Lys, som strømmer ud over Væggens grønne og Tæppernes brogede Farvepragt, spreder en Stemning af noget fantastisk, af Inspiration og Digt over hele Scenen, netop som det passer til Situationen.

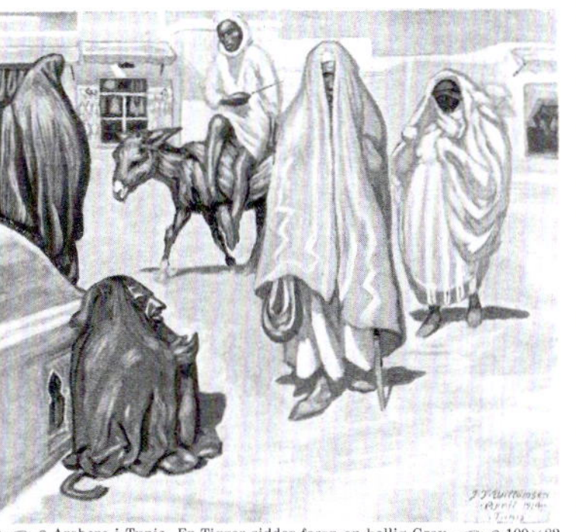
1914 Arabere i Tunis. En Tigger sidder foran en hellig Grav 100×82

Fra en spansk Rejse i 1915 findes i Levinsens Samling et Maleri („Ved Fontænen i Toledo. I Baggrunden Kathedralens Taarn"), som visselig ikke ved sit Motiv, men derimod igennem den Betagelse, man kunde næsten sige Beruselse i Farvefølelse og Stil, med hvilken det er malet, hører til det vidunderligste, Willumsen har frembragt. (Tavle XLVI). Et Anlæg i Toledo med den gotiske Kathedral i Baggrunden og en Fontæne, ved hvis Bassin nogle Kvinder henter Vand, er Motivet. Men allerede den Maade, hvorpaa Taarnets graagrønne Kærne opløser sig i de mørkeblaa Udløbere og disse igen i Himlens grønne og mørkeblaa Uendelighed, er højst aparte, vidunderlig og fin. Fantastisk som et maurisk Eventyr fremtræder Parktræernes Form og Farver, som veksler i Nuancer af grønt, blaat og mørkebrunt med kridhvide eller lysegrønne Lys, ligesom Farvespillet paa Gangenes Sand og Græsplænerne, hvor blodrødt kæmper med det skæreste lysegrønne, og violette og sorte Skygger spiller ind imellem de gule og hvide Lys. Aldrig er et Friluftsmaleri malet med højere Farveinspiration, aldrig har en mere betagende Fantasi omdigtet Virkeligheden og fyldt den med kunstnerisk Henrykkelse.

Excelsior! Stadig højere op mod Fuldkommenheden! Det er Willumsens Devise. At gøre et Billede bedre og bedre, selv at blive bedre og bedre som Kunstner har altid været hans Maal. Tegninger, farvelagte Studier, Akvareller og Pasteller er kun Forberedelser til det egentlige Billede. Paa denne Maade har han altid korrigeret sig selv, arbejdet sig frem til paa den mest fuldkomne Maade at give Udtryk for den Idé, der beskæftiger ham. Han har prøvet sine Figurkompositioner gennem at modellere dem i Voks og Gips. Der findes saadanne Modeller til „Efter Stormen", „De svævende Drenge" og til „Sol og Ungdom", som han har modelleret i de sværeste Stillinger og Forkortninger. Først naar han gennem adskillige Billeder (som i Rækken af Bjergbestigersker), kommer til det Punkt, at Fremstillingen tilfredsstiller ham, giver han Slip paa Motivet.

Til Trods for denne intensive Kamp og Stræben har Willumsen indtil nu været uforstaaet og miskendt af sine Landsmænd. „Man har ikke Brug for mig i Danmark" var hans Ord, naar han fulgte sit Hjertes Lyst og begav sig ud paa Rejser. Han blev bitter over den bristende Forstaaelse af hans Kunst, over Manglen paa Interesse og over den Kulde, som aldrig ophørte. Kun nogle faa Beundrere og trofaste Venner købte hans Arbejder. Han fik ingen offentlige Bestillinger. Med beundringsværdig Standhaftighed og Trofasthed deltog han atter og atter i offentlige Konkurrencer om kunstneriske Opgaver. Han konkurrerede om Freskomalerier i Universitetets Solennitetssal og i Raadhuset, om Dekoreringen af Christian den Niendes Gravkapel i Roskilde Domkirke, og gjorde paa Opfordring et Udkast til Udsmykningen af Tronsalen i det nye Christiansborg. Han viste sin Interesse og Begejstring. Men hver Gang blev han vist tilbage, forbigaaet. Nu begynder Skællene at falde fra Menneskenes Øjne, og de ser Dybden og Skønheden i Willumsens Kunst. Men i Christiansborg, hvor Arbejdet syder ude og inde, har han, den alsidigste, genialeste og den i dekorativ Kunst mest forfarne af alle Danmarks Kunstnere, ikke faaet nogen Opgave.

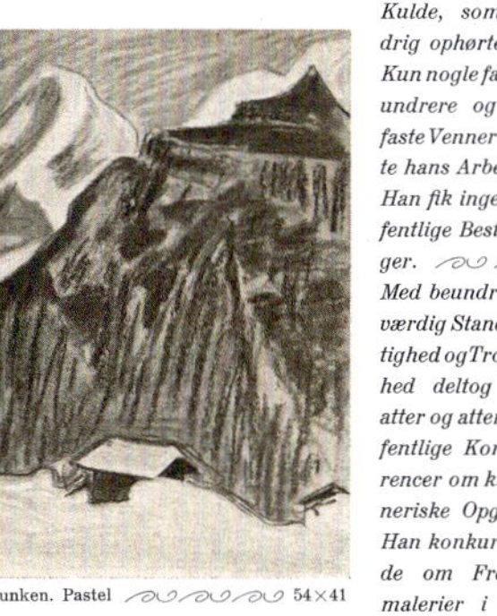
1914 Jomfruen og Munken. Pastel 54×41

⟨44⟩ Det er efterhaanden slaaet fast, at den danske Natur og den danske Folkekarakter skal kaldes blid.

Er der da ikke nok saa megen Regn, Blæst, Storm, som Solskin og Stille? Der er næsten altid en Vind, som skærer ind til Knoglerne.

Er Danske mere blide end andre af Jordklodens Mennesker?

Er der ikke altfor mange, som er hidsige, krakilske og nederdrægtige?

Hvormange af dem er vel Engle?

Er der virkelig saa stor Forskel mellem de Danske og de fleste andre Folk, der lever Norden for Firenze?

Jeg blev igaar betjent af en italiensk Skomager; han kunde, uden at jeg vilde have set noget fremmed ved ham, meget godt have haft sin Forretning i Regnegade eller i Stormgade!

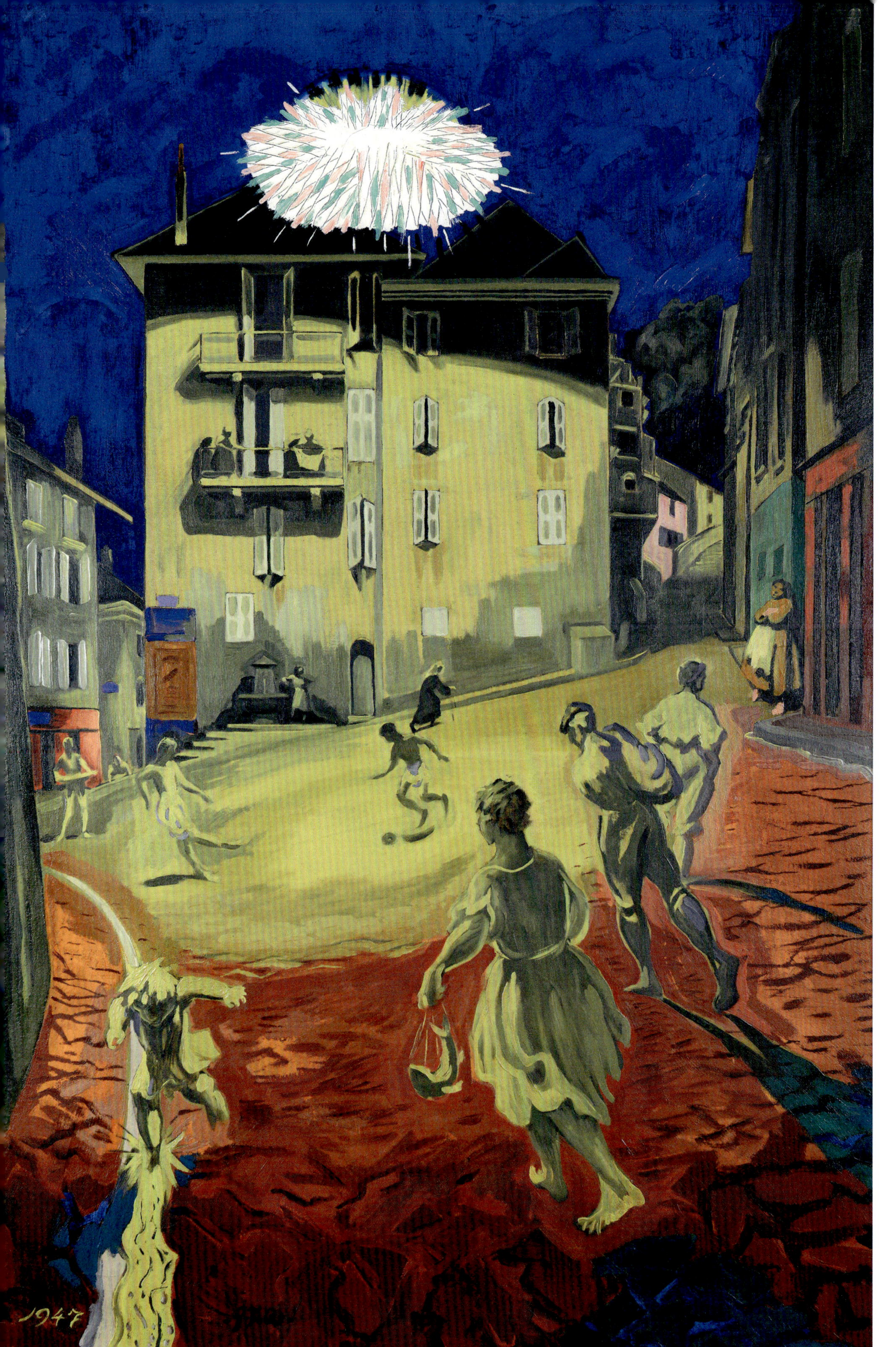
1947

stage himself as an artist who went his own way, uninfluenced—apart from superficially—by French art. Over several pages he specifically rejected the idea that his meeting with Paul Gauguin in Pont-Aven in 1890 had any impact on him artistically. In opposition to any such interpretation, he constantly stressed his own individuality and unique personal development as an artist.[31] The monograph was a heroization of Willumsen's artistic autonomy, paying homage to the art he created as being borne by universal power and absolute originality.

Fighting for a Place in Art History

During the nineteen-thirties, the self-mythologizing of the artist gathered momentum with his plans and campaigns for a Willumsen Museum. When it was finally built in 1957, however, it was not what Willumsen had originally envisioned. The well-travelled artist had been based in the South of France since 1916, and had imagined his return to Denmark being accompanied by pomp and circumstance and a museum not only presenting his works and art collection, but also housing an artist's residence and atelier.[32] Willumsen's plans clearly demonstrate his determination to exercise complete control over his oeuvre and legacy. We can imagine the artist, upon completing a new work, deciding whether it was to be sold or hung in the museum he envisioned being built next to his studio. The idea of staging himself as a working artist in his own museum borders on megalomania, but also symbolizes his need to be in control. When his plans to create a fitting museum failed in the face of constant delays and postponements, Willumsen chose to remain in self-imposed exile. He had two options: to return to Denmark in triumph, or to remain the maladjusted, martyred emigrant who continued to cause a scandal every year when his latest works were exhibited in Denmark (fig. 12).

Unlike Kirchner, Willumsen had no proud, national tradition to relate to. He identified with the nineteenth-century sculptor Bertel Thorvaldsen, but no other Danish artist really interested him. Instead, he turned to the south, focusing on Venetian Renaissance art. Willumsen embraced this canon of Titian and his Venetian successors, and created an extensive collection of older art, albeit one with repeated erroneous attributions of works to artists such as Titian, Leonardo da Vinci, Raphael, Rubens, and Rembrandt. He used his collection to create references for his own art practice, as well as a narrative he wanted to be part of, something he reinforced by restoring and modifying older works in his collection. Rather than being a Danish artist influenced by modern French art, Willumsen worked actively to establish a position for himself in the European art canon.[33]

This rejection of modern French art in order to emphasize his own originality was shared by Kirchner. In *Chronik der Künstlergruppe Brücke*, Kirchner not only failed entirely to acknowledge the influence of French artists such as Paul Gauguin and Henri Matisse, but also ignored the importance of the Neo-Impressionists and Fauvists for the group. In doing so, he refuted earlier analyses of the Brücke artists as the successors of Vincent van Gogh and French predecessors, positioning the group as practitioners of German art with roots in the Middle Ages and with Dürer as a father figure.[34] That the early works of Kirchner and the other Brücke artists have clear echoes of Van Gogh's art is the perfect example of the text's deliberate rewriting of history, demonstrating the complexity of being at the very heart of contemporary art movements, at the same time as promoting one's unique place in art history.

Around 1900, Dürer was the subject of increased attention, and Kirchner's interest in the artist therefore followed the contemporary *zeitgeist* (just as Willumsen's interest in El Greco was typical of his time).[35] This identification with Dürer, however, lasted throughout Kirchner's life, and was expressed in numerous contexts. As the first artist to paint self-portraits reflecting the new Renaissance artist, Dürer's self-representations were

Fig. 12
J. F. Willumsen
Boldspillere på gaden i Cannes (People Playing Ball in a Street in Cannes), 1947
Oil on canvas, 151.5 × 99 cm
KUNSTEN Museum of Modern Art Aalborg

31. Ibid., unpaginated (p. 15). That Gauguin had had a major impact on Willumsen's development as an artist was constantly reiterated by art historians and critics, so denying such claims was crucial for Willumsen.
32. See Hjorth 2006 (see note 10), chapter 6.
33. Anne Gregersen, "J. F. Willumsen's Collections, Collage Aesthetics, and Modifications of the Past," in Gregersen 2018 (see note 15).
34. Weikop 2012 (see note 2), p. 409.
35. Magdalena Moeller, "Kirchner as a German Artist," in Lloyd and Moeller 2003 (see note 18), p. 23. One of the Danish artists who was most interested in Dürer at the time was the painter Jens Adolf Jerichau. Dürer was also among the artists Willumsen was interested in, and whose prints he tried to acquire for his collection.

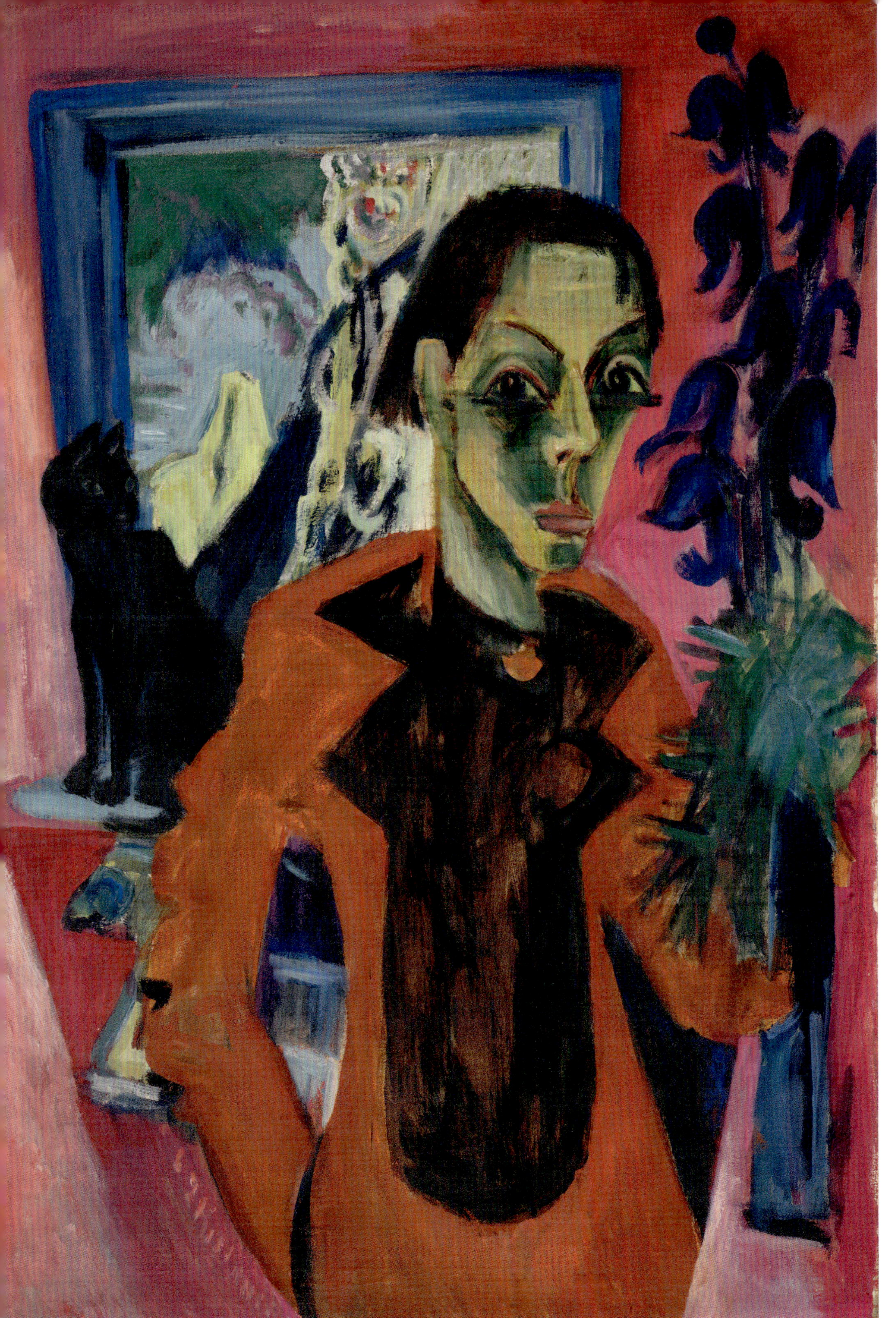

Fig. 13
Ernst Ludwig Kirchner
Selbstporträt mit Katze
(Self-Portrait with Cat), 1920
Oil on canvas,
120.6 × 80 cm
Harvard Art Museums/
Busch-Reisinger Museum,
Cambridge

crucial to Kirchner and something he referenced in his own works. In a 1920 self-portrait, Kirchner stands, as usual, at the very front of the painting with one of his own paintings in the background and his cat Boby by his side (fig. 13). The painting is reminiscent of the first of three famous self-portraits by Dürer from the late fifteenth century (fig. 14). In the self-portrait, Dürer holds a thistle in his right hand—a symbol of marital fidelity, as well as a possible reference to Christ's crown of thorns. In his own self-portrait, the botanically interested Kirchner also holds a plant that looks like the poisonous monkshood, the violet flowers of which hang heavily. According to Greek mythology, this deadly plant grew at the entrance to Hades and was later used as arrow poison and in witches' ointments, making the plant's symbolism as tangible as the firm grip with which Kirchner holds it. Like Dürer, Kirchner portrays himself in three-quarter profile, looking directly at the viewer. Kirchner's portrait appears harsher and more expressive than Dürer's, but both self-portraits express the same self-aggrandizing attitude. Kirchner's yellowish-green, pointed, and mask-like face with its deep eye sockets and penetrating gaze add to the portrait's previously mentioned duality of triumph and defeat, empowerment, and marginalization. It is as if Kirchner insists that the viewer identify with his pain, at the same time as asserting his superiority as a creative individual and status as the descendant of a long, proud tradition.

Being One's Own Critic

For modern artists with a sense for staging the self, autobiographies, monographs, and art-philosophical texts were obvious ways to control the reception of their work and create myths about their persona. Christian Weikop has analyzed Kirchner's use of texts to position himself and control the reception of his oeuvre through *Chronik der Künstlergruppe Brücke,* artist statements, correspondence, contributions to journals, diary entries, and exhibition catalogues. Whilst Willumsen inserted "footnotes" in his monograph, Kirchner edited texts about his work to such an extent that he functioned as co-author, if not ghost-

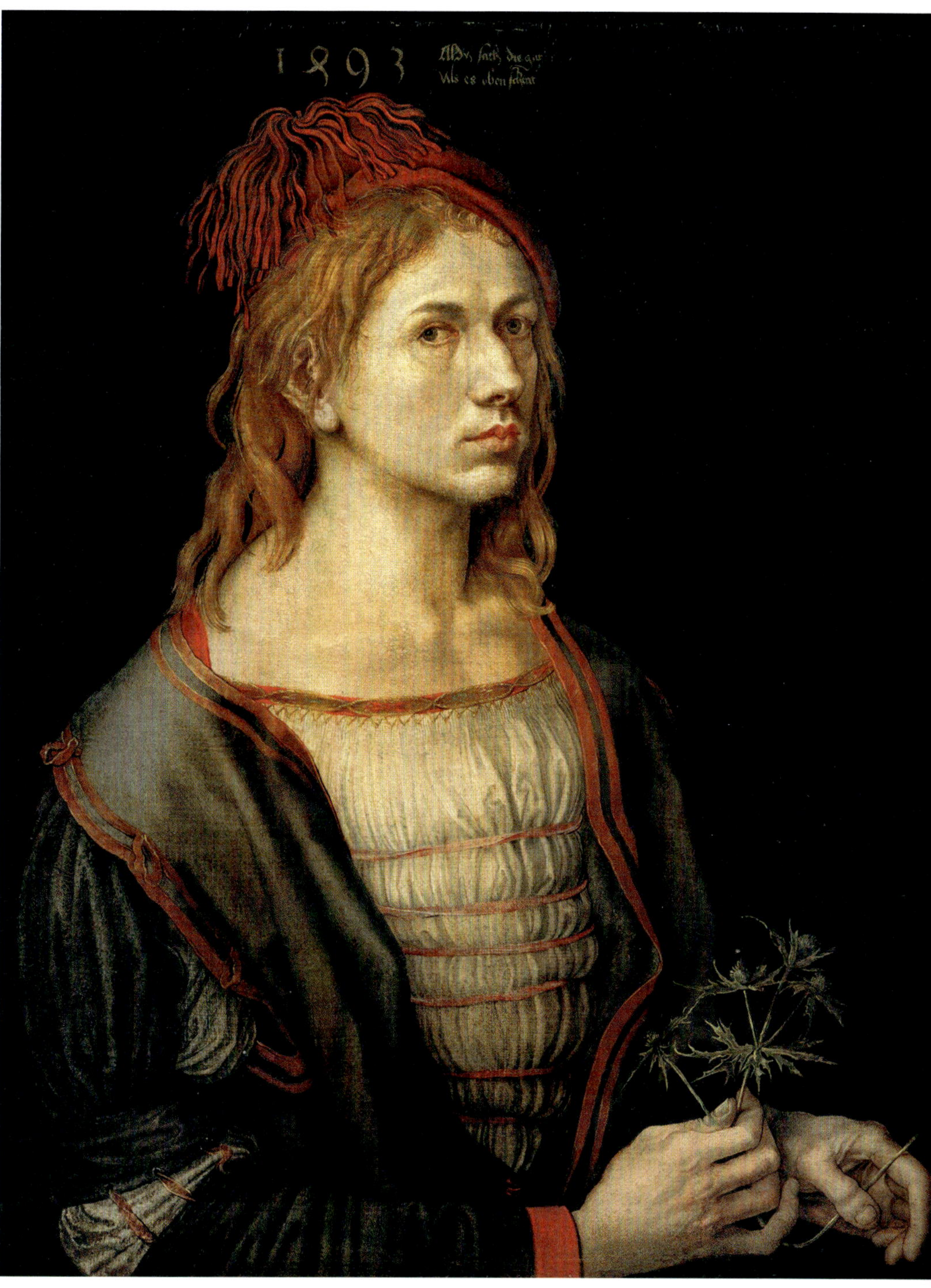

Fig. 14
Albrect Dürer
Portrait of the Artist Holding a Thistle, 1493
Oil on vellum transferred to canvas, 56.5 × 44.5 cm
Musée du Louvre, Paris

writer.[36] Kirchner, however, went a step further than Willumsen, using fiction to reconstruct reality.

In 1920 Kirchner told his friends and acquaintances with enthusiasm about a well-travelled and progressive art critic called Louis de Marsalle, who had a unique understanding of his art. Subsequently the critic's interpretation of Kirchner's "idiosyncratic manner of representation," "hieroglyphic script," and spontaneously refreshing style reflecting the experience of modern life could be followed in his writings. Louis de Marsalle was, however, a pseudonym invented by Kirchner himself. Just as Walt Whitman had done in 1855, when he wrote a notorious, lengthy, and unreservedly laudatory review of his much maligned poetry collection *Leaves of Grass* and published it anonymously,[37] Kirchner invented an art critic to present himself as a remarkably original, German artist expressing the qualities of his country and making a unique contribution to contemporary culture.

Given that Kirchner identified as a *German* artist continuing a national tradition, it seems somewhat remarkable that he invented a *French* critic to write about his work. Yet from his self-imposed exile in Switzerland, the artist continued to try to achieve recognition both within and beyond the borders of his homeland. Furthermore, a French critic would have more authority in maintaining that Kirchner's art had developed independently of con-

36. Weikop 2012 (see note 2), p. 412. As Uwe Fleckner argues in his contribution to this publication, this level of control was especially extreme in relationship to the German author and art historian Carl Einstein, who Kirchner paradoxically ended up appreciating as having a particularly good understanding of his art, and who also validated his belief that he had a unique artistic vision.

37. Walt Whitman [original, unsigned], "Walt Whitman and His Poems," September 1855. *The Walt Whitman Archive*. Accessed 02.04.2020. http://www.whitmanarchive.org.

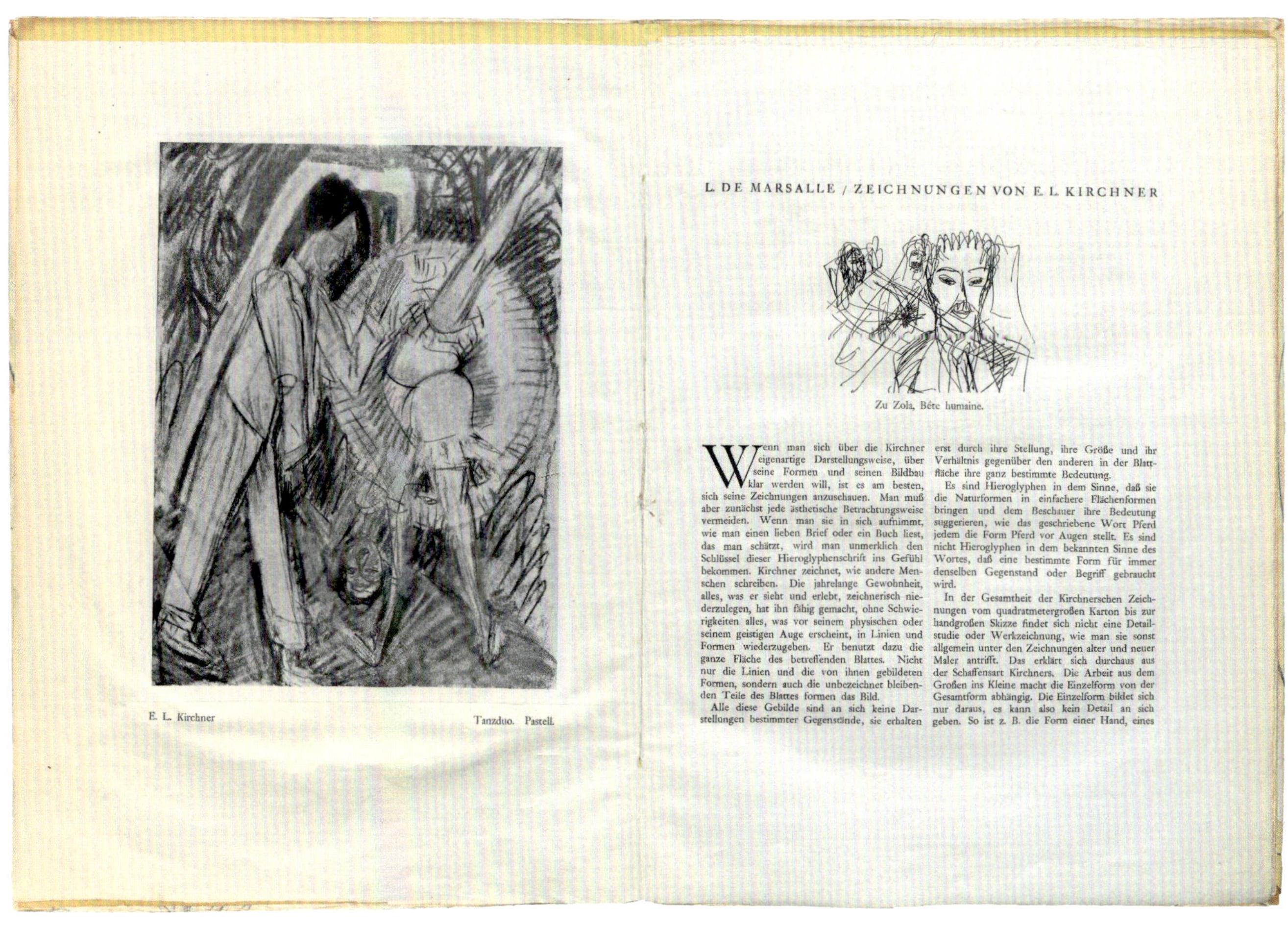
E. L. Kirchner Tanzduo. Pastell.

L. DE MARSALLE / ZEICHNUNGEN VON E. L. KIRCHNER

Zu Zola, Bête humaine.

Wenn man sich über die Kirchner eigenartige Darstellungsweise, über seine Formen und seinen Bildbau klar werden will, ist es am besten, sich seine Zeichnungen anzuschauen. Man muß aber zunächst jede ästhetische Betrachtungsweise vermeiden. Wenn man sie in sich aufnimmt, wie man einen lieben Brief oder ein Buch liest, das man schätzt, wird man unmerklich den Schlüssel dieser Hieroglyphenschrift ins Gefühl bekommen. Kirchner zeichnet, wie andere Menschen schreiben. Die jahrelange Gewohnheit, alles, was er sieht und erlebt, zeichnerisch niederzulegen, hat ihn fähig gemacht, ohne Schwierigkeiten alles, was vor seinem physischen oder seinem geistigen Auge erscheint, in Linien und Formen wiederzugeben. Er benutzt dazu die ganze Fläche des betreffenden Blattes. Nicht nur die Linien und die von ihnen gebildeten Formen, sondern auch die unbezeichnet bleibenden Teile des Blattes formen das Bild.

Alle diese Gebilde sind an sich keine Darstellungen bestimmter Gegenstände, sie erhalten erst durch ihre Stellung, ihre Größe und ihr Verhältnis gegenüber den anderen in der Blattfläche ihre ganz bestimmte Bedeutung.

Es sind Hieroglyphen in dem Sinne, daß sie die Naturformen in einfachere Flächenformen bringen und dem Beschauer ihre Bedeutung suggerieren, wie das geschriebene Wort Pferd jedem die Form Pferd vor Augen stellt. Es sind nicht Hieroglyphen in dem bekannten Sinne des Wortes, daß eine bestimmte Form für immer denselben Gegenstand oder Begriff gebraucht wird.

In der Gesamtheit der Kirchnerschen Zeichnungen vom quadratmetergroßen Karton bis zur handgroßen Skizze findet sich nicht eine Detailstudie oder Werkzeichnung, wie man sie sonst allgemein unter den Zeichnungen alter und neuer Maler antrifft. Das erklärt sich durchaus aus der Schaffensart Kirchners. Die Arbeit aus dem Großen ins Kleine macht die Einzelform von der Gesamtform abhängig. Die Einzelform bildet sich nur daraus, es kann also kein Detail an sich geben. So ist z. B. die Form einer Hand, eines

Fig. 15a-b
Spreads from Ernst Ludwig Kirchner / Louis de Marsalle, "Zeichnungen von E.L. Kirchner," in *Genius—Zeitschrift für werdende und alte Kunst*, 2:2 (1920)

temporary French art. As Weikop points out, in 1923 Kirchner wrote to his friend, the art collector and critic Gustav Schiefler, that he hoped "precisely with the help of this Frenchman, to prove that my art really emerged and developed purely and independently of contemporary French art."[38]

Under the pseudonym, Kirchner wrote no less than six articles published between 1920–33, on aspects of his own art.[39] De Marsalle's last text was written for the catalogue of the retrospective exhibition in Bern mentioned above, a text in which Kirchner was once again portrayed as possessing a uniquely visionary talent, which later in life connected to his early development, thus bringing his artistic powers full circle. After this the Frenchman passed away, and Kirchner avoided revealing the critic's true identity. Via Louis de Marsalle, Kirchner could present himself as he wished to be seen, and also correct the attempts of earlier critics to locate him in a French art tradition or attribute his time with the Brücke group any real significance. He could also create an image of himself as ahead of his time, yet part of it, and as deeply rooted in German art. He thus contributed directly to the creation of a manipulated, romanticized version of his artistic path from the early years in Dresden to his exile in Davos, where according to de Marsalle he was the first painter since Ferdinand Hodler to paint the mountains in a new way.[40]

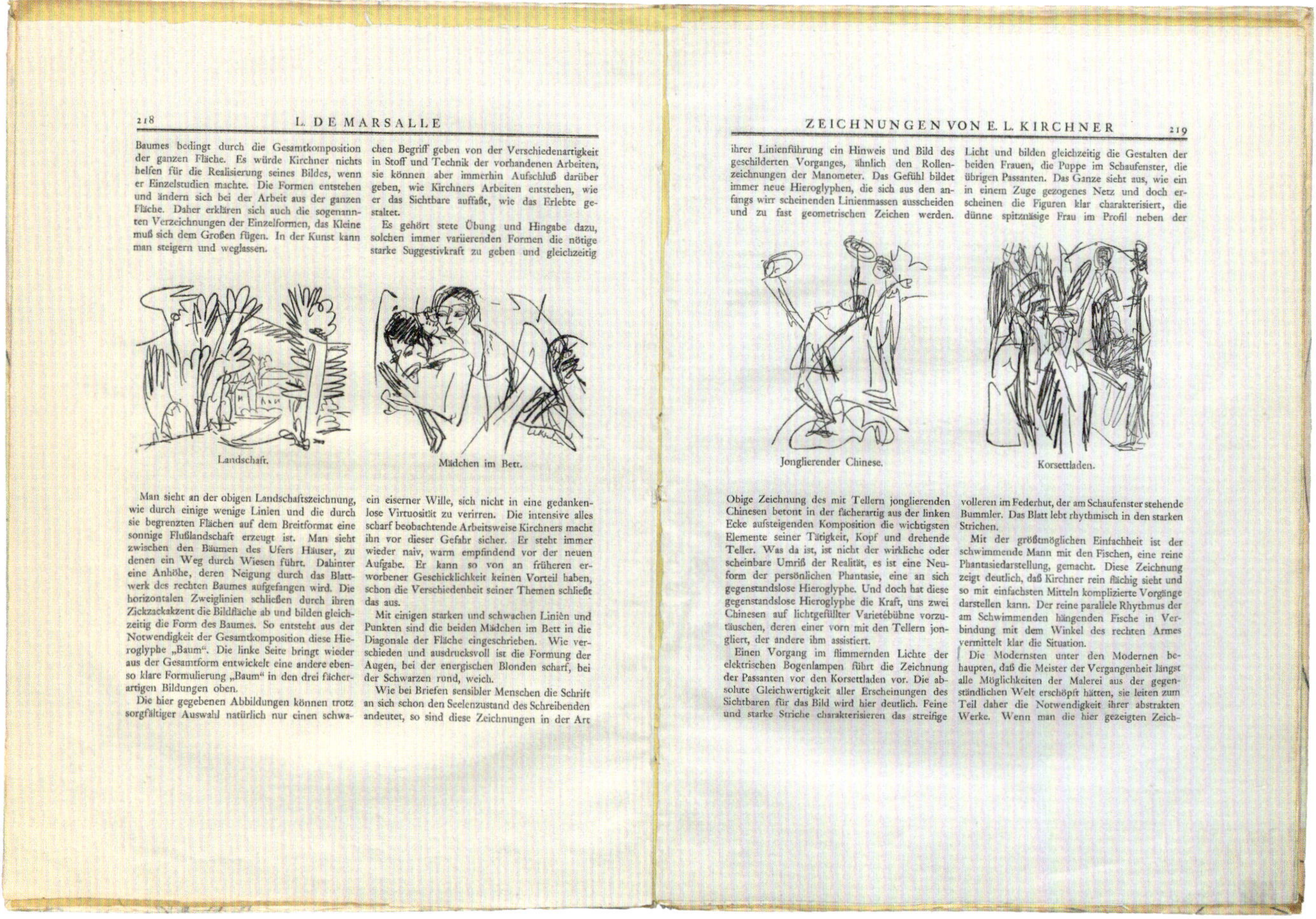

218 L. DE MARSALLE

Baumes bedingt durch die Gesamtkomposition der ganzen Fläche. Es würde Kirchner nichts helfen für die Realisierung seines Bildes, wenn er Einzelstudien machte. Die Formen entstehen und ändern sich bei der Arbeit aus der ganzen Fläche. Daher erklären sich auch die sogenannten Verzeichnungen der Einzelformen, das Kleine muß sich dem Großen fügen. In der Kunst kann man steigern und weglassen.

chen Begriff geben von der Verschiedenartigkeit in Stoff und Technik der vorhandenen Arbeiten, sie können aber immerhin Aufschluß darüber geben, wie Kirchners Arbeiten entstehen, wie er das Sichtbare auffaßt, wie das Erlebte gestaltet.

Es gehört stete Übung und Hingabe dazu, solchen immer variierenden Formen die nötige starke Suggestivkraft zu geben und gleichzeitig

Landschaft.

Mädchen im Bett.

Man sieht an der obigen Landschaftszeichnung, wie durch einige wenige Linien und die durch sie begrenzten Flächen auf dem Breitformat eine sonnige Flußlandschaft erzeugt ist. Man sieht zwischen den Bäumen des Ufers Häuser, zu denen ein Weg durch Wiesen führt. Dahinter eine Anhöhe, deren Neigung durch das Blattwerk des rechten Baumes aufgefangen wird. Die horizontalen Zweiglinien schließen durch ihren Zickzackakzent die Bildfläche ab und bilden gleichzeitig die Form des Baumes. So entsteht aus der Notwendigkeit der Gesamtkomposition diese Hieroglyphe „Baum". Die linke Seite bringt wieder aus der Gesamtform entwickelt eine andere ebenso klare Formulierung „Baum" in den drei fächerartigen Bildungen oben.

Die hier gegebenen Abbildungen können trotz sorgfältiger Auswahl natürlich nur einen schwa-

ein eiserner Wille, sich nicht in eine gedankenlose Virtuosität zu verirren. Die intensive alles scharf beobachtende Arbeitsweise Kirchners macht ihn vor dieser Gefahr sicher. Er steht immer wieder naiv, warm empfindend vor der neuen Aufgabe. Er kann so von an früheren erworbener Geschicklichkeit keinen Vorteil haben, schon die Verschiedenheit seiner Themen schließt das aus.

Mit einigen starken und schwachen Liniën und Punkten sind die beiden Mädchen im Bett in die Diagonale der Fläche eingeschrieben. Wie verschieden und ausdrucksvoll ist die Formung der Augen, bei der energischen Blonden scharf, bei der Schwarzen rund, weich.

Wie bei Briefen sensibler Menschen die Schrift an sich schon den Seelenzustand des Schreibenden andeutet, so sind diese Zeichnungen in der Art

ZEICHNUNGEN VON E. L. KIRCHNER 219

ihrer Linienführung ein Hinweis und Bild des geschilderten Vorganges, ähnlich den Rollenzeichnungen der Manometer. Das Gefühl bildet immer neue Hieroglyphen, die sich aus den anfangs wirr scheinenden Linienmassen ausscheiden und zu fast geometrischen Zeichen werden.

Licht und bilden gleichzeitig die Gestalten der beiden Frauen, die Puppe im Schaufenster, die übrigen Passanten. Das Ganze sieht aus, wie ein in einem Zuge gezogenes Netz und doch erscheinen die Figuren klar charakterisiert, die dünne spitznäsige Frau im Profil neben der

Jonglierender Chinese.

Korsettladen.

Obige Zeichnung des mit Tellern jonglierenden Chinesen betont in der fächerartig aus der linken Ecke aufsteigenden Komposition die wichtigsten Elemente seiner Tätigkeit, Kopf und drehende Teller. Was da ist, ist nicht der wirkliche oder scheinbare Umriß der Realität, es ist eine Neuform der persönlichen Phantasie, eine an sich gegenstandslose Hieroglyphe. Und doch hat diese gegenstandslose Hieroglyphe die Kraft, uns zwei Chinesen auf lichtgefüllter Varietébühne vorzutäuschen, deren einer vorn mit den Tellern jongliert, der andere ihm assistiert.

Einen Vorgang im flimmernden Lichte der elektrischen Bogenlampen führt die Zeichnung der Passanten vor den Korsettladen vor. Die absolute Gleichwertigkeit aller Erscheinungen des Sichtbaren für das Bild wird hier deutlich. Feine und starke Striche charakterisieren das streifige

volleren im Federhut, der am Schaufenster stehende Bummler. Das Blatt lebt rhythmisch in den starken Strichen.

Mit der größtmöglichen Einfachheit ist der schwimmende Mann mit den Fischen, eine reine Phantasiedarstellung, gemacht. Diese Zeichnung zeigt deutlich, daß Kirchner rein flächig sieht und so mit einfachsten Mitteln komplizierte Vorgänge darstellen kann. Der reine parallele Rhythmus der am Schwimmenden hängenden Fische in Verbindung mit dem Winkel des rechten Armes vermittelt klar die Situation.

Die Modernsten unter den Modernen behaupten, daß die Meister der Vergangenheit längst alle Möglichkeiten der Malerei aus der gegenständlichen Welt erschöpft hätten, sie leiten zum Teil daher die Notwendigkeit ihrer abstrakten Werke. Wenn man die hier gezeigten Zeich-

38. "... gerade mit Hilfe dieses Franzosen beweisen zu können, dass meine Arbeit wirklich unabhängig und rein von der zeitgenössischen französischen Kunst entstand und sich entwickelt hat." Kirchner to Schiefler, January 9, 1923. Cited by Weikop 2012 (see note 2) after Ernst Ludwig Kirchner—Gustav Schiefler, *Briefwechsel 1910–1935/38*, ed. Wolfgang Henze (Stuttgart/Zürich, 1990), p. 214.

39. In chronological order, the six texts published under the pseudonym Louis de Marsalle are: "Zeichnungen von Ernst Ludwig Kirchner," *Genius*, 2:2 (1920); "Über die Schweizer Arbeiten von E.L. Kirchner" (Frankfurt am Main, 1921); "Über Kirchners Graphik," *Genius*, 3:2 (1921); "Über die plastichen Arbeiten E.L. Kirchners," *Der Cicerone*, 17–14 (1925); "Vorwort," in *Ausstellung der Graphik von E.L. Kirchner*, exh. cat. Aktuaryus Galerie (Zürich, 1927), and finally a contribution to the catalogue *Ernst Ludwig Kirchner*, Kunsthalle Bern (1933). English translations of two of the texts can be found in Lloyd and Moeller 2003 (see note 18): "E. L. Kirchners Drawings" and "On Kirchner's Graphic Works."

40. Foreword to *Ausstellung der Graphik von E. L. Kirchner* (see note 40). Republished in Lothar Grisebach, ed., *Ernst Ludwig Kirchners Davoser Tagebuch* (Cologne, 1968), pp. 226–27. Cited by Bernard Mendes Bürgi in "Painter of the Alps" in Bernard Mendes Bürgi, ed., *Ernst Ludwig Kirchner—Mountain Life: The Early Years in Davos, 1917–1926*, exh. cat. Kunstmuseum Basel (Ostfildern, 2003), p. 13.

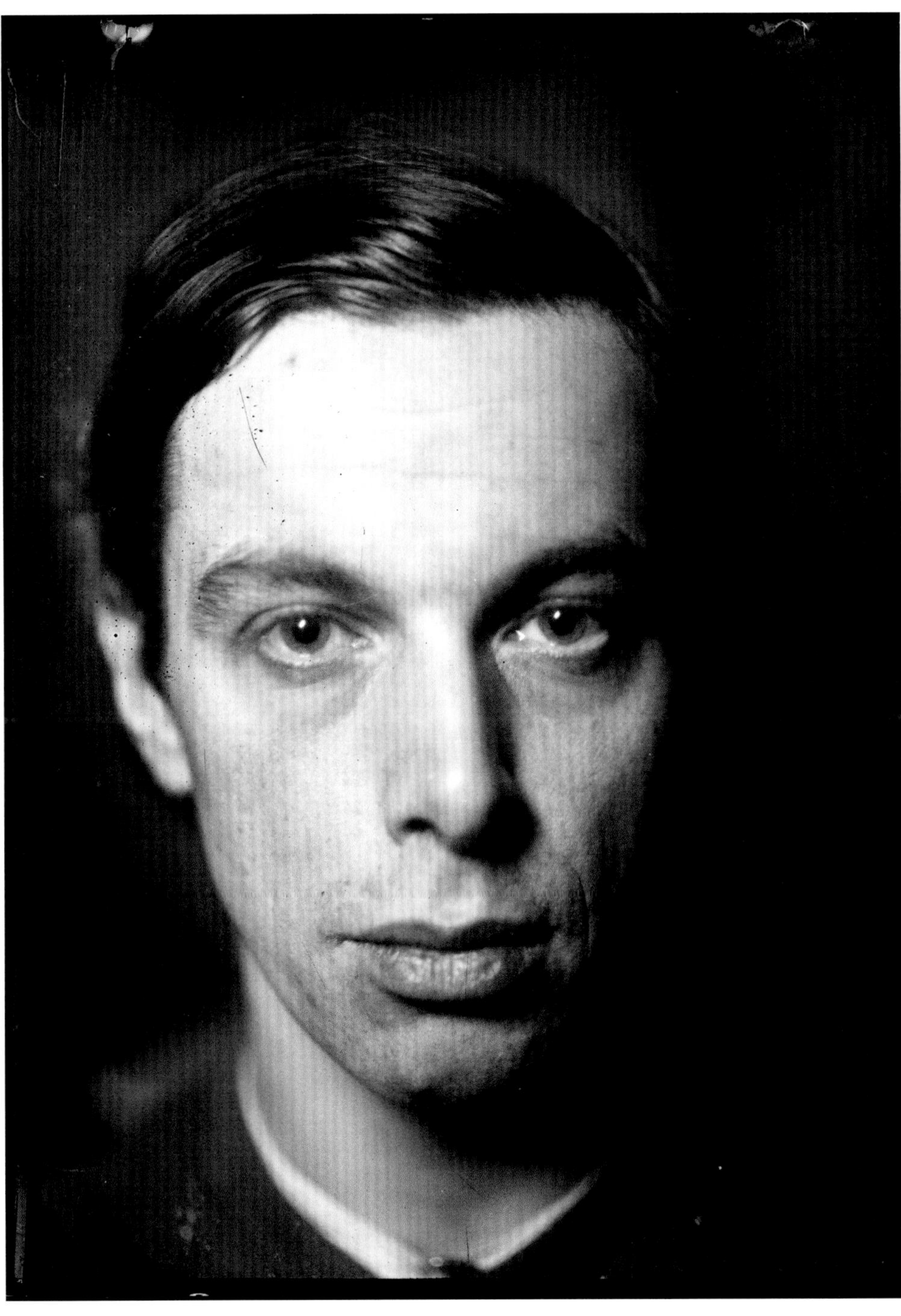

Fig. 16
Ernst Ludwig Kirchner, *Self-Portrait*, ca. 1919
Glass-plate negative, 24 × 18 cm
Kirchner Museum Davos

Two texts on Kirchner's drawings (figs. 15a–b) and graphic works, published under the pseudonym in 1920–21 in the journal *Genius*, praise the artist's spontaneity, technical skill, and constant progress, as well as introducing hieroglyphics in relationship to his art. The impression given is that of an artist who had spontaneously sought out and incorporated old printing techniques, mastering them with superior ease and immediacy. An almost spiritual link is made between the invention of printing in the Middle Ages and Kirchner's use of the technique, but the texts are otherwise free of art-historical references and concepts. Kirchner is presented as an original artist working with what is described in one instance as "naïve delight," and elsewhere as a spontaneous, warm sensitivity without the use of previously acquired skills.[41]

Kirchner used these texts to underline his position as a figurative artist, who unlike "the most modern of the modern" was not averse to representing the physical world, but revealed a new and individual way to bring visible reality into art. The de Marsalle texts also expand on Kirchner's previous self-presentation and view of his own art practice as powerful, unmediated, and direct. The production as well as content of the texts are characterized by a degree of control and megalomania also encountered in Willumsen, although the latter continued to stand as the author of his views on his importance as an artist.

The Road to Self-Mythologization

Like other artists at the time, Willumsen and the seventeen-year-younger Kirchner (figs. 16 and 17) aimed to position themselves on the contemporary art scene and in art history. Their path led from community and group identity to self-imposed exile and self-mythologization. As described in this article, this development can be seen

41. Quoted from the English translation "On Kirchner's Graphic Works" in Lloyd and Moeller 2003 (see note 18), p. 229.

as deriving from but also as a consciously calculated and performative factor in creating an artistic identity. The individualistic quest of both artists developed with time. They also wanted to convince the art world of the validity of this quest, and carve out a position for themselves on an art scene dominated by new movements with abstract, concrete, and conceptual ideals they did not identify with. They continued to take the visible world as the starting point for their figurative, intensely colored, heavily symbolic art, experimenting with different styles and identifying their ideals by building bridges to the art of the past and artists such as El Greco and Dürer.

One of the roles Kirchner and Willumsen identified with was that of the empowered yet marginalized artist. Even though this role was commercially viable and a means of promoting their originality, it ended up being a better fit than Willumsen and Kirchner had ever intended. Both artists had to wait to achieve recognition for what they saw as their full maturation as artists. Instead, it was the time they spent as part of broader artistic movements and art communities that guaranteed them a place in art history. In his native Denmark, Willumsen was famous for his Symbolist works of the eighteen-nineties, whilst Kirchner had his international breakthrough with the Expressionism of the Brücke group.

Individualism, with all its agonies and triumphs, was lived out but also fabricated by Kirchner and Willumsen as a means of making their art unique and essential. This individualistic standpoint and its contemporary rejection contributed to their late works—the style of which is furthest removed from contemporary art movements—failing to receive recognition and being seen as less important than their early works. Their self-mythologizing as individualists was successful, but controlling the reception of their works was a battle that proved impossible to

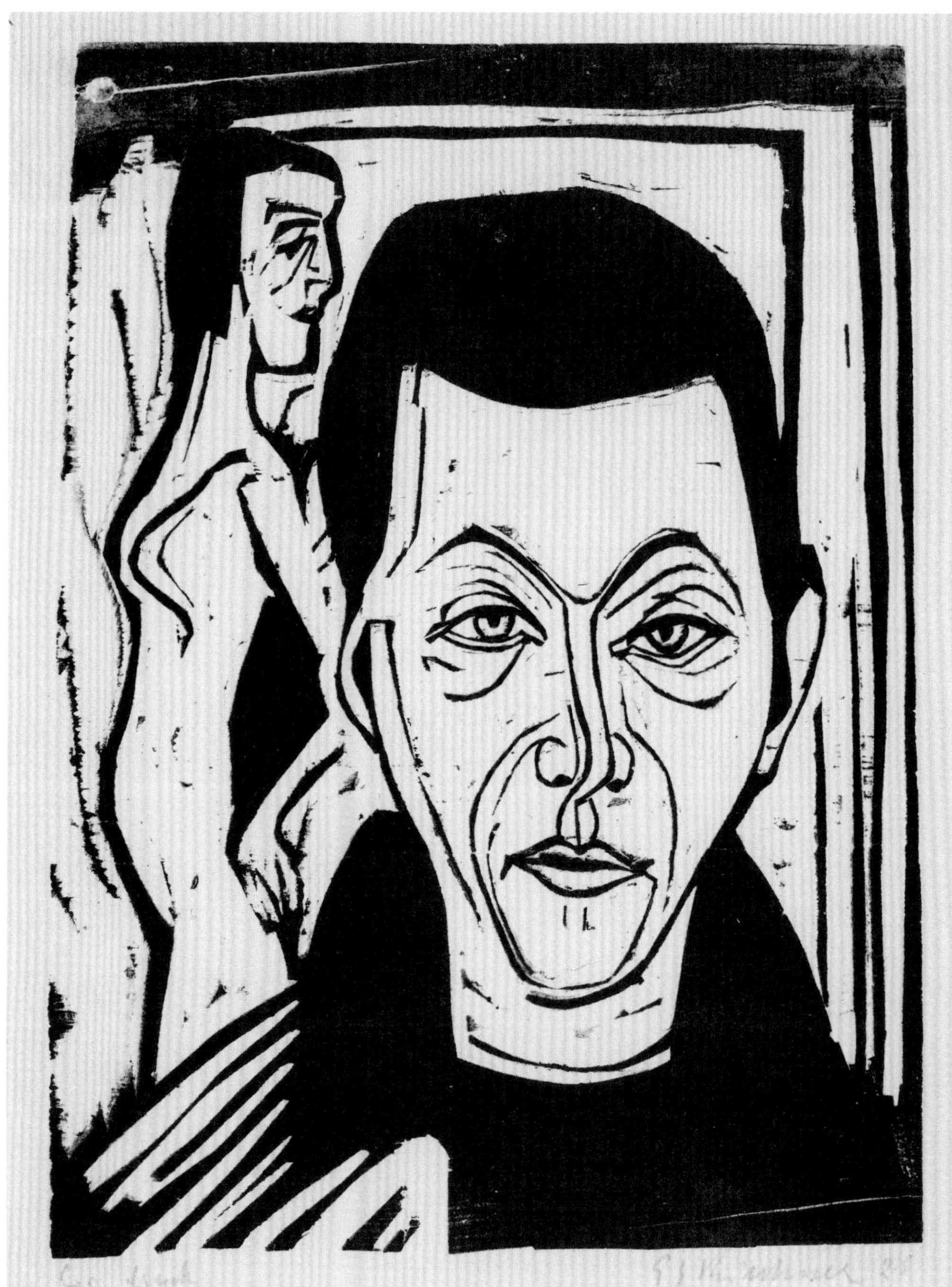

Fig. 17
Ernst Ludwig Kirchner, *Männerkopf—Selbstbildnis* (Man's Head—Self-Portrait), 1926
Woodcut, 39 × 30 cm
Kirchner Museum Davos

win. In recent years, however, Kirchner and Willumsen's late works have started to be reappraised,[42] something that can be seen in the light of a renewed interest in distinctive, individualistic, artistic projects and the figurative art not previously included in classical accounts of modernism. This shift can perhaps also be attributed to the fact that Kirchner and Willumsen's megalomaniacal self-mythologizing fits the performative practices and more diffuse boundaries between the public and private personas of artists today. Kirchner and Willumsen's cultivation of their male genius is perhaps less easy to accept today than, for example, the fluctuating gender roles of the Surrealists, although their awareness of the potential to construct and perform their identities is entirely in keeping with some aspects of contemporary art.[43] Today their autofiction and staged personalities can be seen as a playful, performative strategy, albeit one that originally led to isolation rather than recognition.

A parallel reading of Kirchner and Willumsen's self-mythologizing strategies reveals common features making them typical yet extreme figures on a competitive art market in which the staged outsider and creative genius were potential identities, and where membership of artist groups and communities could be more strategic than idealistic. Any individualistic artistic quest was, however, dependent on a positive reception in the art world, and since this was not forthcoming Kirchner and Willumsen's radical solution was to create it themselves. Kirchner and Willumsen ended their days in self-imposed exile in Davos and the South of France, both apparently facing a defeat that was the direct result of their uncompromising determination to pursue their own agenda. In the context of art history today and its recognition of self-promotion as an artistic strategy, however, this defeat could still have the potential to vindicate their self-mythologization as a genuine artistic project.

42. Regarding Willumsen, see Margrit Brehm et al., eds., *Café Dolly: Picabia, Schnabel, Willumsen*, exh. cat. Willumsen's Museum, Frederikssund (Ostfildern, 2013) and Anne Gregersen, "Painting that Exaggerates, Exceeds, and Insists," in Erlend G. Høyersten, ed., *Wild, Bold, and Late Willumsen*, exh. cat. ARoS Aarhus Kunstmuseum (Aarhus, 2016). For an overview of the reception of Kirchner's late works see Sadowsky 2018 (see note 23), pp. 326–27. The exhibition at Kunstmuseum Basel in 2003 and accompanying publication *Ernst Ludwig Kirchner—Mountain Life: The Early Years in Davos, 1917–1926* had the explicit goal of exploring the late, devalued period of the artist's oeuvre. The director of the museum at the time, Bernard Mendes Bürgi, also made it clear that after 1926 Kirchner moved in the direction of "pronounced stylization and ceaseless self-measurement against the heroes of modern art, especially Pablo Picasso," a justification of the exhibition's focus on Kirchner's first decade in Davos; Bernard Mendes Bürgi, "Painter of the Alps," in Bürgi 2003 (see note 41), p. 13. More recent publications and exhibitions have, however, included more of the late works. See Lloyd and Staggs 2019 (see note 19) and Beisiegel 2018 (see note 23), especially Sadowsky's article.

43. For previous analyses of the performative see, for example, Brehm 2013 (see note 42) and especially her article "A Stage for Directing Self-Images: The Self-Portraits of Schnabel, Picabia, and Willumsen" and Thorsten Sadowsky, ed., *Louis de Marsalle: Visite à Davos*, exh. cat. accompanying *Ernst Ludwig Kirchner—Erträumte Reisen*, Bundeskunsthalle Bonn (Heidelberg, 2018).

Bibliography

Artists and Prophets. A Secret History of Modern Art 1872–1972. Edited by Pamela Kort et al. Exh. cat. Schirn Kunsthalle, Frankfurt. Cologne, 2015.

Bätschmann, Oskar. *The Artist in the Modern World. The Conflict Between Market and Self-Expression*. Translated by Eileen Martin. Cologne, 1997.

Café Dolly. Picabia, Schnabel, Willumsen. Edited by Margrit Brehm et al. Exh. cat. Willumsen's Museum, Frederikssund. Ostfildern-Ruit, 2013.

Echo Room: Thorvaldsen, Willumsen, Jorn, and Their Collections. Edited by Anne Gregersen. Exh. cat. Willumsen's Museum, Frederikssund. Berlin, 2018.

Edvard Munch. Between the Clock and the Bed. Edited by Gary Garrels et al. Exh. cat. The Metropolitan Museum of Art. New York, 2017.

El Greco and Modernism. Edited by Beat Wismer et al. Exh. cat. Museum Kunst-Palast, Düsseldorf. Ostfildern-Ruit, 2012.

Gordon, Donald E. *Ernst Ludwig Kirchner*. Cambridge, 1968.

Ernst Ludwig Kirchner. Edited by Jill Lloyd and Janis Staggs. Exh. cat. Neue Galerie. New York, 2019.

Ernst Ludwig Kirchner, 1880–1938. Edited by Jill Lloyd and Magdalena M. Moeller. Exh. cat. National Gallery of Art. Washington D.C., 2003.

Ernst Ludwig Kirchner. Imaginary Travels. Edited by Katharina Beisiegel. Exh. cat. Kunst und Austellungshalle der Bundesrepublik Deutschland, Bonn. Munich, London, New York, 2018.

Ernst Ludwig Kirchner. Mountain Life. The Early Years in Davos 1917–1926. Edited by Bernard Mendes Bürgi. Exh. cat. Kunstmuseum Basel. Ostfildern-Ruit, 2003.

Grisebach, Lothar, ed. *Ernst Ludwig Kirchners Davoser Tagebuch*. Cologne, 1968.

Hjorth, Ulla. *J.F. Willumsen i Europa*. Frederikssund, 2006.

Jensen, Robert. "A Matter of Professionalism. Marketing Identity in Fin-de-Siècle Vienna." In *Rethinking Vienna 1900*, edited by Steven Beller. New York City, 2001.

Jensen, Robert. *Marketing Modernism in Fin-de-Siècle Europe*. Princeton, 1994.

Jensen, Robert. "Selling Martyrdom." *Art in America* 80 (April 1992).

Jones, Amelia. "'Clothes Make the Man': The Male Artist as a Performative Function." *Oxford Art Journal*, vol. 18, no. 2 (1995).

Kirchner, Ernst Ludwig – Gustav Schiefler. *Briefwechsel. 1910–1935/1938*. Edited by Wolfgang Henze. Stuttgart/Zürich, 1990.

Louis de Marsalle. Visite à Davos. Edited by Thorsten Sadowsky. Exh. cat. *Ernst Ludwig Kirchner – Erträumte Reisen*, Bundeskunsthalle Bonn. Heidelberg, 2018.

Meier-Graefe, Julius. *Entwicklungsgeschichte der modernen Kunst* vol. I and II [1904, 1914–24]. Munich, 1997.

Mentze, Ernst. *J.F. Willumsen. Mine erindringer fortalt til Ernst Mentze*. Copenhagen, 1953.

Meskimmon, Marsha. *The Art of Reflection. Women Artists' Self-Portraiture in the Twentieth Century*. London, 1996.

Patry, Sylvie. *Inventing Impressionism: Paul Durand-Ruel and the Modern Art Market*. New Haven, 2015.

Petersen, Vibeke. "J.F. Willumsen og Tyskland omkring århundredskiftet." *Konsthistorisk tidskrift/Journal of Art History*, 63:3–4 (1994).

Rosenquist, Rod. "Modernism, Celebrity and the Public Persona." *Literature Compas* 10/5 (2013).

Rosenquist, Rod. "Trusting Personality: Modernist Memoir and its Audience." In *Incredible Modernism: Literature, Trust and Deception*, edited by John Attridge and Rod Rosenquist. Farnham, 2013.

Sjælebilleder. Symbolismen i dansk og europæisk maleri 1870–1910. Edited by Peter Nørgaard Larsen. Exh. cat. Statens Museum for Kunst. Copenhagen, 2000.

Weikop, Christian. "Ernst Ludwig Kirchner as his Own Critic: The Artist's Statements as Stratagems of Self-Promotion." *Forum for Modern Language Studies* 48, 4 (September 26, 2012).

Wild, Bold, and Late Willumsen. Edited by Erlend G. Høyersten. Exh. cat. ARoS Aarhus Kunstmuseum. Aarhus, 2016.

Wivel, Henrik. *Ny dansk kunsthistorie bind 5. Symbolisme og impressionisme*. Copenhagen, 1994.

Öhman, Hjalmar. *J.F. Willumsen. Med kommentarer af J.F. Willumsen*. Copenhagen, 1921.

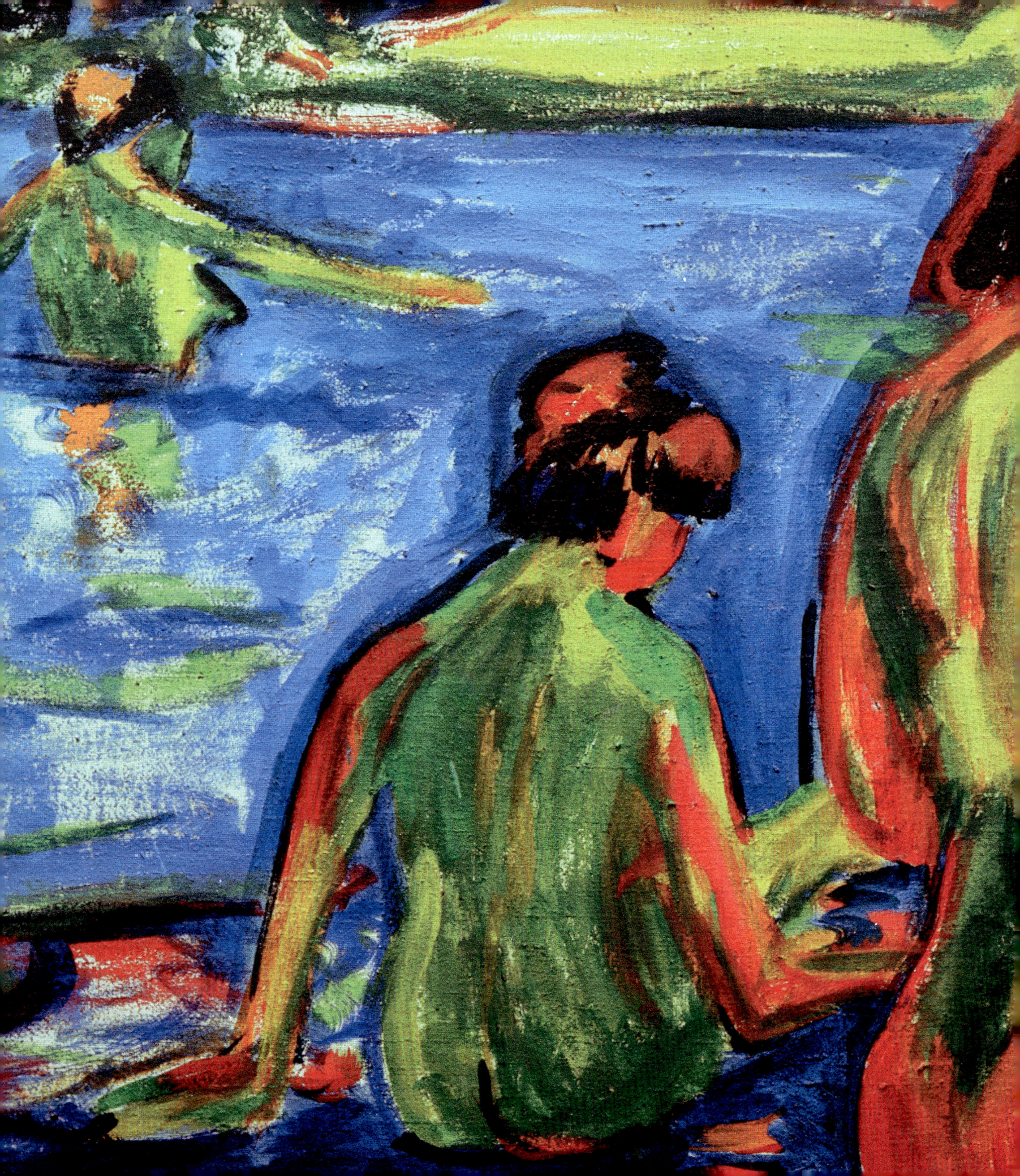

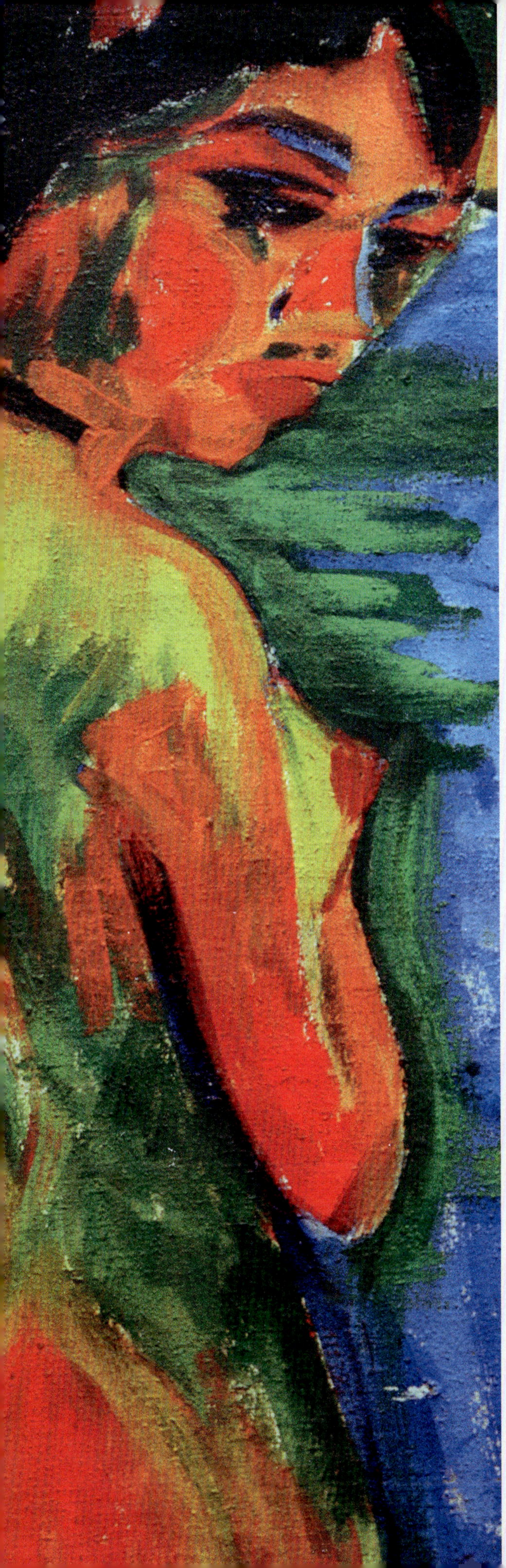

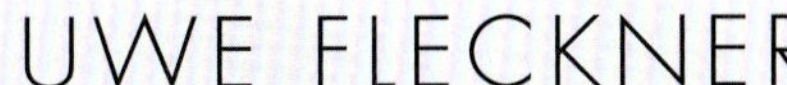

UWE FLECKNER

"... of surprising freedom and joyful multiplicity":

Carl Einstein's Critical Perspective on the Work of Ernst Ludwig Kirchner

Ernst Ludwig Kirchner
Detail of *Im See badende Mädchen*
(Girls Bathing in a Lake), 1909 (dated 1907)
Oil on canvas, 91.2 × 120 cm
Private collection

This essay is based on a chapter of my study on Carl Einstein; see Uwe Fleckner, *Carl Einstein und sein Jahrhundert: Fragmente einer intellektuellen Biographie* (Berlin, 2006), pp. 194–204 ("Der Fall Kirchner").

1. Carl Einstein, *Die Kunst des 20. Jahrhunderts*, Propyläen-Kunstgeschichte, vol. XVI (Berlin, 1926), p. 121. The third edition of Einstein's book is also available in a new, annotated edition; see Carl Einstein, *Die Kunst des 20. Jahrhunderts*, Uwe Fleckner and Thomas W. Gaehtgens, eds., Werke, vol. 5 (Berlin, 1996).
2. Einstein 1926 (see note 1), p. 122 and p. 126.
3. Ibid., p. 113.
4. Ibid.
5. Ibid., p. 132; for more on Einstein's assessment of Kandinsky, see Uwe Fleckner, "Le solipsiste et son critique: l'œuvre de Kandinsky jugé par Carl Einstein," in *Kandinsky: Retour en Russie, 1914–1921*. Exh. cat., Musée d'art moderne et contemporain (Strasbourg, 2001), pp. 38–46; Fleckner 2006 (see introductory note), pp. 87–98 ("Der Solipsist und sein Kritiker").

When the art historian, critic, theorist, and poet Carl Einstein published his *Die Kunst des 20. Jahrhunderts* (Twentieth-Century Art) in 1926, the great age of German Expressionism, the heroic years from 1905 to 1914, was already over. In the nineteen-twenties, Expressionist painters endeavored to assert themselves through their art, in the face of increasing competition from, above all, Cubism. The catastrophe of World War I which had taken the lives of August Macke and Franz Marc, had also led to profound revisions; some Expressionists conservatively backed off from their previous painterly audacities, whereas others—particularly members of the artist' community Die Brücke (The Bridge)—indulged in tired self-citation. Yet Ernst Ludwig Kirchner, who had parted company with his former companions even before the war, was attempting to rise to the challenges of the new age in his self-elected Swiss exile.

In his compendium of contemporary art, as an uncompromising advocate and theorist of Cubism, Einstein dismissed Expressionists almost *en bloc*. Hardly once did he bother to justify his verdicts, which were presented in often very short chapters. With some sparse biographical details and a few aphoristically brief sentences modelled on paradigms from French salon criticism, he attacked Expressionist art and left it to his readers to verify the harsh assessments with reference to attached visual materials and—even more important—to prior theoretical considerations. Erich Heckel, for instance, is dismissed as an "idyllicist" who started "with scarcely surprising coloring" and "probably remained the most closely linked to Nativists"; in Otto Müller, most works lapsed "into meagre blue-and-green sugariness and monotonously mute lines."[1] He wrote of Max Pechstein that he had "the dangerous skill of popularizing every acquired good in an eclectically complaisant manner," was "stuck in broad-based decorative sketches," and that his work finally culminated in "conventional everyday handicrafts"; Lyonel Feininger, in contrast, was attested to have designed his planes made up of "cut crystals" according to the Cubist model, if only hesitantly, but with little "formal knowledge and bold daring."[2]

Yet even the detailed reviews of other artists hardly led to more favorable judgements. Thus Einstein's set of monographs begins with Emil Nolde or, more precisely, with the ellipsis "barbaric magic."[3] His work is characterized in such terse terms, and the metaphorical drumbeat provides the underlying tone which the writer will repeat again and again in the following pages when judging—or rather condemning—the North German Expressionist. The thematic pathos of his paintings, their religiosity, deemed undignified and a supposedly misunderstood exoticism, are lashed at in sharp, often hurtful terms; major formal weaknesses that have supposedly resulted in utterly trivial painting are noted: "In Nolde we see a brew of Nordic sagas and boorishly copied uncouth biblical myths, mixed with colorfully coarse refinement."[4] Franz Marc as a representative of the Der Blaue Reiter (The Blue Rider) group of artists is judged in a more differentiated manner. Whereas his friend Kandinsky had not moved beyond "subjective lyricism," Marc, who had died too early in the war, still dealt in his animal pictures with the spatial and formal problems of the French avant-garde, although he only achieved an instinctively stylized Cubism.[5]

A Jewish Critic of German Painting

However, one of the Expressionist artists that Einstein studied in his *Die Kunst des 20. Jahrhunderts* was an exception to his otherwise more than critical presentation: Ernst Ludwig Kirchner. The author had probably never met the painter, graphic artist, and sculptor personally, but in his case it was the unrestrictedly positive evaluation that gave the artist a strikingly unusual position in the chapter on

"The Germans." The art historian's attempts to get in touch with Kirchner and his intention to include a section on his work in *Die Kunst des 20. Jahrhunderts* at first proved difficult. While compiling his book in November 1922, it seems that Einstein had sent a letter enquiring whether the artist—along with many others—could supply information on his life and work, as well as illustrations. From a letter that Kirchner wrote to Gustav Schiefler on November 29, 1922, we know that he was initially unwilling to do so: "Has a certain Einstein, a writer, perhaps been in touch with you? He has recently asked me for photographs. But I have refused, because this Jew has always criticized German painting, but now wants to make money by writing a book about it. Such a fellow of course takes his illustrations wherever he can find them."[6] Kirchner evidently underestimated the chance he was now being offered, for Einstein, who never wrote his critical texts from a national perspective but always, given his close contacts with the avant-garde of French artists, dealers, and authors, took a European view of art, could have done much to help him realize his international ambitions.

As is known, the artist was very careful in issuing permission for reproductions, and did his best to control art critics' reception of his work. Yet this does not either explain or excuse his prominent antisemitic resentment. A letter sent just a few days earlier by Helene Spengler, Einstein's solicitous friend from Davos, to her son-in-law, the philosopher and one-time director of the Jena Art Association Eberhard Grisebach, confirms the artist's dubious reasons to initially refuse his help in producing the book: "Kirchner received an offer from a Jewish art writer called Einstein to write about him and asking him to send material. You should have seen how proudly he said: I don't need this—luckily I have other people who know me better and will write about me."[7]

That Einstein, the accursed fellow, would ultimately grasp and describe his art better than so many of his hagiographers (even Kirchner's alter ego Louis de Marsalle) is something the artist would admittedly only discover on reading *Die Kunst des 20. Jahrhunderts*. But he initially did let himself be persuaded to sign a contract governing the type and use of illustrations. In May 1925, with the long-planned compendium still unpublished, Kirchner attempted to retract his earlier consent.[8] Although no relevant documents have survived, we may still assume that there was a tenacious exchange of letters on the subject between the author, the publisher and the artist, in the course of which Einstein evidently expressed his assessment of the difficult artist and—in vain—held out the prospect of a further essay on his work. To quote the October 27, 1925 entry in Kirchner's diary: "I have rejected Einstein's article. I could not tolerate this scolding of Die Brücke, despite all his flattery of me, that's why."[9] The artist demanded that Einstein's text be submitted to him before issuing copyright on his works, and the latent conflict between the artist and the author now burst into the open. The first edition of Einstein's principal work of art history eventually had to be published in 1926 without any illustrations of the artist's paintings, graphic works, or drawings, and instead with a notice—the sole footnote in the entire book—in which the author explained the absence of the desired reproductions and firmly dismissed the artist's proposal as unconscionable interference: "Unfortunately, Kirchner's works cannot be reproduced, for the artist's consent could only be obtained on the condition—which precludes free judgment—that the text would be submitted to him for censorship."[10]

Suspicion and mutual distrust thus prevented a dialogue that would probably have allowed another interesting essay to be written. And thus Kirchner's astonishment could not have been greater when he finally received a published copy of *Die Kunst des 20. Jahrhunderts* and found in it a text that failed to meet his expectations precisely because it described his works so expertly and approv-

6. Letter from Ernst Ludwig Kirchner to Gustav Schiefler, November 29, 1922, in Ernst Ludwig Kirchner and Gustav Schiefler, *Briefwechsel: 1910–1935/1938*, ed. by Wolfgang Henze (Stuttgart/Zurich, 1990), pp. 209–211 (p. 210).
7. Letter from Helene Spengler to Eberhard Grisebach, November 24, 1922, in Lothar Grisebach, ed., *Maler des Expressionismus im Briefwechsel mit Eberhard Grisebach* (Hamburg, 1962), p. 141.
8. See letter from Ernst Ludwig Kirchner to Gustav Schiefler, May 2, 1925, in Kirchner and Schiefler 1990 (see note 6), p. 357, and letter from Gustav Schiefler to Ernst Ludwig Kirchner, May 13, 1925, ibid., pp. 357–358. The contract between Kirchner, Einstein, and the Ullstein publishing house has not survived, but was probably worded like such contracts that Kirchner signed on other occasions; see contract with the magazine *Das Kunstblatt*, November 1922, ibid., pp. 207–208.
9. Lothar Grisebach, ed., *E. L. Kirchners Davoser Tagebuch: eine Darstellung des Malers und eine Sammlung seiner Schriften* (Cologne, 1968), p. 99.
10. Einstein 1926 (see note 1), p. 126. In this connection—assuming that the date is correct—a letter from Kirchner to Will Grohmann dated April 9, 1926 raises questions. The artist requests Grohmann to purchase Einstein's book for him, for he would like to see "if my text has survived intact." Einstein must therefore almost certainly have sent the chapter on Kirchner and Die Brücke artists to Davos earlier on, otherwise we cannot account for the fact that Kirchner shows himself, both in this letter and in his diary entry dated October 27, 1925, to be apprised of the harsh criticism of the painters in the group; see letter from Ernst Ludwig Kirchner to Will Grohmann, April 9, 1926, in Karl Gutbrod, ed., *Lieber Freund: Künstler schreiben an Will Grohmann* (Cologne, 1968), pp. 40–41 (p. 40).

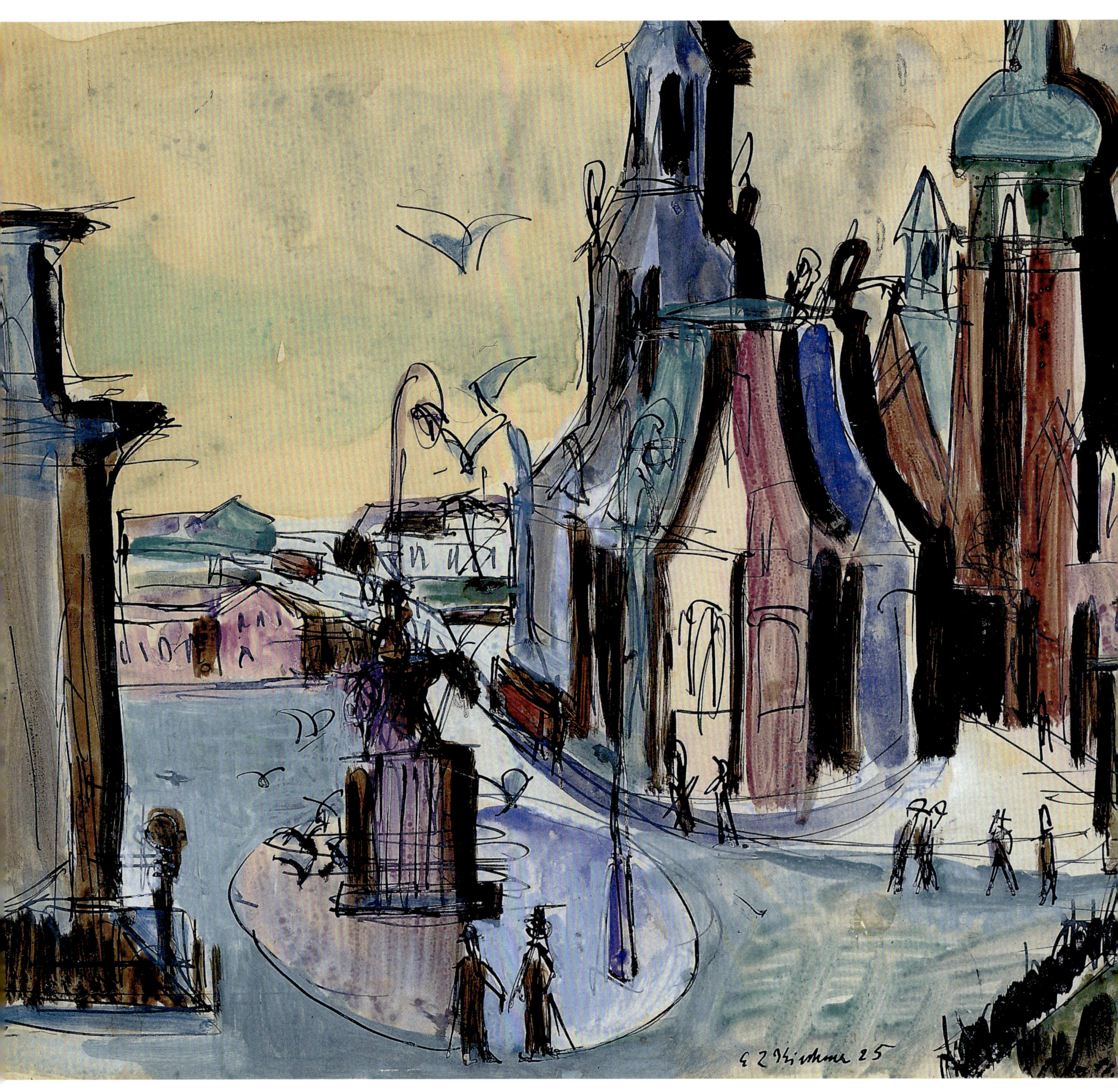

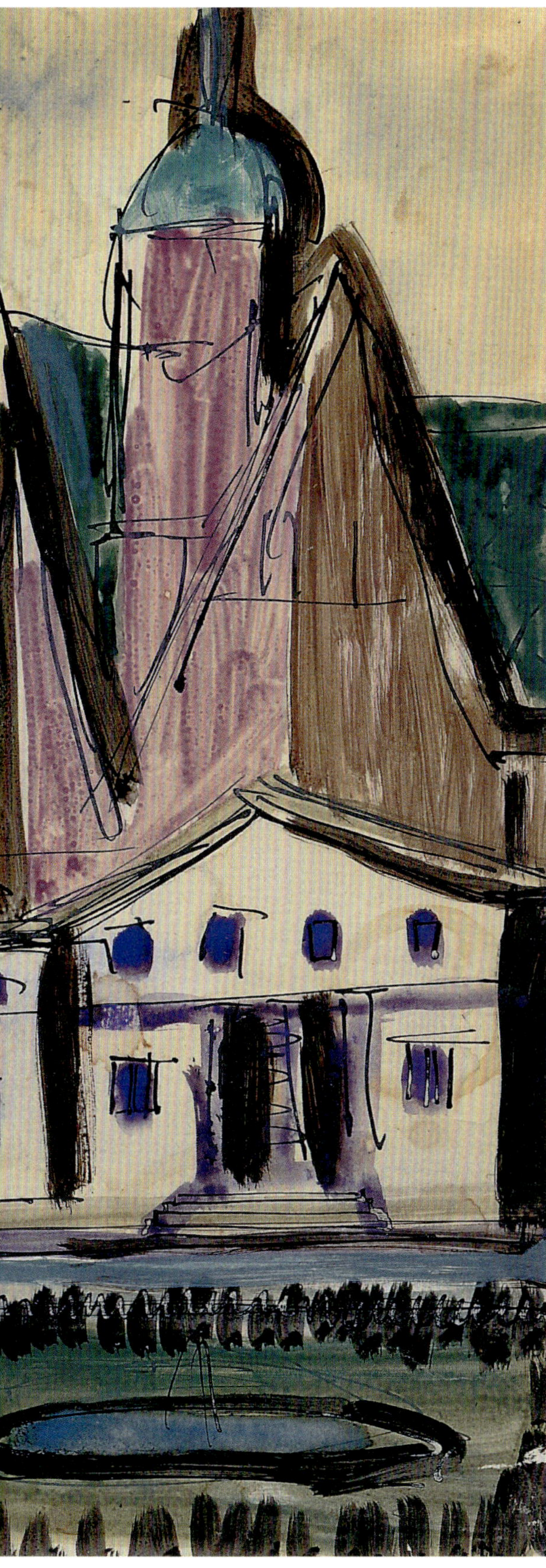

Fig. 1
Ernst Ludwig Kirchner
Ansicht von Dresden (Schlossplatz) (View of Dresden [Schlossplatz]), 1925
Gouache on painting board, 32 × 47 cm
Sammlung Würth, Künzelsau

ingly. Kirchner's response to this surprising text has survived. In a letter dated August 15, 1927, again to Gustav Schiefler, he comments from a Swiss point of view on the pitiful state of German art criticism, and finally cites Einstein's compendium, its language and its appraisal as the only exception:

> That art is today in such a poor state in Germany is in my opinion due to the fact that there are still very few people who approach it in a truly objective and thorough manner; none of the critics and writers there has any notion of technique or form. Thus essays and prefaces are always stuffed with sentimental chatter and personal details, because no one, from the *Reichskunstwart* [government supervisor of the arts] down to the merest hack, can think of anything else. The gentlemen are too conceited to learn anything from artists; and the only one today whose book on Modernism is objective is Einstein, whose *Die Kunst des 20. Jahrhunderts* is first-class. Unfortunately, the man only knows the French well and hardly knows the Germans, although what he has to say about Germans is mostly correct. His judgement is exemplary in its incorruptibility. It is upsetting that we do not have a German who could write thus.[11]

Kirchner's opinion of the writer changed accordingly, even if he did not want to share the latter's preference for French contemporaries. The second edition of the book could therefore be published in 1928 with eight full-page illustrations and even a color plate, for which the artist sent the original of the 1925 gouache *Ansicht von Dresden (Schlossplatz)* (View of Dresden [Schlossplatz]) to Berlin (fig. 1). This offered readers a small but representative selection of early paintings and graphic works right up to the immediate present.[12] However, why Einstein in the third publication in 1931–in which he also substantially reduced his text on Kirchner–had to publish it without reproductions, is unknown, and hard to explain.[13]

11. See letter from Ernst Ludwig Kirchner to Gustav Schiefler, August 15, 1927, in Henze 1990 (see note 6), pp. 483–485 (p. 485).
12. See Carl Einstein, *Die Kunst des 20. Jahrhunderts*, Propyläen-Kunstgeschichte, vol. XVI, second edition (Berlin, 1928), figs. pp. 380–387 and plate XX.
13. See Carl Einstein, *Die Kunst des 20. Jahrhunderts*, Propyläen-Kunstgeschichte, vol. XVI, third edition (Berlin, 1931).

"… the incisive power of this often captivating artist"

But what was so objective, first-class, and incorruptible about his representation that made the artist ascribe to the writer as unique a position within German art criticism as Einstein in turn ascribed to Kirchner's work in the recent history of German painting? His fierce rejection of many German artists, particularly his former associates in the artistic community Die Brücke, was what enabled the painter to see confirmation of the international status he aspired to. Although he had defended his former colleagues before reading the book ("It is truly sad that something like this can have been published in Germany, and understandable that these artists are so despondent and no longer produce anything"), he finally expressed his full agreement with—indeed respect for—the art historian's sharp judgment.[14] Moreover, in *Die Kunst des 20. Jahrhunderts* he could read a thorough analysis of his own work showing that the author had not only acknowledged his work and the intentions behind it, but had also studied it and classified it historically according to carefully chosen criteria. Einstein did not only harshly dismiss Die Brücke, he approached few other artists less firmly; but it was only to Kirchner, and additionally Max Beckmann and George Grosz, that he ascribed a painterly ability going beyond purely eclectic emulation of French achievements.

Einstein describes the art of Die Brücke with an aesthetic finding that strikingly matches the concepts from his early art criticism writings published before the war, and hence chronologically close to the contemporary paintings by Heckel, Schmidt-Rottluff, and Kirchner. Whereas in his art criticism from around 1910 he had called for a return to "grand form," to planarity and tectonics in visual structure, and had seen this fulfilled in what are today largely forgotten artists, as the author of *Die Kunst des 20. Jahrhunderts* he also diagnosed this intention retrospectively in the works of the Dresden group.[15] Admittedly he could now refer to the forerunners and instigators of this type of artistic rethinking, to such painters as Vincent van Gogh, Edvard Munch, or Paul Cézanne and to the unknown masters of African and Oceanic art, in whom —not only in his opinion—the Die Brücke artists had sought crucial painterly impulses.[16] When the art historian explained the claims of the painters around Ernst Ludwig Kirchner by comparing—this time approvingly—their artistic programme with the achievements of French Modernism, his representational mode of comparative argumentation once again became clear:

> These painters tried out the large, free picture. Like Fauvism in Paris, and Van Gogh earlier on, they contrasted the harmonious or conflicting relationships of broader patches of color with descriptive painting. Longing for architecture, they placed the wish for the large picture in contrast to the easel picture: simple bodies, presented in planes. Rather than recording what was seen, they showed things as signs of inner free expression. As with Fauvism, the origins go back to Impressionist techniques that made the colored element independent of the line. The idea was to combine what had been divided up here into simplified large planes.[17]

Yet in the rest of his reflections Einstein leaves no doubt that he sees these intentions as only seldom having been realized. In his view, the emergence of the Dresden artistic community had no formal concept, and its art was to be dismissed as a mere decorative craft when compared with the works of the French avant-garde, and especially with the contemporary spatial concepts of the Cubists.[18] Only Kirchner was expressly absolved from this criticism; in contrast, the other painters in Die Brücke had lacked the necessary creative inventiveness, and had resorted to poor imitation of existing formal idiom. Einstein's polemical attempts to describe what he considered the inadequacies of these painters' art were reflected in the almost unmatchable sharpness of his tone and uncompromising harshness of his judgment. He spoke of "crudely

14. Letter from Ernst Ludwig Kirchner to Will Grohmann, April 9, 1926, in Gutbrod 1968 (see note 10), pp. 40–41 (p. 40).
15. See Fleckner 2006 (see introductory note), pp. 15–36 ("Das kritische Brot der frühen Jahre").
16. See Uwe Fleckner, "Der wilde Körper: Afrikanische Kunst und ihr Einfluss auf das Bild vom Menschen im Werk Ernst Ludwig Kirchners," in Sabine Schulze, ed., *Nackt! Frauenansichten, Malerabsichten, Aufbruch zur Moderne*. Exh. cat., Städelsches Kunstinstitut, Frankfurt am Main (Ostfildern, 2003), pp. 79–93.
17. Einstein 1926 (see note 1), p. 119.
18. Ibid.

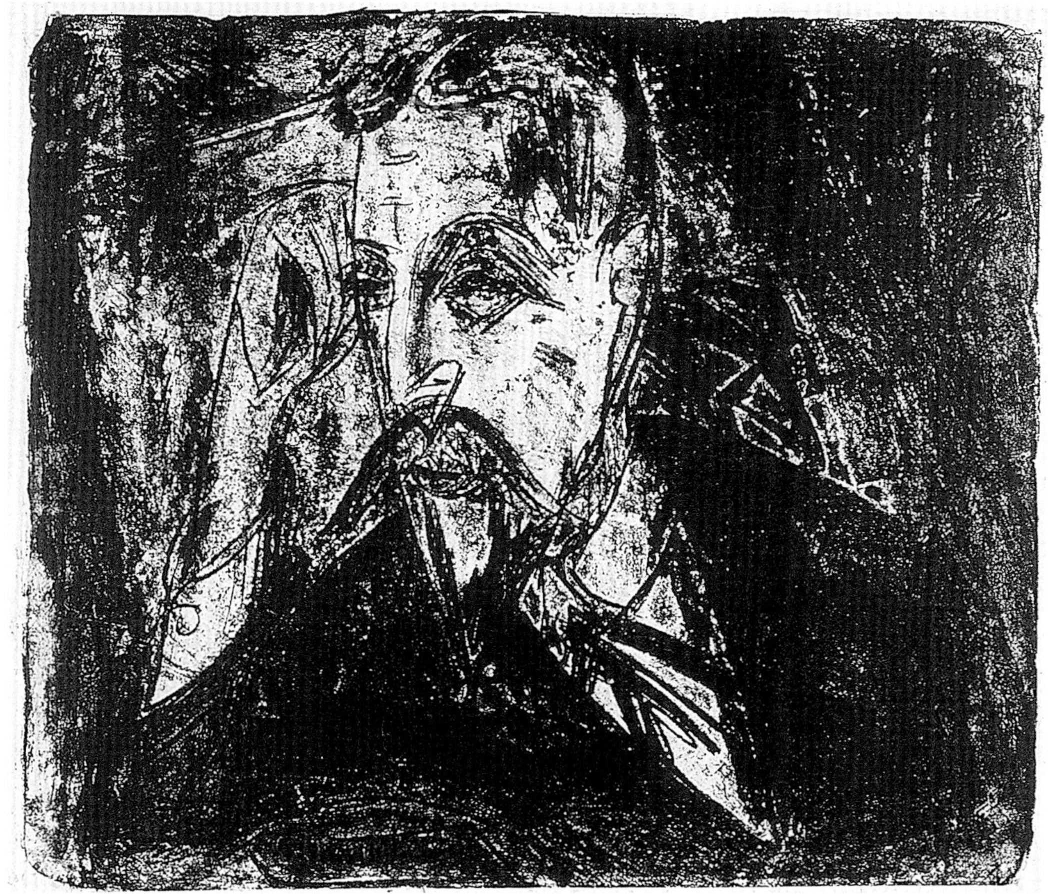

Fig. 2
Ernst Ludwig Kirchner
Kopf Professor Botho Graef
(Professor Botho Graef, Head), 1912
Lithograph, 48.8 × 59.2 cm
Kupferstichkabinett, Staatliche Museen, Berlin

clichéed stylization," "subjective lyricism," and "pathetic reformist idylls"; he noted "inflation of pretentious patches of color," as well as "petty-bourgeois self-satisfaction," "stylization from poverty," and finally "over-narrow, uncourageous subjectivism."[19] In general, the Expressionism of Die Brücke was rejected as a borrowing of Fauvist and in particular Cubist stylistic resources, in which the decisive visual strategies, the visionary findings in form and space, had been neither used nor understood: "It begins and ends in eclecticism, surrounded with literary turgidity and profound banality."[20]

Ernst Ludwig Kirchner, the "seeking man," is—on the contrary—described at the very beginning of the monographic section devoted to him as the outstanding personality within Die Brücke.[21] And the enthusiastic assessment of his art does not suggest to the reader that Einstein had to manage without the suspicious artist's cooperation when writing this chapter. And so in 1926 Kirchner could read to his surprise that the distrusted "Jew," who had previously only criticized German art, had described his work with great sympathy: "From the outset Kirchner displays the greatest sensibility, delicately oscillating color, personally delineated drawing. We are delighted to note the incisive force of this often captivating artist."[22] The singular meaning of Kirchner's work was justified by the fact that as an artist he worked without any schematic doctrine, and full of passion and originality; words from the fields "freedom," "originality," and "sensibility" were used in ever-

19. Ibid., pp. 119ff.
20. Ibid., pp. 119f.
21. Ibid., p. 123.
22. Ibid.

Fig. 3
Ernst Ludwig Kirchner
Im See badende Mädchen
(Girls Bathing in a Lake),
1909 (dated 1907)
Oil on canvas, 91.2 × 120 cm
Private collection

new variations to characterize the painter and his work. In this way the author first examined the painter's drawings and graphic works (fig. 2), to which he assigned a special place in German art precisely because they broke away from the diktat of visual objects in favor of an individual formal stamp:

> In his drawings Kirchner displays free originality like almost no other German. One thing is striking about Kirchner's drawing: he does not give an impression which is subsequently stylized, but the motif appears to him immediately in a personally free version; his sensibility already contains the elements of the interplay, is already filled with free figure, thus vouching for the originality of the person.[23]

The writer of these unusually laudatory lines sees in Kirchner's sheets a visual, indeed visionary, force at work that he otherwise ascribes almost solely to Cubist art. It is not mental dealing with objects, of which Einstein otherwise accuses German artists as a whole, but retinal, sensual receptivity as well as direct, undetached conversion that determines his artistic work. For this, Einstein finds the happy metaphor of the eye as the motor behind craftsmanship: "The original eye, which passionately moves a hand at the same moment, without the hand adulterating or sprucing up the power of imagination; this avoids literature, makes it impossible."[24] Whereas in Einstein's view Expressionist art was bent on imitating and pathetically exaggerating the representational subject, he defines Kirchner's early works, on the contrary, as autonomous artistic creations whose origin lies solely in the artist's individual manner of beholding: "Far from enhancing reality, one marks out one's own way of seeing, one's own viewpoint." Such an approach does not result in surrogates for observed objects, but in thoroughly "convincing equivalents of the power of imagination of surprising freedom and joyful multiplicity"; in other words, idiosyncratic formal and semiotic worlds, the sight of which still triggers in the viewer the required notions of space and things.[25]

Einstein assesses the artist's paintings in a similar way, saying that their form is neither pathetic nor decorative; instead, the artist is applauded for devising visual forms from "temperamentally incisive planes" and "strong rhythms" which the viewer encounters as "vividly aroused organisms." His works resolve the spatial problem of Cubism through "directional contrasts" that point to the "battle of volumes."[26] And, without the reader, at least in the first edition of *Die Kunst des 20. Jahrhunderts*, being able to check what he had read against reproduced visual examples, Einstein describes an individual formal idiom of broken outlines and contrastingly staged lines and planes, with which the painter produced, for example, the works a small selection of which would eventually be seen in the 1928 edition (figs. 3–5). Tellingly, color plays only a subordinate role in his argument, for Einstein's aesthetic considerations, marked here as elsewhere by Cubism, mainly aim at the painterly vision of line, plane, and space. The author endeavors to evoke these as supposedly essential stylistic resources in Kirchner's work, and deduces from his observations that a higher degree of reality is couched in his paintings precisely through the non-mimetic perception of form: "He avoids pursuing too docile curves, interrupts the outline, contrasts various characteristic forms, sharp triangle and rounded line. Kirchner's works are more arbitrary, and perhaps this is why they are more natural than those of other artists."[27]

23. Ibid., pp. 123f. The author did not include Kirchner's lithograph *Kopf Professor Botho Graef* (Professor Botho Graef, Head) in his book until the second edition; see Einstein 1928 (see note 12), fig. p. 381.
24. Einstein 1926 (see note 1), p. 124.
25. Ibid.
26. Ibid., p. 125.
27. Ibid.

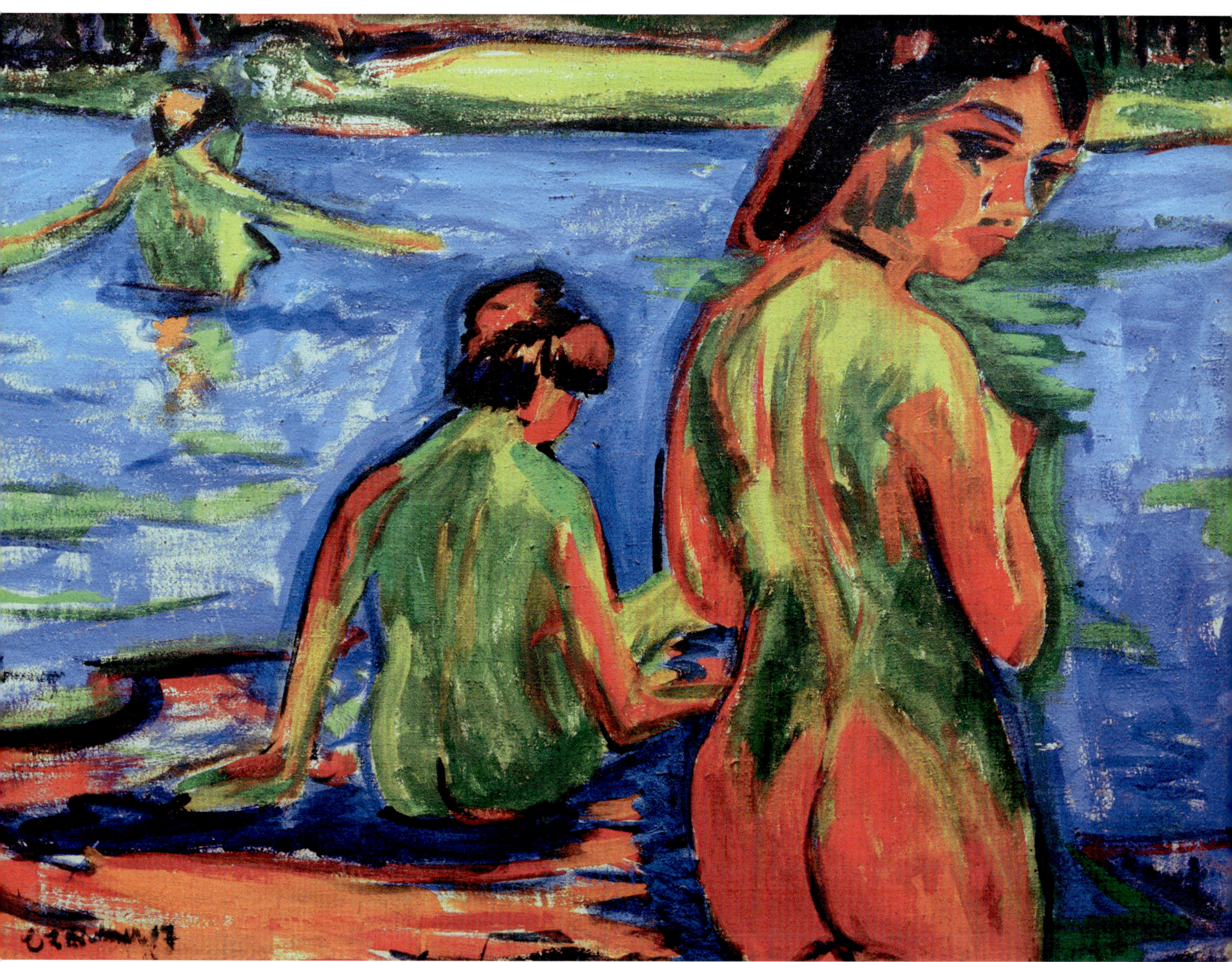

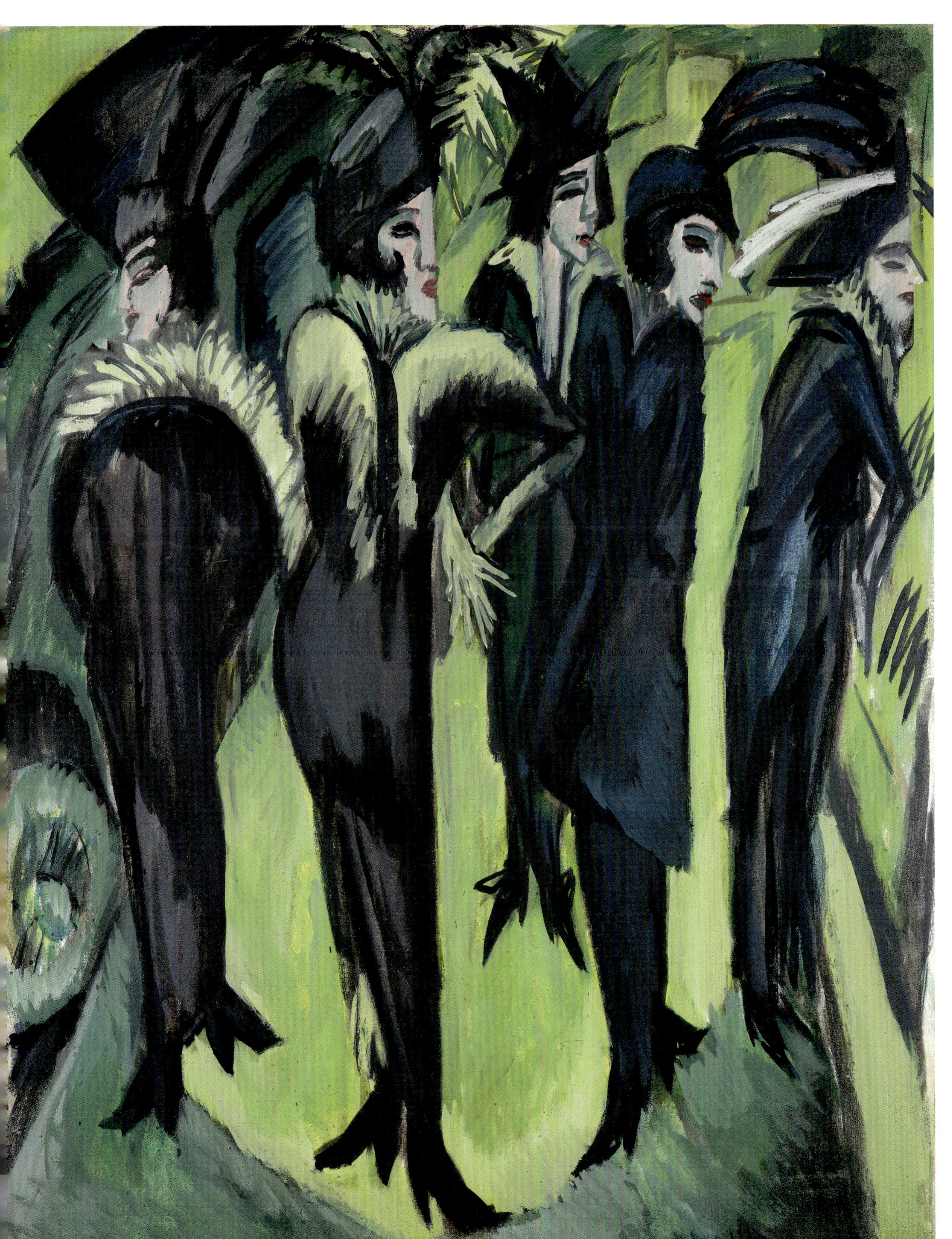

Fig. 4
Ernst Ludwig Kirchner
Fünf Frauen auf der Strasse
(Five Women on the Street),
1913
Oil on canvas, 120×90 cm
Museum Ludwig, Cologne

Fig. 5
Ernst Ludwig Kirchner
Gerda, Halbfigur
(Gerda, Half Length Portrait),
1914
Oil on canvas, 99.1×75.3 cm
Solomon R. Guggenheim
Museum, New York

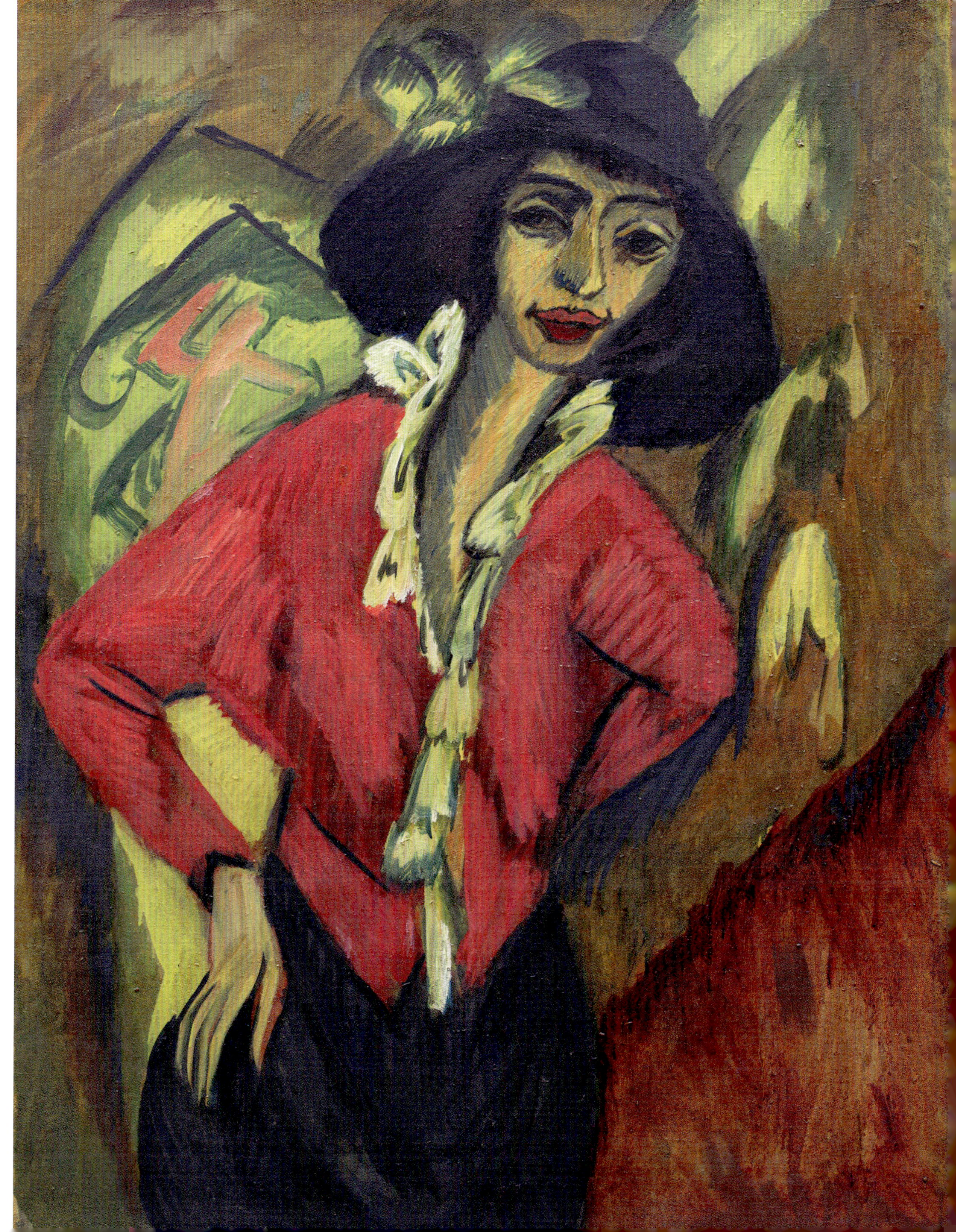

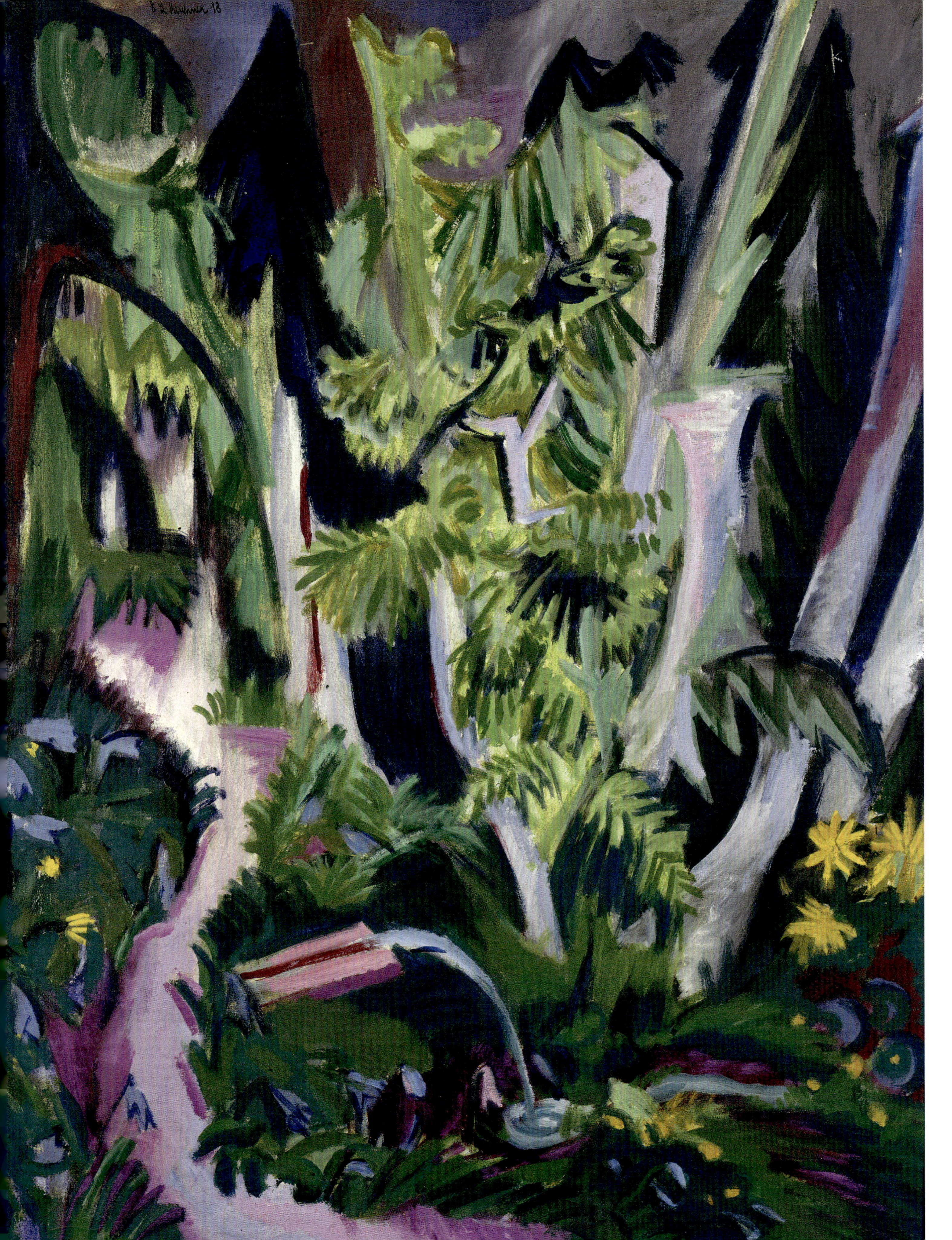

Broader, Heavier, Richer: Kirchner's Late Work

As early as 1926, Einstein came to speak briefly of Kirchner's post-war work, and we learn, as otherwise only from the chapter on "Cubism," that even for the avant-garde critic there is a classical mastery in the restrained balance of form and world, of painterly creation and objective cause (fig. 6).[28] In the Davos mountains, he argued, the artist unbreakably linked his inner, subjective notions of form to the outward features of nature; he had freed himself from his war-induced illness through artistic work on a comprehensive basis: "self-liberation towards broader creation."[29] Stylistically, too, Einstein acknowledges a deep incision in the painter's work, even though the reader can scarcely imagine these observations for lack of illustrations. Kirchner's color had become "heavier," he wrote, his forms "richer," so that his fantasy could establish a vital link with nature.[30] The reconciliation of man with the world, which the author diagnosed in these works, reveals deep philosophical and anthropological insight into the overcoming of the war psychosis that Kirchner shared with many artists and intellectuals from the early Weimar period and, to a certain extent, with Einstein himself: "Increasingly one masters the unity of subject and nature; balanced scales, controlled unity of both forces is seriously attempted."[31]

We do not know which works of Kirchner's the author had in mind when writing such lines. Yet in the 1928 edition, in which the passage on Kirchner's late works was included almost unchanged, Einstein did devote four of the nine illustrations to pictures from the nineteen-twenties, which can certainly be interpreted as a sign of particular appreciation (figs. 7–9). His observation that Kirchner's use of color had become "heavier" can now be traced to the fact that in the nineteen-twenties figurative pictures as displayed by Einstein, the nervous fragmentation of forms into individual brushstrokes, was indeed replaced by application of larger patches of color, with the "richer" formal vocabulary consisting of Kirchner's total abandonment at the time of the staccato successions of strokes learned from Cubism and their replacement with more complex forms of lines and planes.

The aesthetic turn that Kirchner's painting underwent in the nineteen-twenties is clearly apparent from a double page in *Die Kunst des 20. Jahrhunderts* (fig. 10), on which the landscape *Waldinneres*, today known as *Bergwald Frauenkirch* (Mountain Forest Frauenkirch), 1919, which he had already produced in Davos, is confronted with the studio painting *Maler und Modell* (Painter and Model), 1924–27. Einstein's formal criticism thus becomes instantly clear: small brushstrokes build up the vegetable protagonists of natural scenery in the landscape, while in the interior presented in the studio painting—beyond traditional perspective and anatomy—the figures are created by generous tinted planes whose composition is maintained by rhymes in color and form. Yet Einstein did not observe the radical transformation of Kirchner's way of painting, from around the mid-nineteen-twenties onwards, to an ever more abstract, boldly formal idiom with thoroughly ornamental anatomies, which the artist desperately felt challenged to produce—although he made no mention of this—in response to the protean work of Picasso, whom he deeply envied.

Hence, Carl Einstein's extensive rejection of Expressionist painting is in no way due to any, and least of all "Jewish," idiosyncrasy, as Kirchner initially assumed, but is based far more on aesthetic principles, including free and visually autonomous production of forms, mastery of contemporary spatial experiences, and reconciliation of man and the world, of subject and object in the artwork. Ernst Ludwig Kirchner's special artistic path could only be appreciated without restriction precisely because his work did not display any purely eclectic continuation of visual solutions that had already been achieved, above all by the Fauvists and Cubists, did not display any second-hand Modernism but an entirely personal way of seeing and viewing that was unique to him, and is associated by great painterly power. Aesthetic vision, as well as the ability to translate this into valid form, is—if we are to believe Einstein—more important in the artist's drawings, graphic works, and paintings than the spiritual world view of his Expressionist companions.

Fig. 6
Ernst Ludwig Kirchner
Bergwald Frauenkirch
(Mountain Forest Frauenkirch), 1919
Oil on canvas, 120 × 90 cm
Nationalgalerie,
Staatliche Museen, Berlin

28. The author did not include Kirchner's painting *Bergwald Frauenkirch* (Mountain Forest Frauenkirch) in his book until the second edition; see Einstein 1928 (see note 12), fig. p. 384.
29. Einstein 1926 (see note 1), p. 126.
30. Ibid.
31. Ibid.

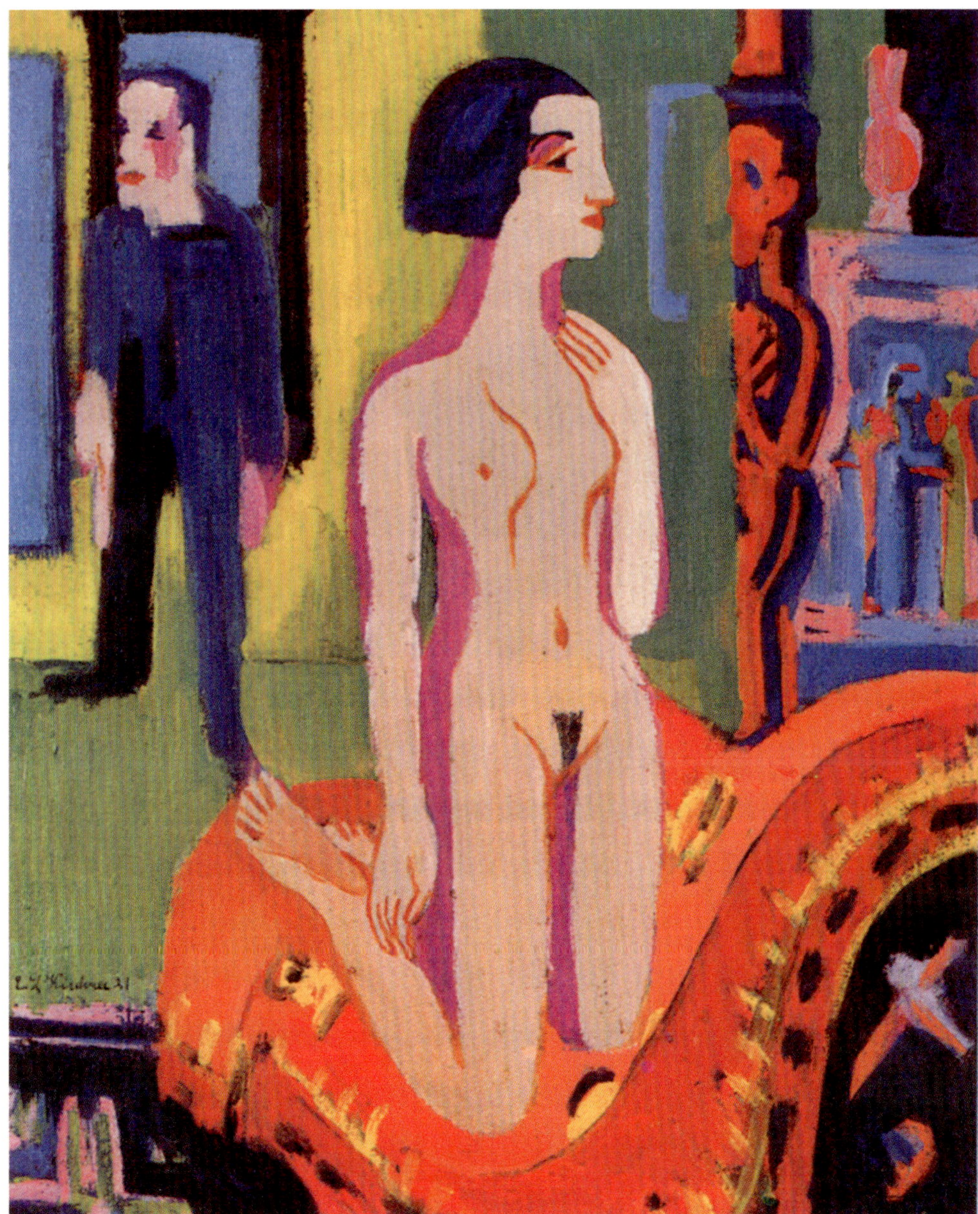

Fig. 7
Ernst Ludwig Kirchner
Maler und Modell
(Painter and Model),
1924–27 (dated 1921)
Oil on canvas, 70 × 60 cm
Private collection

Fig. 8
Ernst Ludwig Kirchner
Die Erscheinung der Sieben im "Eulenspiegel"
(The Apparition of the Seven in "Eulenspiegel"),
1923–24
Oil on canvas, 125 × 167 cm
Private collection,
Chicago

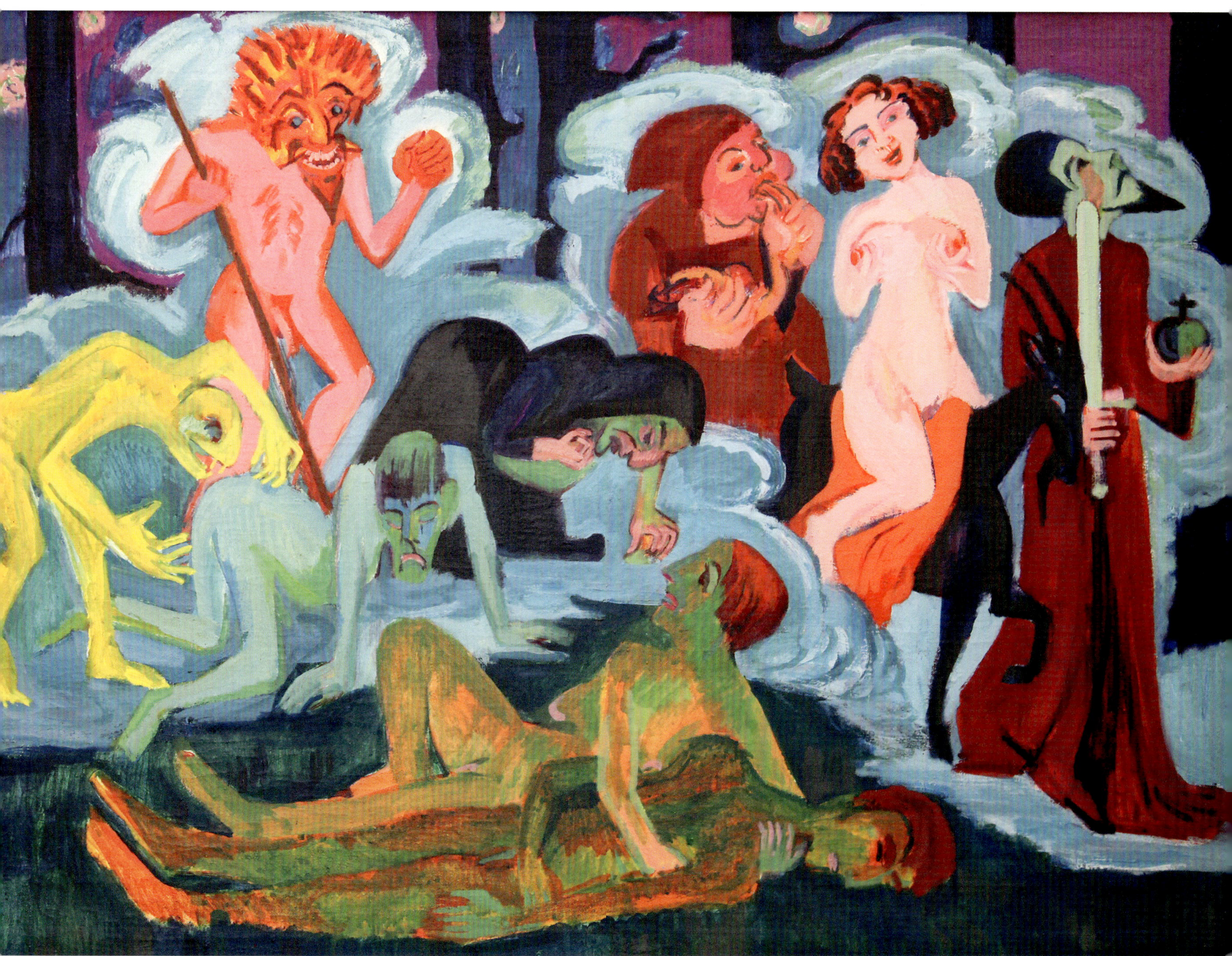

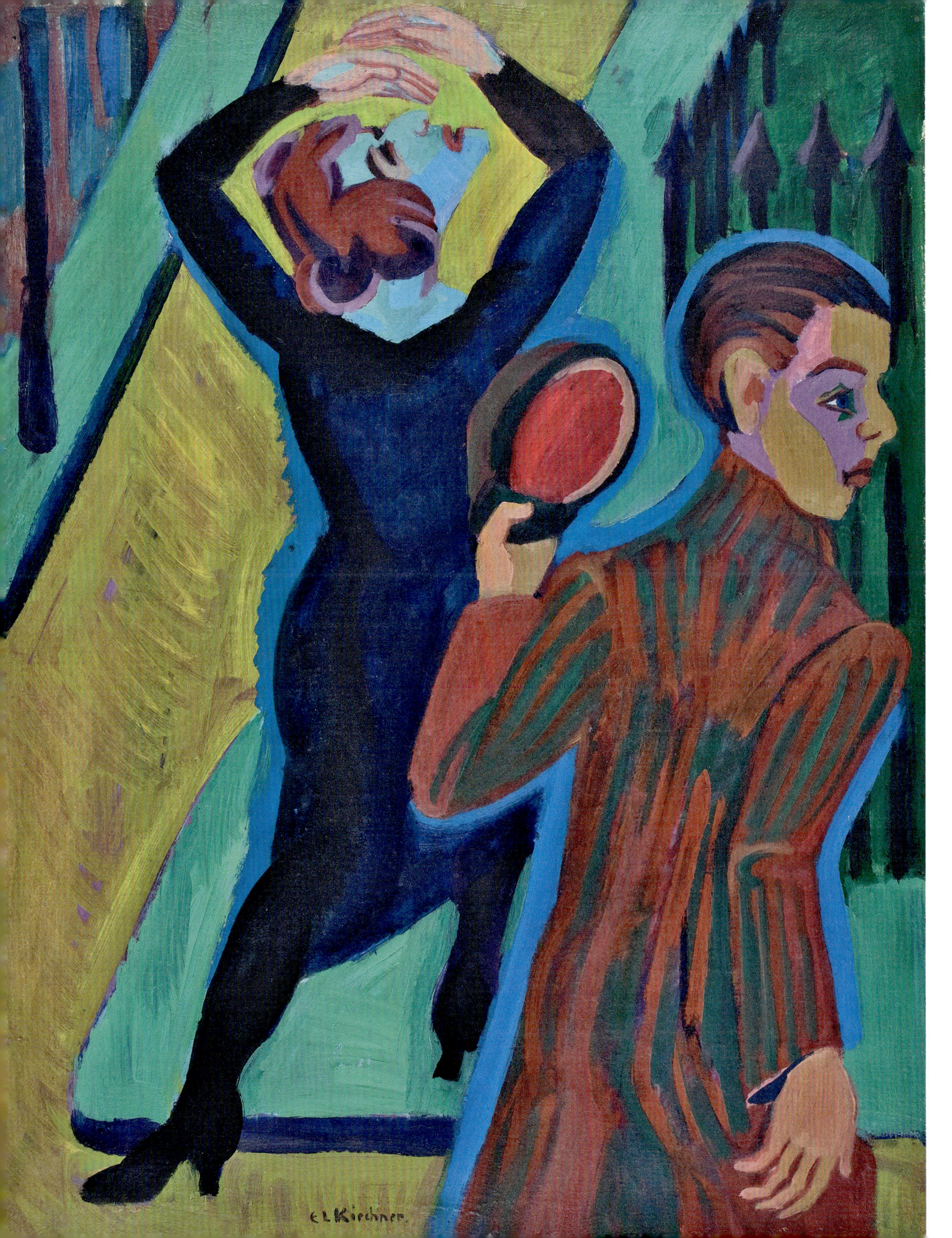
E L Kirchner

Fig. 9
Ernst Ludwig Kirchner
Der Abschied
(The Farewell), 1925–26
Oil on canvas, 120.5 × 90 cm
Kirchner Museum Davos

Fig. 10
Double page from Carl Einstein's *Die Kunst des 20. Jahrhunderts*, second edition, Berlin 1928, with Ernst Ludwig Kirchner's *Waldinneres* (today known as *Bergwald Frauenkirch*), 1919 and *Maler und Modell*, 1924–27

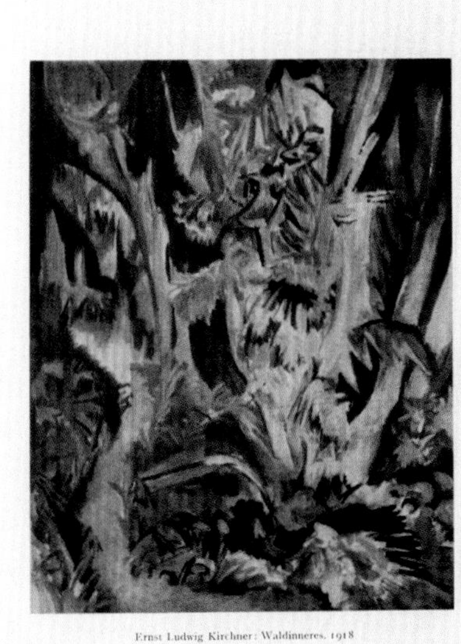

Ernst Ludwig Kirchner: Waldinneres. 1918

384

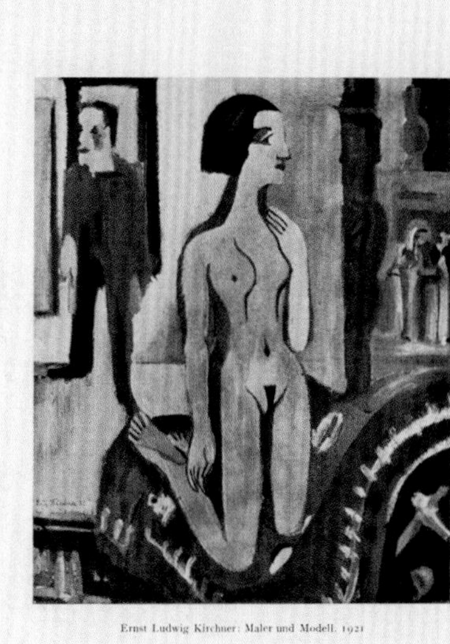

Ernst Ludwig Kirchner: Maler und Modell. 1921

385

Bibliography

Einstein, Carl. *Die Kunst des 20. Jahrhunderts.* Propyläen-Kunstgeschichte, vol. XVI. Berlin, 1926.

Einstein, Carl. *Die Kunst des 20. Jahrhunderts,* second edition. Propyläen-Kunstgeschichte, vol. XVI. Berlin, 1928.

Einstein, Carl. *Die Kunst des 20. Jahrhunderts,* third edition. Propyläen-Kunstgeschichte, vol. XVI. Berlin, 1931.

Einstein, Carl. *Die Kunst des 20. Jahrhunderts.* Edited by Uwe Fleckner and Thomas W. Gaehtgens. Werke, vol. 5. Berlin, 1996.

Ernst Ludwig Kirchner and Gustav Schiefler, *Briefwechsel: 1910–1935/1938.* Edited by Wolfgang Henze. Stuttgart/Zurich, 1990.

Fleckner, Uwe. *Carl Einstein und sein Jahrhundert. Fragmente einer intellektuellen Biographie.* Berlin, 2006.

Fleckner, Uwe. "Der wilde Körper. Afrikanische Kunst und ihr Einfluss auf das Bild vom Menschen im Werk Ernst Ludwig Kirchners." In *Nackt! Frauenansichten. Malerabsichten. Aufbruch zur Moderne.* Edited by Sabine Schulze, exh. cat. Städelsches Kunstinstitut, Frankfurt am Main. Ostfildern, 2003.

Grisebach, Lothar, ed. *E. L. Kirchners Davoser Tagebuch. Eine Darstellung des Malers und eine Sammlung seiner Schriften.* Cologne, 1968.

Grisebach, Lothar, ed. *Maler des Expressionismus im Briefwechsel mit Eberhard Grisebach.* Hamburg, 1962.

Gutbrod, Karl, ed. *Lieber Freund. Künstler schreiben an Will Grohmann.* Cologne, 1968.

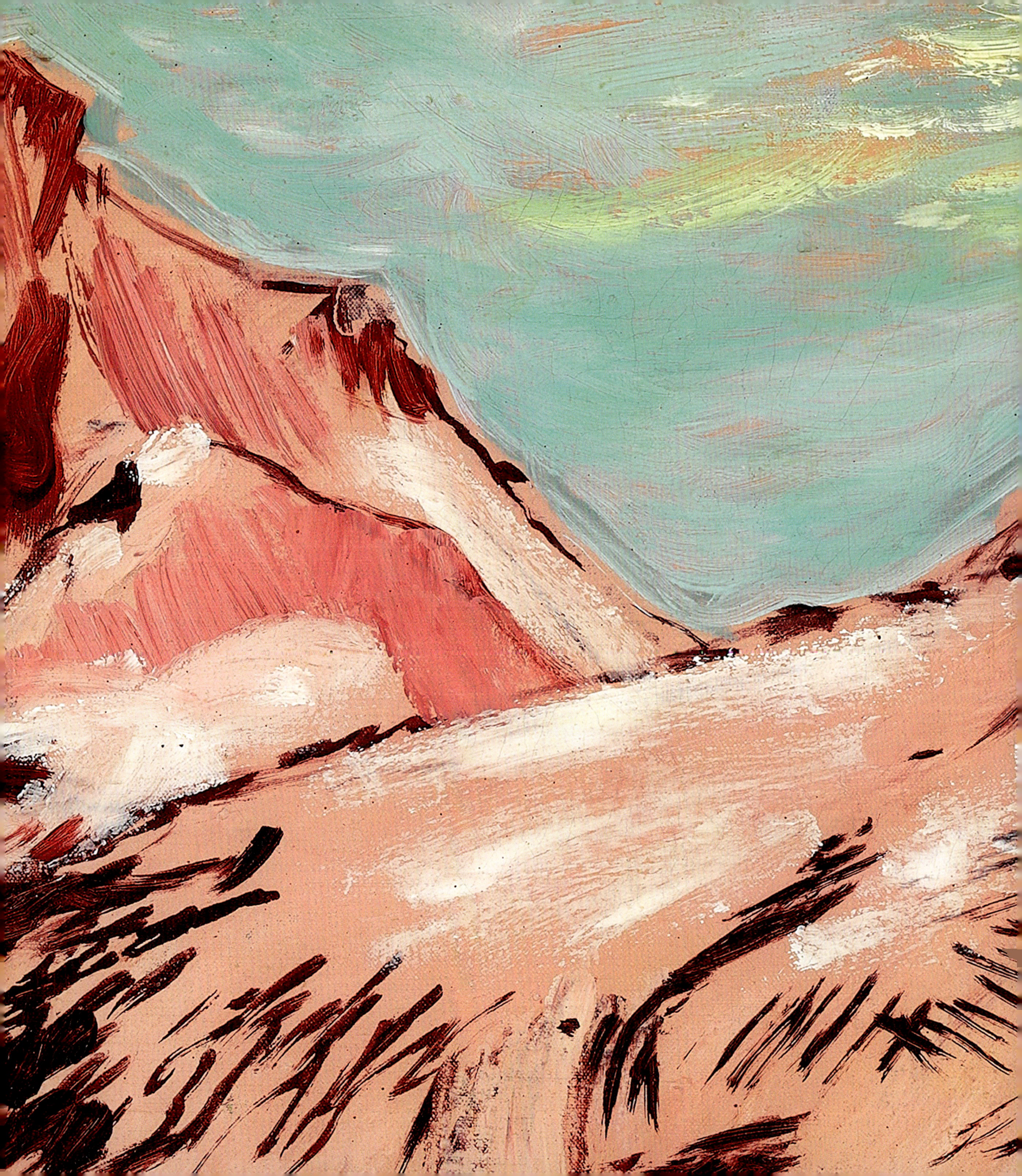

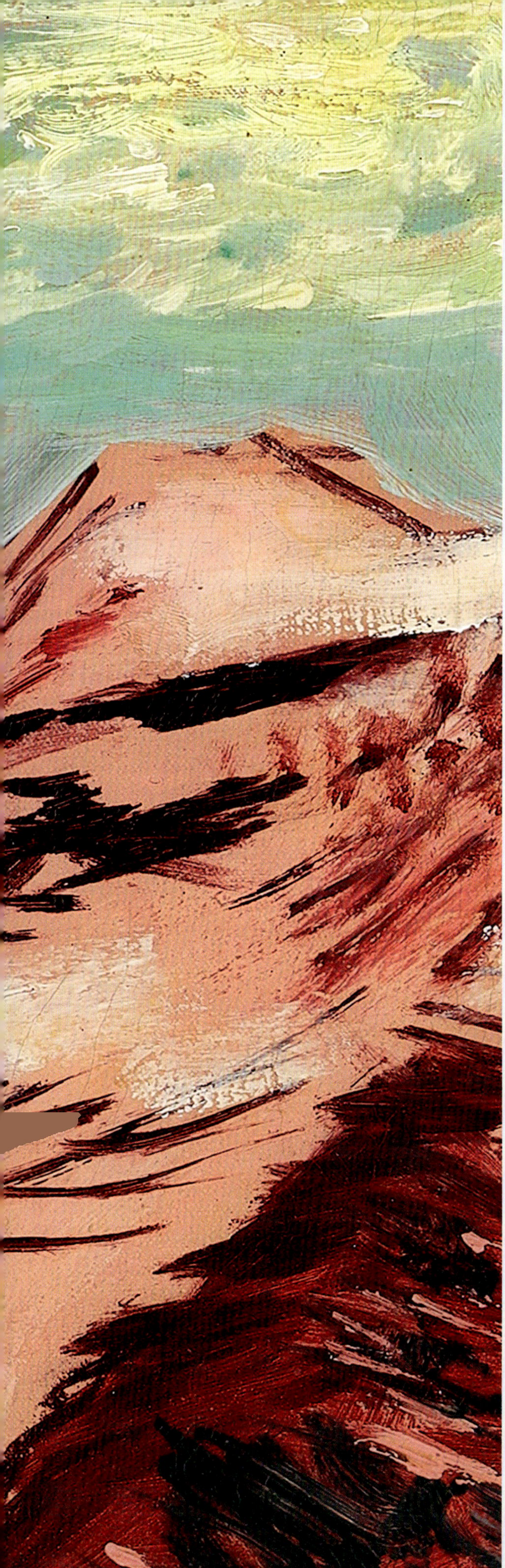

ANDERS EHLERS DAM

"The Mystical Blue Flower of Art": The Aesthetic of the Alps in the Works of J. F. Willumsen and Ernst Ludwig Kirchner

J. F. Willumsen
Detail of *Bjergtinde, Schweiz* (Mountain Peak, Switzerland), 1926
Oil on canvas, 53.5×73.5 cm
Galleri Bo Bjerggaard, Copenhagen

1. Ernst Mentze, *J.F. Willumsen. Mine Erindringer fortalt til Ernst Mentze* (Copenhagen, 1953), p. 90.
2. On this aspect of Willumsen's memoirs see Troels Branth Pedersen, *Bjergtaget: J.F. Willumsen i Norge 1892* (Aarhus, 2006), p. 18, and Merete Bodelsen, *Willumsen i halvfemsernes Paris* (Copenhagen, 1957), p. 10. Furthermore, the fact that Willumsen's memoirs were actually written by Ernst Mentze may have influenced their wording in Danish and its subsequent translation here.
3. Mentze 1953 (see footnote 1), p. 92.

"These mountains became my mountains."[1] This is how J.F. Willumsen speaks of the Alps he experienced during the summer he spent on Lake Geneva in 1891 in the memoirs published to mark his ninetieth birthday many years later in 1953. In a large number of paintings throughout the different phases of his oeuvre, Willumsen strove to represent his experience of elevated mountain landscapes. The mountains were of great symbolic value to the artist, connected to something he found entirely central to the nature of art.

While Willumsen was painting the mountains, another artist arrived in the Swiss Alps. The seventeen-year younger German painter Ernst Ludwig Kirchner visited Switzerland for the first time in 1917, and moved to the sanatorium town of Davos the following year. For Kirchner, who had otherwise largely been a painter of cityscapes, the encounter with the overwhelming nature and rural life of local villagers in the mountains was also of decisive importance, and many of his most beautiful works were created in this landscape.

In the following we will look at the way the Alps influenced both these major artists, who despite being in Switzerland at the same time probably never actually met. Juxtaposed, the similarities and differences between their paintings can throw light on the work of both. Willumsen and Kirchner did not focus on the same aspects of the Alps, but both found the mountain landscape equally aesthetically inspiring. In a broader perspective, as we shall see, both artists were part of a movement celebrating mountains from the late nineteenth century and several decades on, a movement inspired by figures such as the German poet and philosopher Friedrich Nietzsche. Since Francesco Petrarca's account of climbing Mont Ventoux with his brother in 1335—the first known description of landscape in European cultural history—mountains have fascinated writers and artists alike. In the eighteenth century the Swiss artist Caspar Wolf was among the first artists to paint mountain landscapes. During the Romantic period mountains became a sublime symbol of longing in the works of artists such as Caspar David Friedrich, and elements of the Romantics' ideas about mountains can be seen to continue in Nietzschean culture at the turn of the century—and indeed, as this article concludes, into the art of our own age. It is in this panoramic context of diverse interests in mountain landscapes that the work of Willumsen and Kirchner can be located and understood.

I. WILLUMSEN

In some interesting passages of the memoirs mentioned above, Willumsen recounts the experience of the Alps he had during his first visit in 1891. Here it is important to remember that we are dealing with a rationalization of experiences in his youth, a retrospective staging of his life's work by the ageing artist. As a young artist he did not necessarily experience the situations he describes in the same way.[2] This does not, however, mean that his words cannot provide a point of entry for describing Willumsen's mountain paintings. As he recounts, his experience of the mountains in their totality evoked a sense of longing, and he hiked to their summits in the hope of fathoming the landscape. Yet every time he surmounted a peak, he was confronted by a new, even vaster landscape. The mountains themselves thus became associated with longing and illusion, what Willumsen calls "Fata Morgana country."[3] In a sense the mountain landscape was unattainable, retreating every time he approached. Yet in retrospect he claimed his experience of the mountains he portrayed to be central to his art.

He had his first key experience one day when he had hiked to a high altitude and the landscape opened before him. "The mountain country which revealed itself," he recounts, had "a fantastic, dramatic effect in both form and color":

> I felt as if I were in the midst of an earthquake in which the universe seemed to reel, lacking any fixed point. The sense of distance was disrupted by displacements vertical and horizontal. It was impossible to find anywhere for the eye to rest, everything was pell-mell. One could not ascertain what was far away and what was close due to the mists that

> shifted with the sun and changing shadows. Any normal judgement of distance was displaced. That which was close appeared weightless, and that which was far away appeared heavy and solid. Mountain tops in the distance suddenly emerged from the veil of fog with a startling clarity. All the usual laws of nature in the lowlands were suspended in such surroundings.[4]

Here Willumsen describes a sublime experience where what he sees, in all its dynamism and incessant shifts, resembles nothing he had ever experienced before, overwhelming him and demolishing any familiar patterns of perception: an experience of constant movement and change, with no fixed point for the gaze of the artist. Here the fog and mist swirling around the landscape constantly cover and unveil new vistas of distant mountains and rockfaces close by, alternating between haziness and "startling clarity." All the normal laws of perception are rendered void.

The question is whether such a description also sums up features of Willumsen's paintings of mountains. The tremulous, shaken perspective the Danish painter associates with his experience of mountains could also serve as a description of Kirchner's Berlin and Dresden cityscapes, as well as the world of Expressionist painting. Here, however, it is not the natural landscape where everything is "pell-mell," but the chaos and speed of modern city life that disrupts any sense of perspective. Among Willumsen's mountain paintings it is his later works in particular, i.e. those from the nineteen-twenties and nineteen-thirties, that are most reminiscent of the style of Expressionism.

In a work like *Bjergtinde, Schweiz* (Mountain Peak, Switzerland) from 1926 (fig. 1), it is the intense colors of the painting that leap to the eye. The panting is dominated by a large, pink-hued mountain face that occupies around two-thirds of the work. It is not, in fact, a painting of a view or a landscape, but rather of a *massif*. We have no view across the landscape, and any sense of depth is blocked by the steeply rising mountains immediately before us. Areas in the shade are painted in darker reds, and to the right of the foreground sparse dark-green vegetation can be seen spreading across the mountainside. Snow is also scattered across the crags. The entire scene is rendered in marked, coarse brushstrokes, especially the mint-green sky and dark-yellow layer of clouds to the top left. The use of color in the work evokes both Paul Gauguin's Tahiti paintings and the works of Emil Nolde. The different elements converge to create an expressive picture of the massif itself bathed in the golden afternoon light. The landscape we encounter is not calm and peaceful, but an intense, dynamic, and surprising depiction of a mountain face.

In *Mont Blanc i skyer* (Mont Blanc in Clouds) from 1936 (fig. 2), painted by Willumsen ten years later, we see a mountain range "suspended" in swirling clouds. The painting is figurative in as far as we can see what it depicts, but the motif seems strangely alien and simplified. The clouds are applied with simple, arched strokes, like a flurry of thick, bluish white Cs pointing in different directions. The entire painting is in shades of purple and white, and the time of day is difficult to determine. It could be evening. The clouds and snow on the mountainsides are the same color, making the clouds in the sky circling above and around the mountains look like flurries of snow blown off their sides, bringing a sense of dynamic movement to the painting. This creates a turbulent, quivering, and Expressionist view of the deserted mountain peaks, where the sole human presence is that of the viewer.

Whilst there are stylistic elements of Expressionism in Willumsen's mountain paintings, they also possess elements of Romantic idealism, something the artist describes in another passage of his memoirs. Here he recounts finally finding the mountain landscape he was searching for when hiking in Col de Balme, an experience he describes as one of "wonder":

> It was a sight I have never forgotten. An encounter with the mountains that became one of the leitmotifs in my art for the better part of half a century. Surveying the Mont Blanc range was a revelation, like seeing the mightiest building on earth have all its domes and spires covered in dazzling white snow, above

4. Ibid.

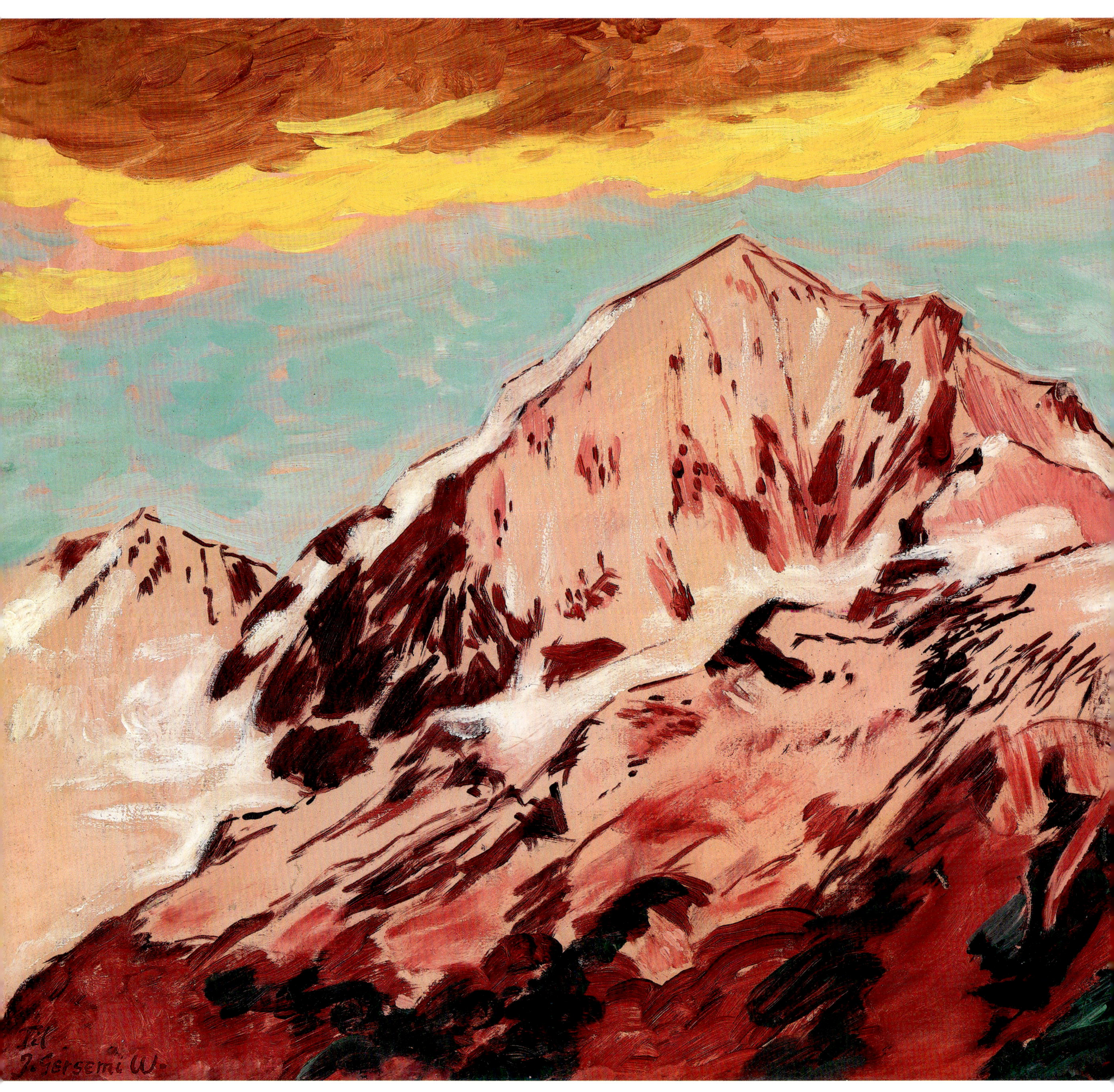
J. Gersemi W.

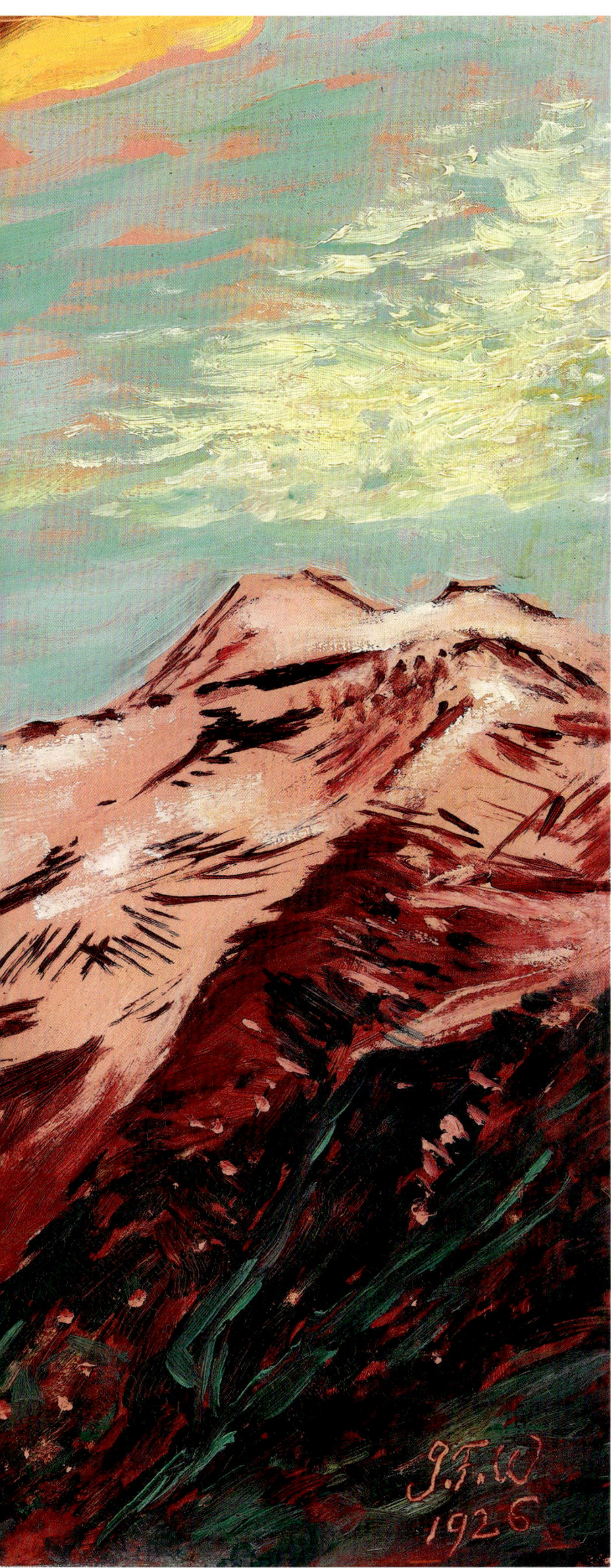

Fig. 1
J.F. Willumsen
Bjergtinde, Schweiz
(Mountain Peak, Switzerland), 1926
Oil on canvas, 53.5×73.5 cm
Galleri Bo Bjerggaard, Copenhagen

> which clouds sailed and the light alternated between pale blue and white and the golden yellow tones of its afterglow.
>
> I have no idea how long I sat contemplating this almost surreal world, but during that time in the mountains I experienced something eternal and everlasting, which like a mirror image enabled me to see and understand some of that which moved me so deeply. It was here that I found the strength to continue on the path that would carry me to the heights where the mystical blue flower of art grows and unfurls in the sun.[5]

As his memoirs show, it was apparently difficult for Willumsen to find the right words to describe the revelation he experienced in the mountains. First he compares them to a monumental and imaginary building, a work of man. Yet the "almost surreal world" of the mountains also functions as a "mirror image." It is, in other words, not the mountains alone that generate this experience of pure nature, but his contemplation of them, during which time stands still. This creates an opening for a mystical vision in which the mountains become symbols of the "eternal and everlasting." Due to their scale and desolate and sublime nature, the mountains incarnate metaphysical qualities also to be found beyond them, i.e. in art.

It is thus in the mountains that Willumsen claims to experience a metaphysical energy from which he can draw "the strength" to continue higher up: the soaring peaks point him in the direction he needs to take as an artist. For what is art for Willumsen? According to his memoirs, it is something to be found on high to which the artist aspires. It is, of course, not literally at the top of Mont Blanc that art comes into being, but rather that mountain peaks become a symbol of the metaphysical inspiration from which art emerges. Willumsen was convinced that it was his physical encounter with the mountains that made him conscious of the direction he needed to take, onwards and upwards to the peaks of the sublime.[6]

Willumsen did not paint mountains because he was a painter of landscapes, but because for him the mountains

5. Ibid., p. 92ff.
6. An entirely different perspective on Willumsen's art, including his mountain paintings, is provided by Gry Hedin's emphasis on his scientific approach to nature: Gry Hedin, "Menneske, natur og videnskab. J.F. Willumsens arbejde med systemer, naturlove og ornamentik," in Lisbeth Lund (ed.), *Naturmøder*, exh. cat. Willumsen's Museum (Frederikssund, 2015), pp. 56–61.

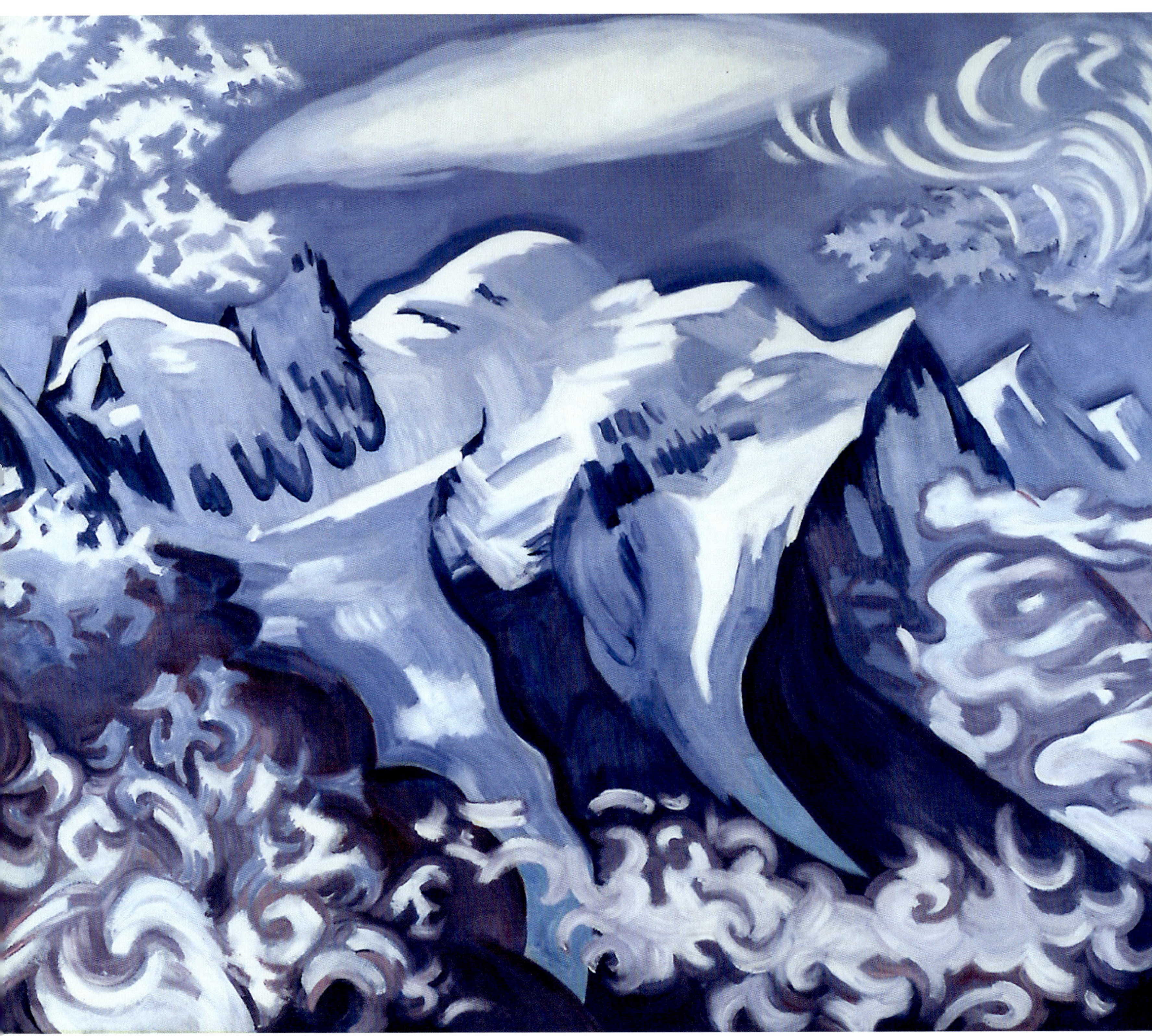

symbolized art itself. In this sense all his mountain works can be seen as *meta* paintings, depicting not the experience of nature, but the essence and creation of art. Inspiration arises like small alpine flowers in the "eternal" snowclad mountains far above the human realm. Here he discovers what he calls "the mystical blue flower of art"—alluding to the Romantic poets' symbol of the blue flower—growing at high altitudes nourished by the proximity of the sun and light. Willumsen's art expresses a continuity between Romanticism's interest in overwhelming and sublime nature (including mountains) and his own distinctive focus on soaring mountains, which is simultaneously Symbolist, Vitalist, and Expressionist in style.

If we turn to Danish literature written around the time Willumsen paid his first visit to the Alps, we find a description of mountains similar to Willumsen's own in Henrik Pontoppidan's novel *Lucky Per* from 1898–1904. The author spends several pages describing how the otherwise technically interested Per experiences a revelation when hiking in the Alps for the first time, a revelation generating the experience of something spiritual, at the same time as confronting an absolute void. Pontoppidan writes that Per experiences: "the vastness, spirit, the mystical powers of Nature to which he was made susceptible by his anxiety. These were masses of immeasurable extension, the immense power of forms and the deep stillness of eternity that called out strange and new feelings and moods in him."[7]

Willumsen's late mountain paintings are, as mentioned, Expressionist in style, with heavy brushstrokes, non-realistic colors, and striking contrasts. Conceptually, however, the works continue the Symbolism of the eighteen-nineties that Willumsen came from, in which reality provides a "mirror image" of the metaphysics of art. An example of a more clearly symbolic mountain painting by Willumsen is the much earlier *Sol over Sydens bjerge* (Sun over Southern Mountains) from 1902 (fig. 3). The style here is expressive rather than realistic or naturalistic, with heavily stylized and symbolic layers and lines. Whereas Willumsen's later expressive paintings create an overall dynamic impression, the landscape in this work is rendered in more detail.

The painting is symbolic in that the metaphysical sphere of the mountains is separate to that of the human and earthbound. The duality is clear, but the rays of light from above—from the sun beyond the frame of the painting—on the bright, white peaks also shine through the cloud cover onto the lake and the town on its shore, illuminating them in a blaze of light. The broad, vertical rays of light from above spread across the world below, marked by the undulating, horizontal lines of the lake. Here, as Leila Krogh notes, Willumsen's "monumental section of the Alps is rendered on a striking scale by the tiny houses at the foot of the mountain."[8]

Willumsen painted *Sol over Sydens bjerge* after visiting Switzerland again in the late summer of 1901. He was accompanied by the sculptor Edith Wessel, who he married in 1903. She was the model for one of Willumsen's most famous paintings, *En bjergbestigerske* (A Mountain Climber) from 1904. According to Hjalmar Öhman, it was on this trip that Willumsen became "spellbound by the Alps."[9] There are a number of sketches from the trip, which Willumsen painted with watercolors, noting the colors in pencil (fig. 4). His detailed studies of the Alps are also recorded in photographs, postcards, and newspaper clippings from the period. These were included in the fourteen large cutting albums Willumsen compiled up until around 1911. Here he grouped and glued images and clippings, as well as photographs he took in loose collages according to different themes or categories. One of the cutting albums was called "Land and Sea" and had the subcategory "Mountains." This is where we find photographs from his 1901 trip to the Alps. They are, as Anne Gregersen writes, "phenomenological investigations of the impact of fog, rain and the rays of the sun on the landscape,"[10] where he often noted the time of day and weather conditions in pencil (fig. 5).

Experiencing the sheer mass of the mountains represented in many of Willumsen's works was something the German Vitalist sociologist Georg Simmel reflected on in his essay "On the Aesthetics of the Alps" (1911).[11] In the Alps, Simmel claims, one encounters an amorphous chaos that defies aesthetic form. In the midst of the massif, what one experiences is "the secret of its materiality" and "sym-

Fig. 2
J. F. Willumsen
Mont Blanc i skyer
(Mont Blanc in Clouds), 1936
Oil on canvas, 126 × 150.5 cm
Willumsen's Museum,
Frederikssund

7. Henrik Pontoppidan, *Lucky Per* [1898–1904], trans. Naomi Lebowitz (New York, 2010), p. 220.

8. Leila Krogh, *J.F. Willumsen. Over grænser*, exh. cat. Ordrupgaard, Charlottenlund/Musée d'Orsay, Paris (Copenhagen, 2006), p. 136. Krogh writes about the paintings *Sun over the Southern Mountains* and *A Mountain Climber* on pp. 135–42. Willumsen's paintings of mountains are also analysed in Dina Vester Feilberg, *J.F. Willumsen—mellem guder og afgrund*, exh. cat. Rønnebæksholm (Næstved, 2012). Most monographs on Willumsen usually dedicate several pages to his mountain paintings.

9. Hjalmar Öhman, *J.F. Willumsen. Med Kommentarer af J.F. Willumsen* (Copenhagen, 1921), p. 91.

10. Anne Gregersen, "J.F. Willumsens udklipsmapper" in *Kunstmagasinet Janus* no. 1 (March, 2009), p. 11. By the same author, "En billedbank i bevægelse. Motiviske krydsbefrugtninger i J.F. Willumsens samlinger af udklip og fotografier," in Christian Gether et al. (eds.), *J.F. Willumsen. Farver & striber*, exh. cat. ARKEN Museum of Modern Art (Ishøj, 2018), pp. 36–47.

11. Georg Simmel, "On the Aesthetics of the Alps," trans. Jens Klenner, in Sean Ireton and Caroline Schaumann (eds.), *Mountains and the German Mind: Translations from Gessner to Messner, 1541–2009* (Rochester, NY, 2020), pp. 187–92. Originally published as "Zur Ästhetik der Alpen," in *Der Tag: Moderne illustrierte Zeitung*, no. 34, January 19, 1911. For a more general perspective on mountains in art see Stephan Kunz et al. (eds.), *Die Schwerkraft der Berge: 1774–1997*, exh. cat., Aargauer Kunsthaus and Kunsthalle Krems (Basel, 1997).

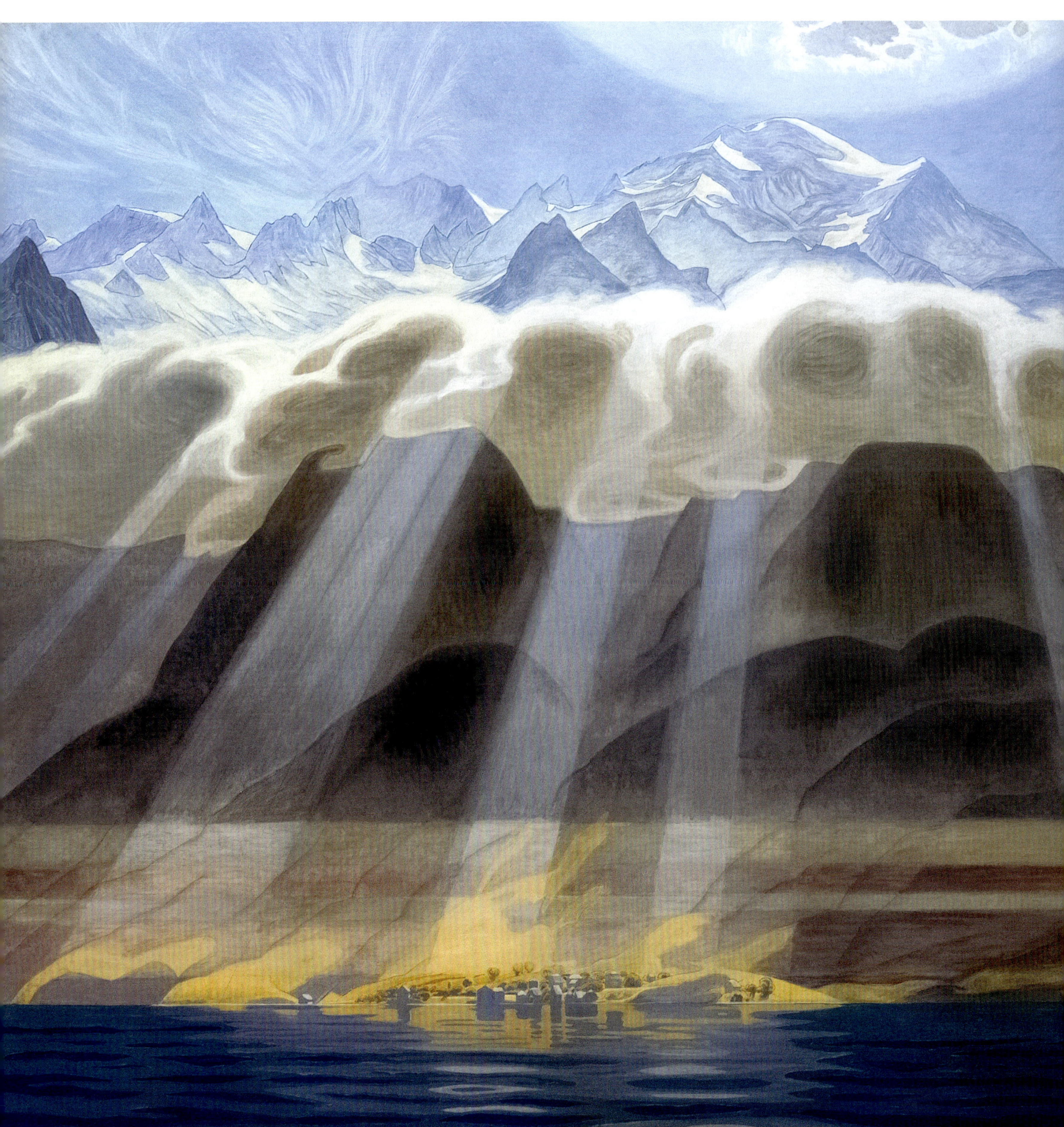

bols of the transcendental" amidst peaks covered with everlasting snow liberated from human nature.[12] According to Simmel, the Alps evade representation in art, and he names the famous Symbolist mountain painters Italian Giovanni Segantini and Swiss Ferdinand Hodler as examples of artists who tried in vain to capture the aesthetic of the Alps. On the relationship between the transcendent landscape and representation Simmel writes:

> To the extent that one may call a landscape transcendent, this is true of the firnscape—admittedly, though, only where simply ice and snow exist, but no longer the green, the valley, and the pulse of life. And because the transcendental, the absolute, into whose atmosphere this landscape entwines us, is beyond all words, it also lies, when not childishly anthropomorphized, beyond all form.[13]

Willumsen's mountain paintings depict not the idyllic and fertile valleys of mountain villagers, but barren peaks devoid of human life. The dualism between the human landscape and snowclad peaks can be seen in *Sol over Sydens bjerge.* The Expressionist style of many of Willumsen's late works from the Alps can perhaps also be seen as an attempt to capture the duality of the mountains as both formless mass and transcendent landscape in the Simmelian sense.[14]

12. Simmel 2020 (see footnote 11).
13. Ibid.
14. I am more positively inclined towards these late mountain paintings than Ulla Hjorth, who writes: "Willumsen's oversimplification in the late works, with their bright poster colors and surface approach, creates a harsh, decorative effect devoid of subtle shades—a schematization that leaves little space for feeling." Ulla Hjorth, *J.F. Willumsen i Europa* (Frederikssund, 2006), p. 130. In recent years Willumsen's works have been re-evaluated, especially in the light of research conducted by Anne Gregersen, who sees his late oeuvre as excessive, contrived, self-assured, theatrical, and postmodern. See, for example, Anne Gregersen: "Painting that Exaggerates, Exceeds, and Insists," in Erlend G. Høyersten (ed.), *Wild, Bold, and Late Willumsen*, exh. cat. ARoS (Aarhus, 2016), pp. 52–69.

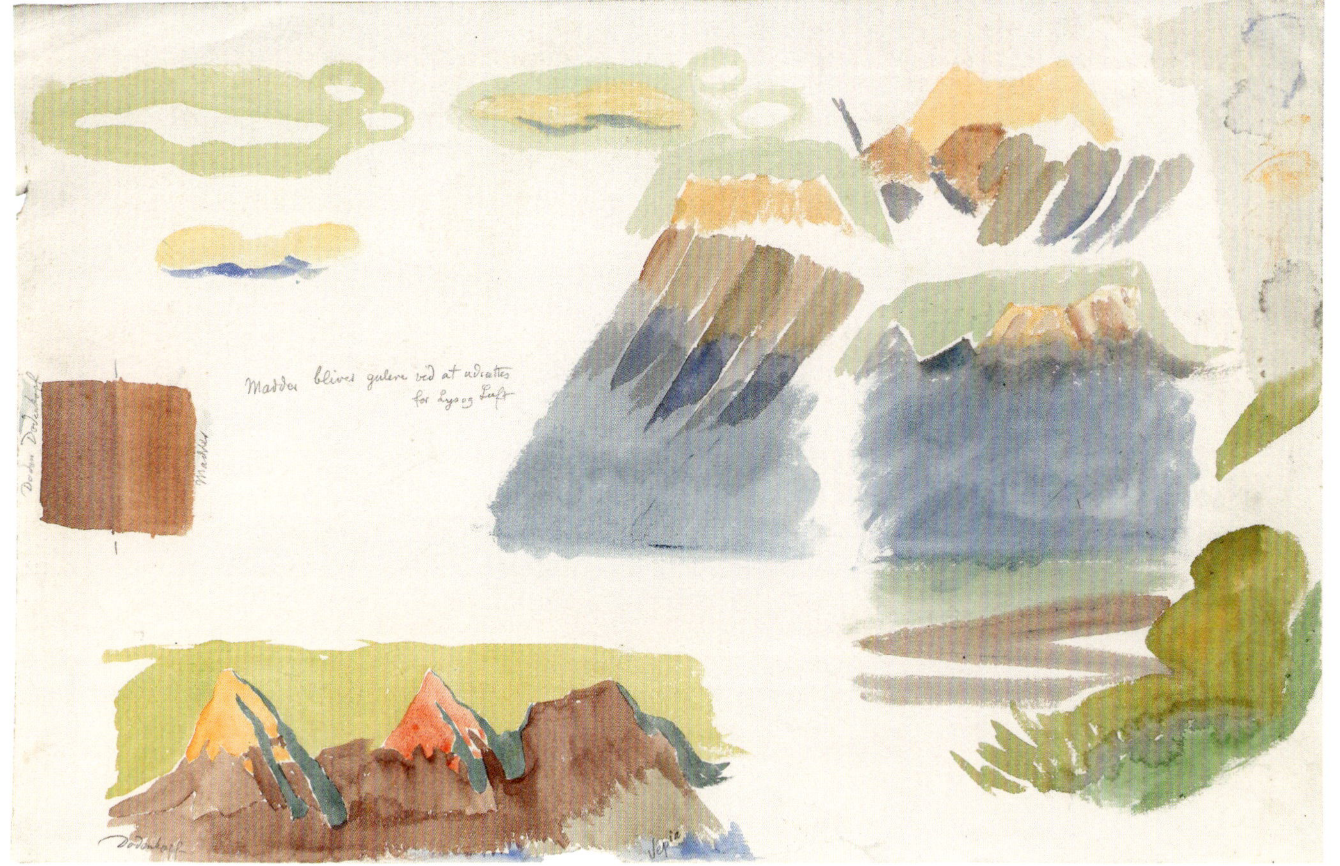

Fig. 3
J. F. Willumsen
Sol over Sydens bjerge
(Sun over Southern Mountains), 1902
Oil on canvas, 209 × 208 cm
The Thiel Gallery, Stockholm

Fig. 4
J. F. Willumsen
Color Study, 1901
Watercolor on paper, 45.7 × 30.2 cm
Willumsen's Museum, Frederikssund

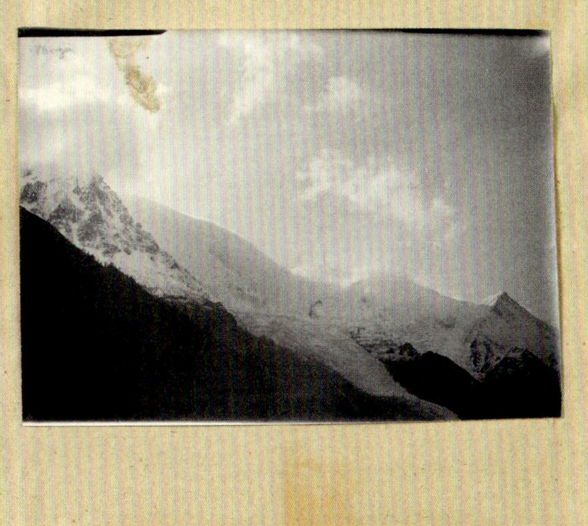

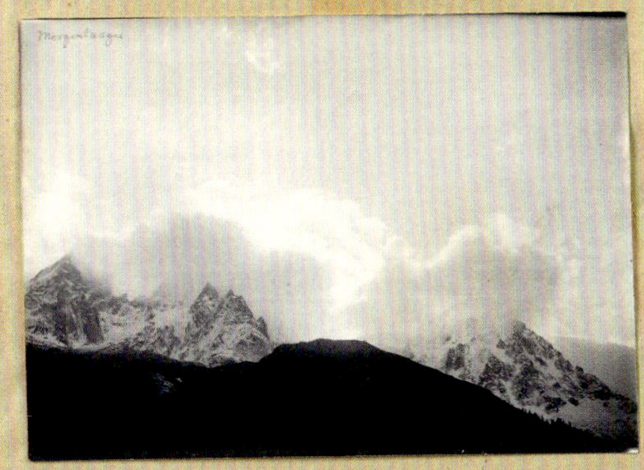

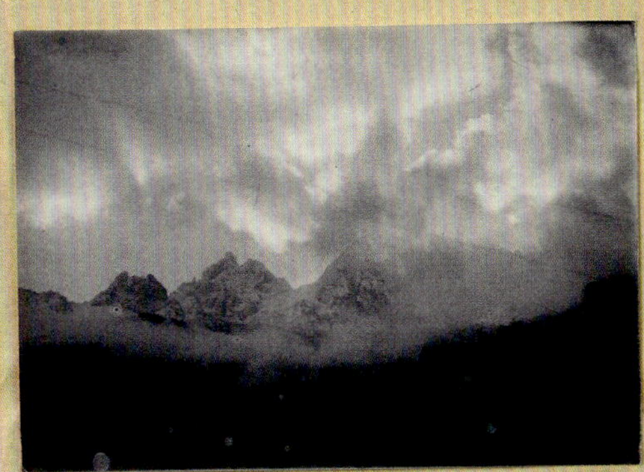

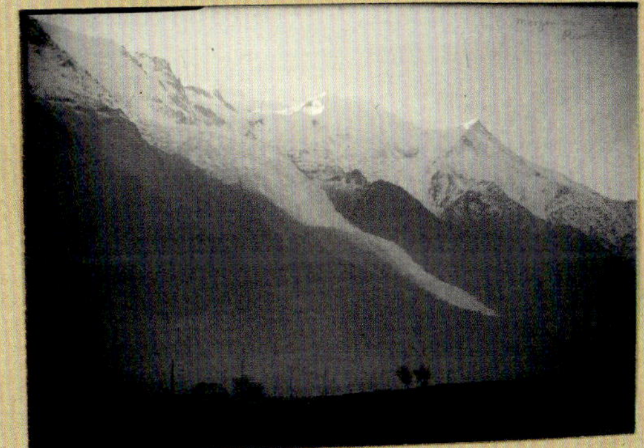

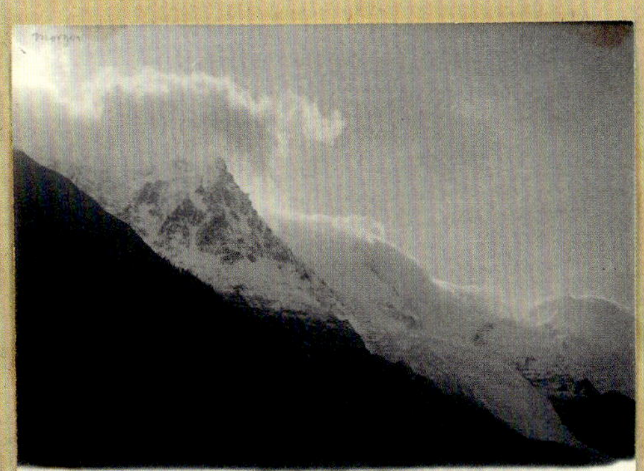

II. KIRCHNER

Whereas Willumsen had his breakthrough under the sway of Symbolism in the eighteen-nineties, and also lived for a number of years at the very center of the movement in Paris, the younger Ernst Ludwig Kirchner had a background in German Expressionism centered on Dresden and Berlin. After the turn of the century, for example with an iconic work such as *Sol og Ungdom* (Sun and Youth) from 1910, Willumsen became part of the Vitalist movement that gained sway around 1900.[15] Kirchner, on the other hand, painted the hectic street scenes, sex workers, and emancipated female dancers of city life. He signed up as a volunteer during World War I, but became dependent on sleeping pills, morphine, and alcohol, and was discharged with depression. At the same time Kirchner, like Willumsen, was also influenced by the ideas of Vitalism current in contemporary health and *Lebensreform* movements. He spent four summers—the first in 1908—on the Baltic island of Fehmarn painting naturists and the lush summer landscape. Despite belonging to different generations and coming from different art movements, there are obvious points of comparison between the work of the two painters. In such comparisons the Expressionist style of Willumsen's late oeuvre comes to the fore, as does Kirchner's personal style and the way both were influenced by the ideas of the Vitalist movement.

After his wartime breakdown, Kirchner was sent to various German sanatoriums and clinics for treatment. Then in early 1917 he came to Davos for the first time, a town at an altitude of more than 1,500 meters in the Swiss canton of Graubünden, where he was taken care of by Dr Spengler and his family. The following year he settled permanently on the outskirts of the town. Here he started to paint his alpine works, as well as designing tapestries and carving wooden furniture and sculptures that he painted and used to decorate his home, transforming it into a *gesamtkunstwerk* (figs. 6 and 7).

The tranquil life he led in the Alps aided Kirchner's recovery. Moving from the depravity of the modern city to a healthy life surrounded by nature and mountain villagers with a timeless way of life, he became part of a movement during the first decades of the twentieth century when what was seen as urban decadence generated a critique of civilization and a quest to find healing in nature and traditional rural life. That Kirchner's pursuit of health took place in the sanatorium town of Davos, where members of the European upper classes, sick or suffering from nervous disorders, came in search of peace of mind and treatment, underlines the distinctly modern nature of Kirchner's retreat from his former life. A similar duality between illness and restorative nature is to be found in Thomas Mann's sanatorium novel from Davos *The Magic Mountain* (1924), which he wrote when Kirchner was living in the area.

This dialectic of Decadence and Vitalism was also related to the widespread Nietzscheanism of the period. From 1869 until his breakdown in 1889, Nietzsche spent many summers in the small town of Sils-Maria in the Alps, around eighty kilometers south of Davos. In both his life and work, the Alps played a central role for Nietzsche, connecting them as he did to health and the strength and courage to live according to a post-Christian, cyclical world view—incarnated in the *Übermensch* or "Superman"—as opposed to the all-too-human, resentful, tradition-bound, Christian life led by the inhabitants of the lowlands.

Much of Nietzsche's bible for the future, *Thus Spoke Zarathustra*, was written in Sils-Maria. The prophetic figure in the book, Zarathustra, has lived in the mountains for many years, but elects to descend to the lowlands of people living stupefied, depraved lives to spread his wisdom. His thinking, he claims, is akin to the highest mountain, a form of communication between "great" men: "In the mountains the shortest way is from peak to peak, but for that route thou must have long legs. Proverbs should be peaks, and those spoken to should be big and tall."[16] Nietzsche, or perhaps rather contemporary Nietzschean thinking, has often been identified as being important to both Willumsen and Kirchner.[17] It would certainly be difficult to understand their interest in the Alps without taking Nietzschean influences into account.

Fig. 5
J. F. Willumsen
Spread from Willumsen's album of cuttings
Land and Sea, ca. 1900–11
Willumsen's Museum, Frederikssund

15. Cf. Anne Gregersen, *Vitale Willumsen—J.F. Willumsens dyrkelse af krop, natur og livskraft*, exh. cat. Willumsen's Museum (Frederikssund, 2008). For more on Vitalism as a movement see Gertrud Hvidberg-Hansen and Gertrud Oelsner (eds.), *The Spirit of Vitalism. Health, Beauty and Strength in Danish Art, 1890–1940*, exh. cat. Fuglsang Kunstmuseum and Fyns Kunstmuseum (Fuglsang/Odense, 2008), as well as Anders Ehlers Dam, *Den vitalistiske strømning i dansk litteratur omkring år 1900* (Aarhus/Copenhagen, 2010).
16. Friedrich Nietzsche, *Thus Spoke Zarathustra: A Book for All and None* [German original, 1883–85], trans. Thomas Common (Herefordshire, 1997), p. 36.
17. The importance of Nietzsche for Willumsen is discussed by Hjorth, 2006 (see footnote 14), pp. 81–89, without, however, addressing the significance of mountains. On Nietzsche and Kirchner see Sharon Jordan, "'He is a Bridge': The Importance of Friedrich Nietzsche for Ernst Ludwig Kirchner," in Jill Lloyd and Janis Staggs (eds.), *Ernst Ludwig Kirchner*, exh. cat. Neue Galerie (New York, 2019), pp. 87–116. On the significance of mountains for Nietzsche see, for example, Sean Ireton, "'Ich bin ein Wanderer und ein Bergsteiger' – Nietzsche and Zarathustra in the Mountains," *Colloquia Germanica*, 42, 3 (2009), pp. 193–212.

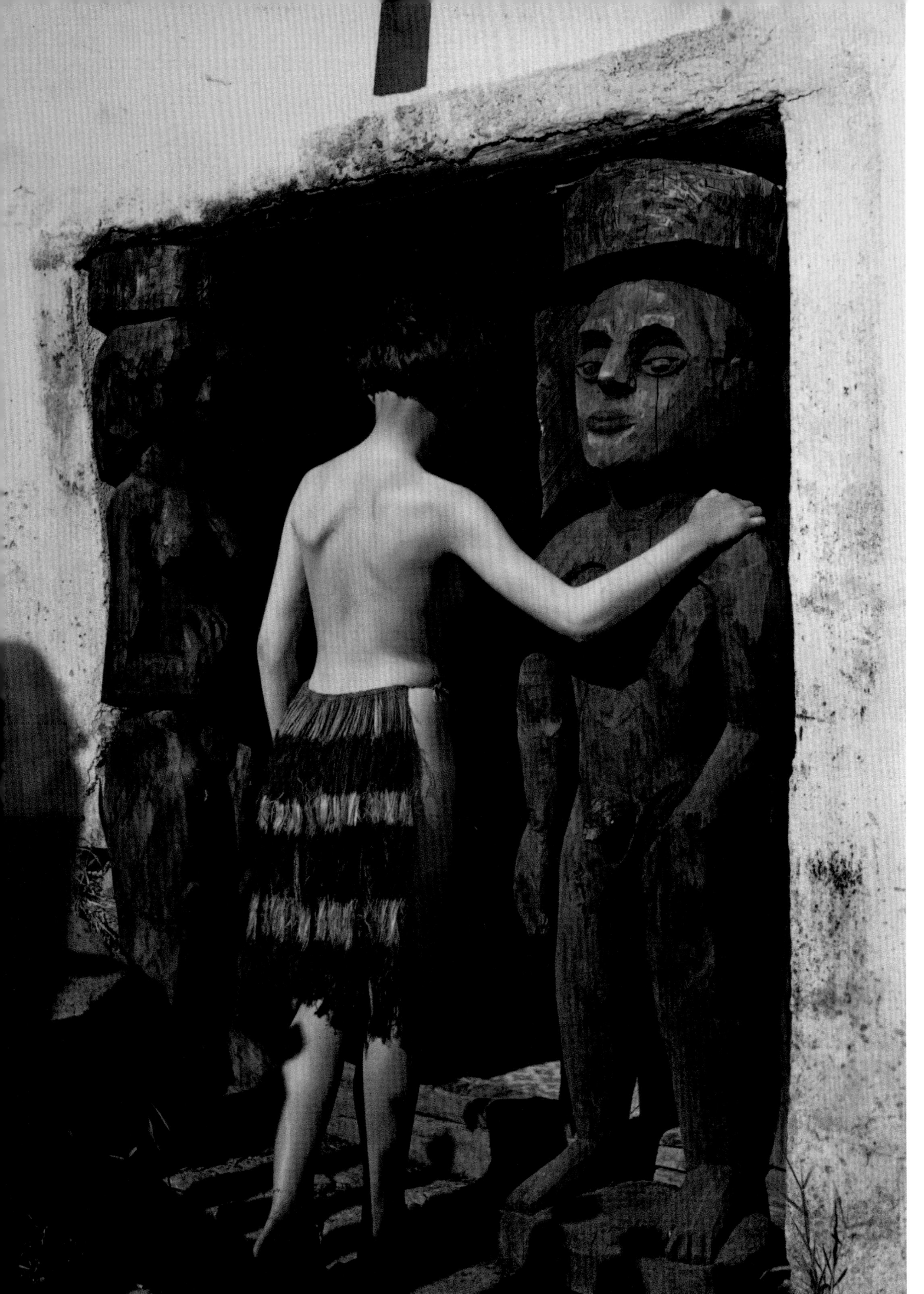

Fig. 6
Ernst Ludwig Kirchner
Nina Hard in Front of the Entrance to the House "In den Lärchen", summer 1921
Gelatin-silver print, 17 × 11.8 cm
Kirchner Museum Davos

Fig. 7
Ernst Ludwig Kirchner
"Sculptor's Studio" next to the "Wildbodenhaus" (Three Sculptures by Hermann Scherer and One by Kirchner), 1924
Glass-plate negative, 24 × 18 cm
Kirchner Museum Davos

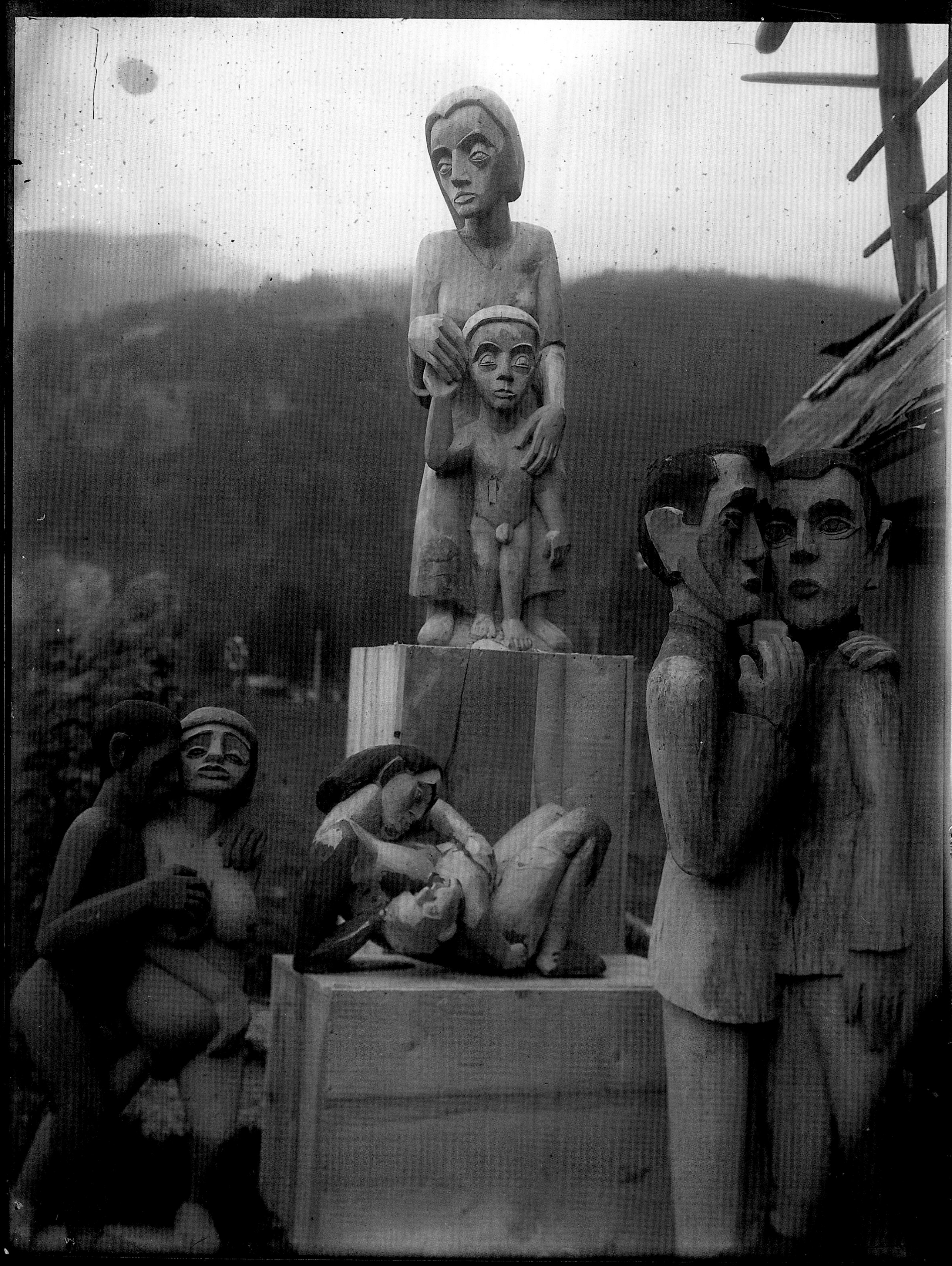

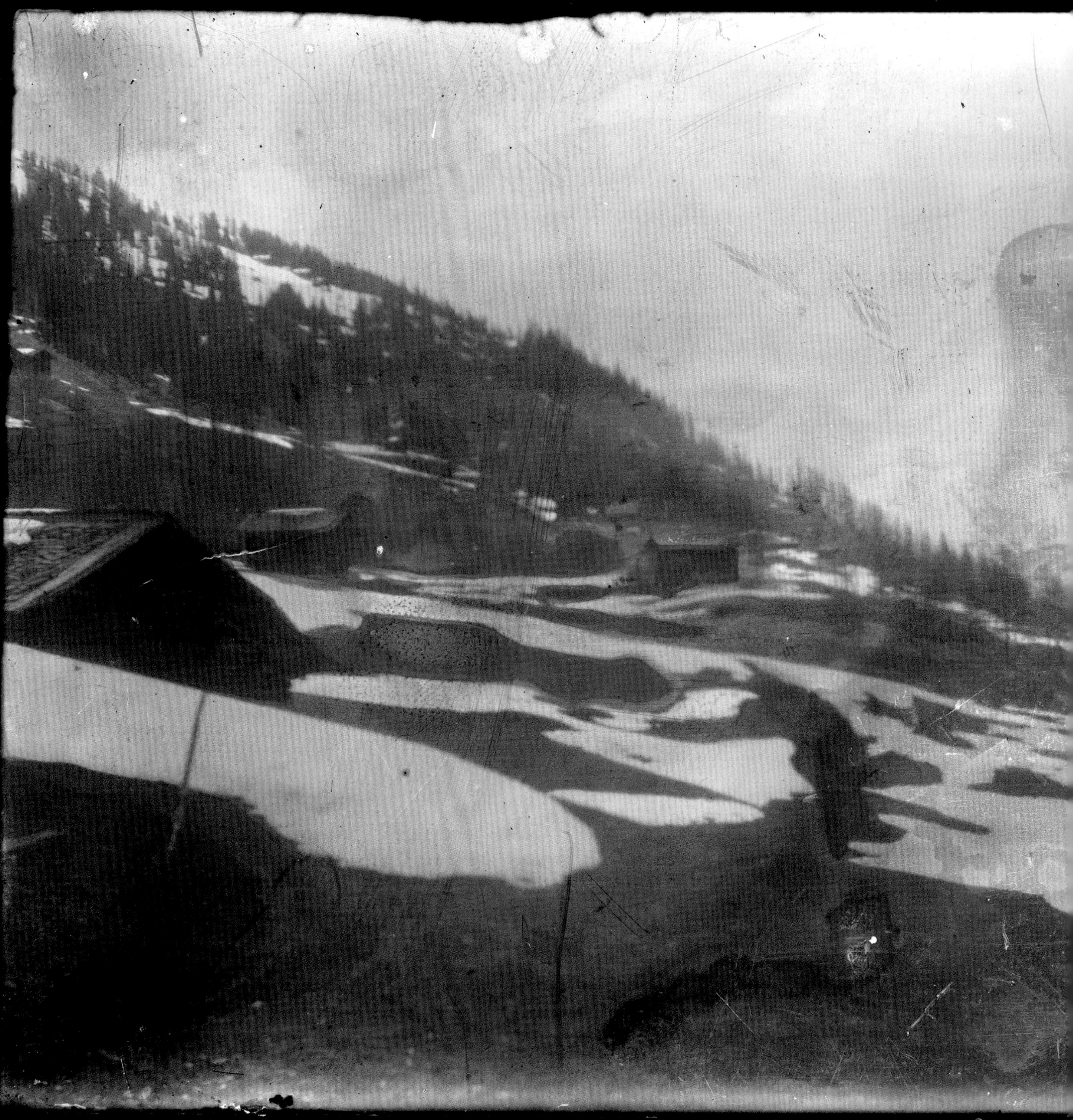

Fig. 8
Ernst Ludwig Kirchner
View from Ernst Ludwig Kirchner's House to Längmatte, 1918–22
Gelatin-silver print, 12 × 16.5 cm
Kirchner Museum Davos

That Kirchner withdrew to Davos did not, however, mean that he withdrew from the art world. On the contrary he cultivated his art contacts, and his works were exhibited in both Germany and Switzerland. He also wrote texts under an assumed name in the hope of influencing how his works were received. Louis de Marsalle was a fictional persona he invented, and in whose name he wrote reviews of his art. In a short article on Kirchner's Swiss works his pseudonym wrote: "The barren yet intimate nature of the highest mountains has had a major influence on the artist. It has intensified his love of his subjects and simultaneously rid his conception of all superfluity."[18]

The extent to which Kirchner's change of lifestyle influenced his painting is debatable. Obviously the subject of his paintings changed, but in many respects Kirchner continued to paint in the Expressionist style he brought with him to the Alps. This can be seen in the often dynamic nature of his mountain landscapes, akin to that of his cityscapes. His palette, however, changed in the direction of clearer colors.

Like Willumsen, Kirchner was fascinated by the mountain landscape surrounding him in Switzerland, and it featured in many of the works he painted here. Also like Willumsen, he photographed the landscape (fig. 8). Unlike the Danish artist, however, who was fascinated by the mountains themselves and their peaks soaring above humanity, Kirchner mainly painted mountain landscapes in which elements of cultivation were present: buildings, people, and animals in the unnavigable, steep mountains. One of Kirchner's favorite motifs is thus the wooden houses spread across the alpine landscape where he lived. The triptych *Alpleben* (Life in the Alps) from 1918 (fig. 9) is a famous example of an homage to mountain villagers tending their cattle and farming the land in an organic landscape with mountains in the background. Unlike Willumsen, who preferred areas above the tree line, Kirchner's works often include tall, slender pines. Whereas Willumsen strives for the sublime—heights that surpass humanity—Kirchner's motifs reveal a fascination with a more domesticated view in which people live at one

18. Louis de Marsalle [alias Ernst Ludwig Kirchner], "Über die Schweizer Arbeiten von E.L. Kirchner," [1933] in Lothar Grisebach, *Ernst Ludwig Kirchners Davoser Tagebuch. Eine Darstellung des Malers und eine Sammlung seiner Schrifte* (Bern, 1997), pp. 231–32.

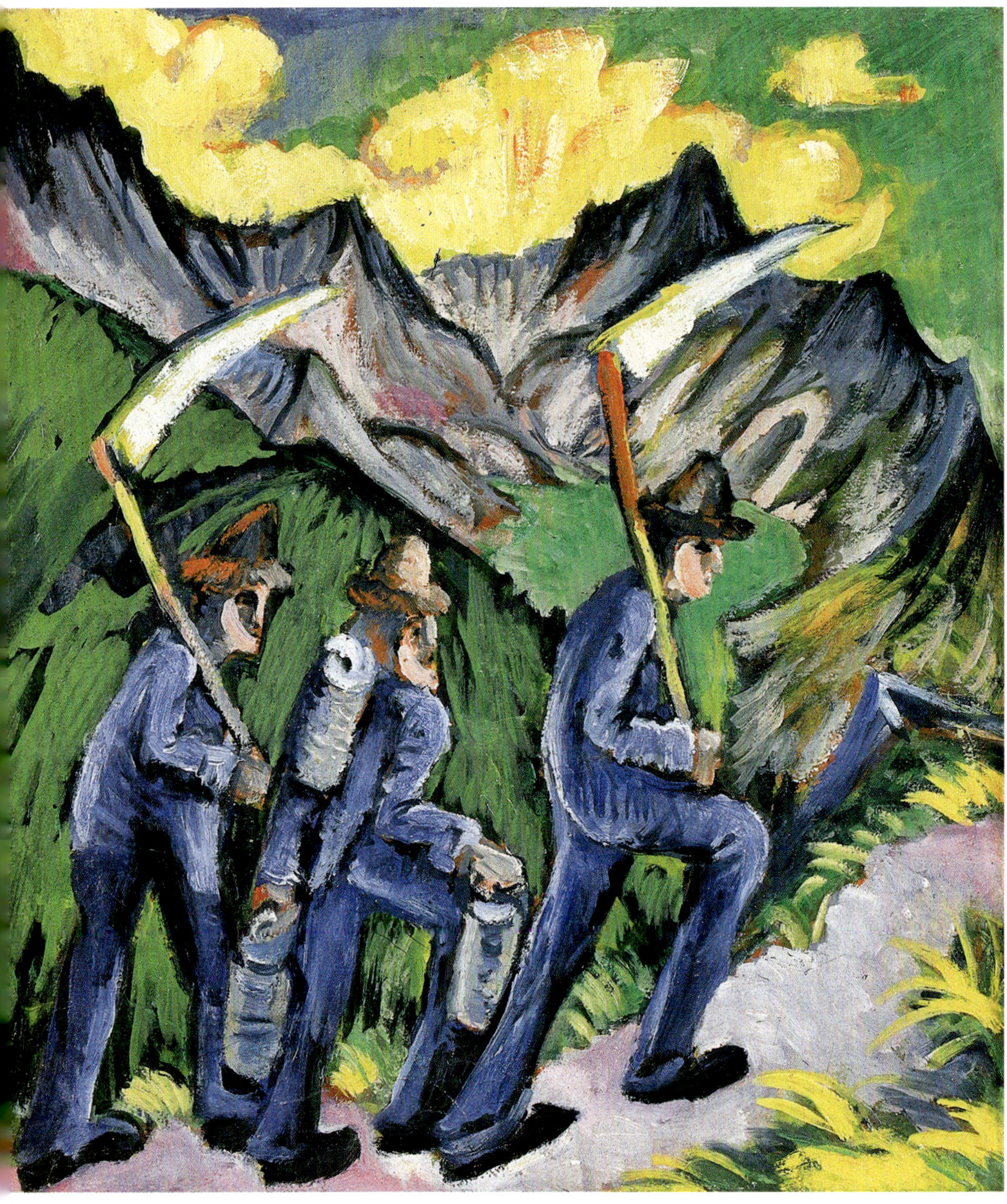

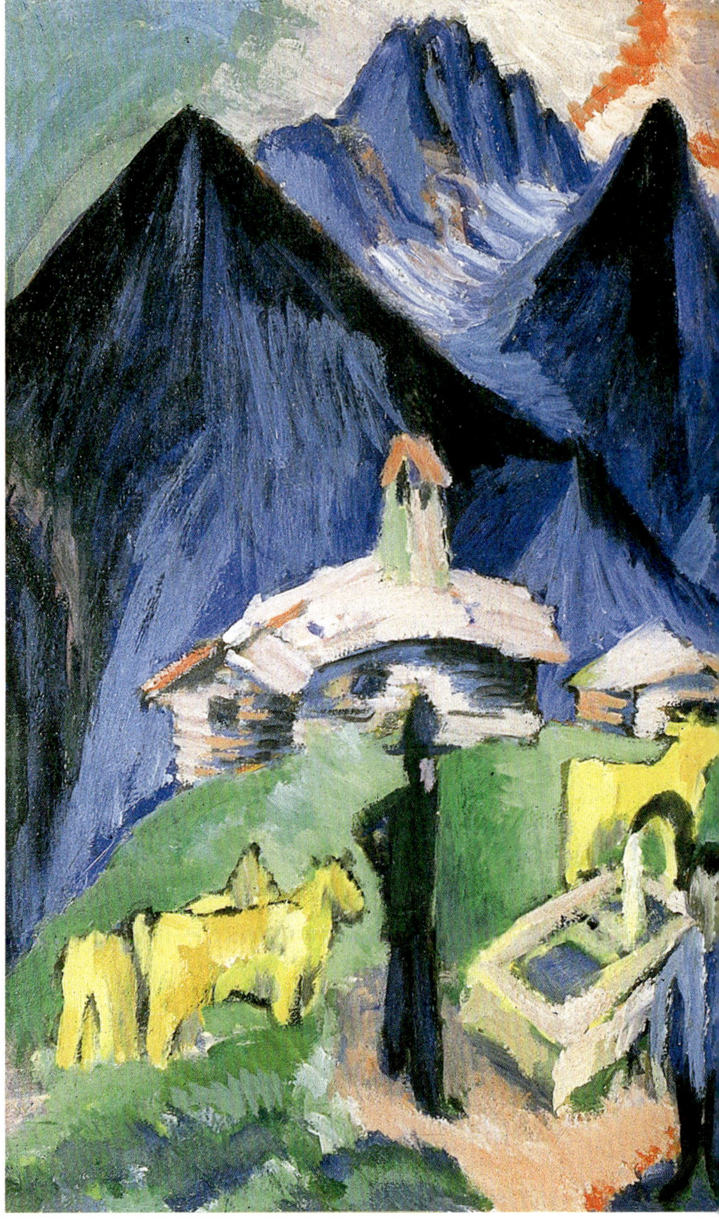

Fig. 9
Ernst Ludwig Kirchner
Alpleben (Life in the Alps),
triptychon, 1917–19
Oil on canvas,
left side panel 70 × 60 cm,
center panel 70 × 80 cm,
side panel 70 × 60 cm
Kirchner Museum Davos

with the landscape according to the rhythms of nature. As such, these works represent an indirect critique of the modern world, albeit one that is in itself a modern phenomenon. At the same time it would be entirely wrong to classify the art Kirchner made in Switzerland as naïve *Heimatkunst*. The Expressionistic style of his alpine works, in keeping with his earlier oeuvre, is modern rather than anti-modern, and his withdrawal to Davos represented a retreat rather than a homecoming for the artist.

Kirchner's works continue the Expressionism of his time in Berlin and Dresden, where he was a key member and co-founder of the Brücke artist group.[19] One of Kirchner's most stunning and famous paintings from his early years in Switzerland is *Winterlandschaft in Mond-*

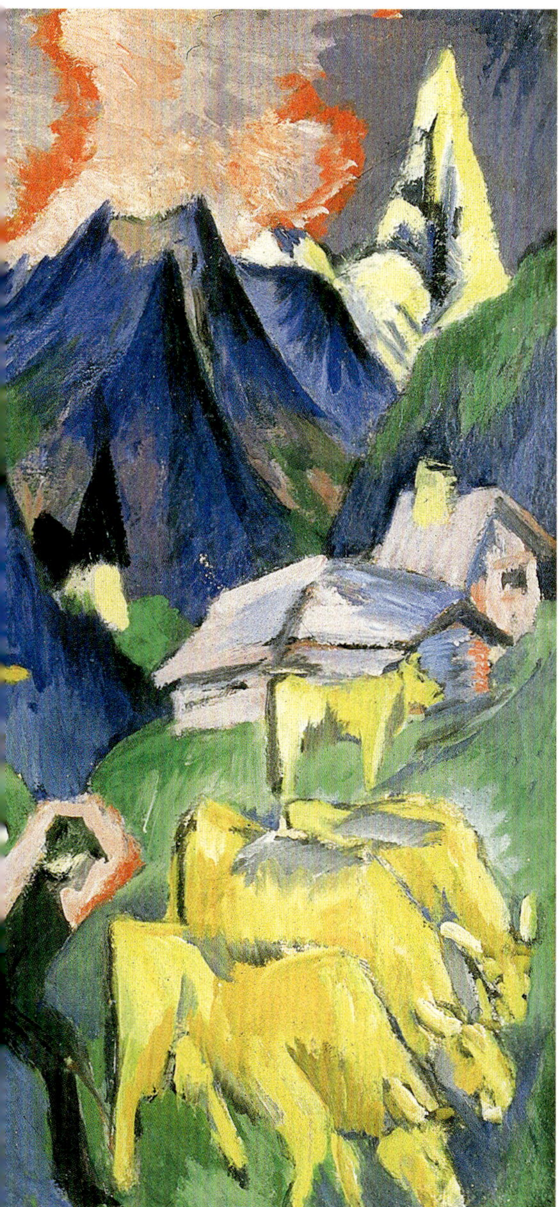

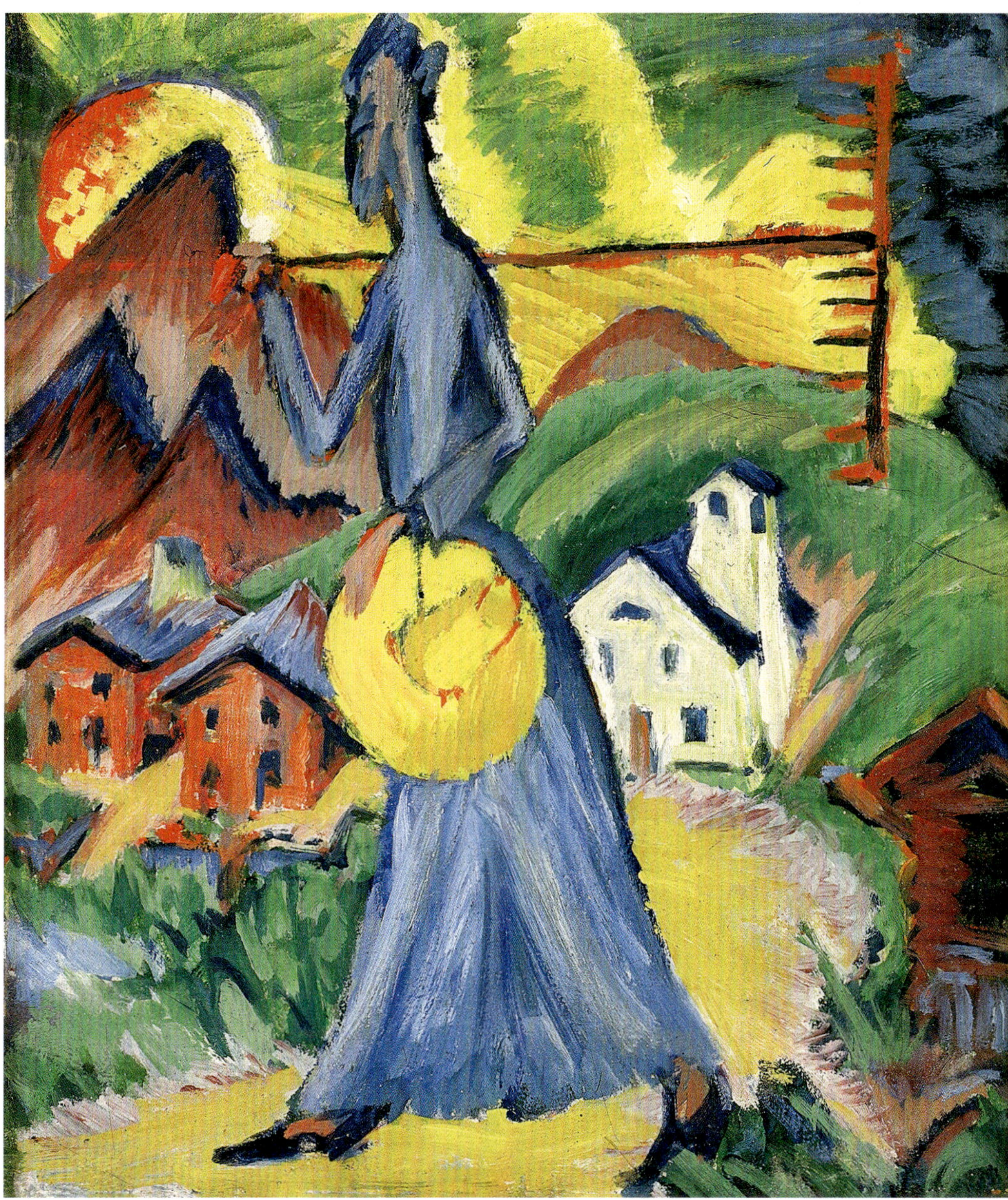

licht (Winter Landscape in Moonlight) from 1919 (fig. 10), a work combining mountains, the cultural landscape, and Expressionism. The painting shows the view from *In den Lärchen*, the house Kirchner rented. The colors in the square painting seem more intense, and the sweeping and pointed forms that point to the moonlit orange sky form an organic winter landscape, simultaneously depicting the coldness of the region and radiating warm intimacy. The work is Expressionist in both color and style. The snow on the mountainsides shifts between shades of bluish white and purple, and the tall pines close by are pink, whereas those in the distant shadows are blue-black. The neighboring houses in the foreground are painted in different shades of reddish brown. Bernhard Mendes

19. On founding the group in 1905 the artists took the name Die Brücke (The Bridge) from Nietzsche's *Thus Spoke Zarathustra* (see footnote 16). In Zarathustra's prologue to the book (p. 8), Nietzsche writes: "What is great in man is that he is a bridge and not a goal."

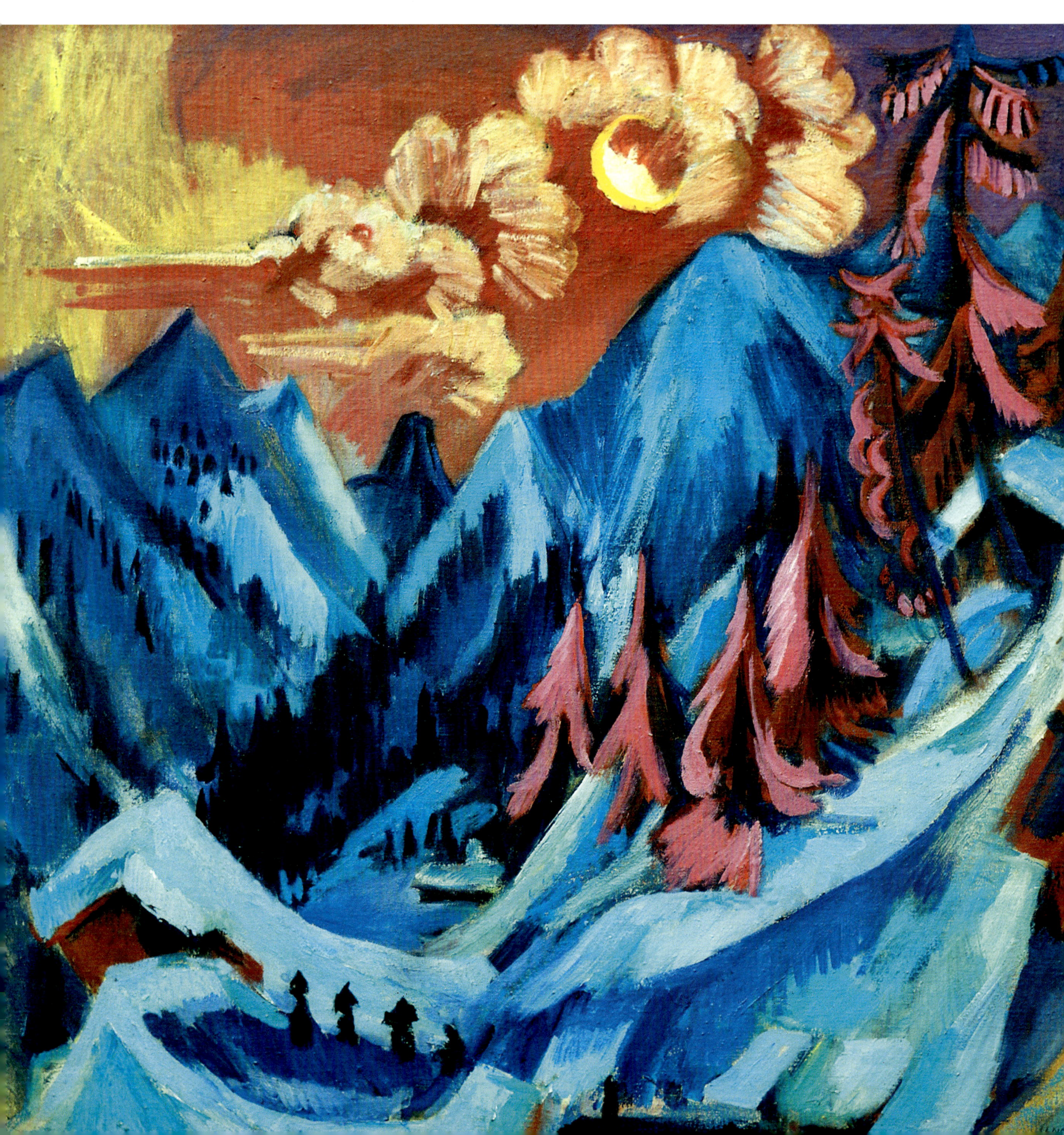

Fig. 10
Ernst Ludwig Kirchner
Winterlandschaft in Mondlicht
(Winter Landscape
in Moonlight), 1919
Oil on canvas, 120 × 121 cm
Detroit Institute of Arts

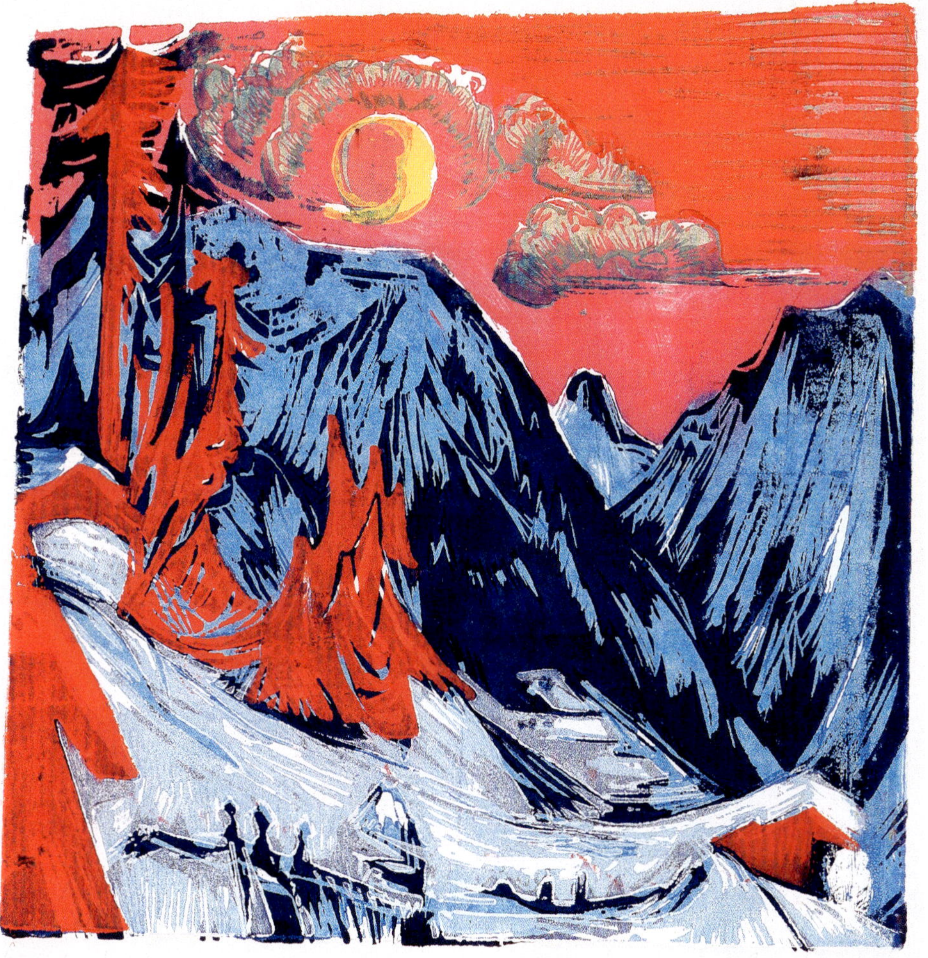

Fig. 11
Ernst Ludwig Kirchner
Wintermondnach
(Winter Moonlit Night), 1919
Color woodcut,
composition 47 × 33 cm
Museum Folkwang, Essen

Bürgi writes poetically of the moonlight in the painting: "This cold, magical coloration is heightened by the shimmering yellow light of the crescent moon, which pierces like flowerlike billowing or beaklike cloud formations and tinges the sky vermilion."[20]

On January 20, 1919, in a letter to Helene Spengler, the wife of the doctor in Davos who treated Kirchner for ailments including morphine addiction, he describes the moon he saw through his window, which forms the basis for *Winter Landscape in Moonlight*. He describes the contrast between life in Berlin, where people are "half-demented," and his new, secluded life in the mountains:

> [T]his morning there was such a wonderful moonset, the moon yellow above little pink clouds and the mountains a pure, deep blue, really glorious. I would so much have liked to do some painting. But it was too cold—even my windows were frosted although I'd kept the fire going overnight. For all that, how immensely glad I am to be here, where the dying splashes of the billows of life outside reach me only by mail.[21]

The painting has a magical ambience created primarily by the use of color, but also by its different elements and winter atmosphere as a whole. Kirchner used the same motif in a series of color woodcuts (fig. 11). In 1937, the year before Kirchner committed suicide, the Nazis confiscated the painting from the Kaiser Friedrich Museum in Magdeburg as "degenerate" art. The peaceful subject was harmless, but the style in which it was painted was considered too modern.

20. Bernhard Mendes Bürgi, "Painter of the Alps," in Bernhard Mendes Bürgi (ed.), *Ernst Ludwig Kirchner. Mountain Life. The Early Years in Davos 1917–1926*, exh. cat. Kunstmuseum Basel (Ostfildern-Ruit, 2003), p. 16.

21. Letter from Ernst Ludwig Kirchner to Helene Spengler dated January 20, 1919 in *Maler der Expressionismus im Briefwechsel mit Eberhard Grisebach*, p. 98 (Hamburg, 1962): "[H]eute morgen [war] ein so wundervoller Monduntergang, auf rosa Wölkchen der gelbe Mond und die Berge rein tiefblau, ganz herrlich, ich hätte so gern gemalt. Aber kalt war's, sogar meine Fenster gefroren, trotzdem ich die Nacht gefeuert habe. Wie unendlich froh bin ich doch, hier zu sein und nur die letzten Spritzer der Wogen des äusseren Lebens zu bekommen durch die Post." The translation here is taken from Bürgi 2003 (see footnote 20), p. 15.

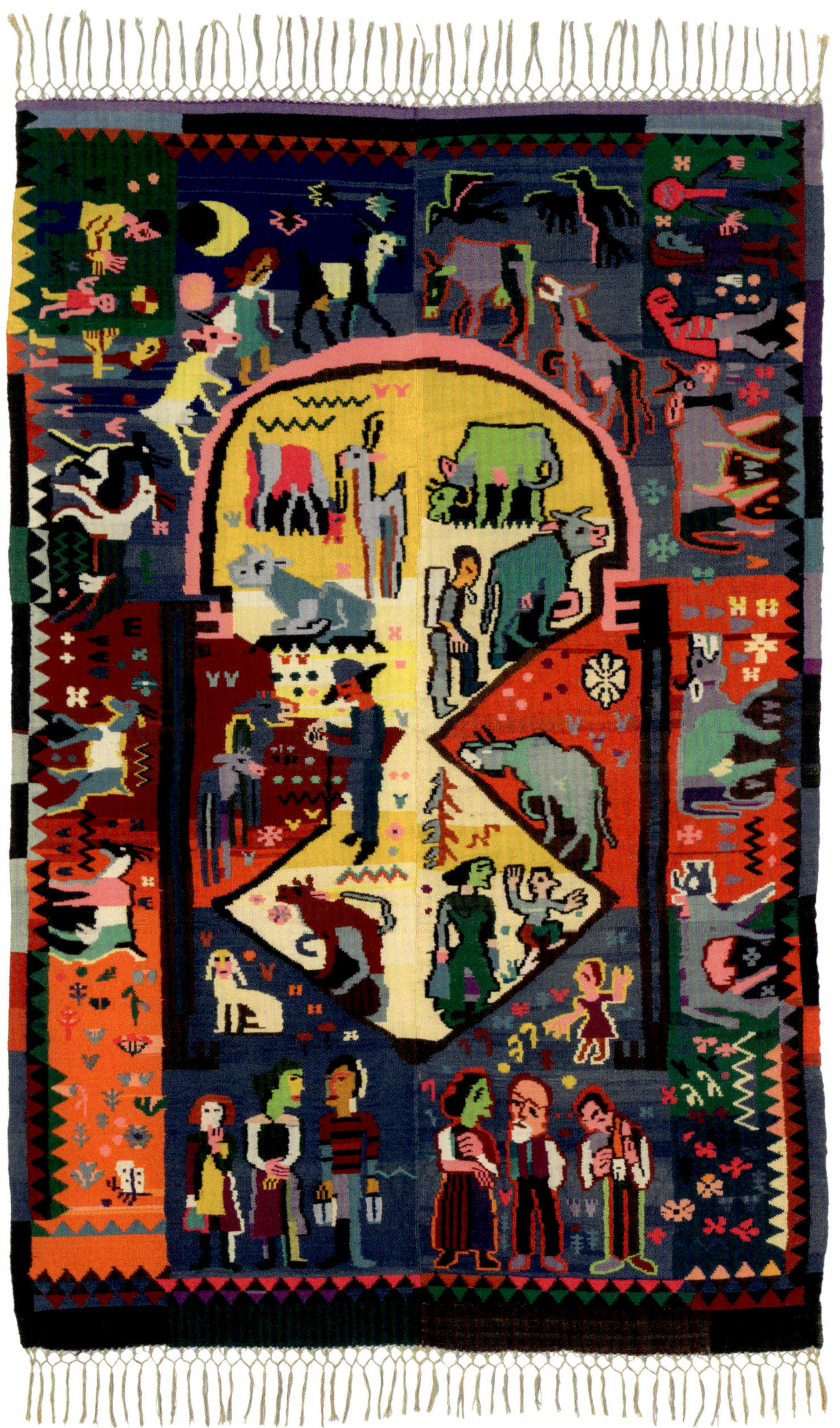

Fig. 12
Ernst Ludwig Kirchner and Lisa Gujer
Alpaufzug (Cattle Drive into the Alps), 1926
Woll, 258 × 172 cm
Zürcher Hochschule der Künste,
Museum für Gestaltung Zürich

Fig. 13
Ernst Ludwig Kirchner
Die Brücke bei Wiesen
(The Bridge in Wiesen), 1926
Oil on canvas, 120 × 120 cm
Kirchner Museum Davos

From around the mid-nineteen-twenties, during his last years in Davos, Kirchner's works became more stylized and decorative. Some of his late works are painted so that from a distance they resemble the tapestries he had also started to design. Kirchner's tapestries were woven by Lise Gujer, who he had met in Switzerland, and the motifs are often based on country life in the Alps. One example is *Alpaufzug* (Alpine Cattle Drive) (fig. 12). The lives of different generations—young children, healthy farmers, and the elderly—form an organically colorful, ornamental pattern in which the farmer's livestock play a central role. Here traditional mountain existence is elevated to an organic art of life in an expressive form with clear naivistic traits.

Just as the tapestries borrow colors and motifs from Kirchner's paintings, his late paintings have also been described as having a particular "tapestry style"[22] where the painting itself is reminiscent of woven tapestries. Here there is no concealment of the two-dimensionality of the image, in which small strokes of color are "interwoven." One example is *Die Brücke bei Wiesen* (The Bridge at Wiesen) from 1926 (fig. 13), where the bridge stretches across almost the entire width of an organic landscape that appears ornamental and without depth: a world of grass-green surfaces interleaved with dark green trees and long snowdrifts in shades of pink and white. The painting also demonstrates Kirchner's growing interest in modern developments at the time. His critique of civilization waned, and he started to include elements such as the train station in Davos. He also used winter sport athletes as a motif. It is also worth noting that Willumsen's famous mountain painting from Norway, *Jotunheim* (1892–1893), was almost certainly inspired by the tapestries he had seen on his travels in the country.[23]

22. A term that originates with the Kirchner specialist Donald E. Gordon. Cited in Bürgi 2003 (see footnote 20), p. 14.

23. On *Jotunheim* and Willumsen's trip to Norway in 1892, including his interest in mountains, see Branth Pedersen 2006 (see footnote 2). *Jotunheim* is also analysed by others, including Krogh 2006 (see footnote 8), pp. 98–104.

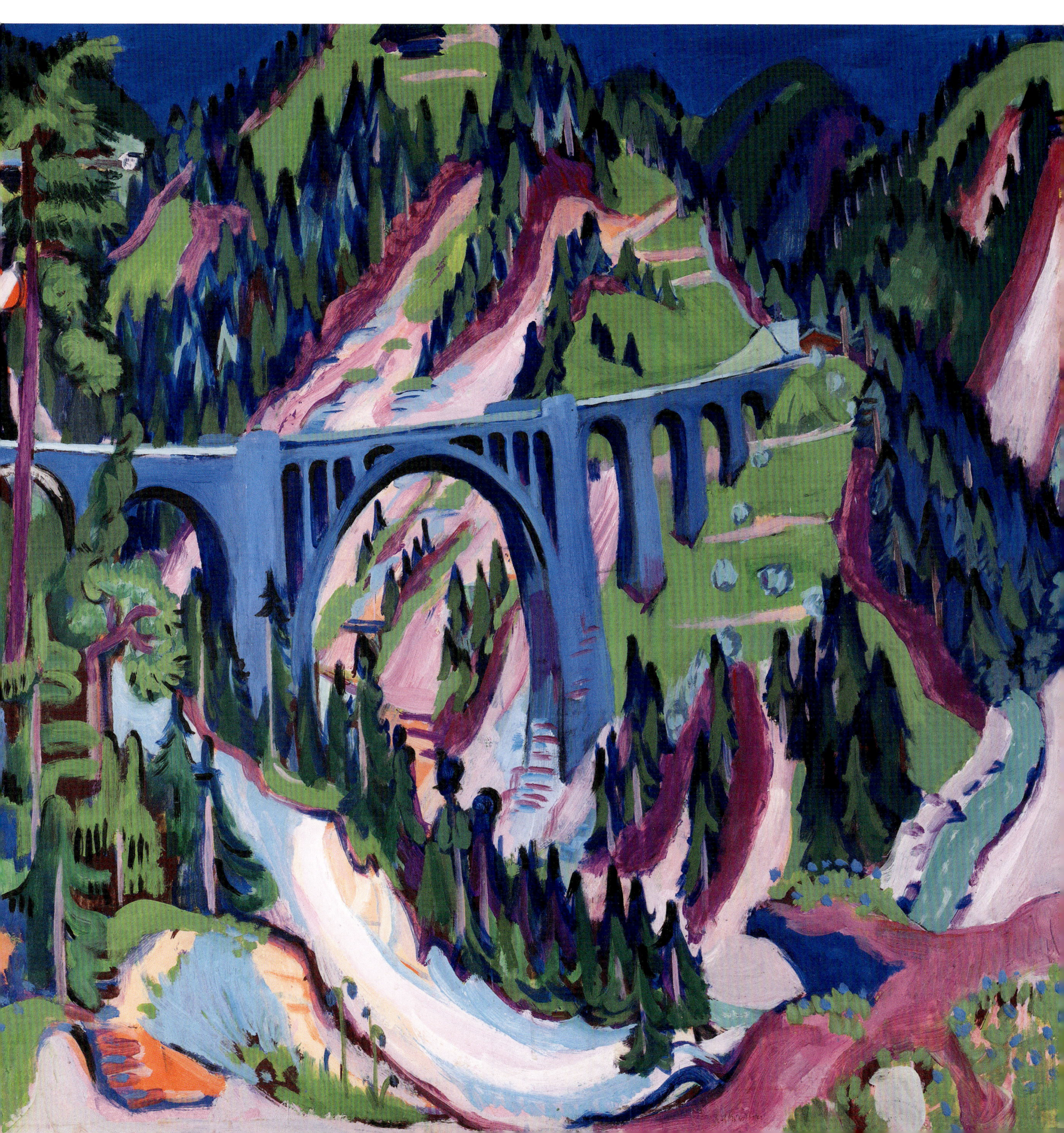

Fig. 14
Gerhard Richter
Davos, 1981
Oil on canvas, 50×70 cm
Art Institute of Chicago

Willumsen and Kirchner were in many ways very different painters who came to mountains as a motif from different backgrounds. Willumsen's point of departure was the Symbolism of the eighteen-nineties. He was not part of any Expressionist movement, unlike Kirchner, co-founder of the Brücke group. Yet interestingly their works have many shared features, albeit more in terms of their Expressionist style than the ideas behind them.

Whilst Willumsen was especially drawn to the highest, most remote peaks covered by "eternal" snow, where he found validation for his metaphysical, idealistic approach to art, Kirchner approached the Alps as a cultural landscape surrounded by mountains, a place where timeless, traditional life unfolded.

Both artists' perception of the mountains was in different ways inspired by the ideas of Vitalism, and both were, in their coupling of life, vitality, and the heights, influenced by contemporary Nietzscheanism. Underlying these were the ideas of Romanticism: for Willumsen an interest in the landscape as sublime, and for Kirchner the idea of organic everyday life in the midst of unspoiled nature.

If we were to draw on the perspective of our own age, it is interesting to note that Gerhard Richter, one of the most important contemporary painters today, has also painted the Alps—indeed the mountains close to Davos. In 1981, in a series of four works entitled *Davos*, Richter painted night images of snowclad mountain crests with the full moon shining through high fog (fig. 14). The paintings are inspired by Romanticism, but their photographic sepia style makes them indisputably modern.

Richter's series presumably references Caspar David Friedrich's similarly brown-toned painting *Zwei Männer in Betrachtung des Mondes* (Two Men Contemplating the Moon) from 1819–20, but with a crucial difference: Richter's work is entirely devoid of people—even the point of view hardly seems human. In this respect Richter's

Davos paintings actually resemble Willumsen's fascination with deserted peaks, and Willumsen also painted several works of the moon above the mountains. So, as we have seen, did Kirchner. Like Willumsen and Kirchner, Richter has taken many photographs of the Alps on which his paintings are based, and has collated them in his *Atlas* project, which has also been published as a book (fig. 15).

Richter has stayed in Sils-Maria often, using the motifs he has found here in his work. Despite the difference between the three artists, Willumsen, Kirchner, and Richter also share a relationship to Nietzsche. Richter started reading Nietzsche as a child when his mother gave him a copy of *Thus Spoke Zarathustra*,[24] and in 1992–93 an exhibition of his works was held at the *Nietzsche-Haus* in Sils-Maria where the German philosopher rented a room in the summer. Richter like his predecessors, inspired by Nietzsche among others, has been drawn to the Alps to paint and photograph, like them in search of "the mystical blue flower of art."

24. Werner Spies, "Ein Ozean aus Glas im Kölner Dom," *Frankfurter Allgemeine Zeitung*, August 25, 2007.

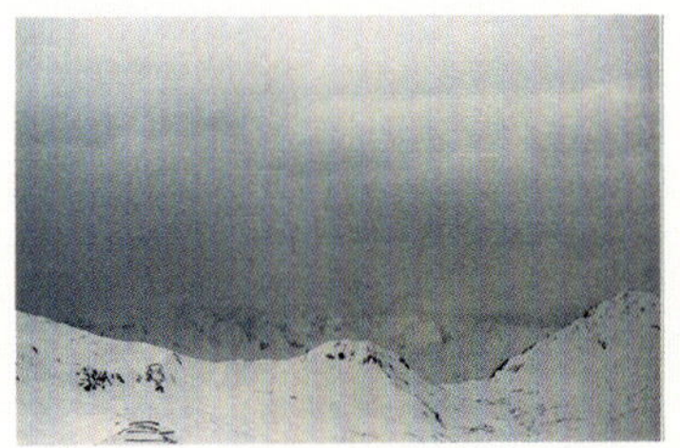
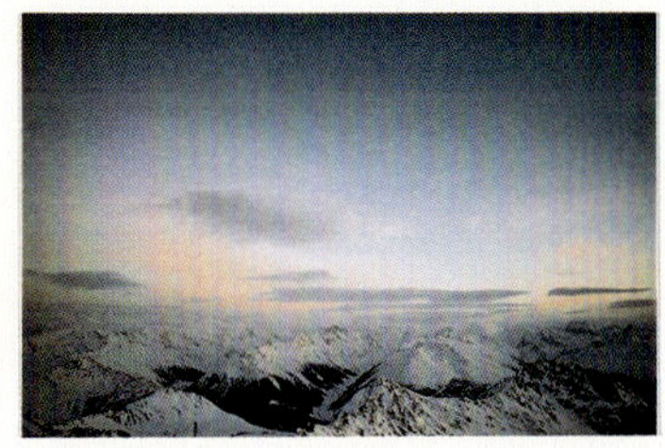
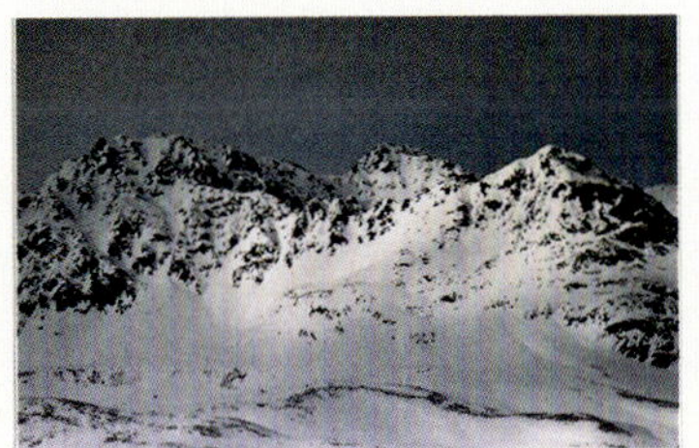
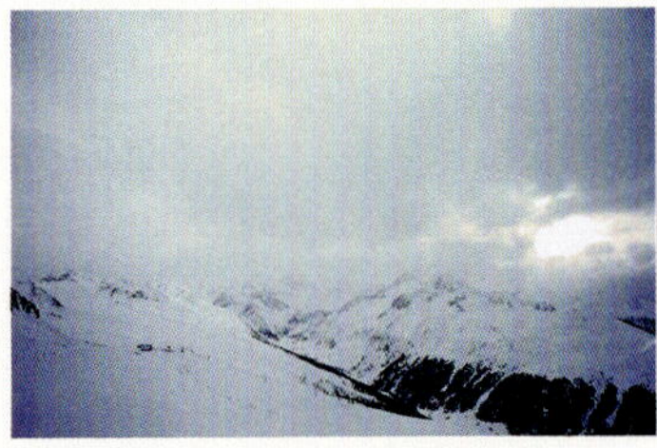
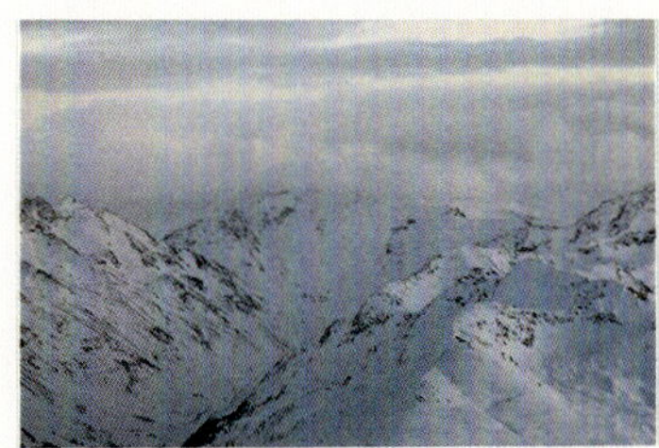
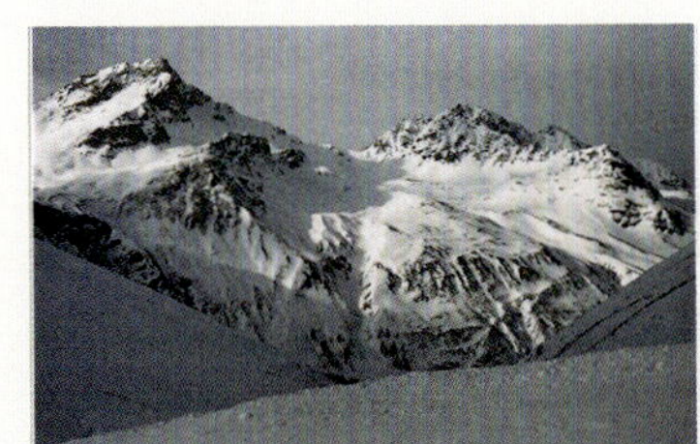
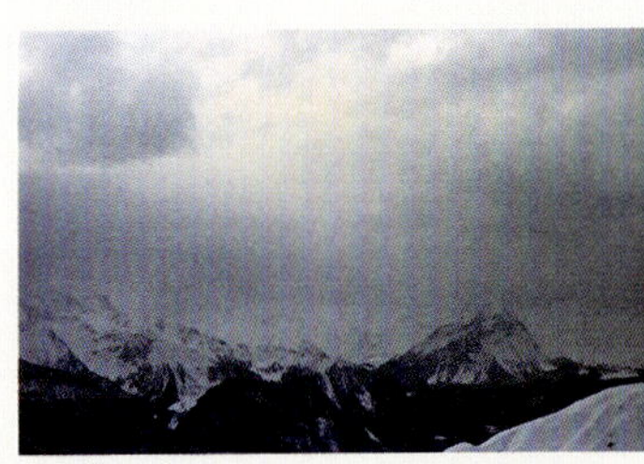
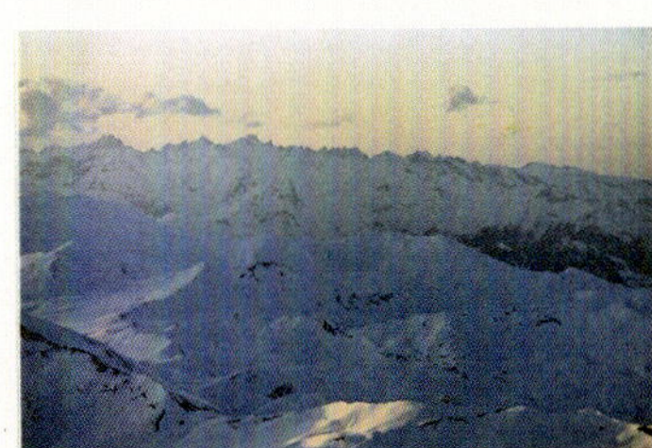
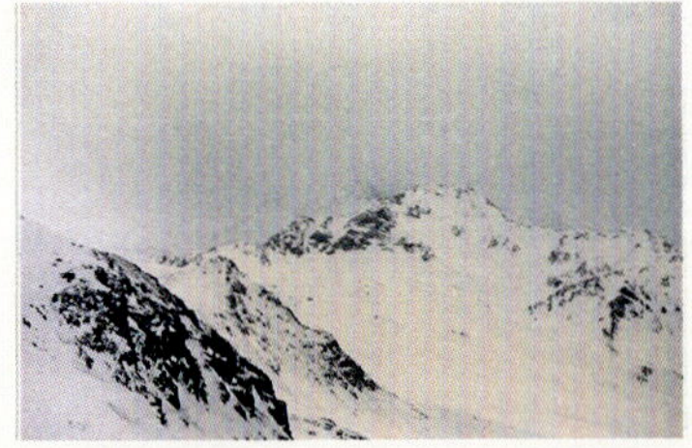

Bibliography

Bodelsen, Merete. *Willumsen i halvfemsernes Paris.* Copenhagen, 1957.

Bürgi, Bernhard Mendes. "Painter of the Alps." In *Ernst Ludwig Kirchner. Mountain Life. The Early Years in Davos 1917–1926*, edited by Bernhard Mendes Bürgi, exh. cat. Kunstmuseum Basel. Ostfildern, 2003.

Dam, Anders Ehlers. *Den vitalistiske strømning i dansk litteratur omkring år 1900.* Aarhus/Copenhagen, 2010.

Die Schwerkraft der Berge. 1774–1997. Edited by Stephan Kunz et al. Exh. cat. Aargauer Kunsthaus, Aarau and Kunsthalle Krems. Basel, 1997.

Gregersen, Anne. "J.F. Willumsens udklipsmapper." *Kunstmagasinet Janus* no. 1 (March 2009).

Gregersen, Anne. "Painting that Exaggerates, Exceeds, and Insists." In *Wild, Bold, and Late Willumsen*, edited by Erlend G. Høyersten, exh. cat. ARoS Aarhus Kunstmuseum. Aarhus, 2016.

Gregersen, Anne. "En billedbank i bevægelse. Motiviske krydsbefrugtninger i J.F. Willumsens samlinger af udklip og fotografier." In *J.F. Willumsen. Farver & striber*, edited by Christian Gether et al., exh. cat. ARKEN. Museum of Modern Art. Ishøj, 2018.

Grisebach, Lothar, ed. *Maler der Expressionismus im Briefwechsel mit Eberhard Grisebach.* Hamburg, 1962.

Grisebach, Lothar, ed. *Ernst Ludwig Kirchners Davoser Tagebuch. Eine Darstellung des Malers und eine Sammlung seiner Schriften.* New edition by Lucius Grisebach. Ostfildern, 1997.

Hedin, Gry. "Menneske, natur og videnskab. J.F. Willumsens arbejde med systemer, naturlove og ornamentik." In *Naturmøder*, edited by Lisbeth Lund, exh. cat. Willumsen's Museum. Frederikssund, 2015

Hjorth, Ulla. *J.F. Willumsen i Europa.* Frederikssund, 2006.

Ireton, Sean. "'Ich bin ein Wanderer und ein Bergsteiger' – Nietzsche and Zarathustra in the Mountains." *Colloquia Germanica*, 42, 3 (2009).

J.F. Willumsen – mellem guder og afgrund. Edited by Dina Vester Feilberg. Exh. cat. Rønnebæksholm. Næstved, 2012.

J.F. Willumsen. Over grænser. Edited by Leila Krogh. Exh. cat. Ordrupgaard, Charlottenlund/Musée d´Orsay, Paris. Copenhagen, 2006.

Jordan, Sharon. "'He is a Bridge': The Importance of Friedrich Nietzsche for Ernst Ludwig Kirchner." In *Ernst Ludwig Kirchner*, edited by Jill Lloyd and Janis Staggs, exh. cat. Neue Galerie. New York, 2019.

The Spirit of Vitalism. Health, Beauty and Strength in Danish Art, 1890–1940. Edited by Gertrud Hvidberg-Hansen and Gertrud Oelsner. Exh. cat. Fuglsangs Kunstmuseum and Fyns Kunstmuseum. Fuglsang/Odense, 2008.

Mentze, Ernst. *J.F. Willumsen. Mine Erindringer fortalt til Ernst Mentze.* Copenhagen, 1953.

Nietzsche, Friedrich. *Thus Spoke Zarathustra: A Book for All and None* [German original, 1883-85]. Translated by Thomas Common. Herefordshire, 1997.

Pedersen, Troels Branth. *Bjergtaget. J.F. Willumsen i Norge 1892.* Aarhus, 2006.

Pontoppidan, Henrik. *Lucky Per* [1898–1904]. Translated by Naomi Lebowitz. New York, 2010.

Simmel, Georg. "On the Aesthetics of the Alps." Translated by Jens Klenner. In *Mountains and the German Mind: Translations from Gessner to Messner, 1541–2009.* Edited by Sean Ireton and Caroline Schaumann. Rochester, NY, 2020.

Spies, Werner. "Ein Ozean aus Glas im Kölner Dom." *Frankfurter Allgemeine Zeitung*, 25. August, 2007.

Vitale Willumsen – J.F. Willumsens dyrkelse af krop, natur og livskraft. Anne Gregersen. Exh. cat. Willumsen's Museum. Frederikssund, 2008.

Öhman, Hjalmar. *J.F. Willumsen. Med Kommentarer af J.F. Willumsen.* Copenhagen, 1921.

Fig. 15
Gerhard Richter
Atlas, Tafel 338 (Davos)
(Atlas, sheet 338 (Davos)), 1973–74
Photo, 51.7 × 73.5 cm
Städtische Galerie im Lenbachhaus
and Kunstbau München, Munich

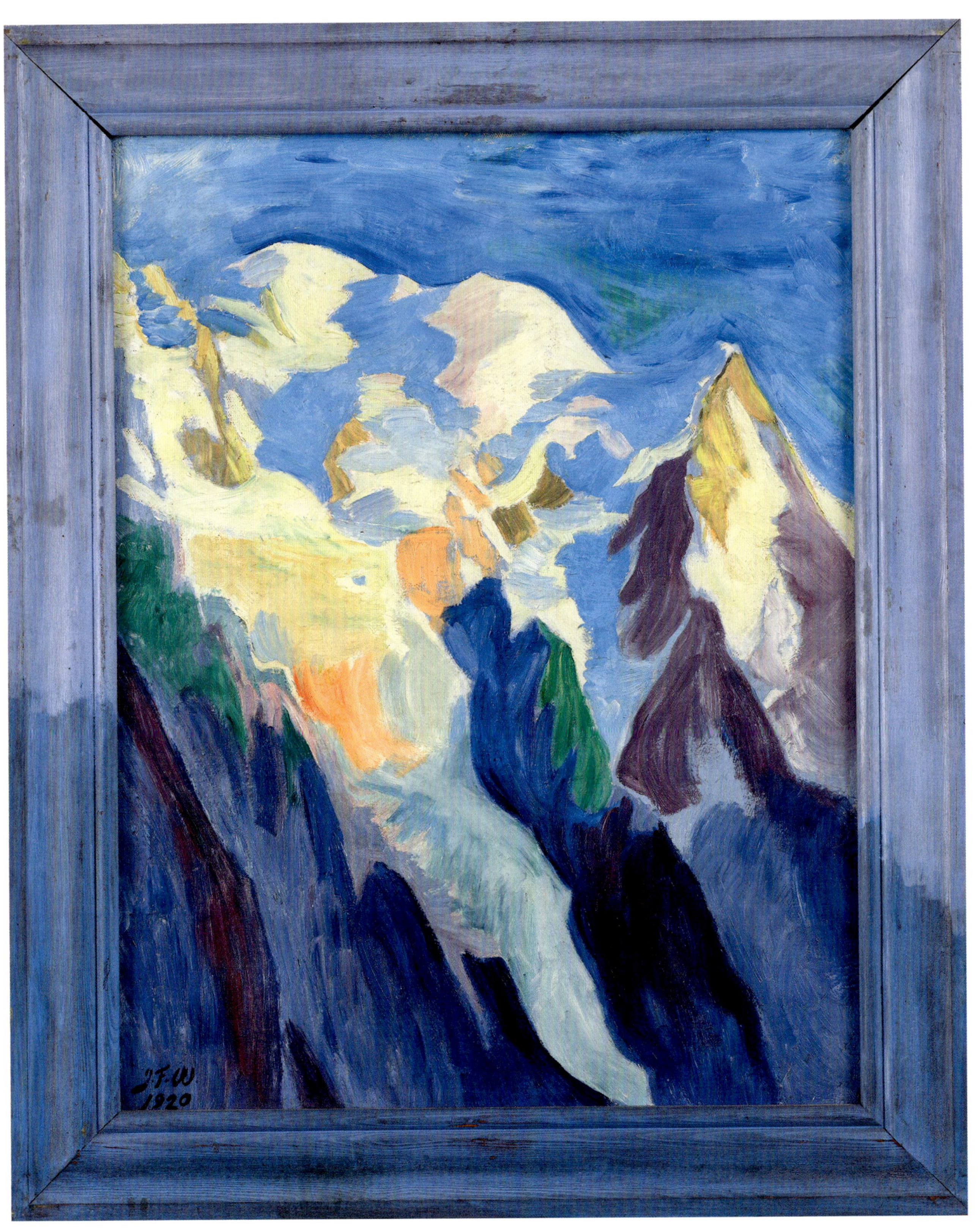

J. F. Willumsen
Mont Blanc i aftensol
(Mont Blanc in
Evening Sun), 1920
Oil on canvas,
61.5 × 46.5 cm
Willumsen's Museum,
Frederikssund

J. F. Willumsen
*Naturens skjolder,
bjergene med de tre
farver* (Nature's Shields.
The Tricolored
Mountains), 1936
Oil on canvas,
126 × 150.5 cm
Willumsen's Museum,
Frederikssund

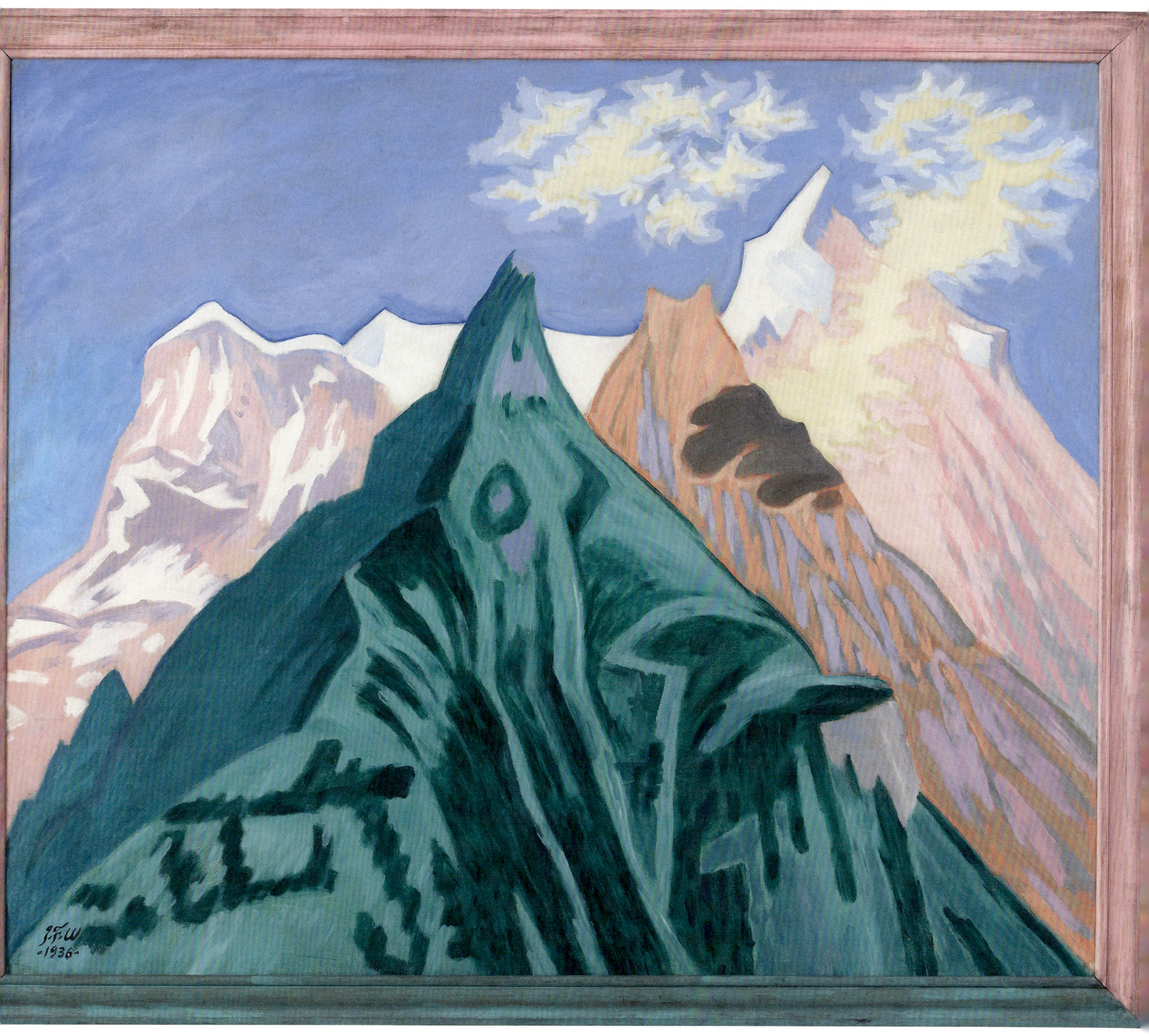

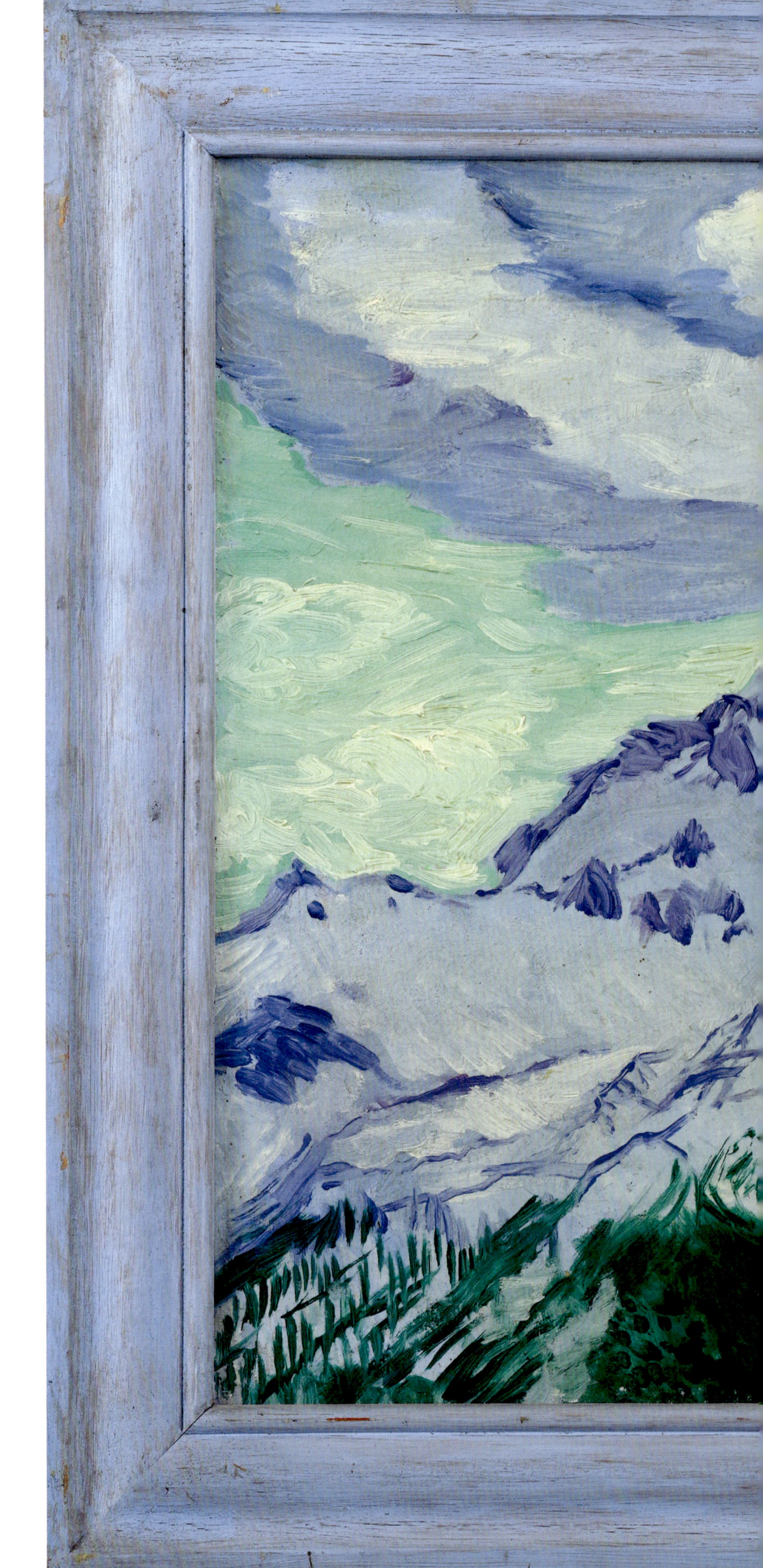

J. F. Willumsen
Bjergkæde i aftensol. Studie efter naturen til billedets midterste del
(Mountain Range in Evening Sun. Study after Nature for the Middle Part of the Picture), 1926
Oil on canvas, 50×73 cm
Willumsen's Museum, Frederikssund

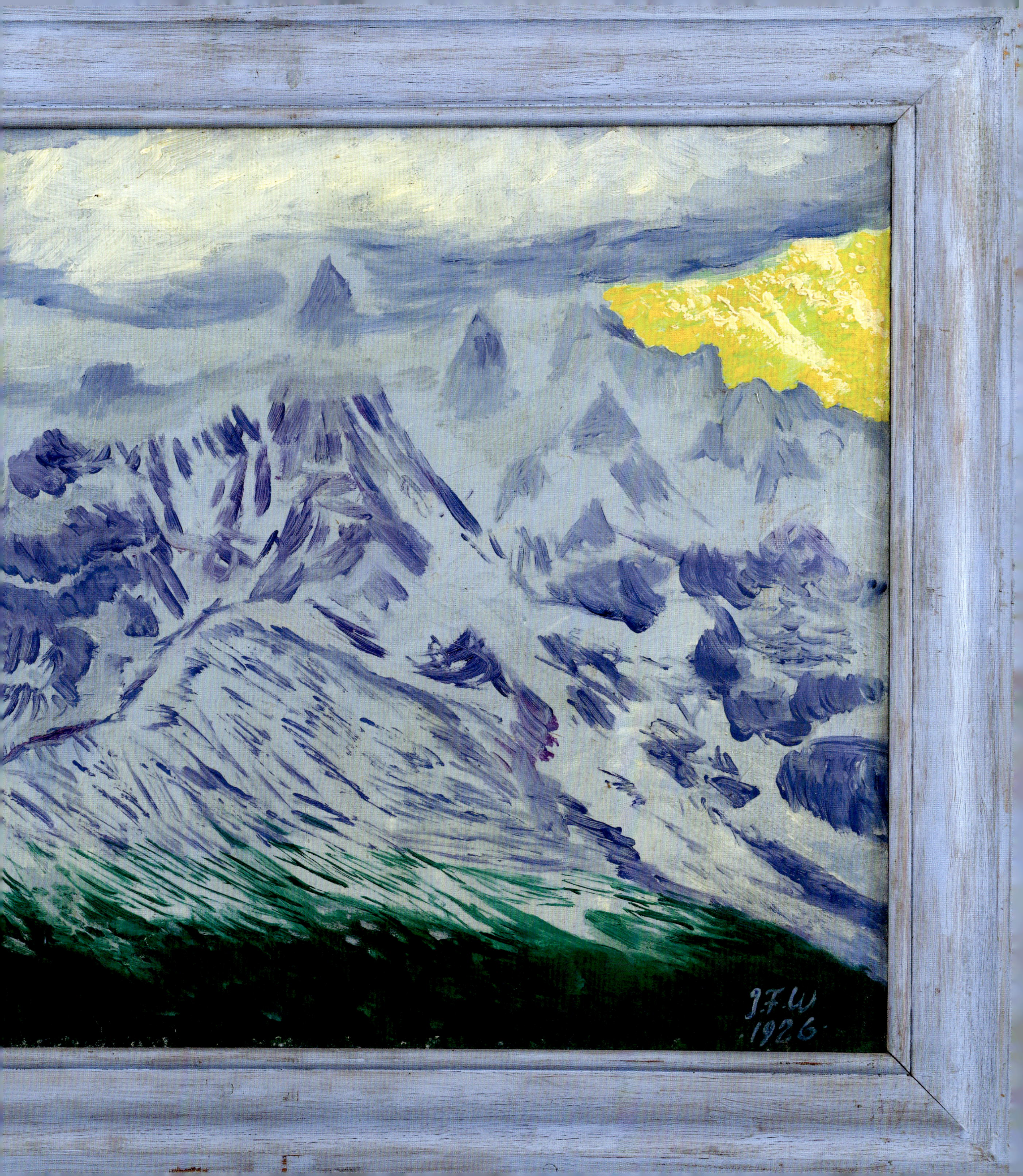
J.F.W
1926

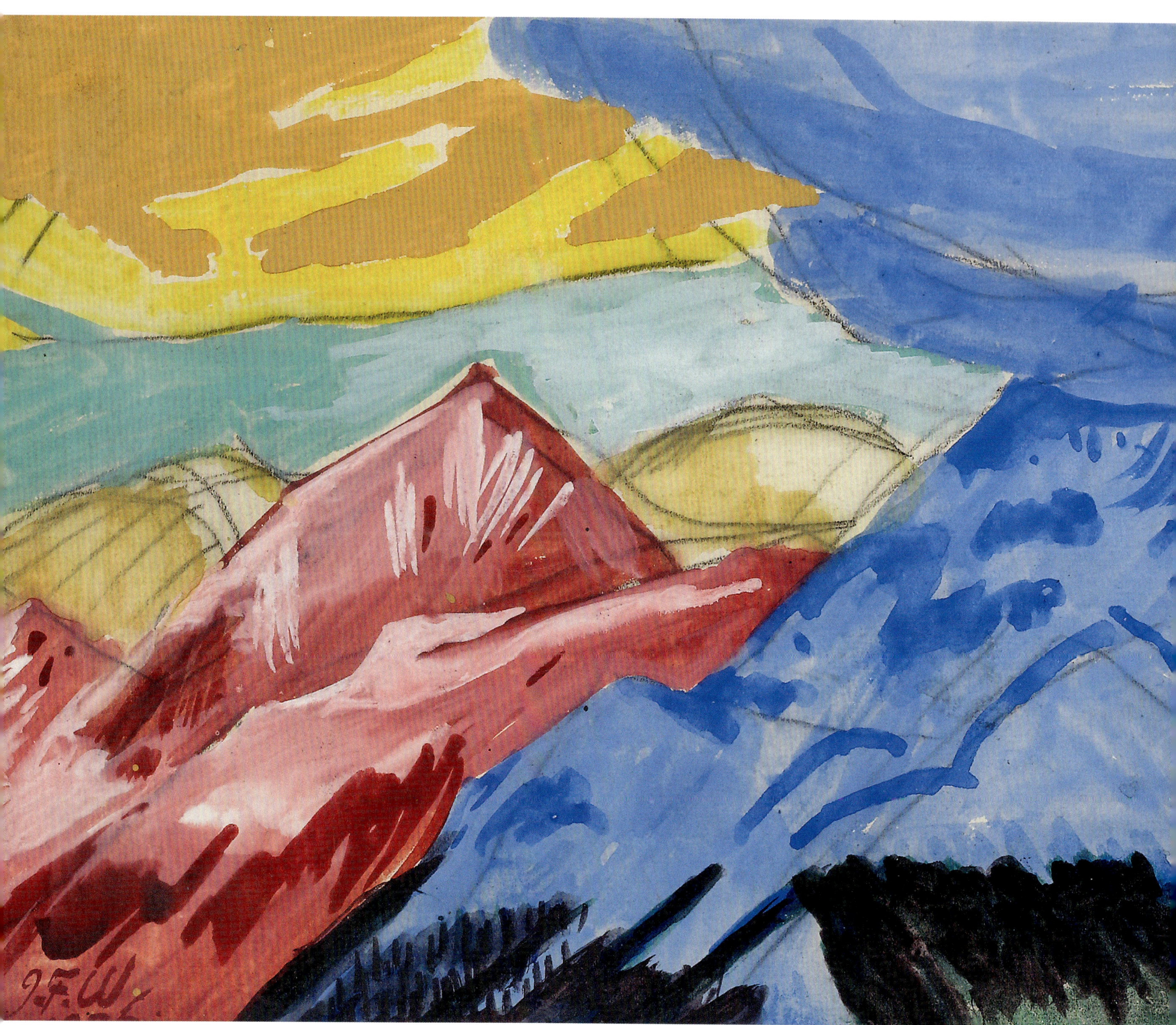

J. F. Willumsen
Bjergkæde i aftensol (Mountain Range in Evening Sun), 1926
Watercolor on paper, 20.2 × 48.5 cm
Willumsen's Museum, Frederikssund

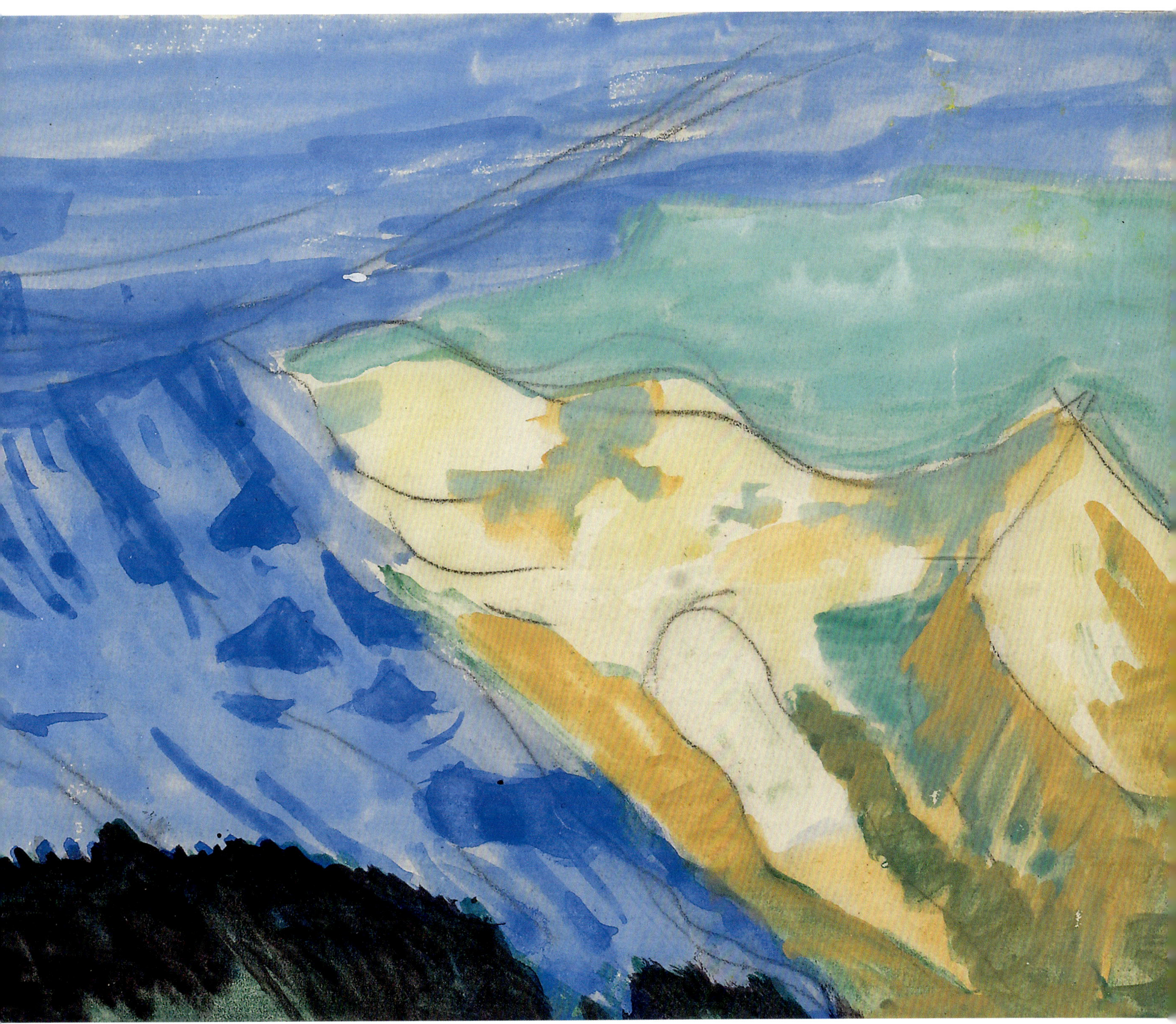

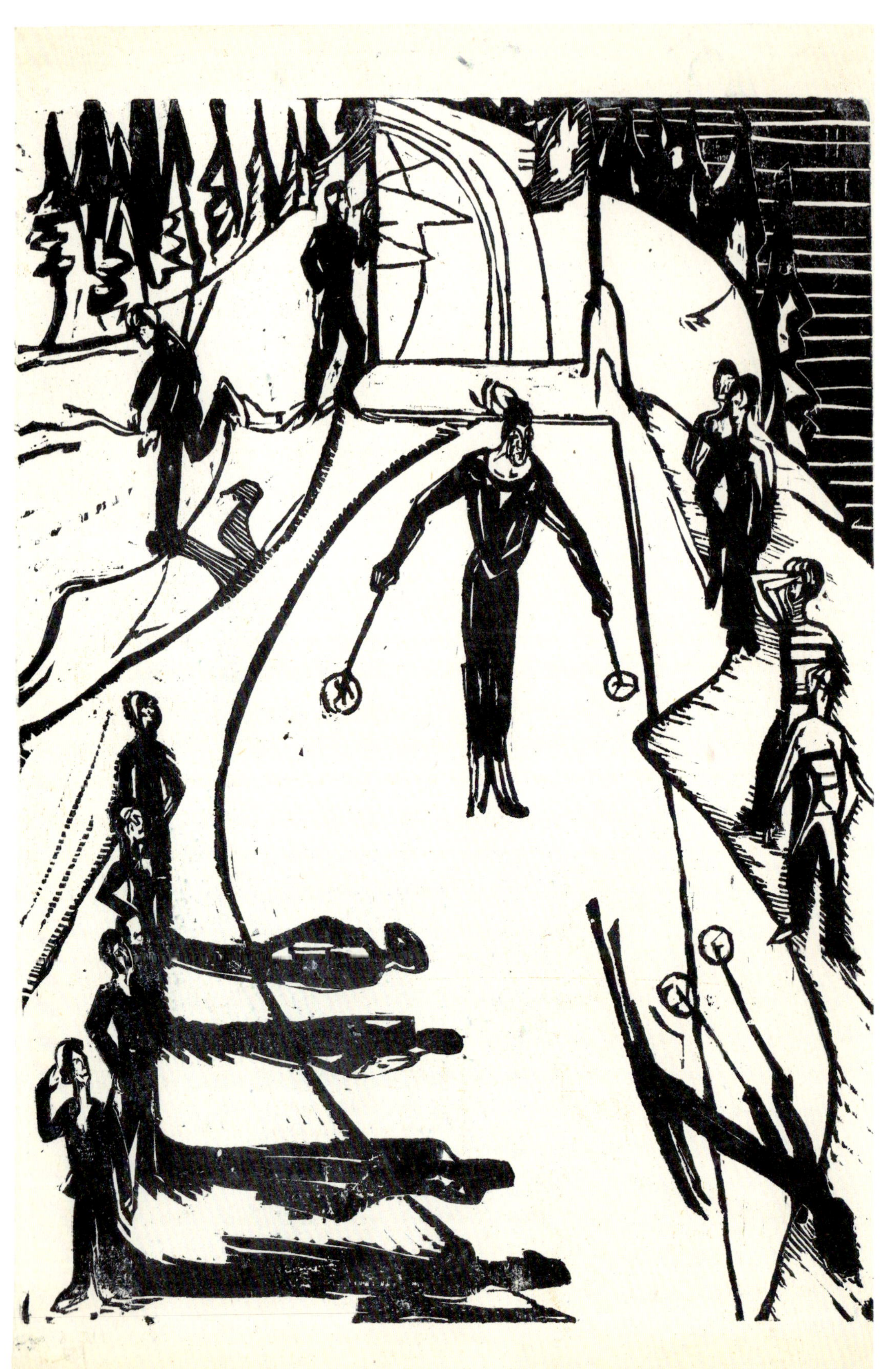

Ernst Ludwig Kirchner
Skisprung (Ski Jump), 1936
Woodcut, 49.9 × 34.8 cm
Kirchner Museum Davos

Ernst Ludwig Kirchner
Clavadeler Berg von Frauenkirch aus (Clavadeler Mountain from Frauenkirch), 1936
Woodcut, 35.3 × 50 cm
Kirchner Museum Davos

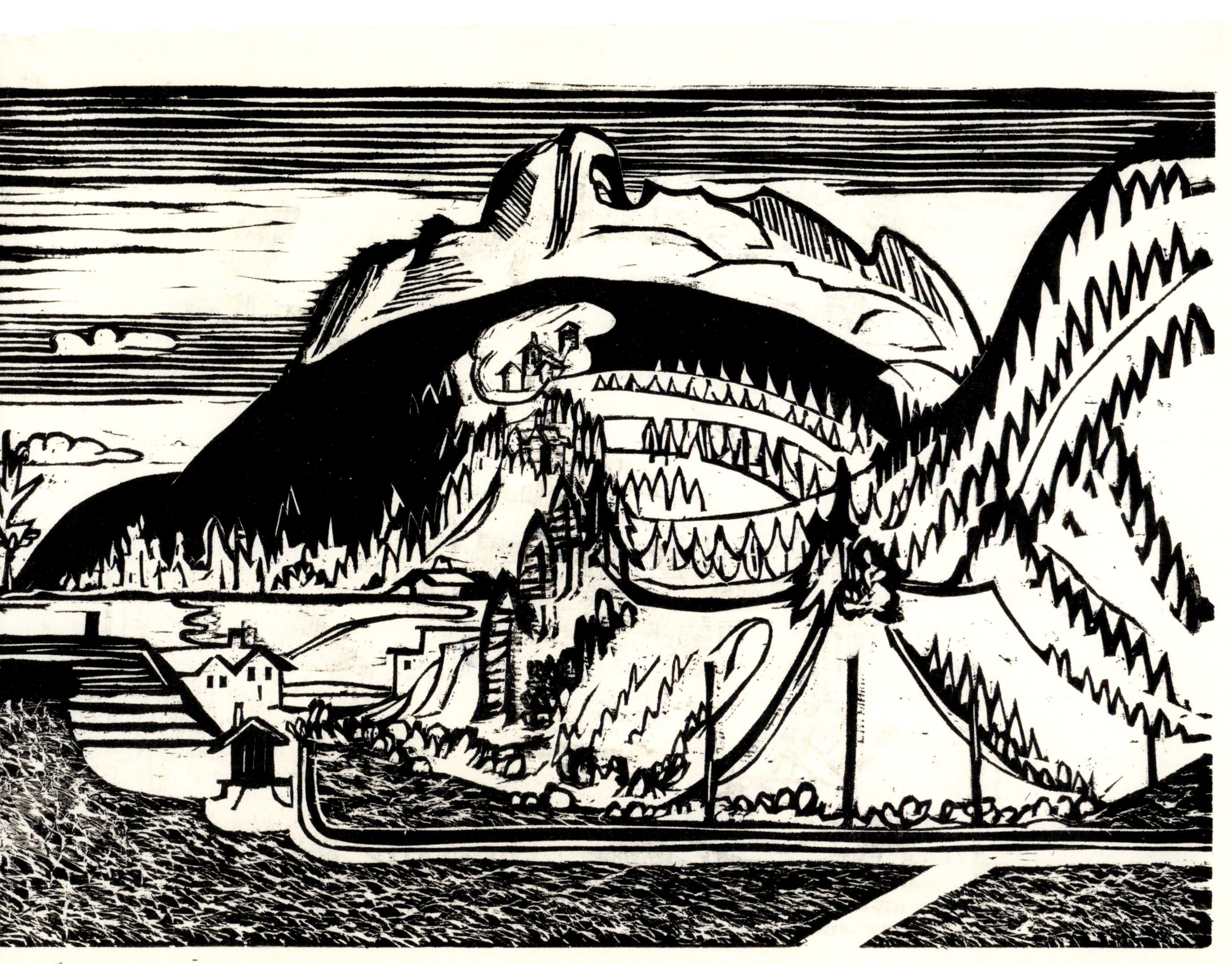

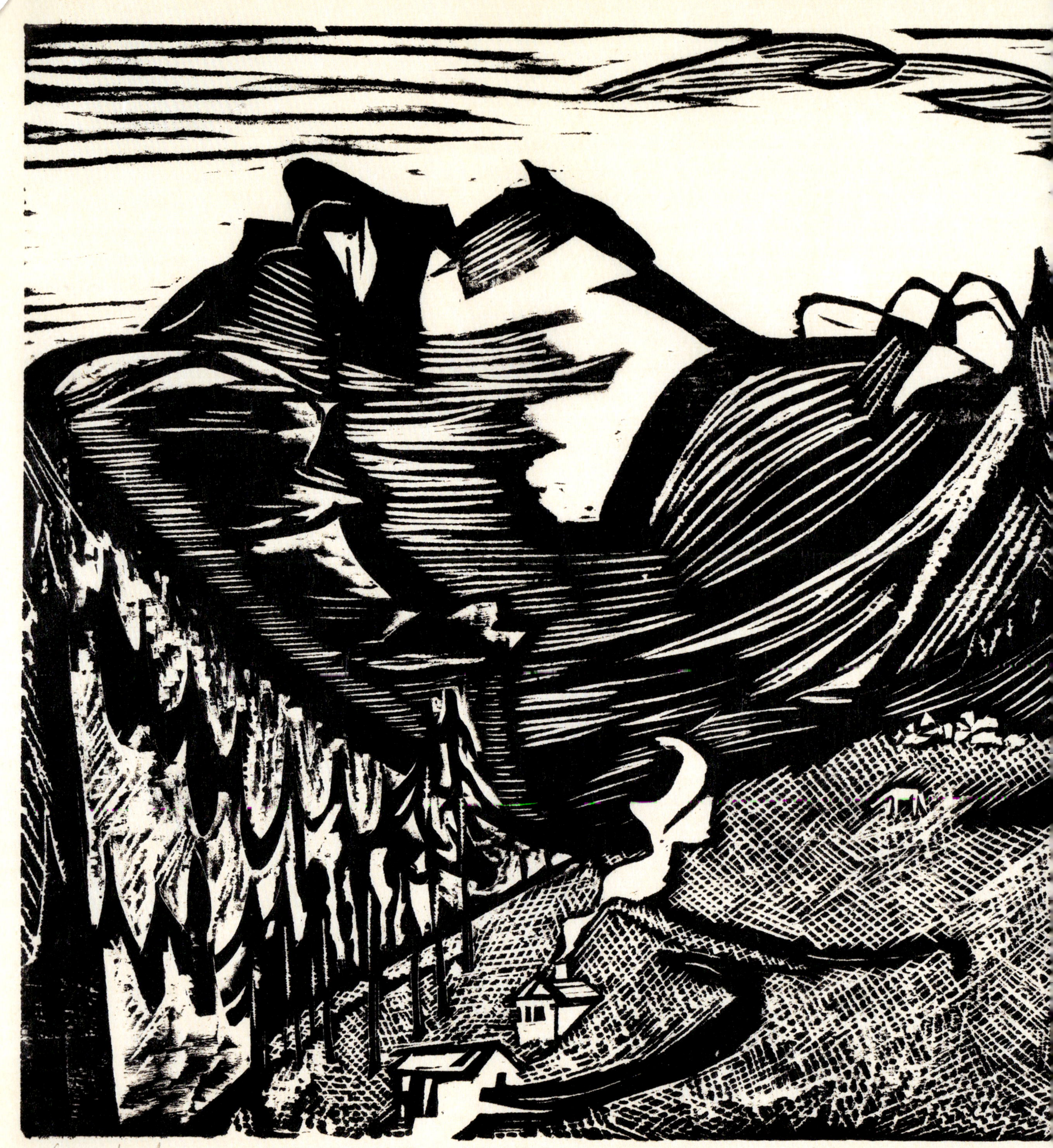
Eigendruck
Herrn Landammann Dr. Brügger mit Dank

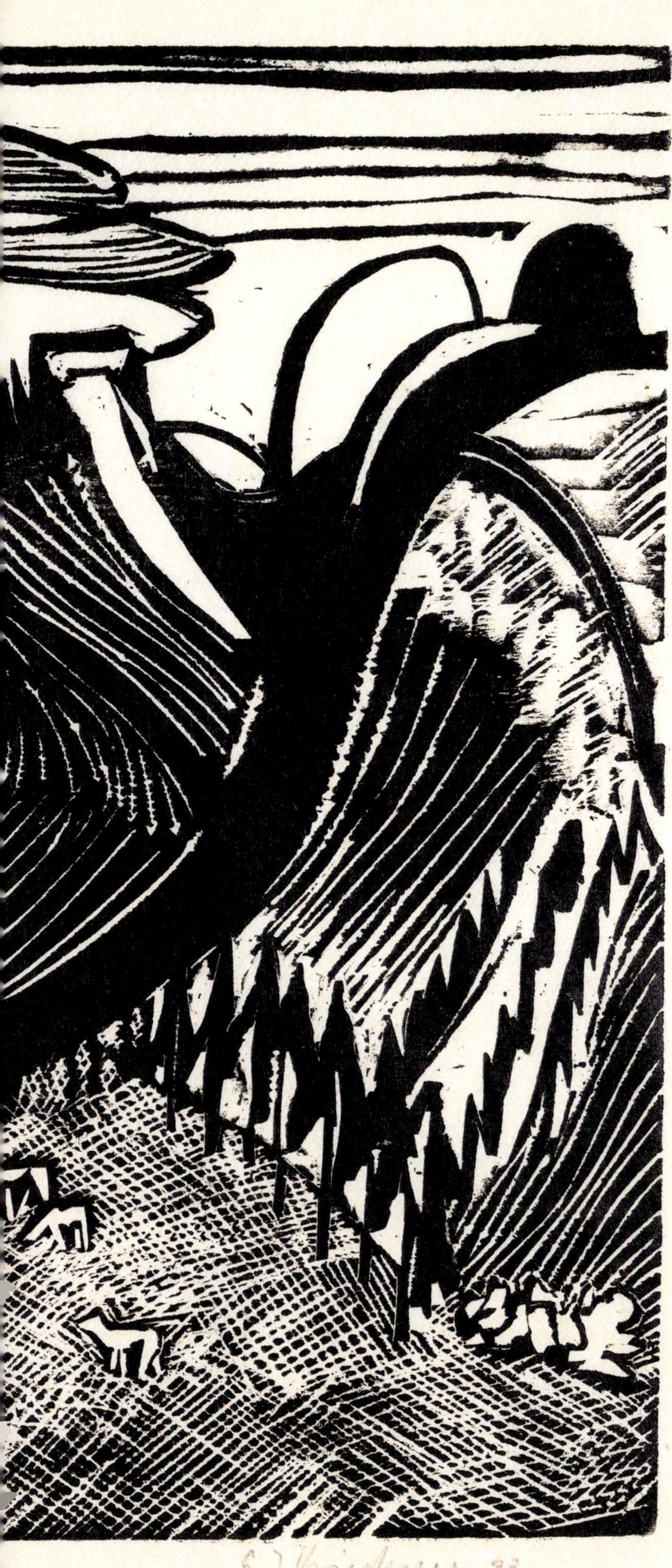

Ernst Ludwig Kirchner
Berglandschaft mit Alp
(Mountainscape with Alp),
1933
Woodcut, 34.7 × 50 cm
Kirchner Museum Davos

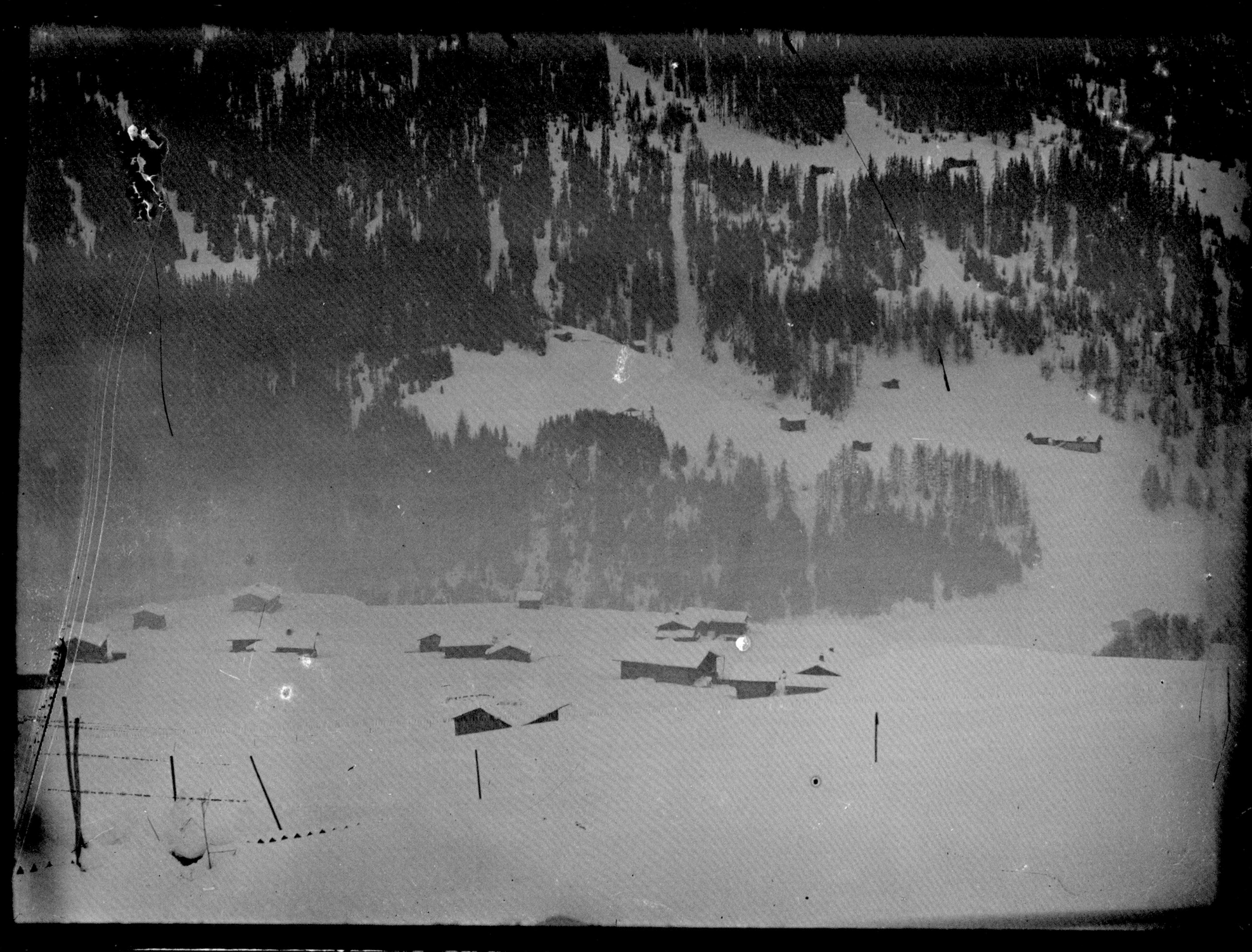

Ernst Ludwig Kirchner
View from Ernst Ludwig Kirchner's House to Längmatte, 1918–22
Gelatin-silver print, 12 × 16.5 cm
Kirchner Museum Davos

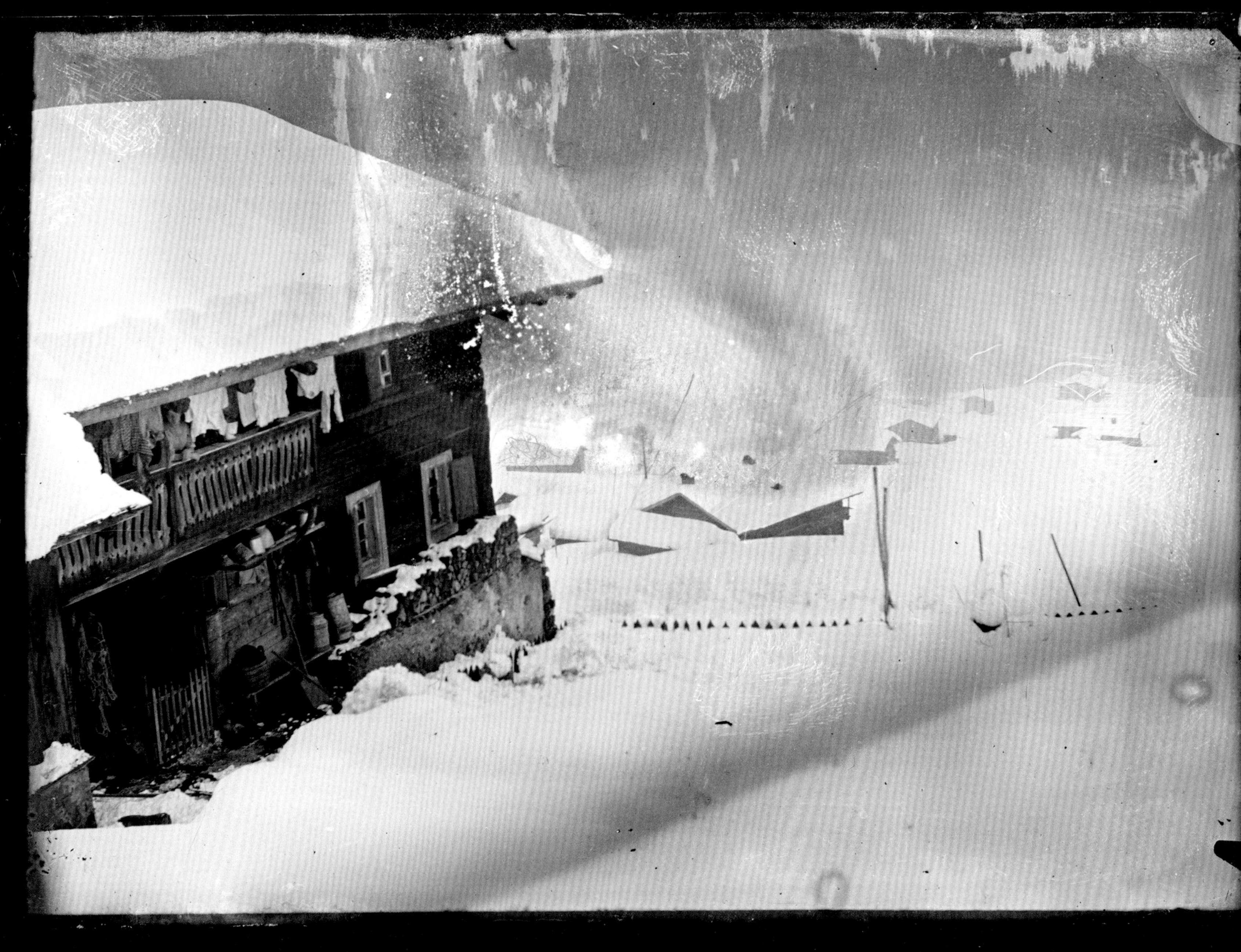

Ernst Ludwig Kirchner
View from the House "In den Lärchen" to the neighboring Courtyard and to Längmatte, 1918–22
Gelatin-silver print, 12 × 16.5 cm
Kirchner Museum Davos

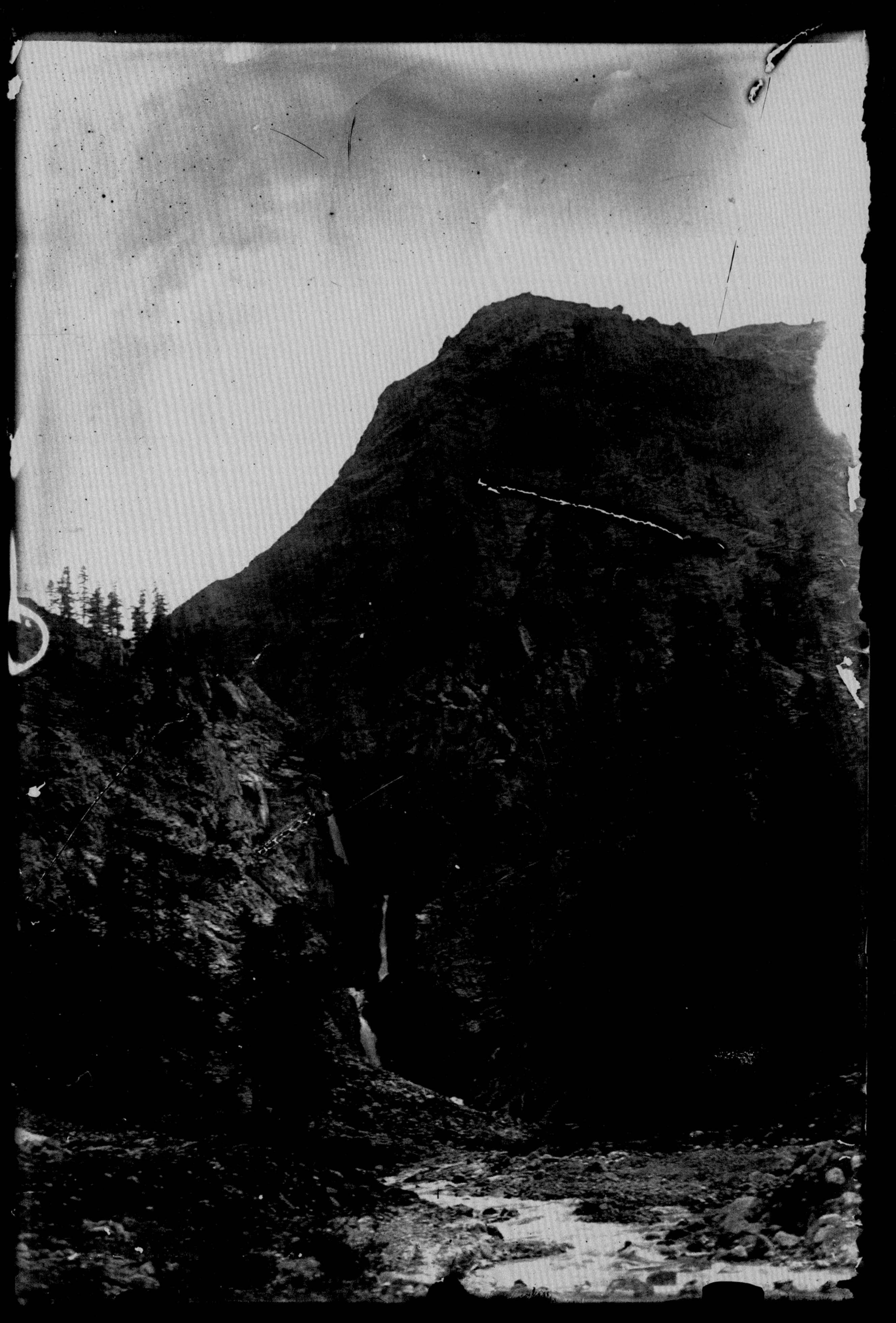

Ernst Ludwig Kirchner
Sertigbach Waterfall, 1928
Gelatin-silver print, 14,8 × 10 cm
Kirchner Museum Davos

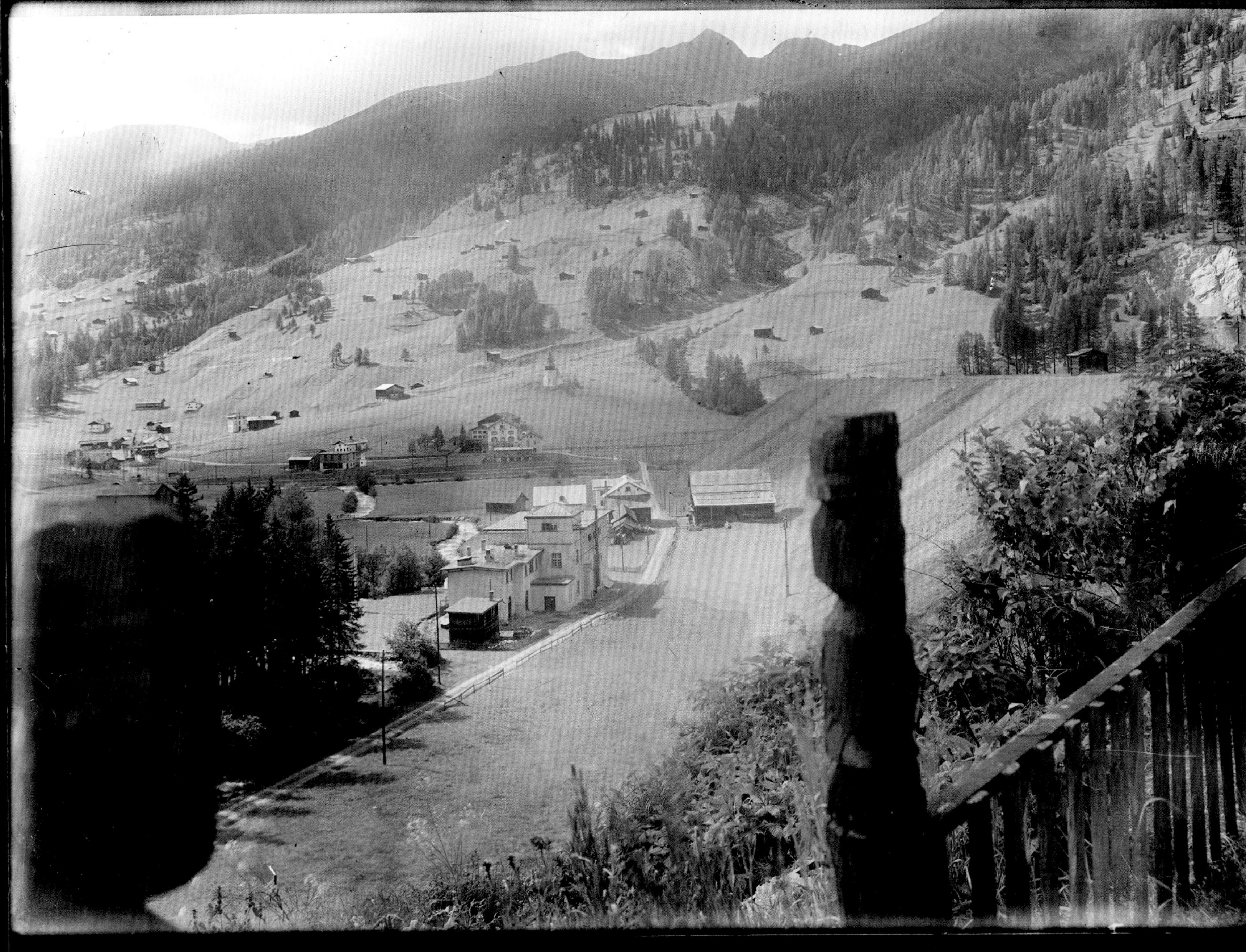

Ernst Ludwig Kirchner
View from Ernst Ludwig Kirchner's House on the Wildboden, after 1924
Gelatin-silver print, 18 × 24 cm
Kirchner Museum Davos

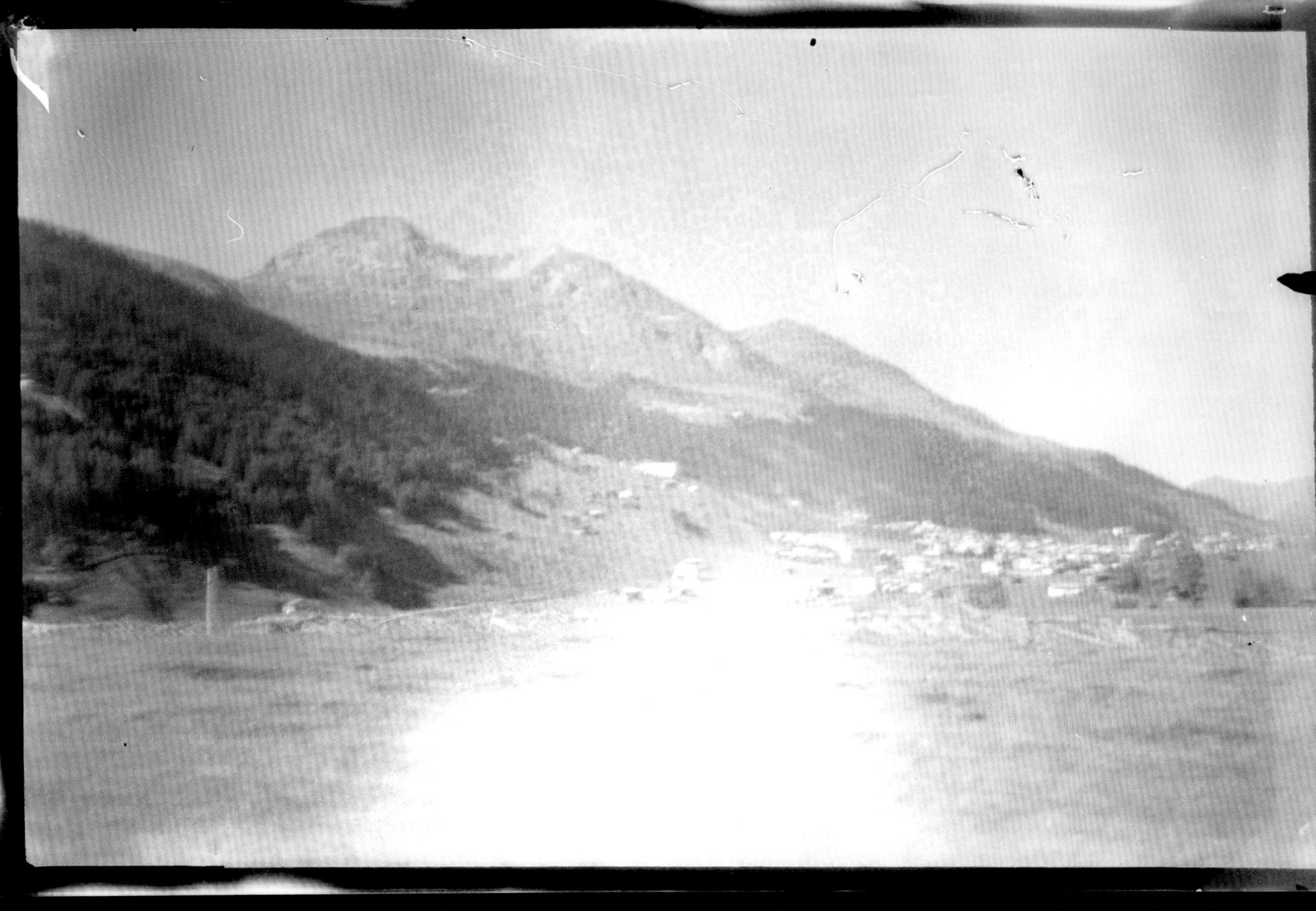

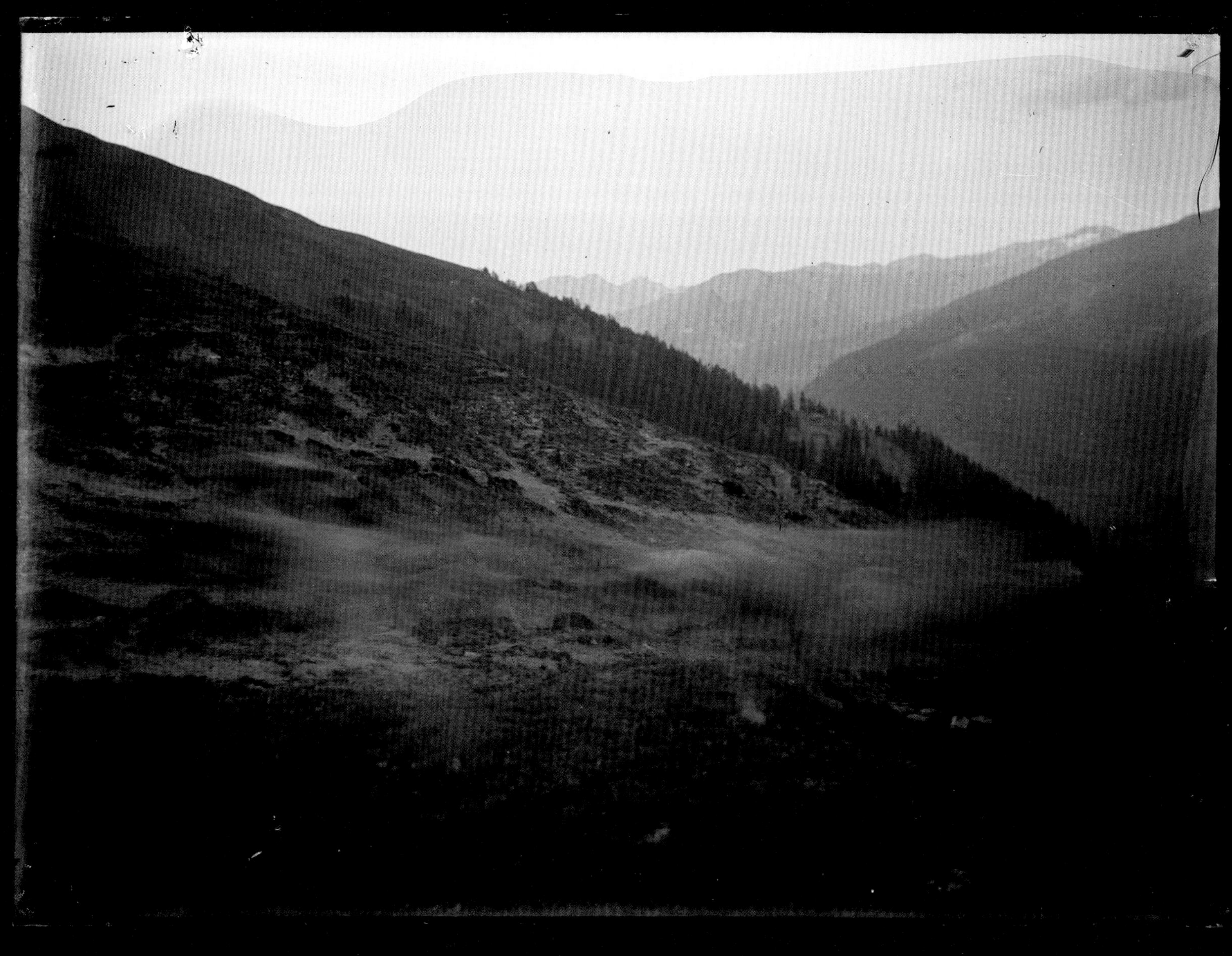

Ernst Ludwig Kirchner
Cows Running on the Stafelalp, ca. 1919
Gelatin-silver print, 18 × 24 cm
Kirchner Museum Davos

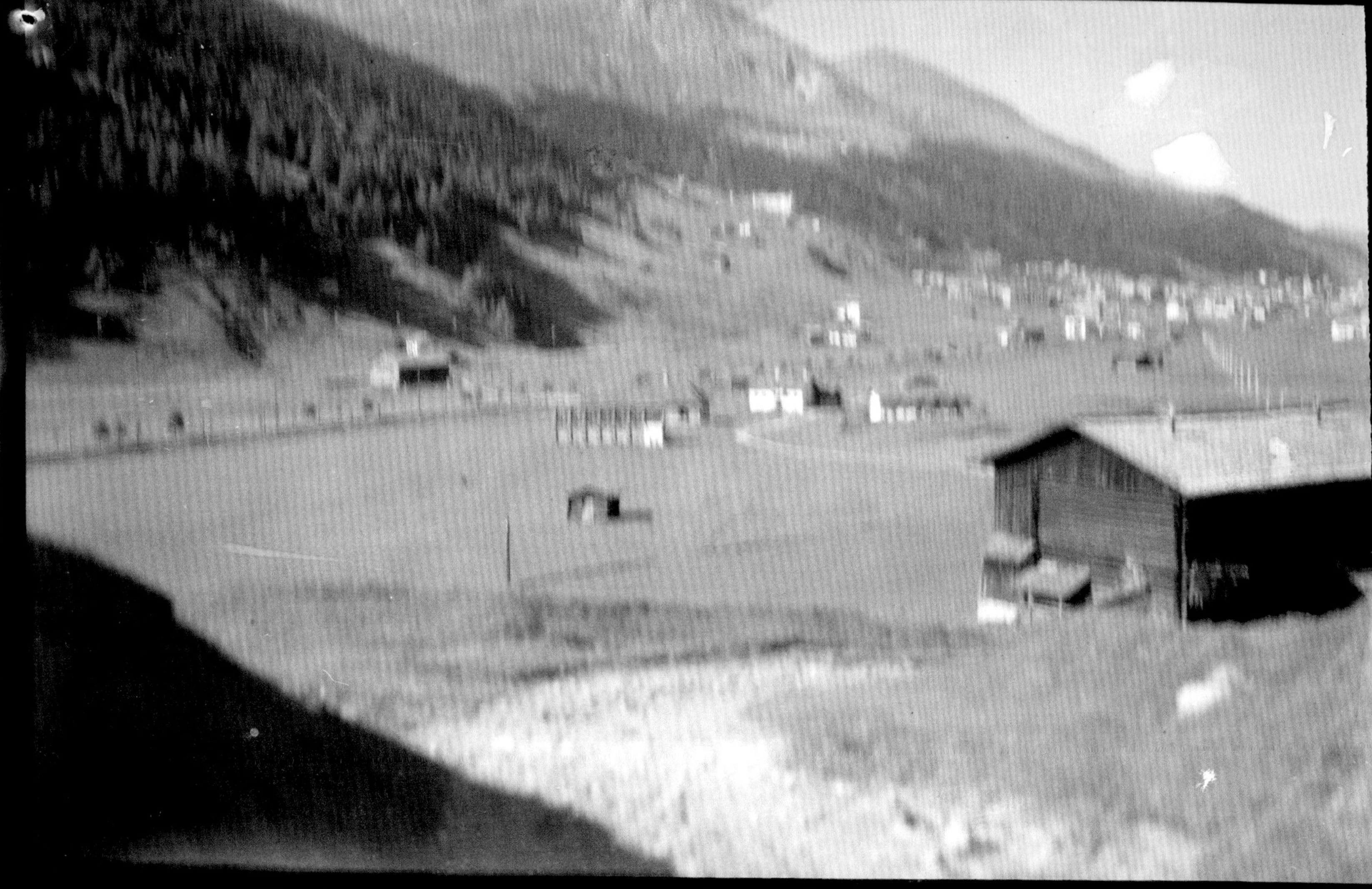

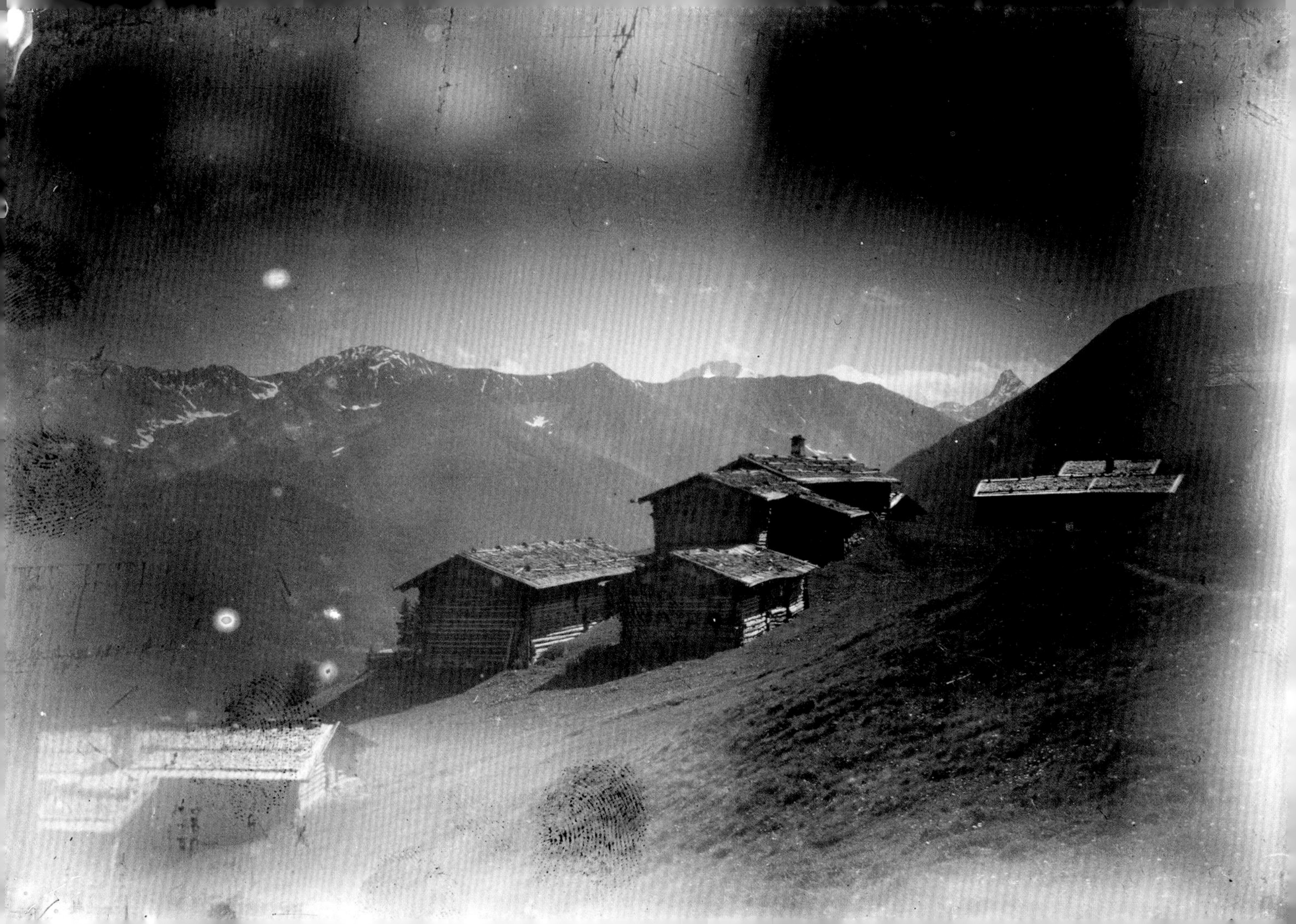

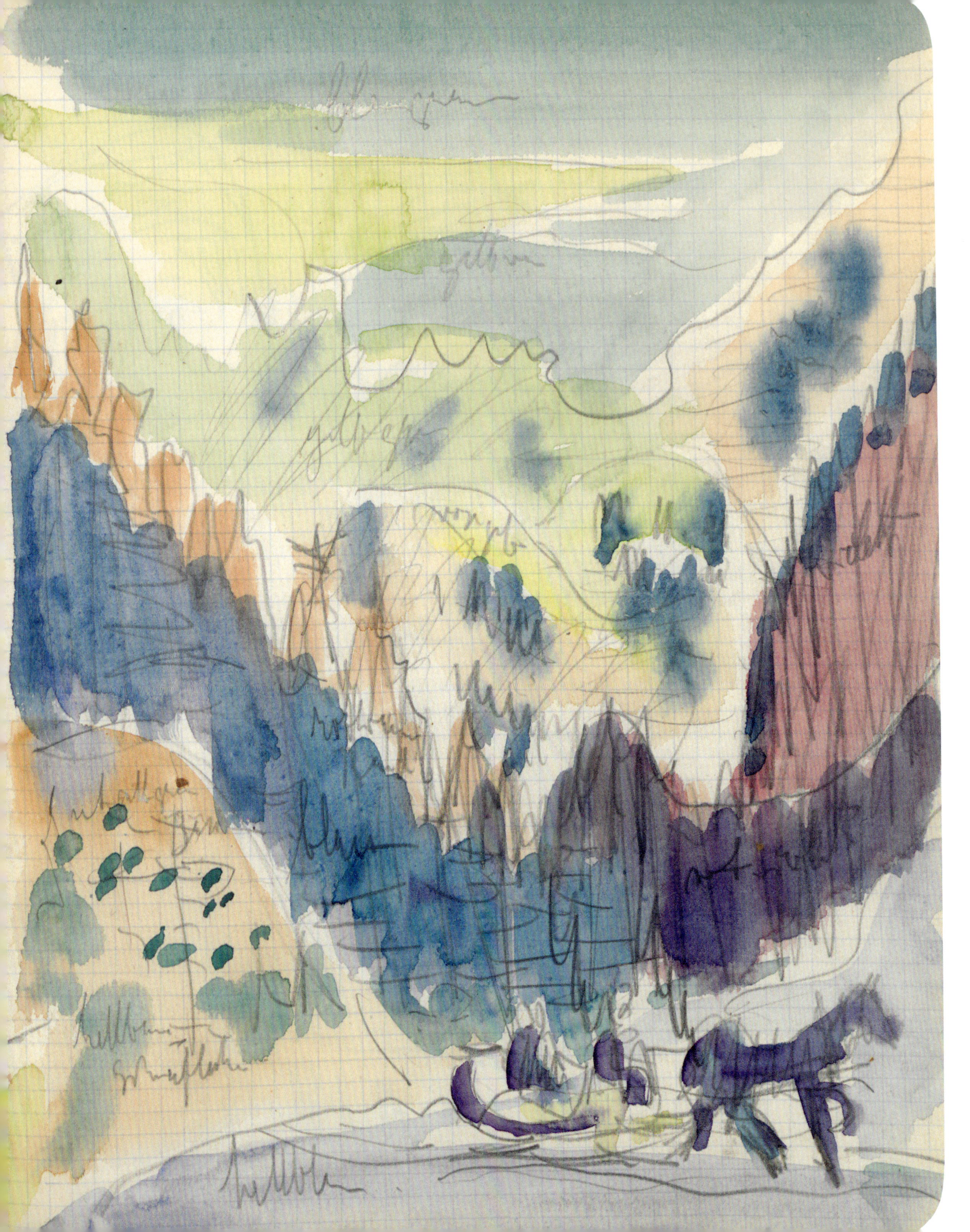

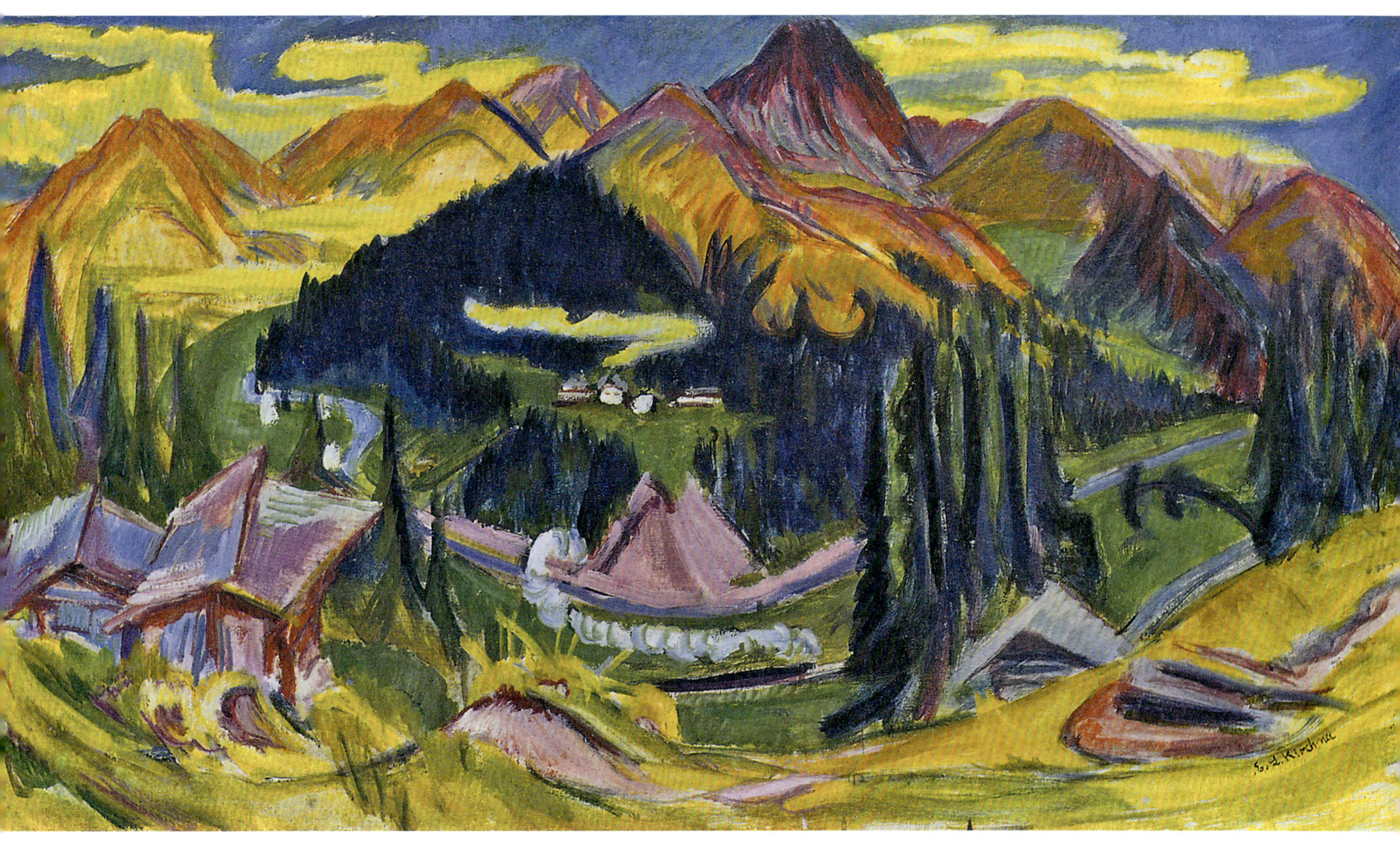

Ernst Ludwig Kirchner
Sketchbook 140,
1927, 1937, p. 2
20.9 × 17.3 cm
Kirchner Museum Davos

Ernst Ludwig Kirchner
Junkerboden bei Frauenkirch/Davos, mit Blick auf Rhätische Bahn (The Junkerboden Mountain near Frauenkirch/Davos, with View to the Rhaetian Railway), 1919
Oil on canvas, 90 × 150 cm
Private collection

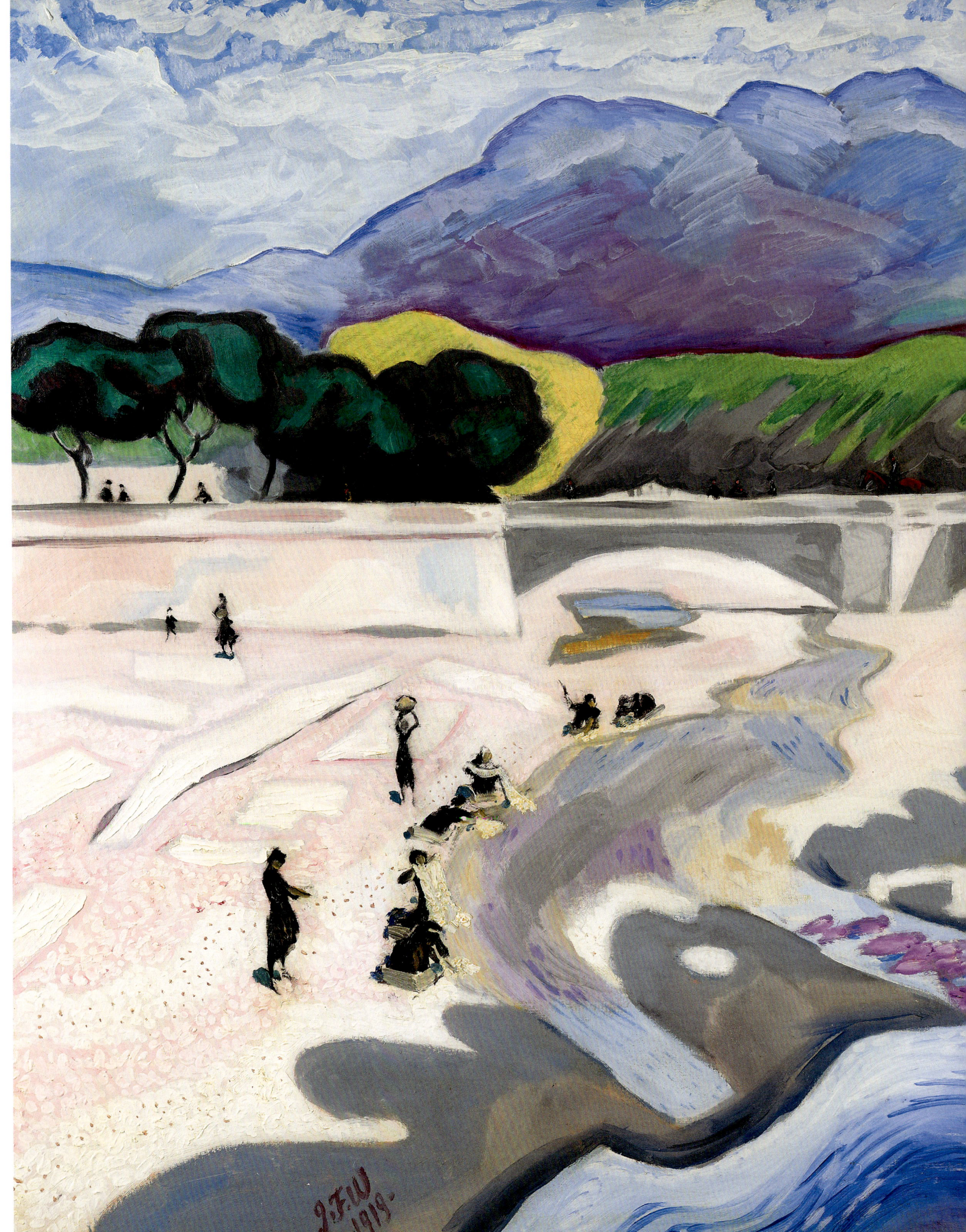

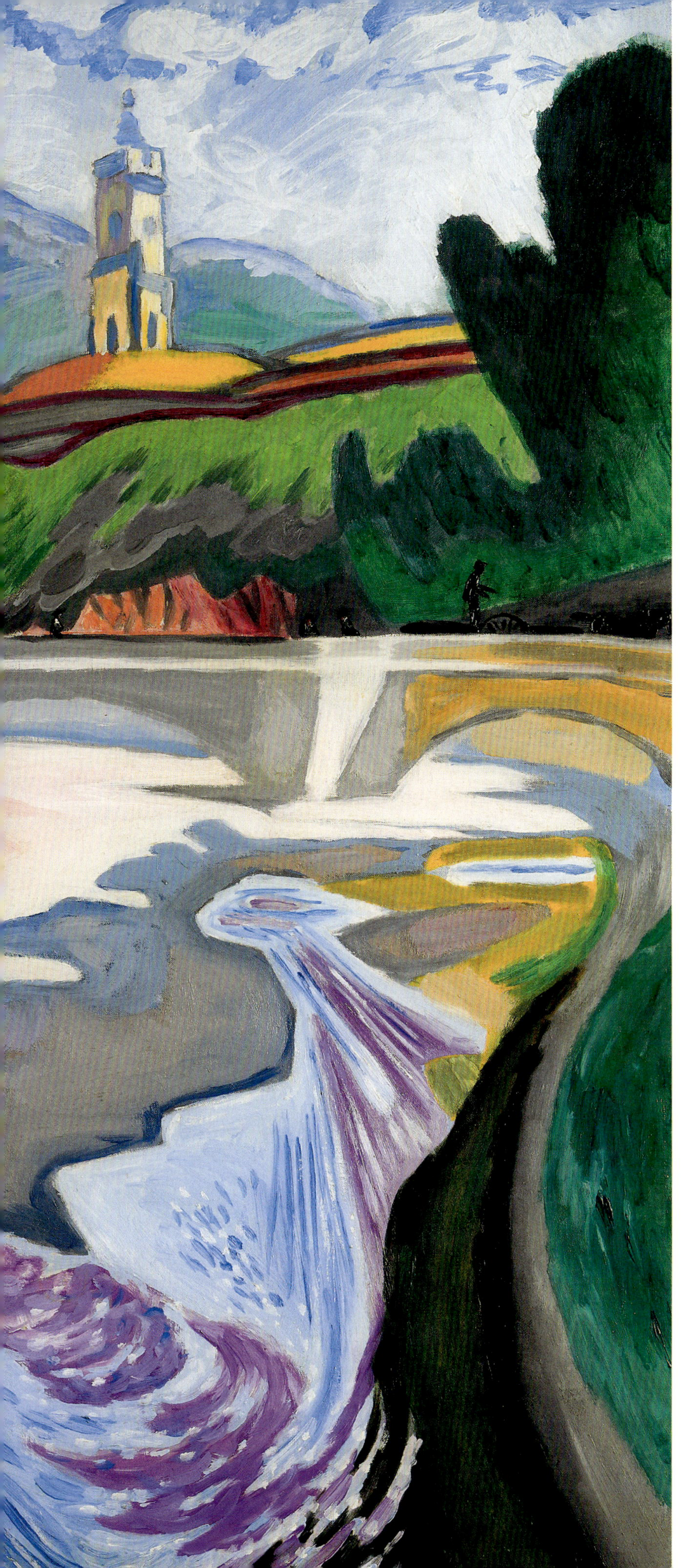

J. F. Willumsen
Vaskekoner ved floden, Nice
(Washerwomen by the River, Nice),
1919
Oil on canvas, 84 × 105 cm
Private collection

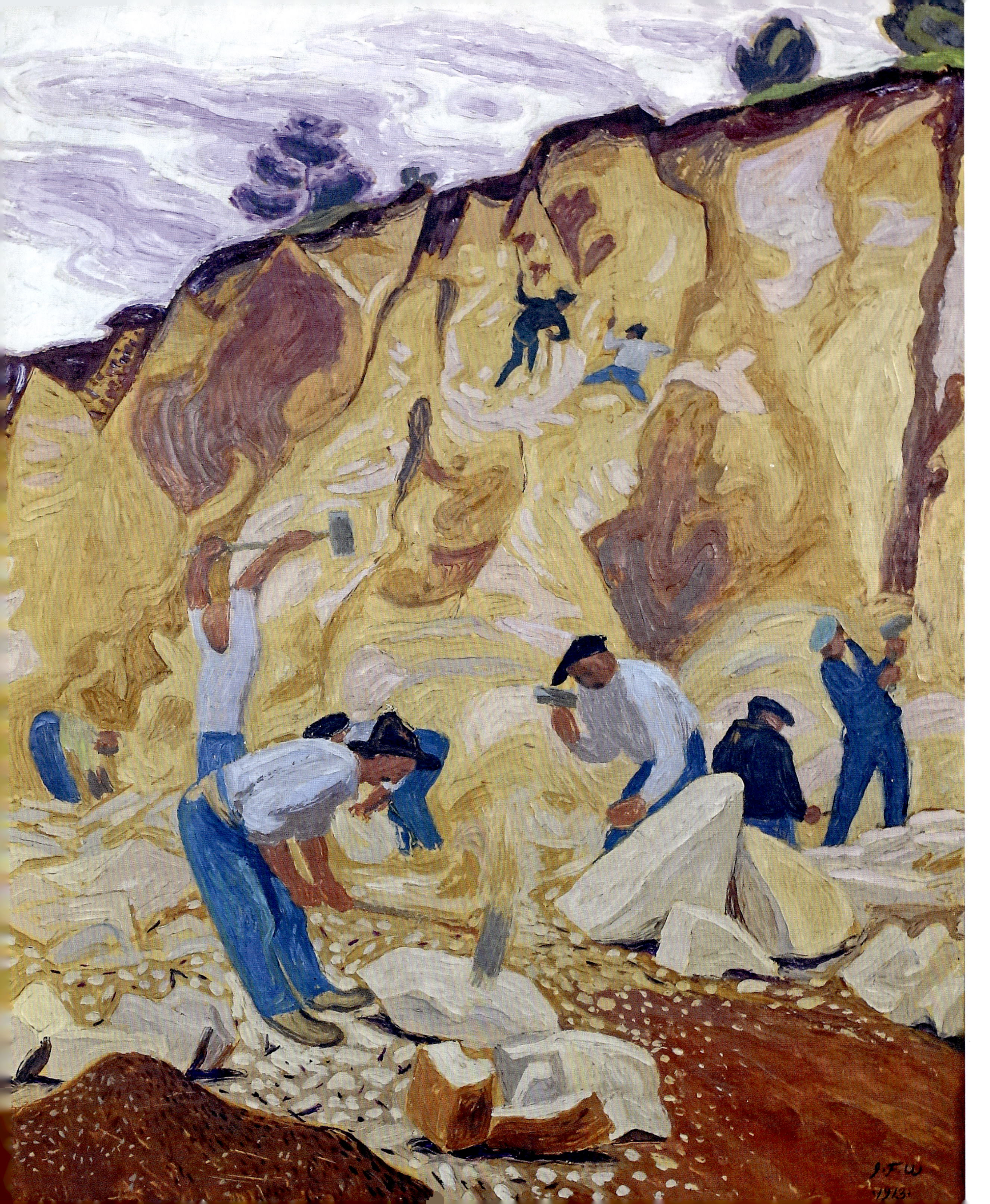

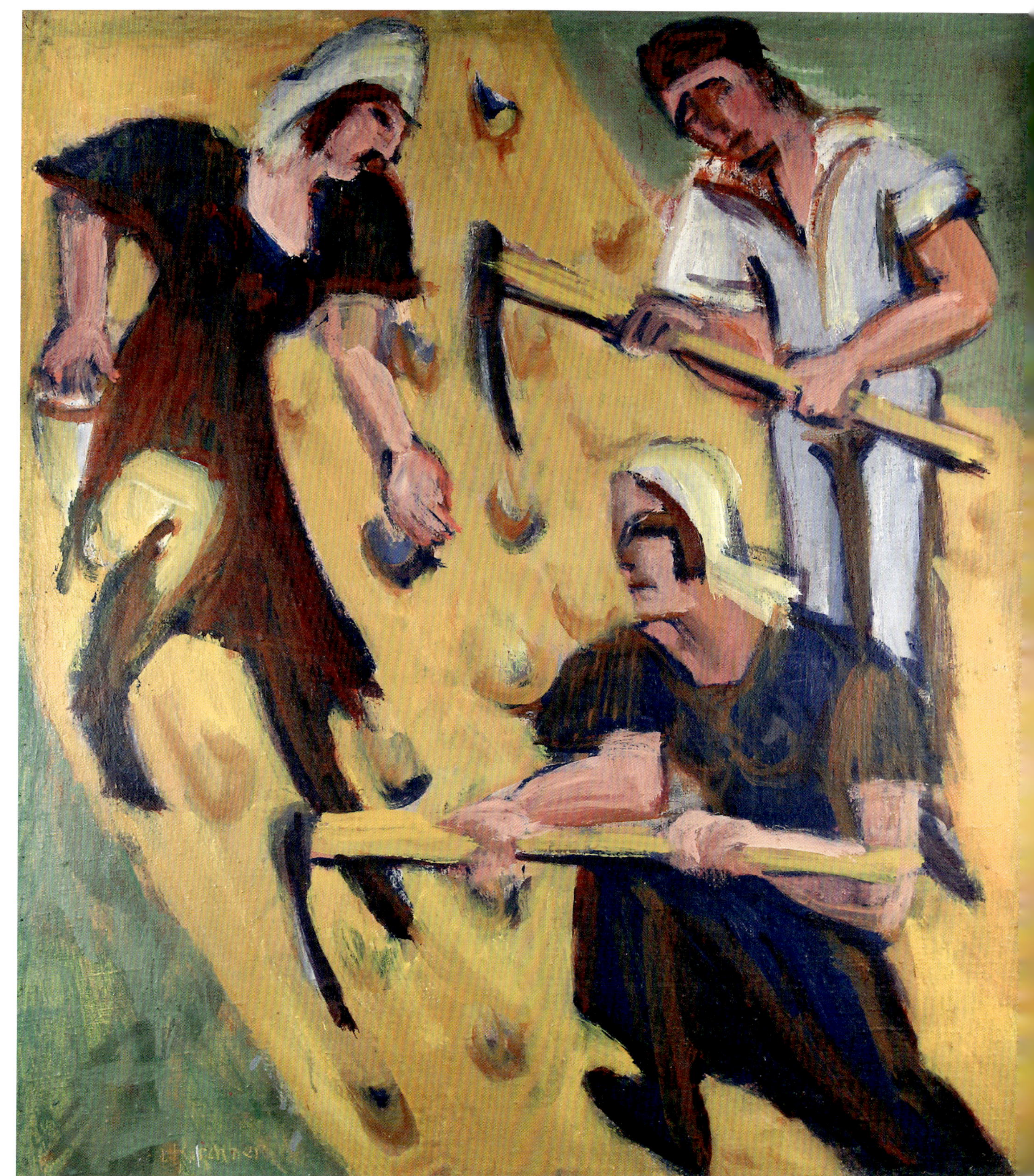

J. F. Willumsen
Stenbrud 2, studie
(Quarry 2, Study), 1913
Oil on canvas, 108 × 91 cm
Victor Petersen's Willumsen
Collection at the Manor
Odden, Hjørring

Ernst Ludwig Kirchner
Hackende Bauern
(Peasants with Picks), 1937
Oil on canvas, 70 × 60 cm
Galerie Henze & Ketterer,
Wichtrach / Bern

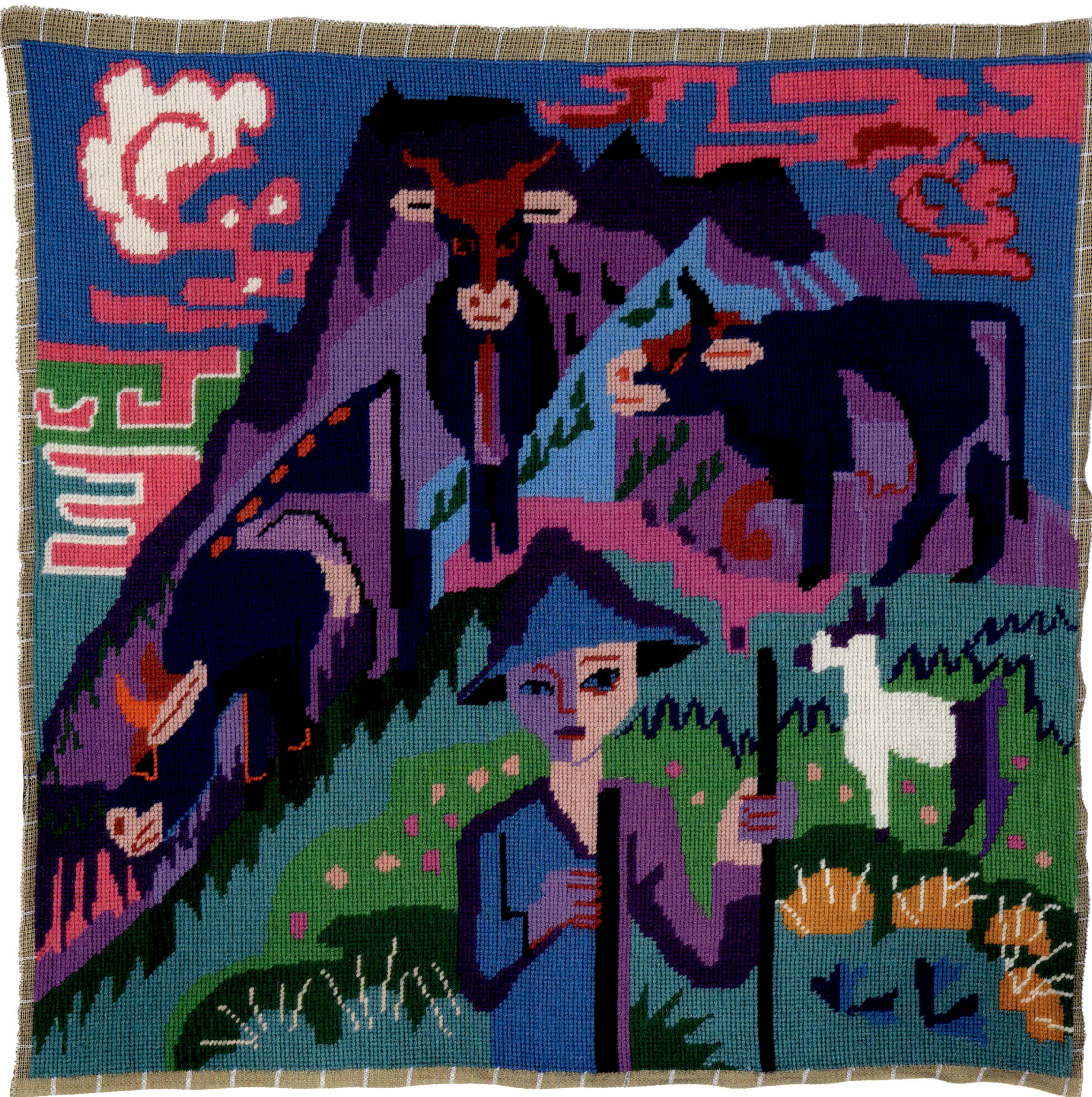

Julia Staub-Oetiker, after
design by Ernst Ludwig Kirchner
Hirte mit Stab in der linken Hand,
mit drei Kühen und einer Ziege
(Shepherd with Walking Stick
in Left Hand, Three Cows,
and a Goat), design 1924 /
woven ca. 1950
Embroidering on canvas,
54.5 × 55.7 cm
Kirchner Museum Davos

Lise Gujer, after design
by Ernst Ludwig Kirchner
Schwarzer Frühling (Black Spring),
design 1929 / woven 1961
Wool, 190 × 96.5 × 1 cm
Kirchner Museum Davos

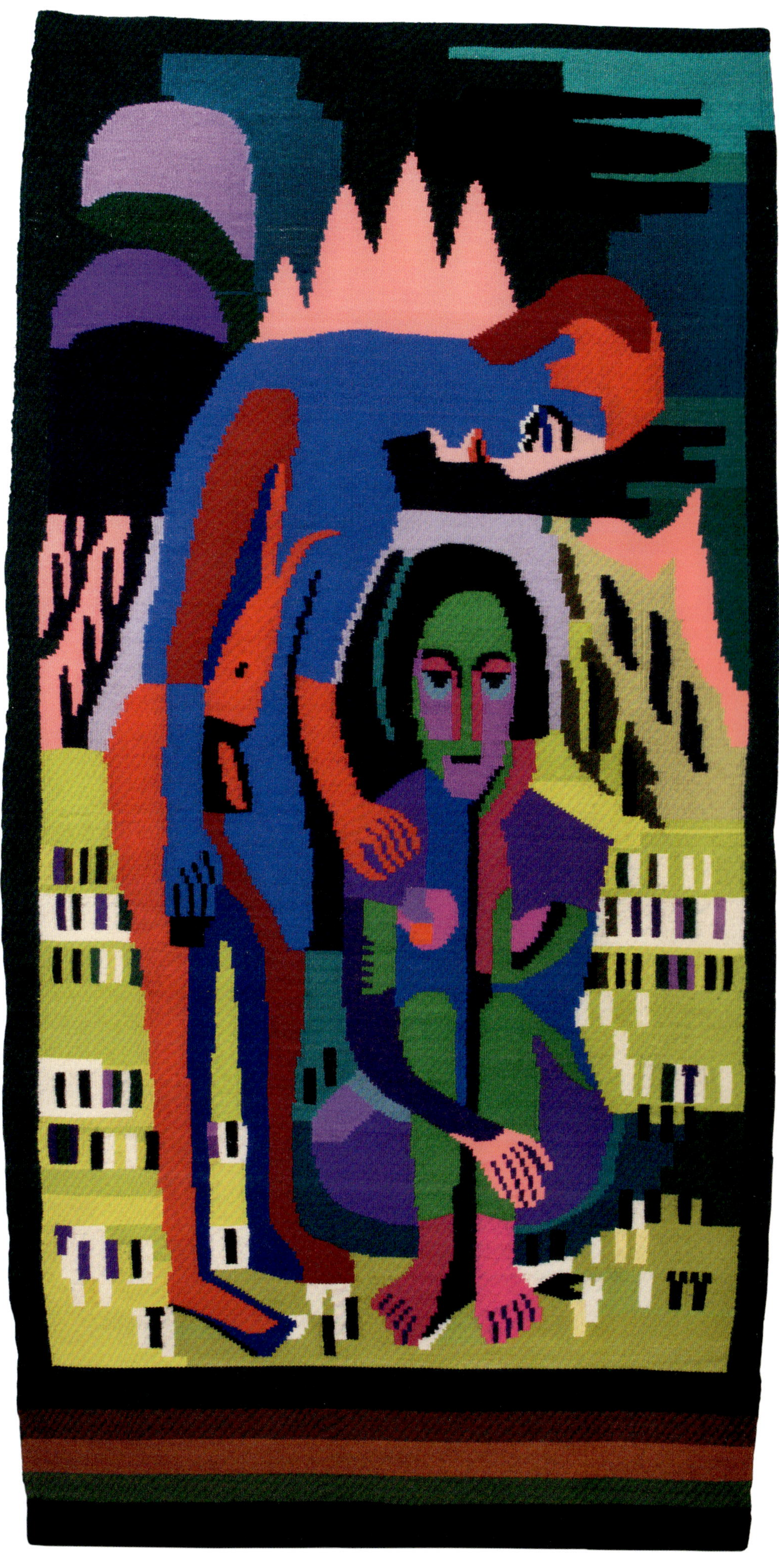

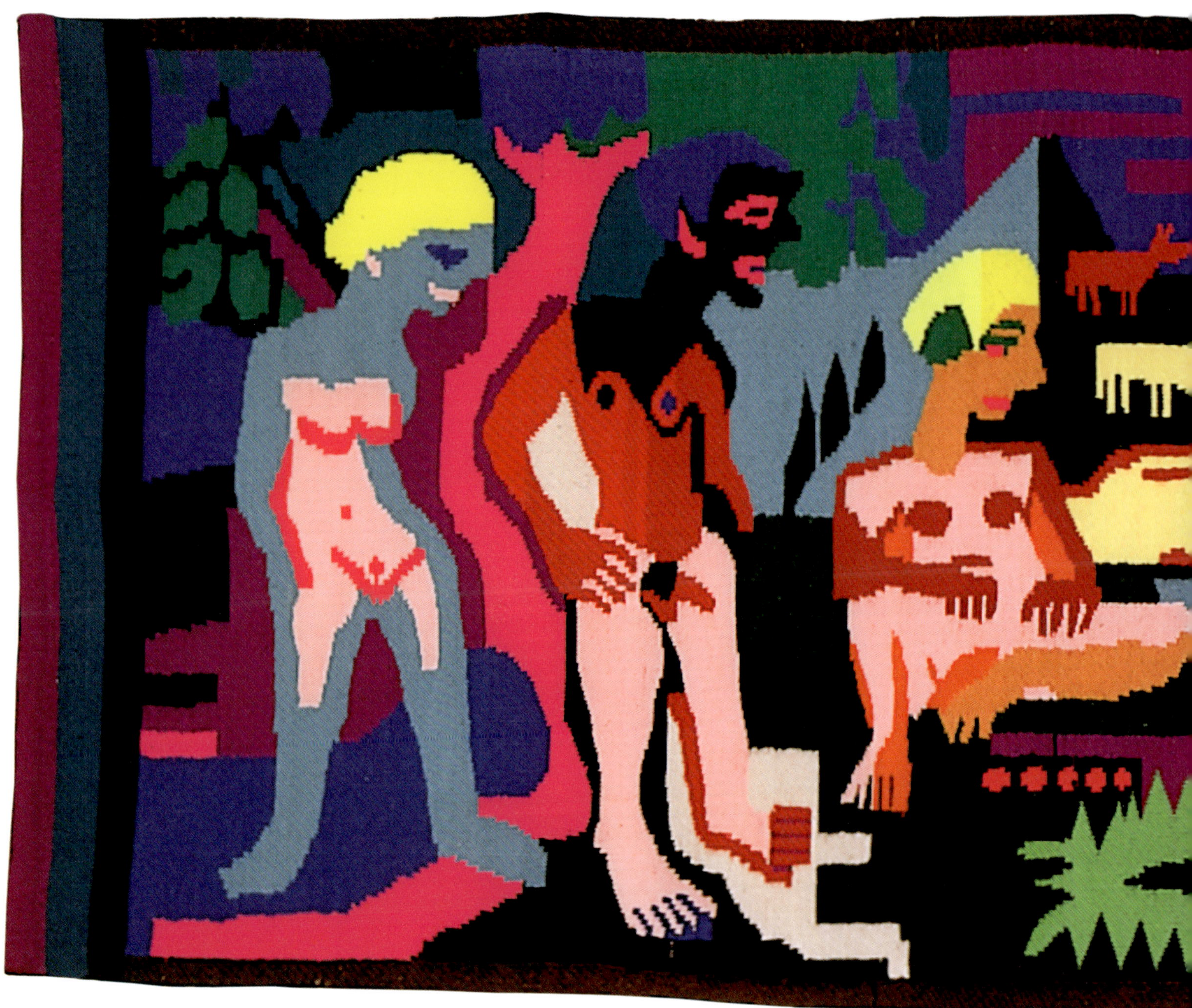

Lise Gujer, after design
by Ernst Ludwig Kirchner
Menschen in Landschaft
(People in Landscape),
design 1923 /
woven after 1953
Wool, 94.5×272.5 cm
Kirchner Museum Davos

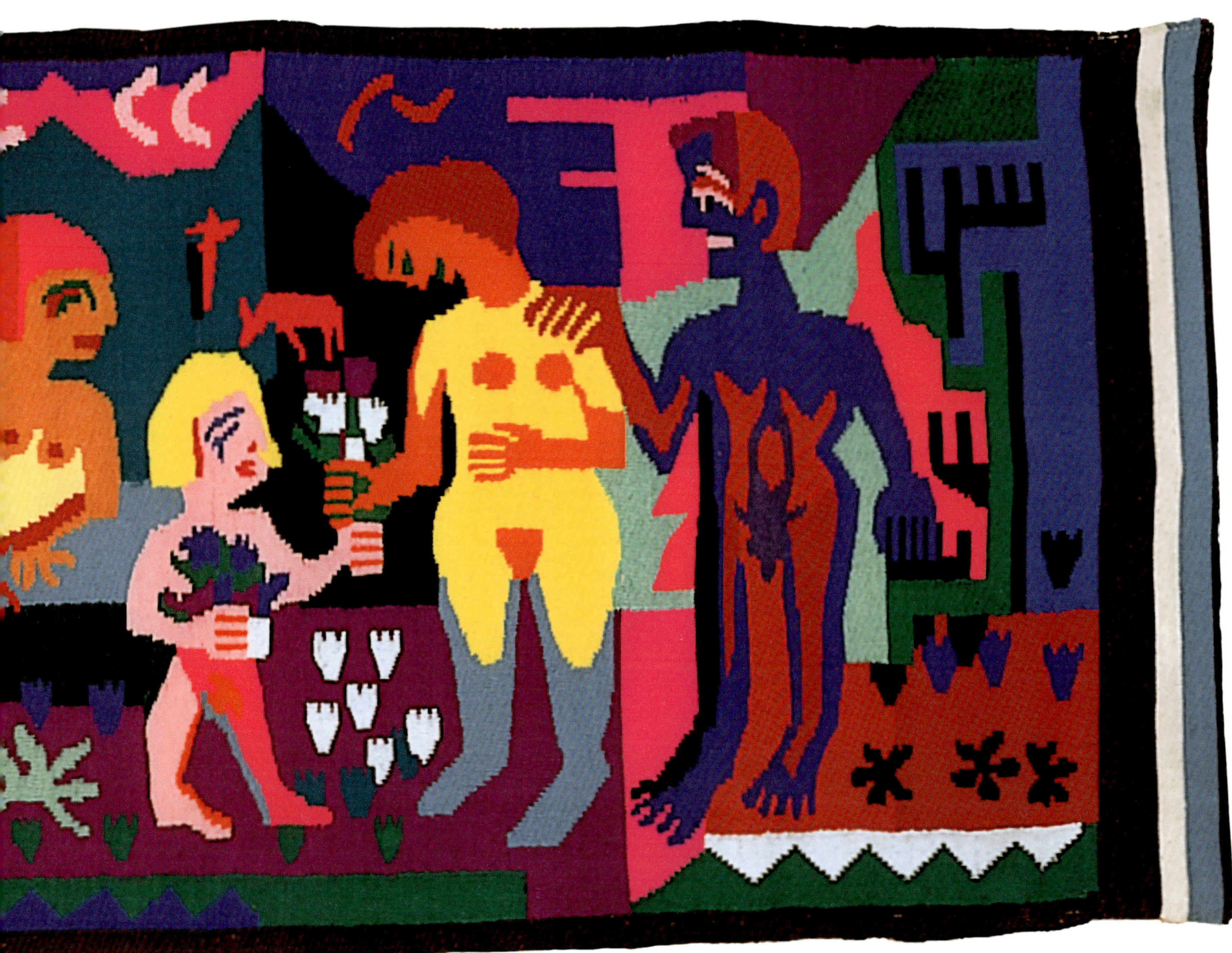

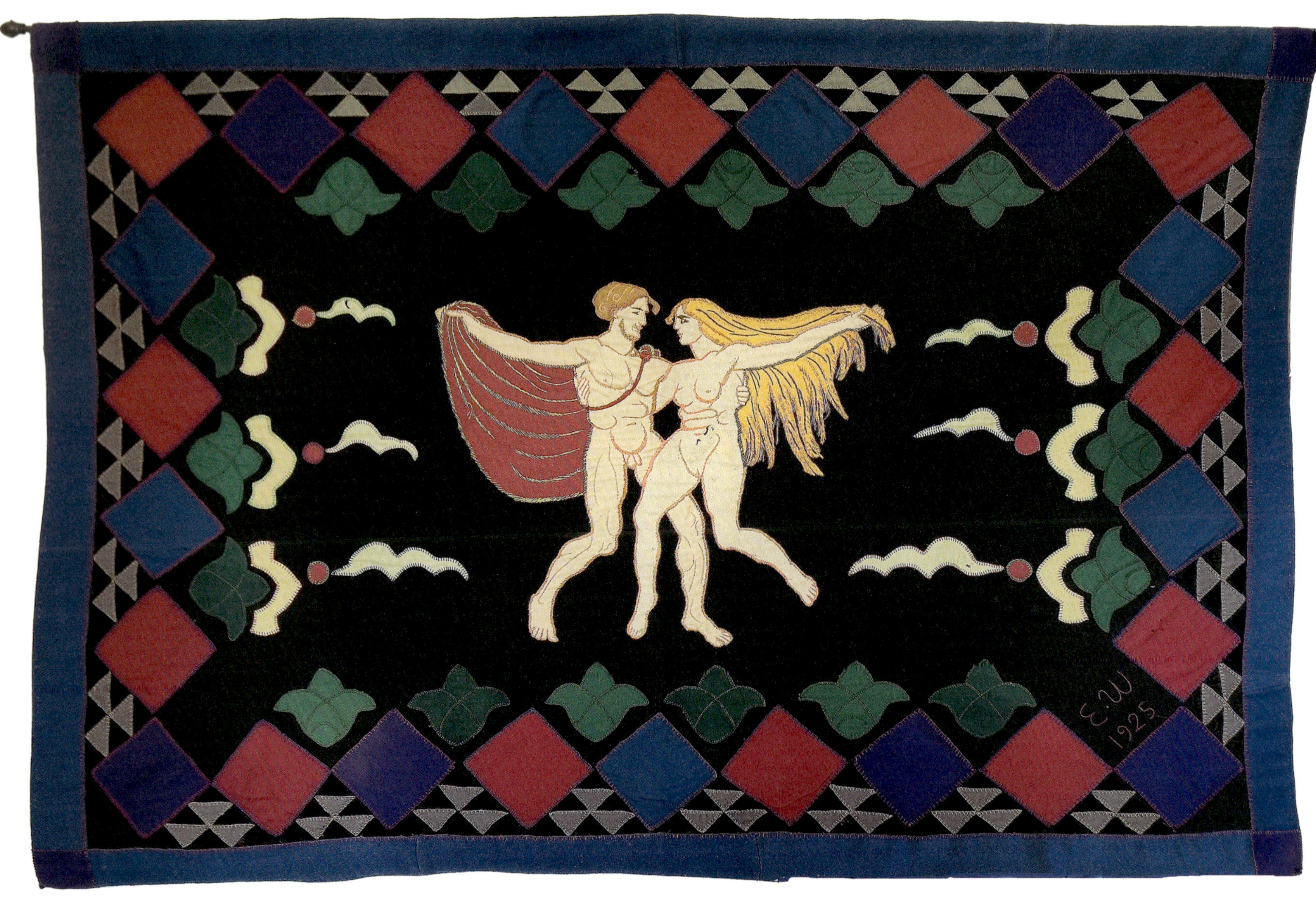

Edith Willumsen, after design
by J. F. Willumsen
Dekorativ dans (Decorative Dance), 1925
Wool on silk upholstery, 95 × 142 cm
Victor Petersen's Willumsen
Collection at the Manor Odden,
Hjørring

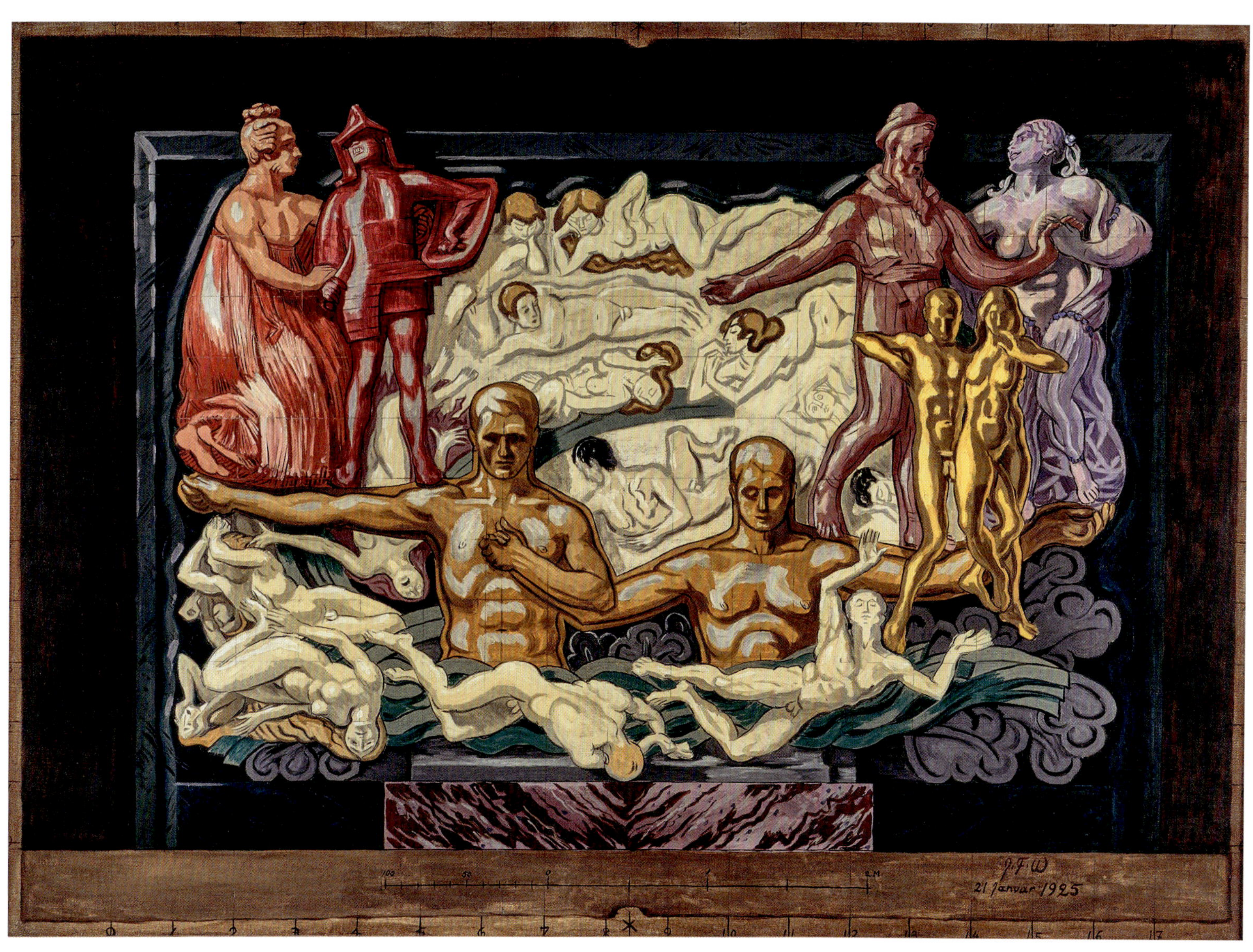

J. F. Willumsen
Det Store Relief. Udkast med forsøg af farver (The Great Relief. Sketch with Trials of Color), 1925
Oil on canvas, 108 × 145 cm
Willumsen's Museum, Frederikssund

Ernst Ludwig Kirchner (1880–1938)

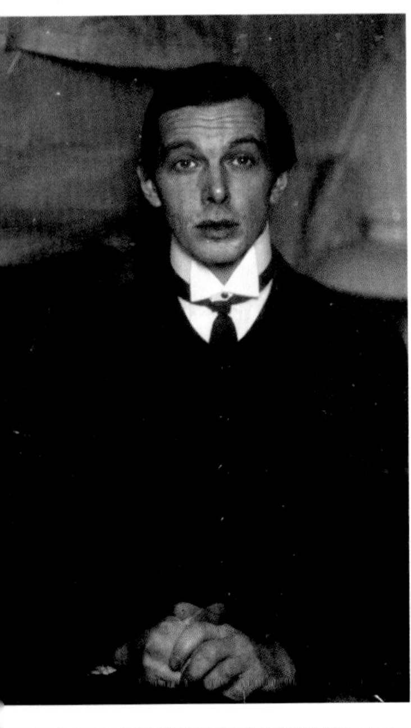

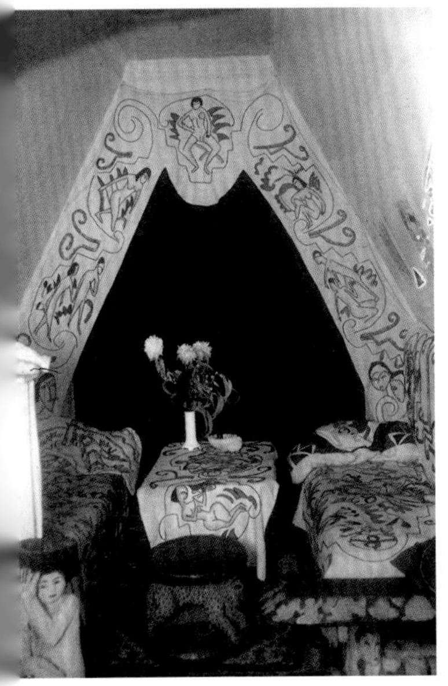

1880 Born on May 6 in Aschaffenburg, Bavaria, the oldest son of engineer and chemist Ernst Kirchner and Maria Elise Malwine Bertha Franke.

1890 Moves to Chemnitz, Saxony, with his family.

1901–04 Studies architecture at Technische Hochschule in Dresden, and from 1903–04 studies art for a semester in Munich. Discovers the French Post-Impressionists, and is fascinated by the print plates of German artist Albrecht Dürer (1471–1528) he sees at an exhibition in Nuremberg.

1905 Co-founds the Brücke artist group in Dresden on June 7. The other founding members are fellow architecture students Erich Heckel, Karl Schmidt-Rottluff, and Fritz Bleyl. His first exhibition with the group is in September, at P. H. Beyer & Sohn in Leipzig. Graduates as an architect.

1906–07 He and the other Brücke artists draw up an art manifesto published as a four-page brochure with a woodcut by Kirchner. Spends several periods by the Moritzburg Lakes close to Dresden.

1908–09 Sees the works of Vincent van Gogh, Paul Gauguin, Georges Seurat, and other Post-Impressionists, as well as the French Fauvists and works by Pablo Picasso and Edvard Munch in a range of exhibitions. First stay on the German island of Fehmarn with his model Emmy Frisch. Embarks on painting *Strasse*, the first of a series of street scenes.

1910 Exhibits with the Berlin Secession. Creates a series of wood sculptures inspired by a visit to Dresden's ethnological museum, Museum für Völkerkunde.

1911 Follows the example of Erich Heckel and Max Pechstein and moves to Berlin in October.

1912 Meets Gerda Schilling and her sister Erna, who later becomes his partner.

1913 Writes *Chronik der Künstlergruppe Brücke* (Chronicle of the Brücke Artists' Group), a source of intense disagreements in the group, which contributes to its disbandment on May 27. Moves to an attic flat in the Friedenau area of Berlin in October, designing his own furniture.

1914–17 Signs up for military service as what he retrospectively describes as an "involuntary volunteer." Granted temporary leave due to mental illness in September 1915 and admitted to a sanatorium in Königstein in Taunus in December diagnosed with alcoholism and addiction to sleeping pills and morphine. In 1917 admitted to Bellevue Sanatorium led by Ludwig Binswanger on Lake Constance in Kreuzlingen, Switzerland. He stays here until June 9, 1918. Starts sketching and painting the Alps and their inhabitants.

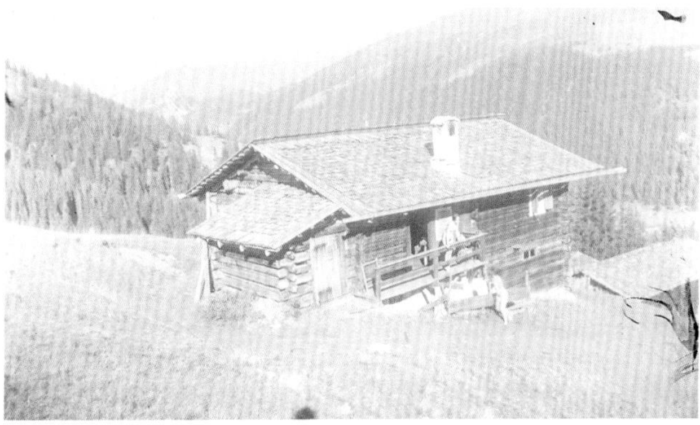

1918 Moves into the cabin "In den Lärchen" in Davos Frauenkirch. Paints a series of Alpine landscapes in rapturous colors, which are considered among his most important works of this period. In autumn he writes *Glaubensbekenntnis eines Malers* (Painter's Creed), published the following year.

1919 Spends the summer in a mountain cabin on Stafelalp. Erna Schilling sends paintings, prints, and drawings from his atelier in Berlin to Switzerland. Starts to repaint, rework, and redate earlier works.

1920 Publishes the first of six articles on his own work under the pseudonym Louis de Marsalle, an attempt to provide an "objective" reading of his artistic development.

1923 Moves into a house on Wildboden in Davos Frauenkirch.

1924 His solo exhibition at Kunstverein Winterthur is met by public outrage.

1925–26 Writes the essay "Das Werk" (The Work of Art) in his diary, outlining his artistic development. After spending several years in Switzerland he returns to Germany, where he lives from December 1925 to March 1926.

1927 Discusses the possibility of painting murals for the newly built Museum Folkwang in Essen with museum director Ernst Gosebruch.

1928 Exhibits the painting *Schlittenfahrt* (Sleigh Ride in the Snow) from 1923 in the German pavilion at the Venice Biennale.

1931 Exhibits in *German Paintings and Sculpture* at the Museum of Modern Art, New York. Becomes a member of the Prussian Academy of Arts in Berlin.

1932–33 Starts preparing for a major retrospective at Kunsthalle Bern in 1933. Publishes his last essay under the pseudonym Louis de Marsalle, who is declared dead in the exhibition catalogue.

1936–37 Offered his first solo exhibition in the US by Wilhelm R. Valentiner, director of the Detroit Institute of Art. The Nazis remove 639 "degenerate" works of art from museums, which are subsequently sold abroad or destroyed. Excluded from the Prussian Academy of Art at the end of June.

1938 After Germany's annexation of Austria on March 12, Kirchner starts to fear the invasion of Graubünden, his refuge in Switzerland, and destroys some of his printing blocks and sculptures. Shoots himself with a pistol on June 15 and is buried in Waldfriedhof cemetery in Davos.

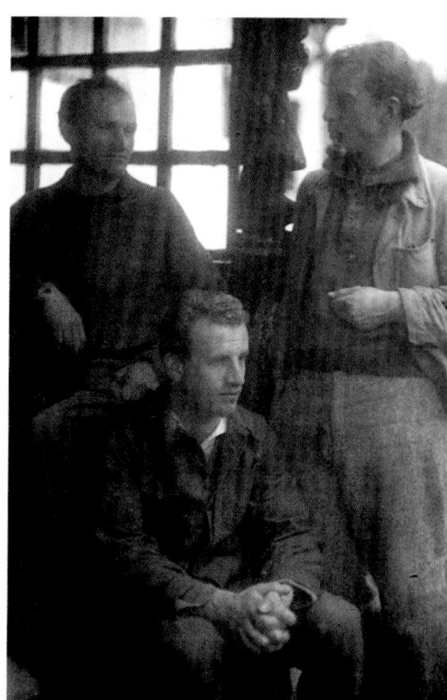

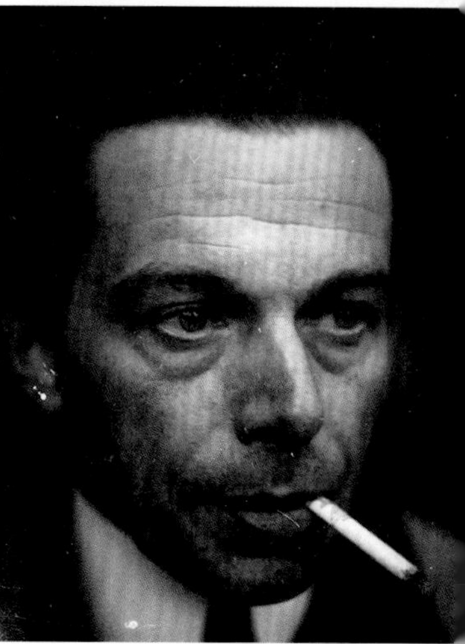

Jens Ferdinand Willumsen (1863–1958)

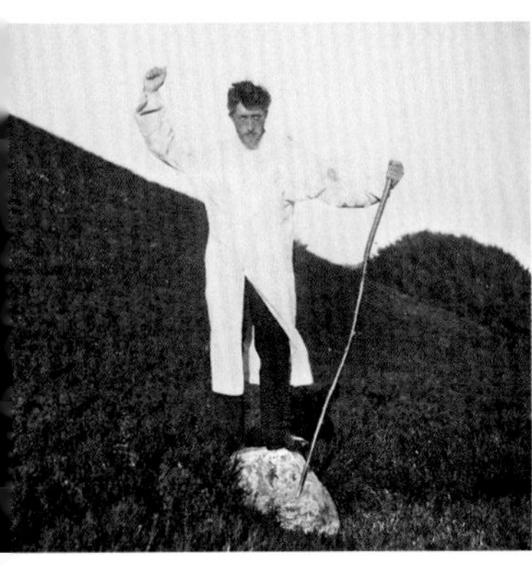

1863 Born in Copenhagen on September 7, son of publican Hans Willumsen and Ane Kristine Jensdatter.

1882 Graduates as an architect from Copenhagen Polytechnic.

1881–85 Studies at the Royal Academy of Fine Arts in Copenhagen. Fails three times to pass the final exam.

1888–89 Travels to Paris and Spain.

1889 First solo exhibition at the art dealer Kleis' Kunsthandel in Copenhagen.

1890 Marries the sculptor Juliette Meyer. The couple have two sons, Jan Bjørn and Bode Bertel. They divorce in 1902.

1890–94 Lives in Paris where he meets the painter Paul Gauguin and other French artists. Visits Norway and Chicago for the 1893 World Fair.

1891 Co-founds Den Frie Exhibition Hall in protest against censorship at the Charlottenborg Spring Exhibition. Exhibits the etching *Fertility*, which contributes to the exhibition becoming a *succès de scandale*.

1893 Buys his first camera and starts experimenting with self-portraits and photographs of his family and friends. Some of the photographs are used as a basis for his paintings.

1895 Designs his own (now demolished) villa in Hellerup, north of Copenhagen.

1897–1900 Artistic director at the Bing & Grøndahl porcelain factory, and key to the success of the company at the *Exposition Universelle* in Paris in 1900.

1898 Designs Den Frie Exhibition Hall.

1900 Exhibits at *Exposition Universelle* in Paris. Moves to New York with Edith Wessel in the hope of an international breakthrough. Starts an extensive collection of images from newspapers and magazines, which he glues into albums of cuttings, as well as a collection of dried plants for a herbarium.

1901–02 Travels to the Alps, Pyrenees, and Italy.

1903 Marries the sculptor Edith Wessel. The couple have two daughters, Ingemor Gersemi and Anne-Mathilde (nicknamed Anse). They separate around 1928.

1903–05 Lives in Paris, where he works with Julius Meier-Graefe to establish a *Salon des Étrangers*. Exhibits eight works at the 1906 Berlin Secession, after which he is invited via Emil Nolde to participate in one of the Brücke artists' exhibitions, an invitation he declines.

1905 Designs his second villa in Hellerup, which serves as his home and atelier.

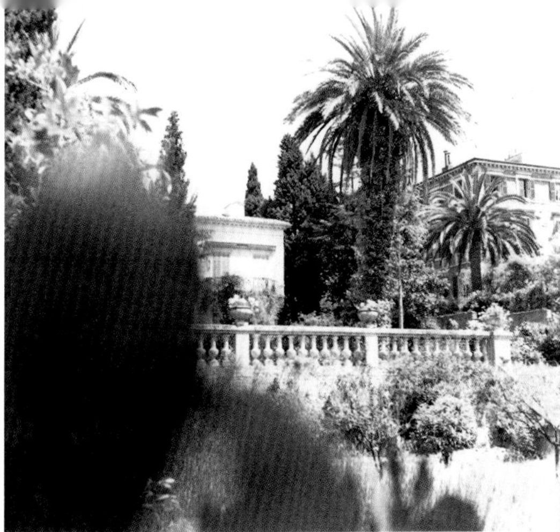

1911–14 Purchases a painting by El Greco and follows in the artist's footsteps to Crete, Italy, and Spain. Travels to Tunisia in 1914.

1911–20 Purchases more works for his "Old Collection," which includes icons, Italian drawings, and Venetian paintings.

1916 Settles permanently in the South of France.

1920 Turns down the offer of a position as professor at the Royal Danish Academy of Fine Arts.

1923 Major retrospective at Den Frie Exhibition Hall. Commissioned by the state of Denmark to make *The Great Relief*, which is carved in marble in Carrara, Italy, during the years that follow.

1920–30 Campaigns for a museum dedicated to his art and art collection.

1927 Publishes a two-volume work on the youth of El Greco. *The Great Relief* is unveiled at the National Gallery of Denmark, causing a scandal. Works on establishing a "Propaganda Bureau" for cultural exports.

1928–30 Starts living with the dancer and painter Michelle Bourret, a relationship that lasts until his death.

1930–32 Four solo exhibitions at Paris galleries. Represented in the 1932 Venice Biennale.

1930–40 Spends time in Venice and Rome, where he paints a number of vividly colored cityscapes. Purchases Asian works for his collection, and continues to campaign for and design a museum dedicated to his work and collection. Paints a series of expressive mountain landscapes in the latter nineteen-thirties.

1942 Moves from Nice to Cannes.

1947 Exhibits his "Old Collection" at Charlottenborg. Due to a series of erroneous work attributions, the collection is dismissed by experts. Draws up a deed of gift donating his works and collection to the state of Denmark.

1954 Moves from Cannes to Le Cannet.

1957 Inauguration of Willumsen's Museum in Frederikssund, designed by architect Thyge Hvass. From the South of France Willumsen pronounces that the museum looks like "a sawmill in Switzerland." He dies before ever visiting the museum.

1958 Willumsen dies in Le Cannet on April 4, and is buried in the grounds of Willumsen's Museum.

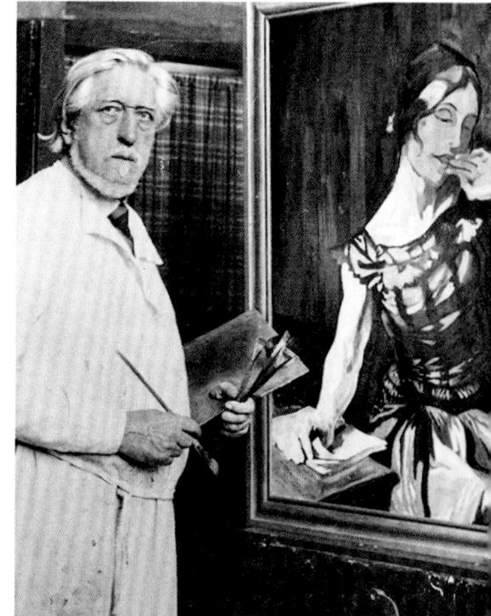

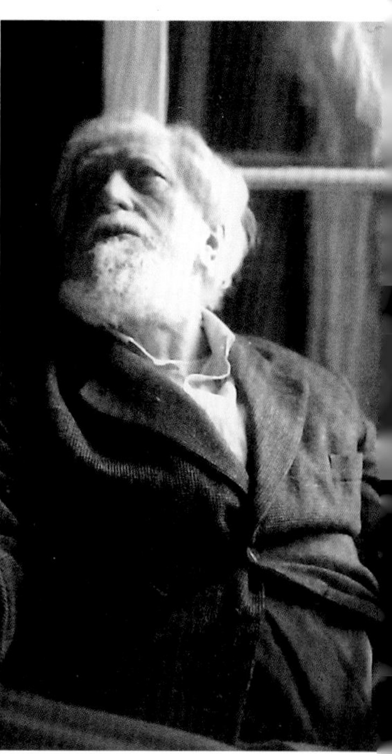

Author Biographies

Anders Ehlers Dam holds a Ph.D. degree in Danish Literature from Aarhus University. He is professor of Danish Literature and Culture at Europa-Universität Flensburg in Germany. His publications include *Den vitalistiske strømning i dansk litteratur* (2010). He has edited books such as *Distancens patos* (2017, with Marianne Stidsen), *Soldat, arbejder, anark. Ernst Jüngers forfatterskab* (2017, with Adam Paulsen), *J.P. Jacobsen og kunsten* (2016, with Gry Hedin) and *Forandre for at bevare? Tanker om konservatisme* (2003).

Uwe Fleckner is professor of Art History at the University of Hamburg, one of the directors of the Warburg-Haus and co-editor of Carl Einstein's and Aby Warburg's complete works. He worked as guest professor at Stanford University and currently at Peking University and was a fellow at the Getty Research Institute, Los Angeles. He is founder and director of the Research Center on Degenerate Art, University of Hamburg, and co-director of the "Bilderfahrzeuge—Aby Warburg's Legacy and the Future of Iconology" international research network. Fleckner is author of numerous books and articles on eighteenth to twenty-first century art history, with French and German art and art theory and political iconography as his main fields.

Anne Gregersen is curator at Willumsen's Museum, Frederikssund. She holds a PhD from the University of Copenhagen, 2015, and a Postdoc at the same university, 2015–19. She also has an M.A. in Art History from the University of Copenhagen, as well as a Master (Diplôme d'études supérieures spécialisées) from Université 10 Nanterre, Paris in curatorial studies. Among her publications are "Becoming Animal through Curatorial Contagion," in Claus Carstensen et al., *Becoming Animal*, exh. cat. Den Frie Centre of Contemporary Art, Copenhagen (2018), *Echo Room. Thorvaldsen, Willumsen, Jorn, and Their Collections* (editor), exh. cat., Willumsen's Museum, Frederikssund (2018), and co-editor of *Curatorial Challenges: Interdisciplinary Perspectives on Contemporary Curating* (2019).

Jill Lloyd is a writer and curator specializing in German Expressionism and turn-of-the-century Viennese art. She is a frequent guest curator at the Neue Galerie, New York where her more recent exhibitions include *Ernst Ludwig Kirchner* (2019–20), *Richard Gerstl* (2017), *Edvard Munch and Expressionism* (2016) and *Vasily Kandinsky: From Blaue Reiter to the Bauhaus, 1910–1925* (2013). She also curated *Ernst Ludwig Kirchner, Expressionism and the City, 1905–1918* (National Gallery of Art, Washington and Royal Academy, London, 2003). She has published widely on early twentieth-century and contemporary art, including her book *German Expressionism, Primitivism and Modernity* (YUP, 1991), which was awarded the National Art Book Prize. Her book publications include studies of Max Beckmann's Amsterdam years and an authorized biography of the Austrian emigré artist Marie-Louise von Motesiczky. Previous appointments include Lecturer in Twentieth-Century Art, University College London, and Editor-in-Chief, Art International Magazine, Paris.

Carsten Thau is professor MSO of Architectural History and Theory at The Royal Danish Academy of Fine Arts Schools of Architecture, Design and Conservation in Copenhagen. He studied philosophy and art history at the J. W. Goethe University in Frankfurt am Main and the University of Aarhus. He is co-author of a number of books on the Danish architect Arne Jacobsen that have provided the basis for exhibitions at the Louisiana Museum of Modern Art, MoMA in New York, and MoMA in Oxford. He has written extensively on architecture, urban history, film, and the philosophy of aesthetics. Most recently he has published books on the notion of time in architecture and the relationship between philosophy and architecture. He has been a guest professor throughout Scandinavia and lectured at art academies and universities worldwide. He has been active as a consultant for Danish museums and contributed to a number of TV programs on Scandinavian architecture.

… of illustrations (Exhibited works are marked with *)

P. 50

* Ernst Ludwig Kirchner
Sketchbook 131, February 1926, p. 52
20.7 × 17 cm
Kirchner Museum Davos
Photo: Kirchner Museum Davos

P. 51

* Ernst Ludwig Kirchner
Sketchbook 076, 1921, 1926–27, p. 31
21.7 × 17.4 cm
Kirchner Museum Davos
Photo: Kirchner Museum Davos

PP. 52–53

* Ernst Ludwig Kirchner
Hedwigskirche Berlin (St Hedwig's Cathedral Berlin), 1927
Woodcut, 25.7 × 42.2 cm
Kirchner Museum Davos
Photo: Stephan Bösch

JILL LLOYD

Detail, pp. 38–39: See fig. 6

FIG. 1

* Ernst Ludwig Kirchner
Tanzende Mädchen in farbigen Strahlen (Dancing Girls in Rays of Color), 1932–37
Oil on canvas, 195 × 150 cm
Gordon 969
Kirchner Museum Davos.
Donation of the Estate of Ernst Ludwig Kirchner 1992
Photo: Stephan Bösch

FIG. 2

Ernst Ludwig Kirchner
Künstlervereinigung Brücke (Artist Association Brücke), 1905
Woodcut, 5 × 6.5 cm
Brücke-Museum, Berlin
Photo: Roman März

FIG. 3

Ernst Ludwig Kirchner
Tanzende (Dancing Woman), 1911
Painted alder-wood, 87 × 35.5 × 27.5 cm
Stedelijk Museum, Amsterdam
Photo: Stedelijk Museum, Amsterdam

FIG. 4

Ernst Ludwig Kirchner
Nelly und Sidi Heckel (Riha), tanzend im Atelier von Erich Heckel, Dresden (Nelly and Sidi Heckel (Riha), Dancing in Erich Heckel's Studio), ca. 1910–11
Glass-plate negative, 13 × 18 cm
Kirchner Museum Davos

FIG. 5

Ernst Ludwig Kirchner
Negertänzerin (Black Dancer), 1909–11/1920
Oil on canvas, 168 × 93 cm
Gordon 74
Sammlung Würth, Künzelsau, inv. 7986
Photo: Peter Falk, Schwäbisch Hall

FIG. 6

Ernst Ludwig Kirchner
Spielende nackte Menschen unter Baum (Playing Naked People Under the Tree), 1910
Oil on canvas, 77 × 89 cm
Gordon 141
Sammlung Moderne Kunst in der Pinakothek der Moderne, Munich – Bayerische Staatsgemäldesammlungen
Photo: Sybille Forster © 2020 Photo Scala, Florence/bpk, Bildagentur für Kunst, Kultur und Geschichte, Berlin

FIG. 7

Ernst Ludwig Kirchner
Werner Gothein, Hugo Biallowons, (E. L. Kirchner?) und Erna Schilling im Kirchners Atelier, Körnerstrasse 45, Berlin (Werner Gothein, Hugo Biallowons, (E. L. Kirchner?), and Erna Schilling in Kirchner's Studio, Körnerstrasse 45, Berlin), 1915
Glass-plate negative, 13 × 18 cm
Kirchner Museum Davos
E.W.K., Bern/Davos, courtesy Kirchner Museum Davos

FIG. 8

Ernst Ludwig Kirchner
Der Tanz zwischen den Frauen (The Dance between Women), 1915
Oil on canvas, 121.1 × 91.4 cm
Gordon 443
Sammlung Moderne Kunst in der Pinakothek der Moderne, Munich – Bayerische Staatsgemäldesammlungen
© 2020 Photo Scala. Florence/bpk, Bildagentur für Kunst, Kultur und Geschichte, Berlin

FIG. 9

Ernst Ludwig Kirchner
Nina Hard (Engelhard), tanzend im oberen Geschoss im Haus "In den Lärchen" (Nina Hard (Engelhard), Dancing in the Upper Floor of the House "In den Lärchen"), 1921
Glass-plate negative, 24 × 18 cm
Kirchner Museum Davos. Donation of the Estate of Ernst Ludwig Kirchner 1992

FIG. 10

Ernst Ludwig Kirchner
Totentanz, Mary Wigman (Dance of Death, Mary Wigman), 1926
Crayon on paper, 47 × 37 cm
Galerie Henze and Ketterer, Bern
Photo: Galerie Henze and Ketterer

IMAGE SECTION II

P. 74

* Ernst Ludwig Kirchner
Nackte Tänzerin (Naked Dancer), 1934
Etching, 38 × 20.4 cm
Kirchner Museum Davos
Photo: Kirchner Museum Davos

PP. 75–77

* Ernst Ludwig Kirchner
Tänzerin im Wald (Dancer in the Forest), ca. 1929
Cellulose nitrate negative, 14.5 × 9 cm
Brücke-Museum Berlin, courtesy Kirchner Museum Davos

P. 78

* Ernst Ludwig Kirchner
Akt in Orange und Gelb (Nude in Orange and Yellow), 1929/1930
Oil on canvas, 91 × 71 cm
Gordon 938
Kirchner Museum Davos
Photo: Jakob Jäggli-Schmelz

P. 79

* Ernst Ludwig Kirchner
Ballspielerinnen (Girls Playing Ball), 1931–32
Oil on canvas, 152 × 89.5 cm
Gordon 993
Kirchner Museum Davos
Photo: Stephan Bösch

P. 80

* Ernst Ludwig Kirchner
Bogenschützen (Archers), 1935–37
Oil on canvas, 195 × 150 cm
Gordon 994
Kirchner Museum Davos
Photo: Kirchner Museum Davos

P. 81

* Ernst Ludwig Kirchner
Bogenschiessende Mädchen im Walde (Female Archers in the Forest), 1934
Etching, 20 × 14.6 cm
Kirchner Museum Davos
Photo: Kirchner Museum Davos

P. 82

* Ernst Ludwig Kirchner
Bogenschiessendes Bauernmädchen vor dem Haus "In den Lärchen" (Country Girl Practicing Archery in Front of the House "In den Lärchen"), ca. 1919–23
Glass-plate negative, 18 × 13 cm
Kirchner Museum Davos

P. 83

* Ernst Ludwig Kirchner
Bogenschützinnen (Female Archers), 1935
Etching, 25.5 × 25.3 cm
Kirchner Museum Davos
Photo: Kirchner Museum Davos

PP. 84–85

* Ernst Ludwig Kirchner
Tennisspiel (Tennis Match), 1927
Etching, 24.8 × 30.9 cm
Kirchner Museum Davos
Photo: Kirchner Museum Davos

P. 86

* Ernst Ludwig Kirchner
Sieger im Wettlauf (Race Winner), 1926–27
Pen and ink on paper, 21.8 × 17.2 cm
Kirchner Museum Davos
Photo: Kirchner Museum Davos

P. 87

* Ernst Ludwig Kirchner
Radfahrerin (Cyclist), 1934
Lithograph, 32.6 × 27.3 cm
Kirchner Museum Davos
Photo: Kirchner Museum Davos

P. 88

* J. F. Willumsen
Michelle Bourret in Dance Position Inspired by Sergei Diaghilev's "Les Ballet Russes," ca. 1934–35
Photo, 17.7 × 12.7 cm
Willumsen's Museum, Frederikssund

P. 89

* J. F. Willumsen
Lola danser (Lola Dances), 1921
Oil on canvas, 155 × 135 cm
Willumsen's Museum, Frederikssund
Photo: Anders Sune Berg

P. 90

* J. F. Willumsen
Jægerpige i skoven (Huntress in the Forest), 1934
Oil on canvas, 190 × 141 cm
Willumsen's Museum, Frederikssund
Photo: Bent Ryberg

P. 91, LEFT

* J. F. Willumsen
Michelle Bourret as Huntress, 1932
Photo, 18 × 12.8 cm
Willumsen's Museum, Frederikssund

P. 91, RIGHT

* J. F. Willumsen
Michelle Bourret as Huntress, 1932
Photo, 14 × 9 cm
Willumsen's Museum, Frederikssund

P. 92

* J. F. Willumsen
De to boldspillende småpiger (Two Young Girls Playing Ball), 1916
Etching, 32.5 × 21 cm
Willumsen's Museum, Frederikssund

P. 93

J. F. Willumsen
To atleter (Two Athletes), 1916
Etching, 23.7 × 17.4 cm
Willumsen's Museum, Frederikssund

PP. 94–95

* J. F. Willumsen
Kuglespillere. Provence (Ball Players. Provence), 1939–46
Oil on canvas, 74 × 91.5 cm
Willumsen's Museum, Frederikssund
Photo: Anders Sune Berg

ANNE GREGERSEN

PP. 96–97

Ernst Ludwig Kirchner
Selbstbildnis als Kranker (Self-Portrait as a Sick Man), 1918–30
Oil on canvas, 59 × 69.3 cm
Photo: bpk | Bayerische Staatsgemäldesammlungen, Munich

FIG. 1

Edvard Munch
Selvportrett i helvete (Self-Portrait in Hell), 1903
Oil on canvas, 82 × 66 cm
The Munch Museum, Oslo
Photo: Juri Kobayashi
© CC BY 4 The Munch Museum

FIG. 2:

Ernst Ludwig Kirchner
Selbstbildnis (Self-Portrait), 1934–37
Oil on canvas, 84 × 61 cm
Bünder Kunstmuseum Chur.
Purchased with support from Bündner Kunstverein
© Bünder Kunstmuseum Chur

FIG. 3

J. F. Willumsen
Selvportræt i malerbluse (Self-Portrait in Painter's Smock), 1933
Oil on canvas, 119 × 117 cm
Willumsen's Museum, Frederikssund
Photo: Bent Ryberg

FIG. 4

Harald Perch
Portrait of J. F. Willumsen, ca. 1917
Photo, 27.8 × 20 cm
Willumsen's Museum, Frederikssund

FIG. 5

* J. F. Willumsen
Også et selvportræt (Also a Self-Portrait), 1916
Etching, 23.7 × 19.3
Willumsen's Museum, Frederikssund

FIG. 6

El Greco (Domenikos Theotokopoulos)
Cardinal Fernando Niño de Guevara (1541–1609), ca. 1600
Oil on canvas, 170.8 × 108 cm
H. O. Havemeyer Collection. Bequest of Mrs. H. O. Havemeyer, 1929
The Metropolitan Museum of Art, New York

FIG. 7
Ernst Ludwig Kirchner
Schlemihl mit dem grauen Männlein auf der Landstrasse (Schlemihl's Encounter with the Little Gray Man on the Highway), 1915
Color woodcut, composition 30 × 31 cm
Museum Folkwang, Essen
©Museum Folkwang Essen – ARTOTHEK

FIG. 8
Ernst Ludwig Kirchner
Bauerntanz im Obergeschoss des Haus "In den Lärchen" mit selbstporträit links (Barn Dance on the Upper Floor of the House "In den Lärchen" with Self-Portrait at the Left), 1919–20
Glass-plate negative, 18 × 24 cm
Kirchner Museum Davos. Donation of the Estate of Ernst Ludwig Kirchner 1992

FIG. 9
Ernst Ludwig Kirchner
Vor Sonnenaufgang
(Before Sunrise), 1925–26
Oil on canvas, 168 × 120 cm
Gordon 783
Sammlung Glarner Kunstverein, Glarus
Photo: Glarner Kunstverein

FIG. 10
J. F. Willumsen in Cannes, 1947
Photo, 18.3 × 23.6 cm
Willumsen's Museum, Frederikssund
Lindequist Foto

FIG. 11A–D
Pages from Hjalmar Öhman, *J.F. Willumsen. Med kommentarer af J.F. Willumsen.* Copenhagen, 1921

FIG. 12
* J. F. Willumsen
Boldspillere på gaden i Cannes
(People Playing Ball in a Street in Cannes), 1947
Oil on canvas, 151.5 × 99 cm
KUNSTEN Museum of Modern Art Aalborg
Photo: Niels Fabæk

FIG. 13
Ernst Ludwig Kirchner
Selbstporträt mit Katze
(Self-Portrait with Cat), 1920
Oil on canvas, 120.6 × 80 cm
Gordon 621
Harvard Art Museums/Busch-Reisinger Museum, Cambridge, MA, Museum purchase
Copyright N/A
Photo: © President and Fellows of Harvard College

FIG. 14
Albrecht Dürer
Portrait of the Artist Holding a Thistle, 1493
56.5 × 44.5 cm
Oil on vellum transferred to canvas
Musée du Louvre, Paris

FIG. 15A–B
Spreads from Ernst Ludwig Kirchner / Louis de Marsalle, "Zeichnungen von E.L. Kirchner," in *Genius – Zeitschrift für werdende und alte Kunst*, 2:2 (1920).

FIG. 16
Ernst Ludwig Kirchner
Selbstbildnis (Self-Portrait), ca. 1919
Glass-plate negative, 24 × 18 cm
Kirchner Museum Davos
Donation of the Estate of Ernst Ludwig Kirchner 1992

FIG. 17
* Ernst Ludwig Kirchner
Männerkopf – Selbstbildnis
(Man's Head – Self-Portrait), 1926
Woodcut, 39 × 30 cm
Kirchner Museum Davos
Photo: Kirchner Museum Davos

UWE FLECKNER

Detail, pp. 122–123: See fig. 3

FIG. 1
Ernst Ludwig Kirchner
Ansicht von Dresden (Schlossplatz)
(View of Dresden (Schlossplatz)), 1925
Gouache on painting board, 32 × 47 cm
Sammlung Würth, Künzelsau
Photo: Volker Naumann, Schönaich

FIG. 2
Ernst Ludwig Kirchner
Kopf Professor Botho Graef
(Professor Botho Graef, Head), 1912
Lithograph, 48.8 × 59.2 cm
Kupferstichkabinett der Staatliche Museen, Berlin
Photo: bpk. Kupferstichkabinett, Staatliche Museen, Berlin – Preussischer Kulturbesitz/ Jörg P. Anders

FIG. 3
Ernst Ludwig Kirchner
Im See badende Mädchen (Girls Bathing in a Lake), 1909 (dated 1907)
Oil on canvas, 91.2 × 120 cm
Gordon 86
Private collection
Photo: © akg-images

FIG. 4
Ernst Ludwig Kirchner
Fünf Frauen auf der Strasse
(Five Women on the Street), 1913
Oil on canvas, 120 × 90 cm
Gordon 362
Museum Ludwig, Cologne
Photo: Rhenisches Bildarchiv, Köln, rba_d024729

FIG. 5
Ernst Ludwig Kirchner
Gerda, Halbfigur (Gerda, Half Length Portrait), 1914
Oil on canvas, 99.1 × 75.3 cm
Gordon 375
Solomon R. Guggenheim Museum, New York
Partial gift, Mr. and Mrs. Mortimer M. Denker, 1978
© 2020 The Solomon R. Guggenheim Museum/Art Resource, NY Scala, Florence

FIG. 6
Ernst Ludwig Kirchner
Bergwald Frauenkirch (Mountain Forest Frauenkirch), 1919
Oil on canvas, 120 × 90 cm
Gordon 582
Nationalgalerie – Staatliche Museen, Berlin
Photo: Joerg P. Anders. Berlin, Nationalgalerie – Staatliche Museen, Berlin
© 2020. Photo Scala, Florence /bpk, Bildagentur für Kunst, Kultur und Geschichte, Berlin

FIG. 7
Ernst Ludwig Kirchner
Maler und Modell (Painter and Model), 1924–27 (dated 1921)
Oil on canvas, 70 × 60 cm
Gordon 769
© Private collection

FIG. 8
Ernst Ludwig Kirchner
Die Erscheinung der Sieben im "Eulenspiegel" (The Apparition of the Seven in "Eulenspiegel"), 1923–24
Oil on canvas, 125 × 167 cm
Gordon 752
© Private collection, Chicago

FIG. 9
Ernst Ludwig Kirchner
Der Abschied (The Farewell), 1925–26
Oil on canvas, 120.5 × 90 cm
Gordon 835
Rosemarie Ketterer Stiftung.
On permanent deposit at Kirchner Museum Davos
Photo: Kirchner Museum Davos

ANDERS EHLERS DAM

Detail, pp. 140–141: See fig. 1

FIG. 1
*J. F. Willumsen
Bjergtinde, Schweiz (Mountain Peak, Switzerland), 1926
Oil on canvas, 53.5 × 73.5 cm
Galleri Bo Bjerggaard, Copenhagen
Courtesy Galleri Bo Bjerggaard

FIG. 2
J. F. Willumsen
Mont Blanc i skyer
(Mont Blanc in Clouds), 1936
Oil on canvas, 126 × 150.5 cm
Willumsen's Museum, Frederikssund
Photo: Bent Ryberg

FIG. 3
J. F. Willumsen
Sol over Sydens bjerge (Sun over Southern Mountains), 1902
Oil on canvas, 209 × 208 cm
The Thiel Gallery, Stockholm
Photo: The Thiel Gallery

FIG. 4
J. F. Willumsen
Color Study, 1901
Watercolor on paper, 45.7 × 30.2 cm
Willumsen's Museum, Frederikssund
Photo: Anders Sune Berg

FIG. 5
*J. F. Willumsen
Spread from Willumsen's album of cuttings *Land og Vand* (Land and Sea), ca. 1900–11
Willumsen's Museum, Frederikssund
Photo: Anders Sune Berg

FIG. 6
Ernst Ludwig Kirchner
Nina Hard vor dem Eingang des Hauses "In den Lärchen" (Nina Hard in Front of the Entrance to the House "In den Lärchen"), summer 1921
Gelatin-silver print, 17 × 11.8 cm
Kirchner Museum Davos. Donation of the Estate of Ernst Ludwig Kirchner 1992

FIG. 7
Ernst Ludwig Kirchner
Das "Bildhaueratelier" neben dem "Wildbodenhaus" (Drei Skulpturen von Hermann Scherer und eine von Kirchner) (The "Sculptor's Studio" next to the "Wildbodenhaus" [Three Sculptures by Hermann Scherer and One by Kirchner]), 1924
Glass-plate negative, 24 × 18 cm
Kirchner Museum Davos. Donation of the Estate of Ernst Ludwig Kirchner 1992

FIG. 8
* Ernst Ludwig Kirchner
Blick vom Wohnhaus von Ernst Ludwig Kirchner auf die Melcherne und Stafelstrasse (View from Ernst Ludwig Kirchner's House to Melcherne and Stafelstrasse), 1918–22
Gelatin-silver print, 11.8 × 16.4 cm
Kirchner Museum Davos.

FIG. 9
Ernst Ludwig Kirchner
Alpleben (Life in the Alps), triptychon, 1917–19
Oil on canvas,
left side panel 70 × 60 cm,
center panel 70 × 80 cm,
right side panel 70 × 60 cm
Gordon 527a–c
Kirchner Museum Davos. Donation from private collection, Bern 2006
Photo: © Christie's Images Ltd – ARTOTHEK

FIG. 10
Ernst Ludwig Kirchner
Winterlandschaft in Mondlicht
(Winter Landscape in Moonlight), 1919
Oil on canvas, 120 × 121 cm
Gordon 558
Gift from Curt Valentin in memory of the artist on occasion of Dr. William R. Valentiner's 60th birthday
The Detroit Institute of Arts
Photo: akg-images

FIG. 11
Ernst Ludwig Kirchner
Wintermondnach
(Winter Moonlit Night), 1919
Color woodcut, composition 47 × 33 cm
Museum Folkwang, Essen
Photo: © Museum Folkwang Essen – ARTOTHEK

FIG. 12
Ernst Ludwig Kirchner and Lisa Gujer
Alpaufzug (Cattle Drive into the Alps), 1926
Woll, 258 × 172 cm
Zürcher Hochschule der Künste, Museum für Gestaltung Zürich
Photo: Courtesy Museum für Gestaltung Zürich, Decorative Arts Collection, ZHdK

FIG. 13
* Ernst Ludwig Kirchner
Die Brücke bei Wiesen
(The Bridge in Wiesen), 1926
Oil on canvas, 120 × 120 cm
Gordon 844
Kirchner Museum Davos.
Photo: Stephan Bösch

FIG. 14
Gerhard Richter
Davos, 1981
Oil on canvas, 50.2 × 69.9 cm
Art Institute of Chicago
© Gerhard Richter 2020 (0082)

FIG. 15
Gerhard Richter
Atlas, Tafel 338 (Davos) (Atlas, sheet 338 (Davos)), 1973–74
Photo, 51.7 × 73.5 cm
Städtische Galerie im Lenbachhaus and Kunstbau München, Munich
Photo: Städtische Galerie im Lenbachhaus and Kunstbau München, Munich

IMAGE SECTION III

P. 166
* J. F. Willumsen
Mont Blanc i aftensol
(Mont Blanc in Evening Sun), 1920
Oil on canvas, 61.5 × 46.5 cm
Willumsen's Museum, Frederikssund
Photo: Anders Sune Berg

P. 167

J. F. Willumsen
Naturens skjolder, bjergene med de tre farver (Nature's Shields. Mountains with the Three Colors), 1936
Oil on canvas, 126 × 150.5 cm
Willumsen's Museum, Frederikssund
Photo: Anders Sune Berg

P. 168–169

* J. F. Willumsen
Bjergkæde i aftensol. Studie efter naturen til billedets midterste del (Mountain Range in Evening Sun. Study after Nature for the Middle Part of the Picture), 1926
Oil on canvas, 50 × 73 cm
Willumsen's Museum, Frederikssund
Photo: Anders Sune Berg

PP. 170–171

* J. F. Willumsen
Bjergkæde i aftensol (Mountain Range in Evening Sun), 1926
Watercolor on paper, 20.2 × 48.5 cm
Willumsen's Museum, Frederikssund
Photo: Anders Sune Berg

P. 172

* Ernst Ludwig Kirchner
Skisprung (Ski Jump), 1936
Woodcut, 49.9 × 34.8 cm
Kirchner Museum Davos
Photo: Stephan Bösch

P. 173

* Ernst Ludwig Kirchner
Clavadeler Berg von Frauenkirch aus (Clavadeler Mountain from Frauenkirch), 1936
Woodcut, 35.3 × 50 cm
Kirchner Museum Davos
Photo: Stephan Bösch

PP. 174–175

* Ernst Ludwig Kirchner
Berglandschaft mit Alp (Mountainscape with Alp), 1933
Woodcut, 34.7 × 50 cm
Kirchner Museum Davos
Photo: Stephan Bösch

P. 176

* Ernst Ludwig Kirchner
Blick vom Wohnhaus von Ernst Ludwig Kirchner auf die Längmatte (View from Ernst Ludwig Kirchner's House to Längmatte), 1918–22
Gelatin-silver print, 12 × 16.5 cm
Kirchner Museum Davos

P. 177

* Ernst Ludwig Kirchner
Blick vom Haus "In den Lärchen" auf den Nachbarhof und die Längmatte (View from the House "In den Lärchen" to the neighboring Courtyard and to Längmatte), 1918/22
Gelatin-silver print, 12 × 16.5 cm
Kirchner Museum Davos

P. 178

* Ernst Ludwig Kirchner
Wasserfall des Sertigbaches (Sertigbach Waterfall), 1928
Gelatin-silver print, 14,8 × 10 cm
Kirchner Museum Davos

P. 179

* Ernst Ludwig Kirchner
Blick von Ernst Ludwig Kirchners Wohnhaus auf dem Wildboden (View from Ernst Ludwig Kirchner's House on the Wildboden), after 1924
Gelatin-silver print, 18 × 24 cm
Kirchner Museum Davos

P. 180

* Ernst Ludwig Kirchner
Blick vom Wildboden nach Davos (View from Wildboden to Davos), after 1924
Gelatin-silver print, 9.8 × 14.5 cm
Kirchner Museum Davos

P. 181

* Ernst Ludwig Kirchner
Laufende Kühe auf der Stafelalp (Cows Running on the Stafelalp), ca. 1919
Gelatin-silver print, 18 × 24 cm
Kirchner Museum Davos

P. 182

* Ernst Ludwig Kirchner
Blick vom Wildboden über den Schiesstand in Islen nach Davos (View from the Wildboden across the Shooting Range in Islen toward Davos), after 1924
Gelatin-silver print, 9.8 × 14.5 cm
Kirchner Museum Davos

P. 183

* Ernst Ludwig Kirchner
Blick von der Sommerhütte Kirchners auf der Stafelalp nach Süden auf das Tinzenhorn (View Looking South of the Tinzenhorn from Kirchner's Summer Cabin on the Stafelalp), ca. 1919
Gelatin-silver print, 12 × 16.5 cm
Kirchner Museum Davos

P. 184

* Ernst Ludwig Kirchner
Sketchbook 140, 1927, 1937, p. 2
20.9 × 17.3 cm
Kirchner Museum Davos
Photo: Kirchner Museum Davos

P. 185

* Ernst Ludwig Kirchner
Junkerboden bei Frauenkirch/Davos, mit Blick auf Rhätische Bahn (The Junkerboden Mountain near Frauenkirch/Davos, with View of the Rhaetian Railway), 1919
Oil on canvas, 90 × 150 cm
Gordon 615
© Private collection

PP. 186–187

* J. F. Willumsen
Vaskekoner ved floden, Nice (Washerwomen by the River, Nice), 1919
Oil on canvas, 84 × 105 cm
Private collection
Photo: David Stjernholm

P. 188

* J. F. Willumsen
Stenbrud 2, studie (Quarry 2, Study), 1913
Oil on canvas, 108 × 91 cm
Victor Petersen's Willumsen Collection at the Manor Odden, Hjørring
Photo: Victor Petersen's Willumsen Collection

P. 189

* Ernst Ludwig Kirchner
Hackende Bauern (Peasants with Picks), 1937
Oil on canvas, 70 × 60 cm
Gordon 1007
Galerie Henze & Ketterer, Wichtrach / Bern
Photo: Galerie Henze & Ketterer

P. 190

* Julia Staub-Oetiker, after design by Ernst Ludwig Kirchner
Hirte mit Stab in der linken Hand, mit drei Kühen und einer Ziege (Shepherd with Walking Stick in Left Hand, Three Cows, and a Goat), design 1924 / woven ca. 1950
Embroidering on canvas, 54.5 × 55.7 cm
Kirchner Museum Davos
Photo: Jakob Jäggli-Schmelz

P. 191

* Lise Gujer, after design by Ernst Ludwig Kirchner
Schwarzer Frühling (Black Spring), design 1929 / woven 1961
Wool, 190 × 96.5 × 1 cm
Kirchner Museum Davos
Photo: Jakob Jäggli-Schmelz

P. 192–193

* Lise Gujer, after design by Ernst Ludwig Kirchner
Menschen in Landschaft (People in Landscape), design 1923 / woven after 1953
Wool, 94.5 × 272.5 cm
Kirchner Museum Davos
Photo: Jakob Jäggli-Schmelz

P. 194

* Edith Willumsen, after design by J. F. Willumsen
Dekorativ dans (Decorative Dance), 1925
Wool on silk upholstery, 95 × 142 cm
Victor Petersen's Willumsen Collection at the Manor Odden, Hjørring
Photo: Victor Petersen's Willumsen Collection

P. 195

* J. F. Willumsen
Det Store Relief. Udkast med forsøg af farver (The Great Relief. Sketch with Trials of Color), 1925
Oil on canvas, 108 × 145 cm
Willumsen's Museum, Frederikssund
Photo: Bent Ryberg

P. 196, CROPPED

Ernst Ludwig Kirchner
Selbstporträt im Atelier (Self-Portrait in the Studio), 1913-15
Glass negative, 13 × 18 cm
Kirchner Museum Davos. Donation of the Estate of Ernst Ludwig Kirchner 1992

P. 196, CROPPED

Ernst Ludwig Kirchner
Mansarde in der Atelierwohnung Kirchners in Berlin-Friedenau, Körnerstrasse 45 (Garret in Kirchner's Studio Apartment in Berlin-Friedenau, Körnerstrasse 45), 1914-15
Glass negative, 24 × 18 cm
Kirchner Museum Davos. Donation of the Estate of Ernst Ludwig Kirchner 1992

P. 197, CROPPED

Ernst Ludwig Kirchner
Nina Hard und Erna Schilling vor Kirchners Hütte auf der Stafelalp (Nina Hard and Erna Schilling in front of Kirchner's Hut on Stafelalp), Summer 1921
Glass negative, 18 × 24 cm
Kirchner Museum Davos. Donation of the Estate of Ernst Ludwig Kirchner 1992

P. 197, CROPPED

Ernst Ludwig Kirchner
Hermann Scherer, Paul Camenisch und Ernst Ludwig Kirchner auf der Veranda vor dem Wildbodenhaus (Hermann Scherer, Paul Camenisch, and Ernst Ludwig Kirchner on the Veranda in front of the Wilbodenhaus), July 1926
Glass negative, 24 × 18 cm
Kirchner Museum Davos. Donation of the Estate of Ernst Ludwig Kirchner 1992

P. 197, CROPPED

Ernst Ludwig Kirchner
Selbstporträt (Self-Portrait), ca. 1928
Glass negative, 18 × 13 cm
Kirchner Museum Davos. Donation of the Estate of Ernst Ludwig Kirchner 1992

P. 198, CROPPED

J. F. Willumsen
Portrait of J. F. Willumsen, 1899
Photo in album
Victor Petersen's Willumsen Collection at the Manor Odden, Hjørring

P. 198, CROPPED

Peter Newland's photo
J. F. Willumsen i sit atelier på Strandagervej med forarbejder til Hørupmonumentet; siddende Edith Willumsen (J. F. Willumsen in his Studio on Strandagervej with Sketches for the Hørup Monument, Sitting Edith Willumsen), 1908
Photo, 22.6 × 16.4 cm
Willumsen's Museum, Frederikssund

P. 199, CROPPED

J. F. Willumsen
Bolig og atelier, Villa le Lido, Cannes (Residence and Studio, Villa le Lido, Cannes), ca. 1954
Photo, 10 × 10.1 cm
Willumsen's Museum, Frederikssund

P. 199, CROPPED

Holger Damgaard
J.F. Willumsen foran maleriet "Skuespillerinde memorerer sin rolle i 'Salome'", 1938 (J. F. Willumsen in front of the Painting "Actress Memorizing her Rolle in 'Salome'"), Nice, March 9, 1919
Photo, 23.5 × 16.9 cm
Willumsen's Museum, Frederikssund

P. 199, CROPPED

Boye Willumsen
J. F. Willumsen, 1957
Photo, 10 × 10.1 cm
Willumsen's Museum, Frederikssund

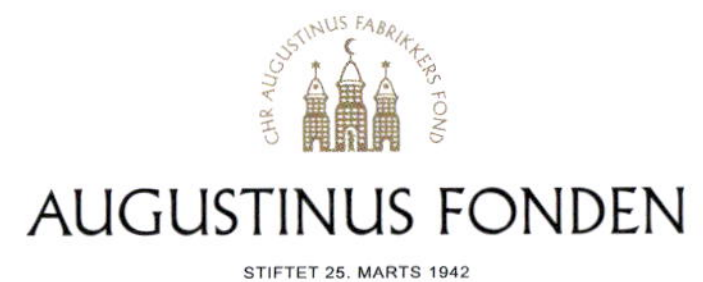

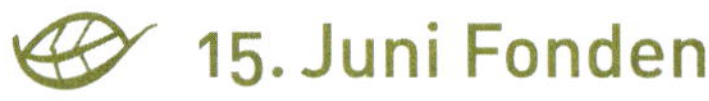

Knud Højgaards Fond
- GRUNDLAGT 1944 -

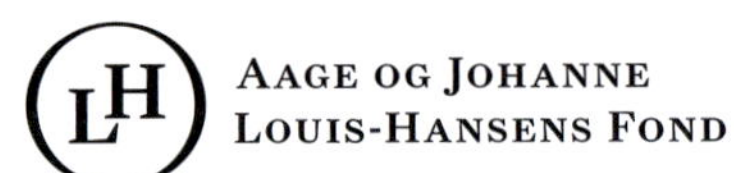

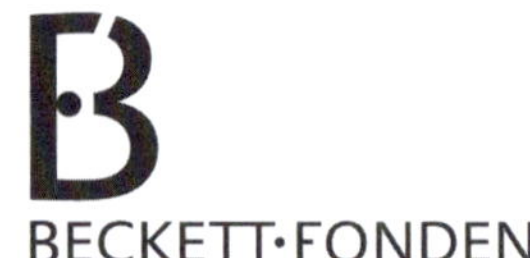

Konsul George Jorck og
Hustru Emma Jorck's Fond

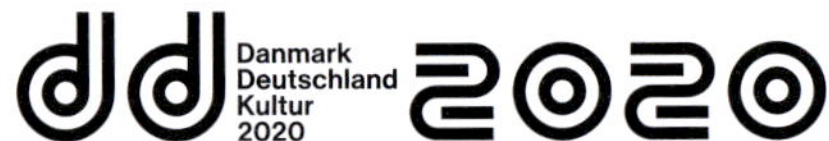

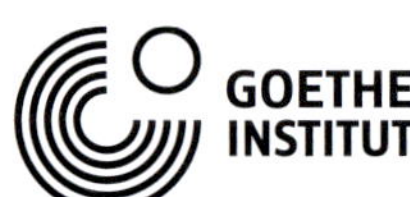

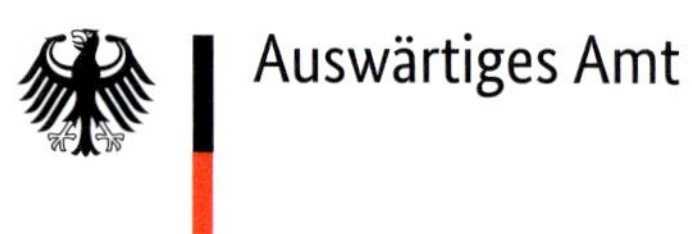

Published in connection with the exhibition
The Late Works of Ernst Ludwig Kirchner and Jens Ferdinand Willumsen: Staging Nature and Life
Willumsen's Museum, Frederikssund · October 10, 2020 to January 31, 2021

Editor: Anne Gregersen
Danish-English translation: Jane Rowley
German-English translation: Kevin Cook
Proofreading: Martin Butler
Graphic design & typesetting: Carl-H.K. Zakrisson
Typeface: Documenta, Futura
Reproductions and printing: Narayana Press
Paper: Arctic Volume White, 150 g

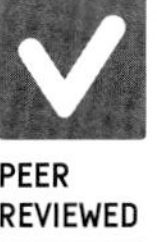

All articles have been peer reviewed in accordance with Danish ministerial requirements. This is to say that a peer, holding a PhD or similar qualifications, has reviewed each text and submitted a written assessment testifying to the academic standard of the contributions.

© 2020 Hatje Cantz Verlag, Berlin, Willumsen's Museum, Frederikssund, and the authors.

© J. F. Willumsen / VISDA

© Boye Willum Willumsen / VISDA

Every effort has been made to contact copyright holders of images published herein. The publisher would appreciate being informed of any omissions in order to make due acknowledgment in future editions of this book.

Distribution worldwide by
Hatje Cantz Verlag GmbH
Mommsenstraße 27
10629 Berlin
www.hatjecantz.com
A Ganske Publishing Group Company

ISBN 978-3-7757-4673-1

Danish edition: ISBN 978-3-7757-4675-5
German edition: ISBN 978-3-7757-4674-8

Printed in Denmark

Thank you to Rasmus Kjærboe, Katharina Lang, Steen Søndergaard Thomsen, Kirsten Jensen, and Adam Jackman.

WILLUMSENS MUSEUM

Cover illustration (front): Ernst Ludwig Kirchner. Detail of *Akt in Orange und Gelb* (Nude in Orange and Yellow), 1929–30
Oil on canvas, 91 × 71 cm, Kirchner Museum Davos
Cover illustration (back): J. F. Willumsen. *Oppe på Campidoglio. Rom* (Up on Campidoglio, Rome), 1931.
Oil on canvas, 73 × 92 cm. Willumsen's Museum, Frederikssund

P. 2: J. F. Willumsen. Detail of *Lola danser* (Lola Dances), 1921. Oil on canvas, 155 × 135 cm. Willumsen's Museum, Frederikssund

P. 4: Ernst Ludwig Kirchner. *Blick in den Eingang von Ernst Ludwig Kirchners Wohnhaus auf dem Wildboden, Davos Frauenkirch, mit dem Schatten des Fotografen und seinem Kater Schaky* (View into the Entrance of Ernst Ludwig Kirchner's House on the Wildboden, Davos Frauenkirch, with the Shadow of the Photographer and His Cat Schaky), after 1931
Cellulose-nitrate negative, 14.5 × 9.8 cm. Kirchner Museum Davos

Some of Ernst Ludwig Kirchner's photographs are shown with the edge of the glass plate to represent the original as fully as possible.